A
HUNDRED BATTLES
IN THE WEST.

ST. LOUIS TO ATLANTA, 1861-65.

The Second Michigan Cavalry

WITH THE ARMIES OF THE MISSISSIPPI, OHIO, KENTUCKY AND
CUMBERLAND, UNDER GENERALS HALLECK, SHERMAN,
POPE, ROSECRANS, THOMAS AND OTHERS;
WITH MENTION OF A FEW OF THE
FAMOUS REGIMENTS AND BRI-
GADES OF THE WEST.

BY

CAPTAIN MARSHALL P. THATCHER,

CO. "B," SECOND MICHIGAN CAVALRY; AID TO GEN. P. H. SHERIDAN.

ILLUSTRATED.

DETROIT, MICH.:
PUBLISHED BY THE AUTHOR.
1884.

Facsimile Reprint by Detroit Book Press

Copyright, 1884.
M. P. THATCHER.

Reprinted by the Detroit Book Press
c/o John K. King Books
901 W. Lafayette Blvd. - P. O. Box 363
Detroit, Michigan 48232

ISBN 0-914905-48-1

Library of Congress Catalog Number 86-050510

DETROIT:
L. F. KILROY, PRINTER,
187 Jefferson Ave.

DEDICATED
TO THE
"GRAND ARMY OF THE REPUBLIC,"
THE RECORD OF WHOSE
DEEDS WILL GROW BRIGHTER
AS EACH
SUCCEEDING GENERATION READS FOR THE
FIRST TIME OF YOUR
TRIALS, SUFFERINGS AND VICTORIES.
FRATERNITY BEGAT AMID SUCH SCENES MUST LEAD
TO THE
GREATEST OF ALL VIRTUES—CHARITY,
AND FROM THIS
LOYALTY FOLLOWS AS NATURALLY AS GOD'S
BLESSING WAITS UPON ALL GOOD DEEDS.
WISHING YOU
MAY LIVE A HUNDRED YEARS
AND NOT AGAIN BE
CALLED TO TAKE UP ARMS,
I REMAIN,
FRATERNALLY YOURS,
THE AUTHOR.

PREFACE.

"All are but parts of one stupendous whole," and it is with the hope that this very small part of the history of our beloved country will find a place in the hearts of not a few, that it is sent out into the world, craving indulgence for imperfections, and justice if merit is discovered.

This work was begun as a history of the Second Regiment of Michigan Cavalry, a regiment that started from an obscure position in the regular army Gordon Granger toward a major-generalship and Philip Henry Sheridan to the proud position of the brightest military genius of the age in which he won his stars.

As the work of searching the records begun, it was found impossible to limit the writings to the doings of one regiment, and so you have here a partial history (written *impartially*) of the war of 1861-5. General Logan truthfully said "the full history of the Great Rebellion will never be known until every regiment and every company has been heard from."

Official and private records have yielded up their treasures freely, and have been carefully compared and revised with the writer's own journal as the groundwork. There was no need of fiction, for truth was stranger far, in every instance worth recording.

Nor has this been written to glorify *anyone*; and it can be read in the knowledge of one fact—the writer was practically an outside witness, serving most of the time as a staff officer, near his regiment, and usually in the same brigade or division; and therefore while he writes principally of what passed before his eyes, he was not always among the most active partakers in the incidents here narrated, and is not, therefore, in any sense writing of himself.

Lieutenant Edwin Hoyt, Jr., who served first as sergeant-major and later as adjutant, and still later as assistant adjutant-general to the brigade commander, has kindly furnished many facts, and his judgment as a clear-headed chronicler, unprejudiced by regimental pride, is recognized, and appreciated.

It has been found simply impossible to separate the record of this regiment from that of others, since it has been shown that by the character of their arms they were constantly brought into contact with every branch of the service, and their history is blended with each and all of them.

It may appear to the most active participants in this regiment's history, that this record is too moderate. Adjutant-General Robertson says "that was always a fault of your historian, when an occasional war correspondent; he did not 'blow' as others would have done." Let others judge.

To the nervous reader, a word. The horrors of the battlefield have been touched upon as lightly as possible. The same temper of mind which unconsciously puts aside tales of horror in the daily papers, murders, disasters, etc., would not delight in perpetuating such disagreeable subjects.

General Sherman said truly when he said, "War is hell." We certainly want as little of it as possible; but aside from that picture of it there are many valuable lessons to be learned, as well as interesting incidents that are worth reading and preserving, and you have this picture from one who has tears to shed for every wound, and whose hand was never lifted against individuals, but against a common enemy.

No doubt many pen sketches herein given to the public for the first time will be criticised by those who witnessed other parts of the field as "not according to my remembrance;" but we all know how individuals differ upon the same subject, viewed from different standpoints, and I have in many instances given way to the weight of evidence as gathered from others whose positions were such as to warrant the probability of their correctness.

There is one point upon which this volume can be referred to with pride—it contains very little that can be called "old." A special effort has been made to print only "unpublished records," and with only two unimportant exceptions that idea has been followed.

THE AUTHOR.

CONTENTS.

PART FIRST.

CHAPTER I.

	PAGE.
THE organization of a company.—Leaf from a diary.—Off for Grand Rapids.	17

CHAPTER II.

DETAILS of Organization.—Sketch of the Captains and Companies.—The Field and Staff. 20

CHAPTER III.

OFF for St. Louis.—An ovation all along the line.—Horses follow in sections of trains.—Incidents by the way.—Camp Benton. 27

CHAPTER IV.

THE finishing touches.—Farewell to Benton Barracks.—Lambs to the slaughter.—Commerce, Mo.—Jeff. Thompson's light artillery.—A night in the mud.—New Madrid.—The baptism of fire. 32

CHAPTER V.

AFLOAT on the Mississippi.—Off for Memphis.—Counter march to Pittsburg Landing.—A muddy business.—Monterey.—Farmington.—In front of Corinth—General Pope. . . . 39

CHAPTEP VI.

THE Mississippi campaign.—The raid on Booneville.—Philip H. Sheridan.—Blackland.—Baldwin. 46

CHAPTER VII.

THE North Mississippi campaign.—"Pine Hills."—Back to Booneville.—The second Booneville.—Rienzi.—A flag of truce. . 58

CHAPTER VIII.

FROM Corinth to Perryville.—Col. Phil gets a star.—Colonel Archie Campbell.—Cincinnati.—Louisville.—General Buell.—Rousseau and Sheridan.—Loomis.—Perryville. . . . 70

CHAPTER IX.

AFTER the battle.—Confederate retreat.—A flag of truce.—"We will bury your dead, move on."—Sweeping the state. . . 88

CHAPTER X.

CARTER's raid.—750 miles in twenty days.—Mountain paths.—Among the lcouds.—Bushwhacked.—Capturing forts.—Humphrey Marshall.—Cutting communications.—Burning bridges. 94

CHAPTER XI.

RECUPERATING.—Pleasant hours short lived.—Farewell to Kentucky.—General Green Clay Smith.—Brentwood.—Thompson's Station. 112

CHAPTER XII.

MIDDLE TENNESSEE.—Three months of post duty with the variations.—Colonel Watkins and Colonel Campbell.—McGarrick's Ford.—Numerous small fights. 122

CHAPTER XIII.

THE Tennessee campaign.—Franklin to Triune.—Triune to Franklin.—Stirring up General Armstrong.—Return to Triune.—The grand forward move.—Rain and mud.—Guy's gap.—A grand cavalry charge.—Shelbyville. 128

CHAPTER XIV.

STEVENSON, ALABAMA.—The army concentrating.—Immense depot of supplies.—Sickness.—Over mountain and moor.—Scouting through Georgia.—Lafayette.—Crawfish Springs and Chicamauga.—Chattanooga ours. 137

CHAPTER XV.

VICTORY out of defeat.—Reflections not designed as critical.—Great soldiers.—Wheeler's Raid.—Destroys a 1,000 wagon train.—A wild chase.—Camp life.—A ferry disaster. . . . 151

CHAPTER XVI.

EAST TENNESSEE.—Climbing mountains—Bushwhacked—Dandridge "Races."—A lively campaign and many hardships. . . 159

CHAPTER XVII.

MOSSY CREEK.—A trick which did not work.—A fight, sharp, short, decisive.—An artillery duel. 167

CHAPTER XVIII.

SEVEREVILLE or Fair Garden.—A midnight retreat.—A morning's advance.—A dead line.—Storming bridge and barricade. . 174

CHAPTER XIX.

VETERANS.—Severeville to Cleveland.—Florence.—Shoal Creek.—Forrest and Roddy.—The non-veterans and the Atlanta campaign.—Lieutenant Darrow.—Captain Fargo's flag of truce.—Pulaski.—Franklin.—Cypress Creek. 179

CHAPTER XX.

THE Hood campaign.—Florence.—Shoal Creek.—Pontoons.—A faithful negro.—Beginning of Hood's advance. . . 191

CHAPTER XXI.

HOOD'S Race with Schofield.—Columbia.—Spring Hill.—The Harpeth.—"Halt!"—The butchery at Franklin.—Stanley.—Wilson.—Cox.—Hatch.—Croxton.—Schofield's report. . . . 197

CHAPTER XXII.

BATTLE of Nashville.—Hood's army demoralized.—Cavalry capturing earthworks.—Capturing prisoners.—What Hood said.—"The retreat."—Thomas's report. 219

CHAPTER XXIII.

HOOD "loses his grip" and resigns.—Forrest's narrow escape.—A battalion charges a division.—Closing scenes. . . 235

CONTENTS. xiii

PART SECOND.

	PAGE.
GENERAL POPE.	247
GENERAL ELLIOTT	248
GENERAL STANLEY.	249
GENERAL EDWARD HATCH.	250
ARMY OF THE CUMBERLAND.	253
COMMANDERS.	254
STONE RIVER—GENERAL ROSECRANS.	256
GORDON GRANGER.	270
PHILIP H. SHERIDAN.	277
SHERIDAN'S HORSE.	291
GENERAL STANLEY.	292
GENERAL WILSON.	294
R. H. G. MINTY.	301
CROXTON'S BRIGADE.	304
INCIDENTS AT FRANKLIN—MRS. SNYDER.	307
W. D. MOODY.	313
A DYING CONFEDERATE.	315
A HORRID SCENE.	316
THE SECOND BATTERY AT SHILOH.	317
THE GLASGOW COLLISION.	318
LEFT ON THE FIELD.	320
A DARING SCOUT.	324
THE ROMANCE OF WAR.	327
SURGEON CHARLES L. HENDERSON.	330
SURGEON WILLIAM BROWNELL.	330
SURGEON W. F. GREEN.	331
NOTES BY W. F. GREEN.	332
SURGEON GEORGE E. RANNEY.	333
NOTES BY GEORGE E. RANNEY.	335
COMMISSARY LAWRENCE.	338
IN THE HOSPITAL.	339
LIEUTENANT R. T. DARROW.	341
TURNING THE TIDE.	343
JIM BROWNLOW CAPTURED.	343
"FIVE DOLLARS FOR THAT REB."	344
"WALK AROUND."	345
BURNT HIS FINGERS.	346
HERE'S YOUR MULE.	348
DESTROYING PONTOONS.	350
COMPLIMENTS TO WIRT ADAMS.	357

CONTENTS.

	PAGE.
LEAVES FROM A DIARY.	359
A SCOUT ON FOOT.	364
"DID THEY STING?"	366
AN INTERRUPTED WEDDING.	367
HORSE SENSE.	368
LUCKY ESCAPES.	370
WEAER'S COVE.	373
A BULL RUN HERO.	378
A LIVELY PRISONER.	379
A FLAG OF TRUCE.	380
SCOUTING IN NORTH CAROLINA.	382
DODGING SHELLS.	384
UNEXPLODED SHELLS.	386
WHO HIT CHALMERS AT BOONEVILLE?	386
RUNNING THE GAUNTLET.	387
A CORPORAL'S GUARD MAKES A RECONNAISSANCE	388
UNDER ARREST.	389
ONE DAY NEARER ATLANTA.	391
WHY CHEATHAM DID NOT GET THERE.	392
GENERAL CHEATHAM'S STORY.	393
CAVALRY AND GUNBOATS.	400
CAPTURING OUTPOSTS.	401
STRAINING A POINT TO SAVE A LIFE.	403
AN OMEN.	406
ALLEGED OUTRAGES.	407
CAPTAIN AVERY.	408
LOOMIS'S BATTERY.	410
A LONELY GRAVE.	411
DIED GAME.—A YOUTHFUL SOLDIER.	413
COURTING DEATH.	414
TOO MUCH GOLD.—DISCIPLINE.	415
THE LAST BATTLE.	416

ILLUSTRATIONS.

	PAGE.
THE AUTHOR.	FRONTISPIECE.
ARMS AND ACCOUTREMENTS.	26
MOUNTED DRAGOON.	31
BENTON BARRACKS.	33
MAP OF NEW MADRID.	34
FORAGERS.	36
GORDON GRANGER.	48
BOONEVILLE, MISS.	64
MAP OF BOONEVILLE.	65
PHILIP H. SHERIDAN.	80
MAP OF PERRYVILLE.	76
NIGHT SCENE AT PERRYVILLE.	83
MAJOR L. S. SCRANTON.	117
SHELLS.	121
COL. A. P. CAMPBELL.	125
CHICAMAUGA.	144
POINT LOOKOUT.	148
MAP OF CHICAMAUGA.	152
MAP OF DANDRIDGE.	162
CAPTAIN JAS. H. SMITH.	165
CAPTAIN J. M. WEATHERWAX.	171
CAPTAIN DAN T. FARGO.	186
LIEUTENANT RUSSELL T. DARROW.	190
MAP OF FRANKLIN.	206
MAP OF NASHVILLE.	219
FIELD AND STAFF.	244
SHERIDAN'S HORSE.	291
LIEUT.-COL. BEN. SMITH.	305
MAJOR W. H. WHITTEMORE.	358
COL. THOMAS. W. JOHNSTON.	359

SECOND MICHIGAN CAVALRY.

CHAPTER I.

THE ORGANIZATION OF A COMPANY—LEAF FROM A DIARY—OFF FOR GRAND RAPIDS.

During the war it was common to hear soldiers talking about how they came to enlist. Some stoutly insisted that patriotism was the first grand incentive to the personal sacrifice; others with a show of modesty "went for the fun of it"—"excitement"—"a chance to see something of the world"—"ambition"—"position"—"distinction"—and now and again we just heard of some one who went to find solace for a "bruised heart." Perhaps a few leaves from an old diary may show the average soldier's reasons, the why and the how, and all about it.

August 25.—* * * I see in every newspaper reports of the grand success in recruiting volunteers for the war just fairly begun in the Southern States. * * *

The old Flag is in danger; already the bones of many of my countrymen are bleaching in the Southern sun. * * * We do not fully realize our country's situation. We hear of battles but they sound like tales of other days. We do not see the smoke of battles nor hear the roar of artillery, the rattle of musketry nor the bugle's call. The drum goes rattling through the street, keeping time with the shrill piping of the fife and the tramp of armed, undisciplined troops. This is all we see or know. But here is something we can all understand. Its every word is an electric shock that tingles the blood and sends it rushing through the veins. A proclamation by Jefferson Davis, styling himself "President of the Confederate States of America." Here it is: "All Northern men will leave the Southern States within thirty days," etc., etc. It is signed August 15, 1861. * * *

The news of the battle of Wilson's Creek comes to us, pictured with all the horrors of civil war. Convalescent, sick and wounded from the battle of Bull Run are straggling home. This is no boys' play. I must enlist. Young and unmarried—why not? * * *

The nearest recruiting office is gathering men for the cavalry. I enter, a stranger to everyone. The man recognized as captain is large, of fine physique; his bearing indicates the leader, "Born to command." The company appear anxious to join the first regiment, nearly full at Detroit. If they fail to enter there, perhaps they will take them in the second, just begun at Grand Rapids. The material of this company thus far is good, judging from one standpoint—they are always ready for a fight. * * * * * * *

We have received word from Colonel Brodhead of the First Cavalry that his regiment is full, therefore we must go into the second, and we are very anxious to get to Grand Rapids before that regiment is also full. * * * * *

Sept. 9.—On our way to Grand Rapids, transportation failing to meet us in time we stay at the Grand Trunk and Milwaukee Junction, sleeping on straw in a little old freight house.

This is our first bivouac—without tents, blankets or supper. In the absence of arms a corporal's guard would have no trouble in "surrounding us."

Sept. 10.—The arrangements for transportation are so exasperating that we make our own contracts for a car and fill it. "Some days must be dark and dreary," but this dark, rainy day did not in the least dampen our ardor, for the racket is much like an excursion to a prize fight or a picnic.

We will leave our friend's diary for the present, believing that the foregoing will serve to show the true spirit that actuated the great mass of those who took their lives in their hands and went out to fight—perchance to die, for the Union.

And this was but one of twelve companies, each of which could doubtless tell a similar story, showing how from a heterogeneous mass the very beginning of the organization of the regiment was made.

CHAPTER II.

DETAILS OF ORGANIZATION—SKETCH OF THE CAPTAINS AND COMPANIES—THE FIELD AND STAFF.

The second regiment of Michigan cavalry was organized by the Hon. F. W. Kellogg, under authority of the Secretary of War, upon a commission as colonel from Governor Austin Blair. About the middle of July, 1861, preparations were made at Grand Rapids for quartering the cavalry troops, but at first these arrangements were very imperfect; a company being placed here and there in vacant buildings—some upon the west side of the river near Pearl street bridge, but more in a row of wooden buildings opposite the gas works on Ottawa street.

One of the first acts of importance to the regiment was the appointment of William C. Davies, of Detroit, as Lieutenant-Colonel, and with him a full complement of field and staff officers—Majors, Adjutants, Surgeons and Quartermasters with their non-commissioned staff sergeants.

As fast as each company received their minimum number, the captains' and lieutenants' names were reported to the governor for commissions.

During this recruiting period the regiment had been gathering together upon the fair grounds where additional barracks had been erected and the preliminary steps toward becoming a soldier had been taken. The first of these was the medical examination; stripped before a board of surgeons, assisted by the surgeons of the regiment. The name, age, hight, complexion, color of the hair and eyes were all duly entered on the rolls.

Straw and army blankets were issued and we laid down side by side, on the floor and in bunks, perhaps to think of pleasant homes, the girl we left behind, or float away to dream-land and scenes of carnage. Our breakfast, dinner and supper consisted of bread, potatoes and meat, tea or coffee, and our meals were at stated hours. We marched into the dining sheds under orders and opposite our respective tin cups and plates, where we halted and sat down at a rough board table. As we look back upon that scene over an interval filled with incidents more stirring, we wonder at the fastidiousness of volunteers, when some officer flushed with the victories of camp life—a winner in the race for shoulder straps—in loud tones proclaims that *his* "men shall not eat with *rusty forks*," and boldly flings the disgraced weapon into outer darkness.

Occasionally some party would fancy themselves wronged by the provisions contractor; for it will be remembered we did not cook our own rations at this camp—"Anderson" as it was called, but they were furnished by contract, and so it often fell out that the soup would be a trifle burned—the coffee just a trifle "off" or the beef a year or two older than necessary—the butter might not have been exactly bad, nor yet very good; still we were all agreed afterwards that "Camp Anderson butter was not the worst we ever saw."

Military discipline was immediately commenced, and the

bugle sounded reveille, roll call, guard mounting and drilling by tacties,—Hardie's tactics—"Right face! left face! about face! front face! eyes right! eyes left! head and shoulders up! forward march! backward march! parade rest!"—Day after day, until the shuffling gait changed for the upright, prompt, sharp steps of a soldier.

The officers had their duties—making out muster rolls, drawing clothing and supplies from the quartermasters, etc.

Soon we had sufficient numbers to form platoons and drill by companies; then battalion drill, and afterwards the full regiment assembled for dress parade; and I think we shall never forget that first parade under command of our little lieutenant colonel, whose short thick stature, fierce black mustache, dangling sword and rattling spurs made him a conspicuous figure; nor how, after listening to a few not very intelligible orders we soon executed a flank movement on our quarters.

The officers visited the city and purchased shoulder straps, feathers, plumes, gold lace and high top boots, and one by one the companies were completed in numbers and outfit except horses and arms.

Company "A," Captain Godley, was the first to march the streets of Grand Rapids in full uniform, under command of Lieutenant Carter. They were a body of large men, mostly from the lumber camps and mills of the Saginaw valley, and made a fine appearance.

Company "G," Captain Fred Fowler, with his farmer boys from Hillsdale in full uniform—white gloves, large plume in the captain's hat, marched in full ranks to the Congregational church and took front seats in the gallery.

Captain Ben. Whitman's Company—"E," from Muskegon, was another body of stalwart lumbermen who looked as if they would be equally at home with rifle, pistol, saber or ax.

Captain Ben Smith; of Company "D," would sit up later and work harder for a joke than any man in the regiment, and his company of Hollanders gave a good account of themselves, whether the captain or his wife was in command.

Captain Goodale, Company "I," was a good natured, jolly old boy from Kalamazoo. His men had their own way mostly in company affairs and seemed to enjoy themselves as they went along, yet they were on hand in every fight.

Captain Peck, of Company "F," was from Lowell with lieutenants from Grand Rapids. His company enjoyed the reputation of being a well behaved, soldierly lot of men, always ready for duty of any kind.

Captain Archie P. Campbell, of Company "K," was from Port Huron and his company had the name of doing more fighting *in* camp and *out* than any other company in the regiment. They were mostly rough lumbermen and log runners from the Black River, St. Clair county, and would stick by their leader in war or peace.

Captain H. A. Shaw Company "B," was from Eaton Rapids. He was once Speaker of the House at Lansing and was ever ready to speak when occasion required, and his boys would do anything they were told to. They occupied the second post of honor—the left of the regiment.

Captain B. P. Wells, of Niles, commanded Company "L." He was one of the few who were apparently satisfied with their positions and looked for no higher honor than to command Company L, who were always ready to obey quietly.

Company "H" was commanded by Captain C. E. Newman, who wore a stunning hat and feather, but had a good company of men from Utica, Macomb county.

Captain R. A. Alger, of Company "C," took commendable pride in his own personal appearance and that of his men. They were mostly from Grand Rapids and the ladies could all point out Captain Alger's company.

Captain F. W. Dickey, of Company "M," was from Marshall; His men were well up in size, personal appearance and drill. If the captain had a weakness it was his love for a good horse.

The field and staff were made up of men from various walks in life and from different parts of the State.

Lieutenant-Colonel W. C. Davies was the real organizer and commander of the regiment. He came from the employ of the Great Western Railroad. His appearance was decidedly "Frenchy" but he claimed to be an Englishman and wore medals of honor upon his breast which had been given him for distinguished services in the Crimea. But he lost his influence to an extent with the regiment by "airing" himself — went to church in full uniform, saber, spurs and all—and never had the opportunity of commanding the regiment in a fight, though we all believed he would have made a good officer.

On the 2d of October, 1861, when Captain Henry R. Mizner, U. S. A., mustered the regiment into the service we had as senior Major, Robert H. G. Minty, a very genial gentleman who endeared himself to the men by his unassuming yet soldierly manners. He lived in his tent in camp and could call his men by name. and was ever ready to impart any instructions or listen to any communications they might make. He was from Detroit and was, like the Lieutenant-Colonel, a railroad man.

Major Selden H. Gorham, of the second battalion, was from Marshall, and came to us with a good record from service as a lieutenant with the three months men at Bull Run. He was a stylish young officer, but a little too much reserved in manners ever to become popular among volunteers.

Major Chas. P. Babcock, of the third battalion, was a very stylish *old* officer. His *slick* iron gray chin whiskers and his prancing iron gray stallion were in exact harmony. His men would do anything for the kind hearted old major, but the war happened about twenty-five years too late for him.

Surgeon Chas. S. Henderson was from Grand Rapids and gave his entire time and acknowledged skill to the faithful discharge of his duty and in this he was ably assisted by assistant Surgeon Wm. Brownell, of Utica.

Peter S. Schuyler, Adjutant, possessed natural qualifications for the arduous duties which devolved upon his position while the troops were being organized, and afterwards Alphonso E. Gordon, Peter A. Weber and George Lee were the battalion adjutants. Gordon was an editor, Weber a popular young business man of bright promise and Lee was a bank book-keeper. They were all from Grand Rapids.

Frank E. Walbridge, of Kalamazoo, was regimental quartermaster. His battalion quartermasters were James P. Scott, of Grand Haven, Seymour Brownell, of Utica, and John A. Brooks, of Newaygo. The four positions were soon consolidated at Corinth in one, when James P. Scott alone remained. Walbridge having been promoted, and Brownell transferred to the Potomac and promoted.

Chaplain Francis Drew, of the M. E. church of Grand

Rapids, held divine service on Sundays, and visited the sick in hospitals. Sylvester's regimental band gave us *selections* at regimental parade or an occasional evening serenade. Prompt responses were made to bugle calls and the discipline of camp life was accepted with becoming grace and an evidence of determination to equal if possible the best drilled and disciplined troops.

CHAPTER III.

OFF FOR ST. LOUIS—AN OVATION ALL ALONG THE LINE—HORSES FOLLOW IN SECTIONS OF TRAINS—INCIDENTS BY THE WAY —CAMP BENTON.

It seemed a long time to wait—those days and weeks when we were drilling, receiving clothing and horses—horses that we could not ride, for as yet we had no saddles nor arms; and every morning as we arose to a bath at the trough in the open air, with a sharp frost nipping our fingers and no fires in all the camp to warm by, we longed for a more sunny clime, with a chance to show the country that Michigan took some interest in the war.

The order came, and on the 14th of November, 1861, we marched to the depot of the Detroit & Milwaukee road, and bidding adieu to friends gathered there, we left for Detroit. At all stations along the road there was a general uproar of cheers, greetings and farewells.

Arriving at Detroit in the evening, we marched in good order to a sumptuous feast spread by the ladies of that city in the freight depot of the Detroit & Milwaukee Railroad, and it was twelve o'clock at night before we were again under way over the Michigan Central, filling the air with cheers as we left, for the good ladies of Detroit, who had feasted us so well.

A train of soldiers was no uncommon sight in those days, yet the enthusiasm was unabated, and throngs of people gathered at the stations, night or day, to give us God speed.

Arriving at Decatur, Michigan, in the morning, we were ordered from the cars for a rest and inspection. The Decatur cannon was ordered out and we were welcomed by a salute, in which a squad of young ladies joined, and their fusilade of kisses went square to the target and never missed a man.

At Niles we took breakfast, which had been prepared by the ladies, who exerted themselves successfully in making our short stay very pleasant. At Michigan City we were well received by the Hoosiers and their ladies, and again at Joliet, and then we plunged out upon the broad moon-lit prairie, whose swelling bosom seemed so like the rolling sea, as we rushed down one grade and up the next, speeding on with never a halt, passing station, town or burning grass, and on into the rock-bound city of Alton on the Mississippi, where we embarked upon those floating palaces, "Meteor" and "Daniel Tatrim," for St. Louis, where after a short, pleasant ride, we arrived in due time, and forming into line marched four miles to "Benton Barracks," the work of General Fremont at the fair grounds.

We numbered 1,240 in officers and men at that time, and the task of transporting that number was no difficult one, yet much less so than the moving of the same number of horses. These were divided into three sections of trains, each train having thirty-five to forty cars.

To load and unload these horses, feed and water them at least once every twenty-four hours on all that long trip from Grand Rapids to Detroit, thence to Michigan City, Joliet, Alton and St. Louis was no small task, as the writer can testify from personal experience. Occasionally a horse would get down and the kicking, squealing and tramping could be heard above the roar of the heavy train. Only one horse was killed of all the number, and stopping the train in the middle of a broad prairie, he was hauled out. After three days from Grand Rapids the battalion of horses was led into camp at St. Louis in good condition. It may not be out of place to remark here that many expressed a wonder that saddles were not furnished at Grand Rapids and the command be permitted to march to St. Louis. For the discipline of that march, if properly conducted, would have been worth quite as much as the benefit received in camp at Benton Barracks (the fair grounds) during the same period. But our camp was laid out on a large open field, level and thoroughly drained, though soft in wet weather, and we were soon in active training for the field. The grounds were one mile long by a quarter wide, surrounded on three sides by wooden barracks, with cooking and dining sheds in the rear and stables farther back.

In the center of the grounds near one end were General Sherman's headquarters, and none will ever forget the long-haired, strong-lunged Indian, who woke us to an early reveille with his bugle that gave forth a blast like a steam fog-horn, and kept it up throughout the day—roll-call, stable call, hospital call, drill, fatigue, sun-set ("Retreat"), and *taps*, when the last light was supposed to be out, and silence reigned supreme.

Who will forget the refrain from all the company bugles and drums as they took up the calls and rattled and blowed to the last long drawn note?

Then the busy scene upon that level plain as company after company and regiment after regiment marched and rode out to drill. Helter-skelter, hither and yon, like a hundred sham battles, deploying, rallying, charging, flanking, wheeling and skirmishing—a grand school of instruction, and we were apt scholars in those days, for our ambition was to excel, and an awkward man or horse was soon broken in, and constant practice soon brought the regiment to a degree of perfection not excelled by even regulars.

Captain Gordon Granger, of the regular army, having been appointed Colonel of our regiment, devoted a portion of his time every day to drilling the officers, and as there was a good sized company of them, more or less amusement was caused by the awkwardness of some who were not as well drilled as most of their men. To see a private soldier roll off his horse and dangle his heels in the air for a second was too common to be funny, but to see an officer in that pleasant (?) predicament was too much for the soldiers who kept at a respectful distance, but they were the only ones who dared to laugh; a frown from "Old Granger," as he was sometimes called, would kill further than an old flint lock.

But it was not many weeks before we were considered soldierly enough to participate in a grand review, and we acquitted ourselves so creditably as to draw special attention from the generals present. From that time on we were no more considered recruits, raw troops, etc., but were given to understand that we were booked for the field.

And with Colt's revolving rifles and pistols, besides sabers, each man was a whole arsenal in himself, and felt superior to equal numbers of the best troops with single-barreled arms in the country. This was no idle boast, as we afterwards proved on many a hard contested field.

CHAPTER IV.

THE FINISHING TOUCHES—FAREWELL TO BENTON BARRACKS—LAMBS TO THE SLAUGHTER—COMMERCE, MISSOURI—JEFF. THOMPSON'S LIGHT ARTILLERY—A NIGHT IN THE MUD—NEW MADRID—"THE BAPTISM OF FIRE."

Colonel Granger, though a gruff appearing man, had succeeded in winning the respect of his regiment by his strict attention to all the details of making a well disciplined body of soldiers out of a mass of awkward men from every walk in life, and the last finishing touches had been added, while arms, ammunition and accoutrements were being drawn and distributed. And now Colonel Granger calls his brother officers of the regular army to look at them as they move about the grounds.

"Pope, look here!"

"Well, what of it?"

"What of it! you d——d fool? You never saw a better looking regiment nor a better drilled regiment in your life!"

More *adjectives* on both sides, then they take a drink and talk of the proposed forward move.

On the 21st of Feburary, 1862, army wagons were packed with camp supplies, and we moved forward, without regrets, even

1 Sherman's Headquarters.   Hospital.   3 Parade Ground.
BENTON BARRACKS, ST. LOUIS, MO.

for the comfortable quarters we had so much enjoyed all winter; and we turned our backs on them forever, as it proved, going, we knew not where, and cared little, though it might be like lambs to the slaughter. And a big, burly, healthy-looking lot of lambs we were, too.

With little delay, we were all packed on board the steamer Empress, the largest and finest of the river fleet, and the next day, as the fog lifted, we steamed down the Mississippi to Commerce, Missouri, where we landed and set out to scour the woods towards New Madrid, where General Pope's army was to join us.

It was reported that Jeff Thompson had been having his own way through that part of the country, and without knowing anything of his force, we naturally moved with caution through the woods, keeping an eye out for ambuscades or any surprise that might be intended for us. We had no definite idea whether Jeff Thompson was the captain of a guerrilla band of swamp rangers, or the regular commanding general of a large force of cavalry, and this uncertainty may have caused some nervous sensations to dance up and down our spinal columns, but it did not appear on the surface, for we moved cheerfully along, with our advance guard out a few rods ahead, and occasional flankers where the ground would permit.

The regiment divided, each battalion going different routes. A heavy rain set in and at dark the different battalions had not reached the point designated for our camp for the night at Benton. Who will ever forget the impenetrable darkness of that night, and the terrible sloughs through which we wallowed in our efforts to follow our guide? Occasionally a halt was sounded and the broken ranks were given an opportunity to stagger out upon terra firma, if they could find it.

Only two battalions reached the camp—late, wet, tired, sore and hungry. The other battalion *roosted* out in the swamps, and thought themselves lucky if they could find a log to perch upon, while the poor animals stood patiently in the mud and water to their knees, "waiting for the light." It came at last, and the "lost" rode into camp with the first gleam of day.

Is it any wonder that men in such a position seize upon anything in the shape of food, and that among the animals brought in, dressed and cut up, was an imported male Cashmere goat, worth $500 for breeding purposes?

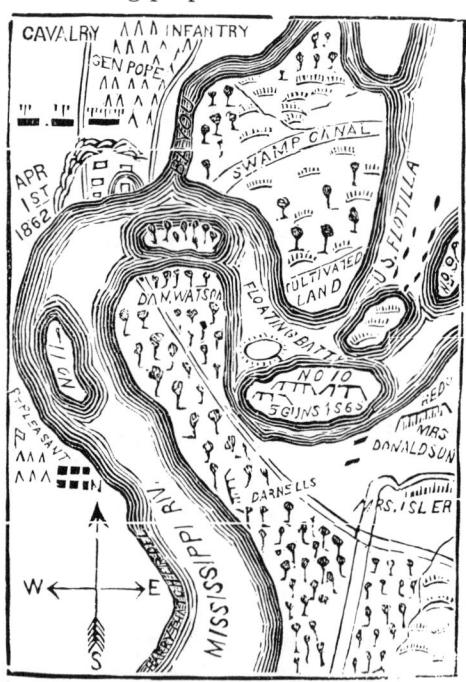

NEW MADRID.

Only a short rest was allowed, and again we set out towards New Madrid, but divided as before, looking for Jeff.

When our advance reached Sikeston, we were confronted by a force of cavalry and three pieces of rifled artillery of small calibre planted on a narrow causeway.

The Seventh Indiana cavalry charged them, capturing the artillery and completely routing them, nor did the enemy offer further resistance until we reached New Madrid, March 3d. A rebel captain, lieutenant and several privates were captured in this charge, from whom it was learned their force was about 10,000 infantry, 900 cavalry and four batteries of field artillery.

The overflow of the Mississippi river bottoms was a serious impediment to Gen. Pope's rapid advance; in fact, it was impossible to bring up heavy guns until the water had subsided, and all the while the enemy's gunboats, some six or seven in number, were able to over-look the country from the decks of their ironclads in front of New Madrid, and while General Pope felt certain he could have captured the place by assault, he felt sure of being driven out by the gunboats with a needless loss of life. Therefore the entire army was drawn up in line on the open plain awaiting developments. Fortunately their firing was "wild," and our position was naturally protected by a slight depression of the ground; we must have looked very unconcerned as we stood there for more than an hour without returning a shot. Then we began to feel their position. Entering a narrow lane on the left, two battalions of cavalry marched to within 200 yards of their earthworks and plainly saw their guns and iron-clads upon the river. Suddenly they gave us a salute with short range fuse shell and the unearthly screech of shell and whirr of broken iron after the explosion were enough to make the stoutest hearts quail. Perhaps ours did, but we did not *tarry* long in that immediate neighborhood, neither did we run. We had drawn their fire on the left and knew their position; we therefore deliberately withdrew. Meanwhile one battalion of our regiment (the first) had made like demonstrations on the right and had a brush with the enemy, capturing a few pickets and driving in the rest. This was known as the "fight at Point Pleasant," Missouri.

Here the writer with a detail of twenty men made his first scout immediately after our locating the main body of the enemy in the fort on the Mississippi river, with an impassable barrier on our left, Wilson's Bayou—a wide swamp or bayou, navigable for small steamers; and our forces extending around to the river on the right. It became necessary to know if there were any straggling troops in our rear and for this purpose a squad of men examined every road, cross road, lane, bit of woods, farm and buildings for a distance of ten miles to the rear, and on this expedition the natural foraging proclivities of a portion of the regiment were soon developed and were the disturbing element that became notorious during the war, yet this same company, Phil Sheridan said, was one of the best squadrons of cavalry he ever had anything to do with.

The work of drawing closer the lines about New Madrid moved steadily onward while the bombardment of Island No. 10, twelve miles away, by our gunboats could be plainly heard, and on dark nights the course of the fuse shells could be traced, as the siege mortars sent their ponderous shells arching through the sky to their work of destruction.

Here Gordon Granger, now a brigadier, gave us an exhibition of his skill as an officer in charge of siege works. The perfect composure with which he went along the line of heavy guns, touching a gun now and then to raise or lower the range, while shot and shell from the enemy's forts plowed the ground all about him, often covering him with clouds of dirt, without so much as drawing from him an indication that he saw or heard anything but his own work, drew from all his men deep though silent admiration; and all the harsh things seen in him or felt in ourselves were buried forever.

With an occasional sortie and repulse, a skirmish on the right and another on the left, the work of reducing the fort went steadily though slowly forward until one evening it began to be whispered about that a general assault was to be made at daylight. By a probably accidental coincidence, the enemy were busy all night in moving their forces across the river, and in the morning when our guns suddenly opened on one part, our infantry made a dash, scaling the works and rushing in, only to find the rear guard of a demoralized army, with all the indications of a hurried departure—half cooked breakfasts, unpacked knapsacks, burdensome trinkets, Texas "cheese-knives," useless arms, accoutrements, etc. They had been busy crossing the river, were followed and captured.

Thus was General Pope's letter to General Halleck verified, and more: He said he would have Island No. 10 in a week—he not only had Island No. 10, but New Madrid as well, and with it three generals, six thousand prisoners, a large amount of munitions of war, 100 pieces of siege and several battalions of field artillery, small arms, tents, wagons, horses, etc.

For this brilliant victory, General Pope received the following telegram from his superior at St. Louis:

MAJOR-GENERAL POPE:

I congratulate you and your command on your splendid achievement. It exceeds in boldness and brilliancy all other operations of the war. It will be memorable in military history, and will be admired by future generations. You deserve well of your country.

           H. W. HALLECK,
             Major-General.

CHAPTER V.

AFLOAT ON THE MISSISSIPPI, OHIO AND TENNESSEE — OFF FOR MEMPHIS — COUNTER-MARCH TO PITTSBURG LANDING — A MUDDY BUSINESS — MONTEREY, FARMINGTON — IN FRONT OF CORINTH.

Our Missouri Campaign was ended, and we made all haste to join Grant and Buell at Pittsburg Landing, but before we had embarked news came that the battle of Shiloh had been fought and our troops were in possession of the grounds.

While embarking at New Madrid, a gunboat was seen coming slowly round the bend of the river from Island No. 10. That she was a rebel gunboat, we had every reason to believe, and in our break-camp condition we were not prepared for that kind of a visitor. As she came on, a shot was sent whizzing across her bows, but she did not deign to reply and another was sent crashing into her sides at low water mark. Still no reply, and we began to surmise that she was abandoned. Sending out a small boat, we discovered this to be true, and as she drifted on to a bar and sunk, we went on with our work, feeling assured now that the river was ours as far down as Cairo at least.

We had captured quite a number of transports with New Madrid and Island No. 10, and now they became quite useful in moving our troops. Our regiment alone filled two or more (for we were not sure of high water) and we were soon past Cairo and made no halt until we were not many miles from Memphis. Why we did not land near there and march across to Pittsburg Landing was known only to the generals in command. We did not even tie up where it was possible to land. High water had covered the banks and we tied to trees that stood in water ten to twenty feet deep. To those whose boats brought up the rear, and had the pleasure of seeing a long curved line of jack-lights, lanterns and fire-holes from the main decks, the picture will probably remain a bright scene against a very dark back ground (a cypress swamp) reminding them of that far off long ago until the last solemn "Roll Call."

We curled up in our blankets feeling pretty safe. We knew we could run away from gunboats, bushwhackers could not get within two miles of us by land, and as for other transports molesting us, we felt that we could whip nearly "all creation" coming in that shape.

With the earliest light we set out on our return up the Mississippi to Cairo, up the Ohio to the Tennessee, and after eleven days reached Pittsburg Landing and passing a little above, disembarked at Hamburg Landing, April 21st, 1862, where for the first time the actual *business* of a cavalry soldier with us began.

We never knew when we lay down at night, usually without tents, whether we were to be allowed the luxury of an all night's sleep, (even though our blankets and the hard ground was all there was beneath us, and the changing sky above us), or were to be called at midnight or the earliest streak of day. We had enlisted for the war and were always cheerful under the most severe hardships. To be in the saddle all night was too common for even novelty; and to be engaged driving in scouting or reconnoitering parties was an every day occurrence, while a dash upon the enemy, testing the strength of their position, driving in pickets, destroying railroad tracks and bridges, losing a few, capturing a few, watching, advancing and drawing the enemy's fire while the infantry and artillery maneuvered for position—all this and more, became our daily schooling in the business of a soldier, and about all the credit we ever got, in those days, was ridicule from the infantry because we were not numerically strong enough to whip the whole rebel army without the aid of infantry or artillery. "Here, get back in the rear and give a *man* a chance," was the usual salutation as we, having accomplished our object, dropped back to await further developments.

One of the first encounters we had, meeting with any considerable force, was about the first of May, 1862. Our regiment went out with the second Iowa, taking the road that led through a small burg called Monterey, on the road to Corinth. It had been raining and the roads were soft, but the sun came out warm and clear as we started, early in the morning, to push the enemy as far as possible and return. We surprised their pickets, and rushed on towards their camp. Found them moving and their camp-fires and deserted camp equipage, cast off guns, bayonets, belts and cartridge boxes showed they were in a hurry to get somewhere, we knew not where, but soon found out. A running fight of two or three miles took us through Monterey and half a mile beyond, where our advance, under Captain Alger, rushed wildly into an artillery camp commanding a little hill, well protected by infantry.

Opening a sharp fire on us, the companies in front turned and got out of the way, while the companies in the rear moved under cover of a ravine, until they were again in the rear and deliberately marched back to Monterey, where the regiment re-formed in good order and returned to camp.

That scout came the nearest to being a panic in its termination of any movement we ever made, and as such, was a valuable lesson to us in teaching self control and guarding against a rout.

Very soon after this, about the 5th of May, 1862, our camp was established at, or near Farmington, beyond which our outposts, the cavalry vidette and pickets of the army, were stationed. Near our regiment was the well-known "Big Tree Signal Station," from which most of the enemy's works at Corinth could be inspected.

Not far in our advance, a half mile perhaps, was the open field upon which our heavy siege guns were planted, and across whose uneven surface, furrowed here and there by rains, some of the fiercest struggles of the war were fought. From this camp we were sent on those daily reconnaissances.

If Beauregard was discovered throwing up earthworks or forts this regiment was often selected to "feel of him," General Pope knowing that no retreat would be sounded until likely to be crushed by overpowering numbers. Sometimes the artillery would be sent up and a sharp artillery duel followed while we stood calmly by ready to support if needed. Occasionally the enemy felt of our works, when a skirmish was sure to follow, that, occurring anywhere else, would have been called a battle. The most important of these was fought on the 9th day of May and has been known as the Battle of Farmington. We give General Pope's report of that engagement:

HEADQUARTERS ARMY OF THE MISSISSIPPI,
Near Farmington, May 9, 1862.

MAJOR-GENERAL HALLECK:

The enemy is felling timber on my left and rear, about where a road conducts across Seven-mile Creek, to the highlands toward the railroad. I have a strong cavalry picket, a regiment of infantry, and a section of artillery on the road, about three miles from my left.

JNO. POPE,
Major-General Commanding.

HEADQUARTERS ARMY OF THE MISSISSIPPI,
May 9, 1862.

MAJOR-GENERAL BUELL:

Enemy is forming a pretty strong line of battle at Farmington, having driven in our pickets. Please march Nelson's division in this direction immediately, and be ready.

JNO. POPE,
Major-General Commanding.

Without entering into details it appears from correspondence between Generals Halleck and Pope, that the Army of the Mississippi (Pope's corps) was looked upon as holding the key to our advance when the time came, and General Halleck was taking all necessary precautions to bring the three divisions of his army into touching distance, and General Pope was expressly instructed not to bring on a general engagement until he had notice that all were ready, and therefore it was against General Pope's wishes that so stubborn a resistance was made at Farmington.

To check the enemy from a farther advance was his only thought; but our men could not understand the difference between a maneuvering retreat and that terrible word *defeat*, and, therefore, many a poor fellow lost his life, whom General Pope would gladly have saved. And for the same reason, doubtless, he does not refer to that engagement except as an unimportant skirmish. Thirty-five thousand against ten thousand was terrible odds, yet we were all mad because we could not hold our extreme advanced ground.

There was a tendency at this time among a certain class at Washington to belittle any of the minor engagements of that campaign, and probably no officer suffered more from this cause than General John Pope. To those who saw the obstacles which nature threw in the way of an active campaign in that locality, the energy with which General Pope pushed roads across swamps that appeared impassable, and placed heavy siege guns where but a few days before light artillery could scarcely go, the reason for this apparent over-caution, this apparent slowness of the "on to Corinth movement," was well understood. For an army as far from their base of supplies as ours was to have rushed into a trap, might have proved a national calamity, and it is a well established rule among the best military men to guard well their rear and flanks; hence the duty that cavalry performs in an advance of the magnitude of the north Mississippi campaign, was a very important and exceedingly arduous one. Night and day the movement must be continuous. If the enemy make a demonstration upon the left, neither swamp nor wood must form an impassable barrier. If they attack the right, the cavalry must be there also, to meet, fight and hold them until the main force can be brought into action.

This battle of Farmington was a peculiarly trying one. The enemy made a demonstration in full force and so sudden that when the cavalry moved forward to meet them and charged over the roughest part of the field they found line after line of infantry moving forward with unbroken tread; while their artillery rapidly formed on the flanks and poured a deadly enfilading fire of grape and canister into our ranks. We will never forget our "twin" Second Iowa cavalry at that moment, how they charged and re-charged the third time though every gully was filled with horses and men. It was a second Balakiava and before the enemy could shake them off our infantry was there and what came so near being a disastrous defeat was turned into a stubborn resistance and finally a victory for our arms. Our heavy guns were at one time held by the enemy, but they were all re-taken and the rebels sent staggering back into Corinth, leaving their dead and wounded upon the field.

With a dangerous swamp in our rear and only one available road, a retreat, we thought, meant annihilation. But it was characteristic of that army, they never knew when they were whipped; and so, they fought on, inch by inch, until the tide turned.

That battle really decided the fate of Corinth, by teaching Beauregard what kind of material he had to contend against. If Grant and Buell could hold their own at Shiloh *without* Pope what could they not do *with* him?

CHAPTER VI.

CORINTH—THE MISSISSIPPI CAMPAIGN—PHILIP H. SHERIDAN—RAID ON BOONVILLE—EVACUATION OF CORINTH—BLACKLAND.

Who that was encamped near Farmington has forgotten the following order and its midnight calls:

HEADQUARTERS ARMY OF THE MISSISSIPPI,
MAY 9th, 1862.

TO DIVISION COMMANDERS:

The discharge of a piece of artillery at these headquarters will from this time forth be the signal for the immediate assembling of this entire command under arms and at their posts.

By order of

GENERAL POPE.

C. A. MORGAN, Aide-de-Camp.

As this order was read to the troops immediately after the battle of Farmington it may well be supposed that the signal was obeyed with alacrity. If the long roll sounded in Beauregard's camp it was very likely to be sounded in ours very soon after. If our pickets were driven in at any hour of night or day, the dull reverberations of that headquarters gun would be replied to by a yell throughout camp as if every man slept with one eye and one ear wide open.

On the 15th of May a negro that had been captured by the rebels from an Ohio regiment escaped from Corinth and reported an unusual stir within the rebel camp, and talk of a movement south.

General Pope was anxious to move forward upon Corinth but he could not until General Buell had cleared a way and made roads to move forward simultaneously.

Day and night our cavalry, or some portion of it, was at the front pressing the enemy's outposts, establishing and holding positions, scouting or doing picket and vidette work.

The following is one of many scouts made at the time:

Headquarters Army of the Mississippi,
Farmington, May 22d, 1862.

Major-General Halleck:

The cavalry force I sent to Yellow Creek has returned. It went as far as the Tennessee river.

 * * * There was no enemy. * *

The country was almost impassable. The command then went to Iuka and returned along the railroad as far as Glendale. At Barnesville a few mounted pickets were seen and pursued for several miles in the direction of Jacinto, where there is a regiment of cavalry under McNeil, formerly of the "Rifles." * *

Jno. Pope,
Major-General Commanding.

Colonel Gordon Granger's commission as Brigadier-General dated back to March 26th, 1862, and from that time on the regiment was commanded by Lieutenant-Colonel Gorham. General Granger and Governor Blair felt that the command of this regiment should be in the hands of a thorough West Point soldier with no uncertain record, and looking around for such a man,

General Granger remembered Captain Philip H. Sheridan, of General Halleck's staff, and as Governor Blair happened to be at Farmington he recommended Captain Sheridan for the position and the following order was immediately issued:

> MILITARY DEPARTMENT OF MICHIGAN,
> ADJUTANT-GENERAL'S OFFICE,
> May 25th, 1862.
>
> Captain Philip H. Sheridan, U. S. A., is hereby appointed Colonel of the Second Regiment Michigan Cavalry, to rank from this date. Captain Sheridan will immediately assume command of the regiment.
>
> By order of the Commander in-Chief.
>
> JNO. ROBERTSON,
> Adjutant-General.

This order was made out at Pittsburg Landing and delivered to Captain Sheridan by Captain Alger, and Quartermaster Frank Walbridge, on the 26th, and next day—May 27th, Colonel Sheridan walked into camp and was introduced to the officers. In his quiet, unostentatious way he soon won the respect and confidence of the entire command.

By the following order it will be seen that our new colonel got himself immediately into business:

> HEADQUARTERS ARMY OF THE MISSISSIPPI,
> Farmington, May 27th, 1862.
>
> GENERAL GORDON GRANGER:
>
> You will send a brigade of cavalry, to proceed by some secluded route, to a point on the Mobile & Ohio railroad, at least forty miles south of Corinth, with instructions to destroy the railroad bridges, trestle works, telegraph wires, etc., wherever it is practicable, and to render the railroad useless as far as possible.
>
> In your orders to the officer commanding the brigade, you

MAJ.-GEN. GORDON GRANGER, U. S. V.,
COLONEL SECOND MICHIGAN CAVALRY.

will give him the necessary instructions as to his movements, being careful that he is to return by a different route from that pursued in his forward movement.

Respectfully,

JNO. POPE,

Major-General Commanding.

On the following day he writes to General Halleck, that one regiment returned from Iuka, thus leaving but two regiments, the Second Michigan and the Second Iowa Cavalry, to make the hazardous expedition into the enemy's country; to strike the advance of a retreating army of 35,000 men.

Who can ever forget the thick darkness of that moonless, starless night when our command cut loose from all encumbering baggage and set out by a circuitous route, avoiding towns and camps of the enemy, upon a trip that was to thoroughly test the endurance of horses and men?

Not a sound above a whisper, or the steady tramp of hoofs, the jingle of spur and saber, to keep heavy eyelids from closing, as hour after hour, by two and two we went wearily along, not knowing what moment an ambush might frustrate all our plans, of which we subalterns and men could only guess. Of such a thing as the evacuation of Corinth we had not dreamed, or doubtless when we reached Booneville on the morning of the 29th we should have felt more nervous.

The following shows what we really had to encounter:

HEADQUARTERS, CORINTH,
May 30th, 8:40 A. M.

MAJOR-GENERAL HALLECK:

My advance, the thirty-ninth Ohio and forty-second Illinois, entered town and planted the United States flag on the Court house at 6:40 this morning. They were the first troops in the place. I am throwing forward my cavalry and artillery in pursuit. The enemy retired by the Mobile road yesterday.

JNO. POPE,
Major-General.

Therefore when our little handful of men attacked the forces at Booneville and held the place for two hours, while the trains, depot and munitions of war were being destroyed, the greater part of Beauregard's army was within a mile or two of us, retreating rapidly toward our raiding party.

Colonel Elliott, of the second Iowa, was in command of this expedition, Colonel Sheridan second in command—and as the regiments were very much reduced in numbers by sickness and detail upon detached service, there were less than 1,200 men in the expedition.

In his report to General Halleck General Pope writes:

"They blew up one culvert, destroyed track, switches; burned up depots, locomotives and twenty six cars loaded with supplies of every kind; destroyed ten thousand stand of small arms, three pieces of artillery, a great quantity of clothing and ammunition and parolled two thousand prisoners who could not keep up with the cavalry. The enemy had heard of his movement and had a train of box and flat cars, carrying 5,000 infantry and artillery, running up and down to prevent his reaching the road. The whole road was lined with pickets. For several days Colonel Elliott's command subsisted on meat alone, such as they could find in the country. For daring and dash this expedition has been distinguished in the highest degree."

This was strictly true, although Beauregard in his report belittled the affair, and made *glaringly false statements.*

Colonel Elliott, in his report of this expedition, speaks in very flattering terms of the command under him, and makes special mention of the services of Colonel Sheridan, Lieutenant-Colonel Hatch, second Iowa, and Captain A. P. Campbell, the latter commanding a detachment of the second Michigan, that did some special service on our right (the enemy's front center) in repulsing the enemy while the work of destruction was going on, and says, the route taken covers a distance of two hundred miles, traveled between the early morning of the 28th and the evening of the 31st of May, 1862; and refers to it as the first expedition of the kind in the war of the rebellion.

The following is Colonel Sheridan's report of the Booneville Raid:

HEADQUARTERS SECOND MICHIGAN CAVALRY,
Camp near Farmington, Mississippi,
June 1st, 1862.

SIR:—I have the honor to report the following, as the operations of my regiment at the capture of Booneville, Mississippi, on the morning of May 29, 1862:

My regiment was formed a short distance in rear of the town, and on the left of the second regiment of Iowa cavalry, when I received directions from Colonel Elliott, commanding, to take one half of the regiment and pass to the south of the town, and destroy a bridge on the Mobile & Ohio Railroad, leaving the other half of the regiment in reserve, to support me, should it be necessary.

I proceeded rapidly in the direction indicated until I reached the road, then down the road one and a half miles, but found no bridge or culvert. I then learned that there was no bridge, except the one at Baldwin, some nine miles further down, and that defended by three regiments and one battery. Directions were then given to the companies to destroy the road by tearing up the track, bending the rails and burning the cross-ties. This was done with alacrity at four different places, by both officers and men, and continued until I received orders from the Colonel commanding to join him at once at Booneville.

While these operations were going on, a dash was made by a squadron of rebel cavalry at our rear and on the right of the reserve of my regiment, but was handsomely met by the reserve command of Captain Campbell, who dismounted a portion of his command, and when the enemy came within range, received them with a volley which caused them to break and run in all directions.

While passing to the south of the town and along the railroad, I captured about five hundred Confederate soldiers, one hundred of whom had good percussion muskets, the balance I think had thrown their muskets away. They were placed along the road to defend it, but made no resistance. I turned them loose after breaking up their guns, as we could not be burdened with them, in our rapid return to this camp.

I have the honor to report that the officers and men of my regiment without a single exception behaved well.

I respectfully bring to the notice of the Colonel commanding, Captain Campbell, commanding the reserve, Captain Alger, who commanded the line of skirmishers in my advance, and Adjutant George Lee, who rendered important services. My regiment returned to camp without any casualties.

Very respectfully, your obedient servant,

P. H. SHERIDAN,
Colonel Commanding.

To LIEUTENANT C. F. MARDEN,
    Adjutant Second Brigade, Cavalry Division,
        Army of the Mississippi.

General McPherson was at the time in charge of all the railroads in General Halleck's army. He said if it had not been for the engine and cars we cut off at Booneville, he could not have supplied the army, as the Tennessee River was then too low for transports to move, and there was not rolling stock enough south of the Ohio River to move the immense supplies required.

On our return to Corinth (or Farmington) we learned of the evacuation and then realized that we had been giving Beauregard's whole army a brush. Our loss was very slight, and after one night's rest—such perfect rest as comes to weary bodies after long privations, with a feeling of perfect security for one night's undisturbed slumber—we were again in the saddle and off for the front. Passing over the scene of our daily struggles —here our outpost camping ground, there a well worn path where chain guard, videttes or grand rounds had made every tree, stump, log and knoll as familiar as the cow paths at our old northern homesteads; and just across the little opening a glistening musket or a little puff of smoke must surely greet us if we go farther. But these forbidden grounds are free once more and we go cheerily along—through deserted rebel camps, earthworks, fallen trees, abattis and on through more threatening forts, near which mysterious graves were made to give up their buried treasure of heavy siege guns, too heavy for rapid flight.

If we had passed days and weeks at the front we were for a time at least well toward the rear. How long we were to remain so was soon revealed to us; for on we go through Corinth with scarce a halt, and on toward the scene of our late raid, nor did we halt until we were within sound of guns again.

On the 4th of June we passed the still smoldering fires of Booneville, and saw the ground covered with shot and unexploded shell thrown from the cars, the explosions of which it is said led the Confederates to believe they were attacked in force, and it really did sound like a fierce engagement with artillery and musketry. Had they but known we were a mere handful; had we but known how near we were to Beauregard's main army, how different the result might have been for the "Twin Seconds!"

On the morning of the fifth of June we were again pressing the enemy toward Blackland. Encouraged by the constant giving way of the enemy's rear guard, Colonel Sheridan pushed on by the main road leading from Booneville to Blackland, our right flank.

And here a digression seems necessary. History reveals the fact that General Pope, though sick in his tent at Booneville, had suggested to his superior in command that by united action, a vigorous push would undoubtedly result in the capture of a large portion of Beauregard's broken, disheartened army. Assurances of support upon the right and left flanks were not promptly given, and thus left to himself Pope was in doubt how far Halleck desired the movement carried south. The army, or that portion of it acting with Pope, had been everywhere successful, yet we were usually very cautious. General Pope had written to General Halleck that he could probably take possession of all the country as far south as Baldwin, but to hold it was another thing; it was a long distance from his base of supplies and therefore he had given instructions to his subordinate officers not to push beyond certain points but to return to Booneville and go into camp. Therefore when Colonel Sheridan went out on the Blackland road it was to find out what the strength of the enemy was in that direction and return.

The colonel did not propose to fritter away much time scouting and skirmishing, feeling cautiously here and there and give the enemy a chance to organize for a determined stand. Yet it must be confessed he had undoubtedly been deceived as to the condition of the banks of a little muddy stream, nearly dry, that lay in our path, across which there was but one bridge, a little log, mud-covered affair not to exceed twenty feet in length.

With a few men out on the flanks the column at once put a stop to the scattering fire and dashed forward through the narrow forest road, capturing here and there a picket or a straggler and keeping up a running fire for a mile or more, then with a shout and our saber battalion in the advance, closely followed by the heavier dragoon portion of the regiment, we went whirling down upon them, nor thought of halting until the little bridge was crossed, the hill gained and we found ourselves within pistol range of a heavy park of artillery supported by a division of infantry. There they were, in plain sight, only a few rods distant through the trees; there was evidently some consternation among the infantry; but the artillery met us with shell, and its support, or those immediately near, gave us a volley—bullets and buckshot being about equally divided. The shelling of the woods was calculated to strike terror into the hearts of older soldiers than we were, yet remarkably few showed outward signs of fear. A very close call was that for Colonel Sheridan, who, when the enemy opened with shell, had his hat knocked from his head by a piece of broken shell, and as an orderly handed it up—"Rather a close call, Stephenson"— was his only remark, and few were aware how near we came to losing our Colonel at the beginning of his career. "The bridge!" That one thought seemed to seize every one, and before the command had fairly died away in the thick smoke that surrounded us, a battalion under Campbell had dismounted and were in line ready for any forward movement on the part of the enemy.

Colonel Sheridan quietly withdrew his troops under cover of the woods, the dismounted men covering the retreat safely, and in a short time all were back across the bridge; a few, however, trying the stream, found it almost bottomless and only succeeded in getting out with extreme difficulty. One of the most remarkable escapes occurred to an orderly, whose horse, a new one, could not be checked when the artillery opened so close. Dashing into the muddy stream, he climbed the bank, panting and nearly exhausted, only to lose his footing at the very top, and reeling, fell backward a distance of twenty or thirty feet nearly perpendicular and struck upon his head, but his rider, a small, youthful soldier, slipped from the saddle at the very crest of the bank and landed square upon his feet unharmed. One look satisfied him the horse was or would be dead shortly, and he mounted an unsaddled mule and rode away. This showed conclusively what a splendid opportunity was lost to the enemy that they did not attempt, at least, to capture the whole of us by a rapid forward movement at the time our bugle sounded the recall, but it would have cost them dearly.

The expedition was successful and had ended without doubt in thoroughly arousing the enemy to a sense of the dangers that beset them if they lingered there long, which they did not do, for in a day or two we were over the same ground again and not an enemy in sight.

It appears the enemy had withdrawn all forces toward Baldwin, forty-one miles south of Corinth, the direction in which Rosecrans's division had been moving. The second was therefore soon ordered to join the advance down the Mobile & Ohio and on the 7th we were on the gallop along that railroad, and passing through Baldwin with scarce a halt, soon brought up at the little station, Guntown, about five miles farther than we were ordered to go, and therefore, finding no enemy in sight, with every evidence of a hasty departure, with the midsummer sun beating upon the little band of Michigan men, who had not slept nor eaten but little for thirty hours, we returned. Our knapsacks and canteens were about empty and twenty miles lay between us and our wagon trains. The country had been stripped by the retreating enemy, and even a raw onion was looked upon as a luxury to be enjoyed only by the tireless forager; and many a Yankee took his first lessons in drinking buttermilk and eating "corn pones" as we sauntered back to our camp near Booneville, where our summer outpost campaign began, June 9th, 1862.

CHAPTER VII.

THE NORTH MISSISSIPPI CAMPAIGN—PINE HILLS—BACK TO BOONE-
VILLE—THE SECOND BOONEVILLE—RIENZI—A FLAG OF
TRUCE.

June 10, 1862: The enemy were now encamped at different towns twenty five to forty miles to the south and southwest of Corinth, and contented themselves with an occasional scout in our immediate front, but their campaign had been generally disastrous, not only losing many of their best troops, either in action or by desertion, but greatly disheartening them by their loss of territory, arms, accoutrements and fortifications.

Though we held the key to the north Mississippi country— Corinth—with the railroads leading north, east, west and south, yet the climate had begun to tell heavily upon our troops, and out of 1,200 fighting men of six months before, the regiment could not muster over 450 to 500 effective men. The most healthy locations for a camp were selected for all the troops and it fell to our lot to take up a position between Corinth and Hamburg Landing, on a range of dry pine hills, where we might not only recruit the shattered health of the men but also the strength of our worn and jaded horses; adding new ones in place of those entirely worthless.

Near by were the field hospitals—long rows of large square tents spread beneath the few scattered trees, and from which more men were carried out to their "long homes" than had fallen upon the battle field; and as many more were sent away to the North as soon as they were able to creep from their cots upon which they had tossed for many weary days in the delirium of fever; or, moving about camp, living skeletons, around whose emaciated forms the coarse army clothing hung and flapped like animated scare-crows, hunting for something.

Those were trying days for our troops. Generals saw their divisions melt into brigades; brigades to regiments and regiments to battalions. Men lying beneath the shade of hospital tents saw stretchers brush past and asked no questions. It might be brother, father or faithful comrade; self preservation taught them only to ask themselves, "will my turn come next?" and the heart grew callous and indifferent, though men were buried by the score.

The few remaining days of June went speedily by, however, as we were simply recuperating, and our *duties* were little more than a picnic from the 9th to the 29th of June. But for those twenty days of light duty we paid dearly afterward. From the left and rear to the extreme front was only a jump of little more than a day. We were getting settled down in camp, a bit homelike, on the 1st day of July, 1862, near Booneville, when early in the morning—immediately after Sergeant Smith (afterward Captain Smith) had gone out with his company to relieve the picket, stationed about three miles and a half south and west of Booneville, under Lieutenant Scranton (afterward Major Scranton), word came back that our pickets were being driven in.

It appears that during the previous week a company of the Third Michigan Cavalry had been partially captured at the same point during the night while on picket duty, and, that frequent night raids had been made on outposts all through that country. As we looked upon this as a sort of guerrilla warfare that deserved to be stamped out, several of the Second's officers had expressed a desire to be attacked in the same manner. In fact we were all getting somewhat *conceited* with our death-dealing revolving rifles. Therefore when Colonel Sheridan said in his quiet way, "Captain Campbell, you may take two companies more out and see what's going on," there was a look of eager determination upon the face of every man that was something wicked to behold.

When Captain Campbell arrived on the scene he discovered that Lieutenant Scranton had already repulsed the enemy twice, though falling back each time and that his (Campbell's) arrival was very opportune, for the enemy were swinging quite a heavy column around to our left and were likely to capture or demoralize that part of Lieutenant Scranton's command, which he was then hurrying in from the right to a more favorable position on the Booneville road.

But let us hear what Colonel Sheridan had to say respecting the second Booneville:

HEADQUARTERS SECOND BRIGADE, CAVALRY DIVISION,
Camp on Kings Creek, Mississippi, July 2d, 1862.

SIR:—I have the honor to report that in obedience to your instructions, I established my brigade consisting of the second

Iowa and second Michigan cavalry regiments at Booneville, Mississippi, June 28th, and threw out strong pickets on the numerous roads approaching that place.

On the morning of July 1st, a cavalry command of between four thousand and five thousand men under General Chalmers advanced toward Booneville on two converging roads. The head of their column on the Booneville and Blackland road came in contact with my pickets three and one-half miles southwest of Booneville. This picket under command of Lieutenant Scranton, second Michigan cavalry, fell back slowly, taking advantage of every tree to fire from until they came to the point where the second road on which the enemy were advancing intersected this road. At this point our picket had a strong position and good cover and were presently reinforced by a second company, and subsequently by three companies more, all of the second Michigan, under command of Captain Campbell.

The enemy had, up to this time, only shown the heads of his columns. At this point, our resistance was so great, that the enemy was obliged to deploy two regiments on the right and left of the road. Information was then sent to me, that the enemy were in force. I sent word to Captain Campbell to hold the enemy, until I could support him, and if necessary to fall back slowly. Previous to this time, I had stationed one battalion, second Iowa, in Booneville. I then directed Colonel Hatch to leave one company of his regiment in camp, and take the balance of his regiment and the battalion in Booneville, except two saber companies, and form in rear of Campbell, cover his flanks and support him by a charge, should the enemy break his line. While this was being done, the enemy attempted to drive Captain Campbell from his position by a charge through the open field. In this they did not succeed, but were gallantly repulsed with great loss, my men reserving their fire until they were within twenty-five or thirty yards, when they opened a fire on them with their Colt's revolving rifles. They then commenced turning the flanks of Captain Campbell's position, when he retired to another strong position in his rear.

As soon as the enemy saw him retiring, they again charged him, but he succeeded in repelling them by collecting his men together in groups, when a hand to hand conflict took place, the men in some cases using the butts of their guns. At this time, Lieutenant-Colonel Hatch, second Iowa, came up with his supports, and this position was maintained for a considerable length of time.

The enemy again commenced his flanking movements, passing around our left, crossing the railroad and approaching the left of our camp. I then determined to turn their left flank, and make a bold dash at their rear; this was handsomely executed by Captain Alger, second Michigan, with four saber companies, two from second Michigan, and two from second Iowa. The Captain passed around their left flank by a circuitous route, until he came directly on their rear, on the Blackland road. He then charged the enemy with sabers, and drove them until their overwhelming numbers obliged him to retire. At the same time that I gave the order to Captain Alger to attack their rear, I directed Lieutenant-Colonel Hatch, second Iowa, to move a portion of his regiment to their left flank, and if a good opportunity occurred to make a charge. This movement was finely executed, and a dash made successfully at their left flank.

The charge of Captain Alger directly in their rear, and the dash made at them on their left, by Major Coon, second Iowa, together with the determined and stubborn resistance of Captain Campbell, with his one hundred and sixty riflemen in front, so much disconcerted the enemy, that they commenced falling back, leaving a large number of their dead and wounded officers and men on the field, and were followed up a distance of four miles. At this point the enemy crossed a difficult swamp, and night coming on, the pursuit was abandoned, and the troops ordered to return to camp.

Our loss in this affair was killed, one; wounded, twenty-four; missing, sixteen; total casualties, forty-one.

The loss of the enemy must have been severe, as we were occupying good positions all the time, and well covered, while they used the open ground for their deployment. They have taken a number of wagons from the people to carry off their dead and wounded. Among the wounded that fell into our hands, are two Lieutenants, who will die.

I respectfully bring to the notice of the General, the good conduct of the officers and men of my command : Colonel Hatch, second Iowa; Major Coon; Captains Gilbert and Queal, second Iowa; Captain Campbell, Captain Alger, Captain Wells, Captain Schuyler, and Lieutenants Scranton, Hutton, and Nicholson, of the second Michigan, all behaved with great gallantry,

Major Hepburn, A. A. A. General Lee, and Lieutenant Thatcher, who acted as aids during the day, are deserving of great praise.

I am sir, very respectfully, your obedient servant,

P. H. SHERIDAN,
Colonel Commanding Second Brigade,
CAPTAIN R. O. SELFRIDGE, Cavalry Division.
A. A. G., Cav. Div., Army of the Mississippi.

* * * * * * * * *

HEADQUARTERS ARMY OF THE MISSISSIPPI,
July 2d, 1862.

The General commanding, announces to this Army, that on the 1st instant, Colonel P. H. Sheridan, second Michigan cavalry, with eleven companies of the second Michigan, and eleven companies of the second Iowa, was attacked, near Booneville, by eight regiments of rebel cavalry under Chalmers, and after an eight hours. fight defeated and drove them back, leaving their dead and wounded on the field.

The coolness, determination and fearless gallantry displayed by Colonel Sheridan, and the officers and men of his command, in this action, deserve the thanks and admiration of the Army.

* * * * * * * * *

By order of General Rosecrans:
W. L. ELLIOTT,
Brigadier-General and Chief of Staff.

HEADQUARTERS SECOND BRIGADE, CAVALRY DIVISION,
July 2d, 1862.

GENERAL:—The enemy have retreated, and in all probability to Guntown and Saltillo. There are none of them to be found between Booneville and Blackland.

I have two companies of infantry and a battery of artillery for support furnished by General Asboth, which is all that is necessary at the present time.

We were attacked by General Chalmers, with the following regiments:—Brewer's 200; Say's 800; Adam's 874; Green's 800; first Alabama battalion, 180; Kentucky battalion, 180; Carson's 800; Balsac's 800; and probably two others.

P. H. SHERIDAN,
Colonel Commanding.

BRIGADIER-GENERAL W. L. ELLIOTT,
Chief of Staff, Army of the Mississippi.

This report was very concise, but Colonel Sheridan did not state that he was more fit for the hospital than active service that morning; and when we remember the plans, how they were laid, with each officer's special duty so interwoven with the whole plan of operations, we are compelled to acknowledge that right here was evidence of true military genius in this young officer's career at the very threshold of life—the very first engagement he ever had the opportunity of planning and executing, and of greater importance than an Indian fight.

What Corinth was to the whole Northern army, that also was Booneville to Corinth. Roads lead to Blackland, Guntown, Tupelo, Jackson and the great strategic points of all the Mississippi valley; and the opportunities for flank movements by the Confederates were very limited. Hence, the defeat of Chalmers by Sheridan, was looked upon as a great victory, regardless of the numbers engaged, or the losses upon either side.

A study of the following map, roughly sketched from memory, will enable us to realize the full importance of the position and the brilliancy of the engagement that ended so victoriously for our troops:

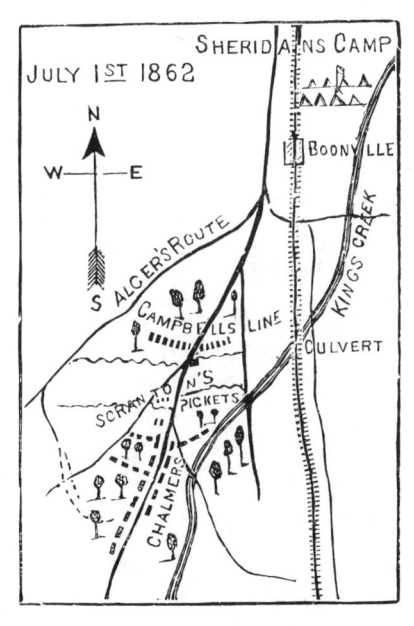

BOONEVILLE.

By referring to Colonel Sheridan's report to General Rosecrans, it will be seen that the force opposed to us, under General Chalmers, was no small scouting party but was composed of the fighting men of eight regiments—at least 4,500 men, and when these formed in solid column and charged down upon our little band of less than 500 (166 at that particular point) in that winding woods road with oak openings on either side, through which either artillery, infantry or cavalry would have no trouble in operating, it is not saying too much surely to write that stubborn engagement down as among the most heroic struggles of the war.

That deadly fire, the emptying of saddles, that half living blockade of fallen horses and men—who, that saw it, can ever forget the struggling mass, groaning, cursing, shouting and creeping from beneath the heaps of dead and dying horses and men? Surely this is more than a skirmish. And our men! Take a look at them. Their horses—where are they? Not far off. And if they have been driven from one position their next is not far in the rear, and every tree and bush hides a whole battery of small arms, while along the line, with a look of fierce determination, strides the "big captain," pistol in hand, and near him the other officers—the non-commissioned officers and men—who so ably assisted him in that hand to hand encounter with ten times their number. No wonder the rebels thought it Yankee brag, when afterward told how small the number was opposed to them on that day; and when Captain Alger, with his four companies, dashed in upon the enemy's rear, the work of strategy was complete. Bewildered, uncertain as to our real strength, discouraged, outgeneraled, the gay Chalmers, who came so near being captured by Alger's command, turned his horse and allowed his men to save themselves as best they might.

For their part in this action Captain Campbell was promoted to lieutenant-colonel and Captain Alger was promoted to major. Prompt recognition of valuable services was characteristic of Sheridan. With Campbell, standing like an enraged tiger, at bay in his lair; and Alger and his trusty followers impetuously assaulting him in rear, Chalmers did well to retire and look better into his situation. If he did not know Sheridan before, he knew him then.

On the morrow, when the writer, as aid to Colonel Sheridan, went over the grounds with an escort to see how many wounded were left, every house was found to be a hospital, while all that were able to be removed had gone and many of the dead were buried or carried away.

In reviewing that engagement after a lapse of more than twenty years, the thought occurs to us that there could have been no greater proof of the wisdom and fitness of military skill and judgment than was shown in the arming of these sturdy men of Michigan with just such arms as they had; drilling them in just the tactics by which they were drilled and giving them just the colonel that was given them. And let it be recorded in the annals of American history that a battalion of dismounted Michigan cavalry held their own against a division of cavalry and infantry, on equal grounds, without earthworks, fence or thick woods; and this was our loss: killed, 1; wounded, 25; missing, 16; total casualties, 42. And thus was the key to this important outpost held without reinforcements, which reached us late in the afternoon, though it is quite probable that the whistle of the locomotive and the cheering of the men in camp had something to do with accelerating the movements of the enemy toward their rear.

This victory gave us comparative rest for a month, during which time we moved camp three times, looking for the most desirable location that could be found. Good water and a dry camp were not always obtainable in that land of swamps.

But Rienzi came the nearest to being a perfect camping ground that we found in all that country, while pleasant roads, an abundance of open fields for parade and drill grounds (to say nothing of horse races) made camp life quite endurable for those who were blessed with moderate good health.

Many incidents, not strictly historic, will be reserved for Part Second of this volume, that will forever stamp Rienzi as *the* camp of all others filled with stirring events of camp life on the frontier, including "A Flag of Truce," "Capturing Outposts," etc., and this chapter is closed with Colonel Sheridan's report of the repulse of the rebel Colonel Faulkner.

HEADQUARTERS SECOND BRIGADE, CAVALRY DIVISION,
August 27, 1862.

CAPTAIN:—I have the honor to report that my cavalry pickets on the Ripley road were attacked yesterday, about two o'clock p. m., by a large force of the enemy, say seven hundred to eight hundred. The pickets were rapidly driven in, followed by a small detachment of the enemy, to the vicinity of my camp. The command was quickly turned out, and Colonel Hatch directed, with two battalions of his regiment, to attack the enemy, supported by Colonel Lee with two battalions of the seventh Kansas. Upon the approach of this force, the enemy exchanged a few shots with them and broke and ran, closely pursued by Colonels Hatch and Lee, who were directed to drive the enemy beyond the Hatchie. The second Michigan was held in reserve.

The enemy made a stand at Nowland's Store, but were attacked so vigorously that they again broke and fled, this time scattering in every direction. From this point to within five miles of Ripley there was a complete rout, the road was strewn with shot-guns, dead horses, hats, coats, blankets, etc. Colonel Faulkner, commanding this rebel force, was so hard pressed that he separated from his command on one of the little by paths and made his escape. He left us his hat, however, as did nearly the whole of his command.

The pursuit was continued to within five miles of Ripley, and until after dark, when the command was ordered to return to camp with their jaded and worn-out horses.

Our loss in this affair was two badly and four slightly wounded, and four or five missing, some of whom I think, will probably come in. The loss of the enemy I am unable to state; it was understood they were guerrillas; unfortunately eleven prisoners were brought in. About two hundred shot-guns, twenty horses, and a large number of pistols were also brought in.

The effect of this rout must be very discouraging to the enemy. I doubt if ever they will fully collect together again. All but three companies were raw levies. The effect on our men was very exhilarating.

I cannot speak too highly of the promptness with which the command turned out, being ready and in pursuit of the enemy in fifteen minutes after the first information of the enemy's approach was received.

P. H. SHERIDAN,
Brigadier-General Commanding.

CAPTAIN W. C. RUSSELL,
Assistant Adjutant-General.

OFFICIAL:
F. D. GRANT,
Lieutenant-Colonel, A. D. C.

As usual, the second Michigan was immediately sent out after the return of the chasing party and the country was scouted beyond Ripley. But the second Iowa and seventh Kansas had done their work thoroughly; no enemy was found, except in the distance a shadowy horseman, repeating the tactics of yesterday.

CHAPTER VIII.

FROM CORINTH TO PERRYVILLE—COL. PHIL. GETS HIS FIRST STAR—CAPT. ARCHIE CAMPBELL MADE COLONEL—INCIDENTS BY THE WAY—AFLOAT ON THE OHIO—CINCINNATI—LOUISVILLE—GENERAL BUELL—ROUSSEAU AND SHERIDAN.

The comparative quiet our troops had enjoyed in the north Mississippi country since the victory of Sheridan over Chalmers at Booneville had been a great blessing to the Confederates under Beauregard, giving them time to mature plans, offensive, rather than defensive, and they improved it in a bold campaign, far to our left, not stopping to menace Nashville or any other stronghold we might have had.

September 1st, 1862, Bragg's army, crossing the Tennessee river, marched triumphantly, without check or hindrance, through the states of Tennessee and Kentucky, nor stopped until they had neared the gates to Ohio and Indiana at Cincinnati and Louisville.

The abandonment of Corinth was not to be thought of, but among the troops withdrawn from that key to the South, Sheridan requested and obtained leave to bring with him his old regiment. He had now won his first star, and was ordered to take command of an infantry division.

Early in September, 1862, the outposts south of Corinth were drawn in and preparations made for leaving a strong garrison force at Corinth, while the main part of that army started on a race with Bragg for Kentucky.

Railway transportation was used as far as possible and the 9th of September found the Second at Columbus, Kentucky, having filled every car, outside and in, to its utmost capacity, riding on top of box cars, many of them, with that reckless abandon and boisterous hilarity so common to soldiers under such circumstances. It was more like an armed picnic excursion than a headlong rush to battle.

At Columbus we embarked on government transports, and this embarkation was a scene long to be remembered, for its novelty and excitement.

Thirteen transports lay at the levee, receiving their burdens of horses, mules and government wagons. From frowning bluffs looked down upon us great black iron "dogs of war;" and at their base, upon a level plateau, lay scattered about heaps of torpedoes, shot and shell. Braying mules and neighing horses were hurried—carried if necessary—along the plank on board, occasionally falling, feet uppermost, in the muddy waters below—disappearing for a moment, then clambering out to be led and pushed, more vigorously and with less patience, along the giddy walk; and when night closed in all were on board, the plank hauled in, and with a bright Southern moon for our light, myriads of twinkling stars, flashing jack-lights and glaring furnace fires, the ropes were cast off and we set out for the Ohio river.

The entire trip was a grand holiday rest, and never did troops enter into the spirit of fun with greater zest than on this occasion.

In ten days, after passing through some little excitement occasionally from scattering guerrilla fire along the bank, we halted at Louisville, only to learn that Cincinnati was threatened, and on to that point we pushed without disembarking.

But we were immediately ordered to return to Louisville, where we found the city under great excitement. According to rumor the whole rebel army was ready to march in and take possession. But our forces were now arriving in large numbers, and the city began to breathe more freely. Earthworks were hurriedly thrown up around the suburbs, from river to river, while the cavalry began to push out, scouting and finding the river road southwest clear nearly to Elizabethtown.

The Second made a dash upon that place, capturing the outposts and a portion of the troops stationed there. A Confederate flag waved defiantly from the court house, but Sergeant-Major Hoyt, with a few men from Company F, rushed in, regardless of how many might be secreted there, and tore it down, bringing it away triumphantly. We retired leisurely to our camp at Louisville, and immediately began our heavy picket duty, whole regiments going out and standing to horse all night.

On one of those darkest of Southern dark nights we took the Bardstown pike, and found the enemy strongly posted within a few miles of the city. We crept up as near as possible and received a raking fire of grape shot from a battery, but fortunately they fired low and only one man was killed—Lieutenant Daniel Moody, of Company E,* the first blood of the Kentucky campaign. Knowing their position and having no desire for night battle, we retired a short distance and stood to horse all night, but no further demonstrations were made on either side.

Colonel Sheridan had now received his commission as Brigadier-General, to date back to the Booneville fight, and Captain Campbell was made colonel from the same date.

We received some recruits and new horses and once more the regiment was finely mounted and in good shape. The struggle immediately began. On the first day of October, 1862, the grand army of Don Carlos Buell marched out of Louisville with 58,000 men—a grand pageantry of war—flags flying, bands playing, gaily caparisoned horses dancing, and the heavy rattle and clank of artillery wheels mingling with martial strains of fife and drum beat.

Proudly the Second responded to the order—to "take the front," upon the center, while from every road troops came pouring out of the city. Would this be another "Bull Run?"

Out upon the Bardstown pike we marched, and soon met the enemy's outposts. Firing, then retire to give the alarm, and then began that memorable Kentucky campaign—cavalry attacking skirmish lines; sometimes mounted, oftener dismounted, steadily moving forward, pressing the enemy's rear guard, and a continuous running fight of seven days followed, over every foot of ground from Louisville to Perryville, during the week

* He had that day received notice that a lieutenant's commission was on the way for him, but he was never entered upon the roll as such.

that intervened, by night or by day, sleeping as we could catch it, by the road side, in the fence corners and in grove, or woods; always without tents, and generally with only hard bread, bacon and coffee for our rations—the country having been stripped by Bragg's army. Clouds of dust filled the air—no rains for weeks, and the only liquid refreshment found to moisten our parched throats was from muddy, stagnant pools, in rocky dry creek bottoms, through which the whole Confederate cavalry had tramped. Was it any wonder that men swallowed Kentucky apple-jack in draughts that would have killed a man under ordinary circumstances?

We neared the hills beyond which Chaplin Creek wound along, and to it we were looking with eager eyes, hoping in a few hours to revel in the luxury of clear water.

A wreath of smoke; a sharp crackling report; a whizzing, screeching sound, followed by a bursting shell close to our lines, warned us that the enemy had found a good place to make a stand.

This being Kentucky soil, it was proper that a Kentucky regiment should have the first opportunity to crush the invaders. A well mounted regiment of them—the seventh—dashed away in good style, down across the valley and up the opposite hill.

It was probably their first charge, and therefore we should not lay it up against them, if immediately on striking the enemy and finding them strongly posted with grape and canister in abundance, they very soon "struck for their homes," hatless and considerably demoralized.

It was a very unsoldier-like thing for the men of the Second to laugh and shout, and they were immediately given an opportunity to do better; but whether from pride or otherwise they moved up with a few companies thrown out, dismounted and staid.

The battle of Perryville has never been fully understood by the general public. It has been treated by newspaper historians as a mere skirmish. How many are there that ever knew that nearly 10,000 men were either killed or wounded, and that the struggle was almost continuous either on the right or left, and often at both wings, from sunrise until long after dark? Fourteen hours of fire and smoke, with lead and iron hail, without food or water, deserves more than a contemptuous notice.

It will not be attempted to do that battle entire justice in this volume, but we feel it due our regiment and all the troops that participated in that fierce struggle to record in brief some of the general movements, and, if possible, direct attention to the causes which led to our failure in securing not only victory for our arms but a crushing defeat for the enemy.

The Second, with two companies thrown out in advance, had driven the enemy's rear guard across Doctor's Fork of Chaplin Creek, on the Springfield road, late in the afternoon of October 7th, and beyond that haystack which has been made historic. Here we were checked by sharpshooters. At first their firing was so far away on the hills, removed from the main body of their troops, that we could not hear the reports of their guns, but their bullets were uncomfortably close with their hissing music. One of our companies was deployed on the right and one on the left of the road, and creeping forward, dismounted, we determined to dislodge them, when down upon us with a Texas yell came a squadron of rangers, their leader mounted upon a fine gray stallion. Giving them a well directed volley they were scattered, the commander falling with a mortal wound. His comrades abandoned him, for many of them were apparently hard hit, but the horse stood mutely by, until the dying captain was removed to a house near, which at once became a hospital, and this was the first victim of Perryville.

The charging party returned to their forces on the hill; their artillery opened on the mounted portion of the Second as they stood near our skirmish line, and it began to look as if we were to close the day in a general engagement. Our line was soon strengthened by infantry and artillery, but it was now too late for any further advance that night, and the cavalry were glad to give up the post of honor for one of rest.

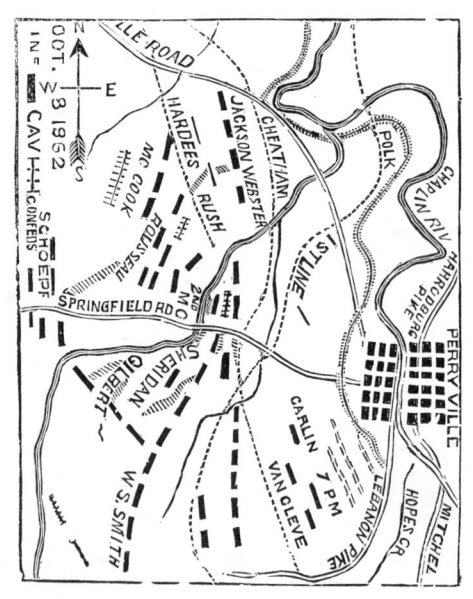

PERRYVILLE.

Early in the morning of October 8th, "those revolving rifles" were wanted at the front again. We found the enemy had retired a short distance, but we soon uncovered their position after crossing Doctor's Fork, where we were met by a brisk fire from musketry, lodged in a wooded hill beyond, at easy range. The regiment was immediately ordered to "dismount and fight on foot." Horses were left in the rear and the men only checked their steps when it was discovered an unusually large body of sharpshooters were decimating our ranks.

The advance, consisting of six companies, under command of Major Alger, pressed forward to the foot of the hill.*

"Under cover" was shouted along the line, and every puff of smoke was met by another. Two regiments of sharpshooters confronting each other meant no boys' play.

We were now face to face with the Arkansas sharpshooters. A hand, a hat, or the smallest part of a body exposed, on either side, was sure to receive a bullet.

During this short stop seventeen men of Company D went down; other companies lost, but not so heavily. But we had five bullets to their one, and their fire was very soon silenced by our steady pouring of lead into their hiding places, and the enemy were glad to creep rapidly along the ground, and behind trees until the brow of the hill put them in temporary safety. But in doing so they lost heavily. The enemy formed a new line near by. Then, as if seized by a sudden impulse, the entire regiment sprang to their feet, flew over the fence and mounted the ridge, nor checked their steps until they had

*Major Alger was immediately after promoted to lieutenant-colonel of the sixth cavalry, and later to the colonelcy of the fifth, serving in the Shenandoah with Sheridan, and later was brevetted for meritorious service to brigadier and major-general.

driven the enemy down the hill on the other side. Then the enemy's new line met us, and it was too hot for so small a number, even with revolving 'rifles. Again the men were ordered under cover, and a part of the regiment withdrawn. This was a signal for the Confederates, and leaping to their feet they rushed in strong force upon our battalion and we hastily retired. Here Captains Weatherwax and Barrows were each shot through the thigh. Captain Weatherwax hobbled off on one leg with the bullets plowing the face of the hill all around him. Captain Barrows was also brought away.

And now our own infantry, the second Missouri and forty-fourth Illinois, came to our relief, and gallantly took the front with, "You have done enough, boys, for this morning," and at sight of them the enemy fell back rapidly.

Not a waver along the line; but that steady tramp! tramp! tramp! moving on up over the hill. The scattering ceased and the only sound to be heard was the muffled tread of armed men. Again the rattling fire, but not a step was broken, and now we see those men with iron nerve raise their polished arms to a level with their eyes and—Woo-o-o! as if one hand had moved the whole; and forward upon double quick they go—loading and firing at will, as they run. The enemy were driven from the ridge, and now as we look to the right we see our Phil and staff riding along the crest of the hill and know at once that these are a part of his division.

The wounded are removed. Barrett's and Hiscock's batteries are ordered up the right of the Springfield road and Loomis's battery on the left, where we moved and formed in his front and rear as a support, and here that old prince among artillerymen fired away, over our heads, across the valley, warning the enemy by his wonderful close shots that they were no match for him at long range and that they were being watched. For an hour or more an artillery duel was here carried on, the enemy's artillery occupying the hills near Perryville.

What was occurring in front of Sheridan we can only conjecture, but we knew that his artillery was busy, and that occasionally there were flank fires, met by our infantry with crash and cheer, and our lines were as yet unbroken. General Sheridan's official report of his part in that engagement has been kindly furnished and will tell the story from his own pen.

As yet there were no demonstrations upon our center from the enemy's infantry, but Loomis's eagle eye swept the field, and his gruff voice fairly shook the hills as, turning to General Rousseau, who had just rode up from the left, he roared, "General, what is that away up that pike across yonder?"

"Well, I should say it's dust!"

"I should say so. Oh, I'm not so full but I could tell that, ha, ha!" and that magnificent voice again burst out full above the bang and crash of his "Coldwater pets."* The cloud of dust grew. The enemy's artillery fire from the Perryville hills slackened.

Again that muttered thunder from Loomis:

"General, that's a large body of troops, and that's—yes, Harrodsburg pike. I guess we have tread on the tail of Mr. Bragg's coat, ha, ha!"

"Here orderly, where's my glass?" from Rousseau.

"Mine is at your service, General," and taking it from his

*It will be remembered that Loomis's battery was known as the "Coldwater" artillery.

hand, he gazed long and carefully, never dreaming that there was a hidden enemy much nearer. Returning the glass apparently satisfied that he must move his division up from the left to meet them at the best possible vantage ground, he jocosely remarked:

"Well, Loomis, you are all right, you can give them a small sized hell right here. I'm a *little lame*, reckon I'll have to be going," and he jogged off back to his division and was soon seen moving quietly along, half a mile to our left, with instructions from McCook (his corps commander) to go as near to Chaplin Creek as possible (our men were suffering for water.)

Rousseau expected some resistance, but he was not prepared for an attack from the whole of Hardee's corps.

As they neared the bluffs they probably followed their skirmish lines closer than was prudent. In fact, closer than Rousseau intended they should. But the enemy kept giving way and it was impossible for our troops to resist the temptation to follow.

Suddenly, while Rousseau was making observations to his right, Hardee's corps arose, as if from the earth, and poured a murderous fire into Rousseau's division. Almost at the first volley Generals Tyrrell and Jackson fell, and Colonel Webster, commanding a brigade, with them.

Among the regiments composing Rousseau's division were several that had been pushed hurriedly forward from their recruiting rendezvous at the North, without discipline, scarce knowing enough of military tactics to execute a successful "Right face!" Left without brigade commanders, and a murderous fire pouring upon them, it is no wonder they were

PHILIP H. SHERIDAN,
COLONEL SECOND MICHIGAN CAVALRY.
LIEUTENANT-GENERAL, UNITED STATES ARMY.

driven back like sheep before the disciplined troops of General Hardee, with the flower of the Confederate army. But, General Rousseau had made one mistake, a very common one—a lack of caution—and he instantly resolved to correct it or die in the attempt. He rode fearlessly along the lines as the men fell back, firing the air fairly blue with lead, and shouting his commands. It was the moving spirit of the hour. They obeyed him. Every man stood firm and the enemy recoiled before that stubborn band, that stood firing over their fallen comrades.

A large part of our artillery had fallen into the hands of the enemy, when the balance of McCook's corps came to the rescue and a part of the field and artillery were re-taken.

Within a few miles lay Buell, with half his army. Anxious eyes were turned as if the tramp of reinforcements could be heard; but none came and we only knew that Hardee had been reinforced and McCook was holding his ground at the left, while the roar of artillery and the rattle of musketry were appalling.

Between McCook's position on the left and Sheridan's on the right was a space of half a mile, over which no heavy fighting had occurred, and this must be held if possible by the cavalry, with the gallant Loomis on our right sweeping the plain in our front and the hills beyond; or when occasion required pouring a deadly enfilading fire into Hardee.

The loss of that hill was a serious one to the enemy. It was the pivot upon which swung the fate of the day. Had it been crowned with impregnable works, it could not have been of more value to us.

Firing increased in front of Sheridan. The awful roar in

front of Rousseau told of renewed struggles. Cheers rent the air; lines wavered, gave way and rallied again in quick succession.

The position of the cavalry was an unenviable one. Shot and shell from either wing came, crossing each other, and dropping in our midst. Still the cavalry remained, ready to strike when and where most needed.

The blood red sun sank lower in the western horizon, half obscured by smoke and dust. Would it "stand still," or bring this struggle to an end? Every nerve seems drawn to its fullest tension as we stand, and watch, and wait. Every moment seems an age. Gladly would we sweep down upon the enemy's flanks and end this suspense.

But lower sank the sun, and as the twilight shadows gathered round, scattering shots from skirmishers in front of Sheridan began to attract our attention.

The boom of a single cannon from Barrett's battery continued at regular intervals. A dark line of infantry crouched behind the artillery. Cheers of an assaulting enemy break upon the air close to Sheridan. Our artillery was apparently silenced. Had they abandoned their guns? Would there be no further resistance? Great Heavens! how the earth trembles, as from the throats of ten guns, double shotted with canister, there pours forth a sheet of liquid fire. The cheering ceased; but for a moment only, when, bravely facing death, the enemy come again, only to be met with another, as terrible as the first.

Then was heard the voice of Sheridan—"Up boys, and give 'em hell!" and springing to their feet our infantry dashed upon the wavering lines, putting them to flight and covering the ground with the fallen.

Our attention was now attracted to the left where the firing grew hotter, and we move up to assist Rousseau; but the sound of musketry died away as the darkness settled down, and the artillery alone kept up a defiant roar at close range until long after dark; while the bursting shells were above and about us, or plunged with a whirling heavy thud into the hill in our rear.

At last silence came, broken only by the low, moaning wave that came up from five thousand upturned faces; and spectral figures, bearing lanterns and stretchers, moved about, searching out the living from among the dead.

NIGHT SCENE AT PERRYVILLE.

From Buell's official reports it appears that he had 58,000 men, but there were 22,000 new troops that were almost entirely without drill or discipline, and we had not intended fighting at the point where the battle was forced upon McCook's and Gilbert's corps; and, that for two hours during the severe repulse to Rousseau's division Buell had no word from McCook and supposed our advance was simply having a severe skirmish.

While all military authorities that knew Buell gave him credit for being one of the best organizers that our army contained, nearly all united in condemning him for not throwing forward his available troops when it became evident we must fight or suffer the demoralizing influences of a retreat. Yet many thoughtful military men, on sober second judgment, admit that General Buell received more than his share of condemnation. That at least McCook should receive adverse criticism for precipitating that battle without consulting his superior, and that General Gilbert and General McCook failed to act in concert; in fact that Gilbert left the right to be managed by division commanders, who, though perhaps never so able, were not kept fully posted respecting the center and left;—in short that these two corps were not properly in supporting distance of each other.

Our loss in this engagement was 916 killed; 2,943 wounded; 484 missing.

Polk's corps of Bragg's army contained 35,000 effective men, the best in their service; and with these Polk really fought that battle, while Bragg was away at Frankfort with the remainder of his army, organizing a state government and expecting at least 20,000 recruits to his army, for whom he had brought arms with him. But he was greatly disappointed at the indifference of the Kentuckians and left the State in disgust—his army greatly demoralized, and he lost about 15,000 men in all, including desertions. His losses in killed and wounded were never correctly known, but must have been at least double ours, as they were the assailants, and whole brigades were practically annihilated—notably in front of Sheridan when his batteries opened upon them with canister, at sunset, and were charged on the flank by Carlin's brigade at the critical moment and driven wildly through Perryville, where a large train of wagons and 140 men and officers were captured.

The following is the report of operations of the eleventh division, army of the Ohio, in the Battle of Perryville, Kentucky, October 8th, 1862:

HEADQUARTERS ELEVENTH DIVISION, ARMY OF THE OHIO,
Camp on Rolling Fork, six miles south of
Lebanon, Ky., October 23, 1862.

CAPTAIN:—I have the honor to make the following report of the operations of my division, in the action of the 8th instant, near Perryville, Kentucky:

In accordance with the instructions of the General commanding I directed Colonel Dan. McCook, with his brigade and Barrett's battery, to occupy the hights in front of Doctor's creek, so as to secure water for our men. This was done very handsomely, after a short skirmish at daylight in the morning, giving us full possession of the hights. In about two hours afterwards the enemy advanced in considerable force, through a line of heavy timber on the eastern slope, to drive us from this position. I had, however, in the meantime ordered forward Colonel Laibold's brigade and Hescock's battery, so that I felt myself well prepared, and strong enough to receive him. I then directed Colonel Laibold to advance two of his old regiments and drive the enemy from the timber, and at the same time put the batteries into position. Colonel Laibold succeeded in driving the enemy back down the hill and across Chaplin creek, after an obstinate contest, in which the loss was severe on both sides, and Captain Barrett with one section of his battery, and Lieutenant Taliaferro with one section of Hescock's battery, drove the enemy from every position he took.

About this time General McCook, with his corps, under

artillery fire from the enemy, made his appearance on my left, when I advanced Captain Hescock's battery to a very good position in front of the belt of timber above mentioned, where he had an enfilading fire on the enemy's batteries on the opposite side of the valley of Chaplin creek and advanced, at the same time, six regiments to support him. The fire of Captain Hescock was here very severely felt by the enemy, who attempted to dislodge him by establishing a battery at short range; but Hescock's firing was still severe, and his shots so well directed and effective, as to force the enemy's battery from its new position in ten minutes.

The enemy then placed two batteries on my right flank, and commenced massing troops behind them with the apparent intention of making an attack on that front, when, by the direction of Major-General Gilbert, I reoccupied the crest of the hill.

I had no sooner gotten into position than the enemy attacked me fiercely, advancing with great determination almost to my very line, notwithstanding a large portion of the ground over which he was advancing was exposed to a heavy fire of canister from both of my batteries. I then directed a general advance of my whole line, bringing up the reserve regiments to occupy the crest of the hill.

On our advance the enemy commenced retiring, but in good order. I could not follow up this advantage to any great extent, as the enemy were advancing on our left, General McCook's right having been driven back some distance, but directed the fire of my artillery across the valley on this advance of the enemy, forcing it to retire, thus very much relieving General McCook. This ended the operations of the day, it being dark, and the enemy having retired from the field.

I cannot speak with too much praise of the good conduct of the officers and men of my whole division, all of whom were engaged. The new troops vied with the old troops of the division in their coolness and steadiness.

My brigade commanders, Colonels Greusel, Dan. McCook,

and Lieutenant-Colonel Laibold, behaved with great gallantry, leading their troops at all times.

Neither can I speak too highly of Captains Hescock and Barrett, and the officers and men of their batteries.

I respectfully bring to the notice of the General commanding the excellent conduct of Surgeon Griffiths, medical director of the division, who was untiring in his care for the wounded on all parts of the field; also the following officers of my staff: Captain Beck, Aid-de-camp, Lieutenant George Lee, Acting Assistant Adjutant-General, Lieutenant Van Pelt, Division Commissary, and Lieutenants Denning and Burton, for their activity in bearing orders, and other valuable assistance rendered me during the day.

The total casualties in my division were as follows:

Killed, 44; wounded, 274; missing, 12. Total, 330.

I inclose herewith a list of same, giving names, rank, company and regiment.

The report is also accompanied by the reports of brigade and battery commanders.

I am, sir, very respectfully, your obedient servant,

P. H. SHERIDAN,
Brigadier-General Commanding.

CAPTAIN J. EDWARD STACEY,
Assistant Adjutant-General, Third Corps.

CHAPTER IX.

AFTER THE BATTLE—CONFEDERATE RETREAT—A FLAG OF TRUCE—"WE WILL BURY YOUR DEAD; MOVE ON"—SWEEPING THE STATE.

When our troops lay down to rest after the fatigue and excitement of the day we were in blissful ignorance of the results of the battle. We were bivouacked near our starting point of the morning, and most of us lay in a dry creek bottom, or along the fence corners, resting on our arms, horses only partially unsaddled, and we fully expected to renew the struggle at daylight. The rumbling clank of artillery wheels, the tramp of infantry, the click of bayonets at the stacking of arms —all told of movements which we could only guess meant maneuvering for position or guarding against surprise, and therefore when daylight came and found us ready, but no firing, we began to think perhaps a victory had been won. Moving cautiously forward we were soon upon the battle-field, but no enemy in sight, except the stark and stiff unburied dead, side by side with our own heroes, and we could not refrain from remarking if our forces had been all engaged this dead line would not have been so near nor the deaths so divided.

But what desecration. These walnut groves, fit haunts for childhood's sports—cut, torn, marred by war's grim ravages. Heaps of mangled flesh and rags steel the hearts of men and rob them of their humanity. Did there ever such another nutting party as this crack and pick beneath these grand old walnut trees? Bridles thrown over the arm, horses nibbling at the smoke and dust begrimed blue grass, hogs rooting among the leaves, nuts and dead soldiers; and, kneeling here and there, bronzed cavalrymen cracking walnuts with all the relish of truant school boys. This is no exaggerated picture.

Soon we move on and find our approach to the clear waters of Chaplin creek undisputed, and horses and men dash into the first clear water they have drunk in a week. Then we were ordered to move on and find the enemy. Pushing forward more rapidly we soon came up with their rear guard on the road to Harrodsburg and were again face to face with sharpshooters, but we were in no humor to lose time with them, and moving forward rapidly dislodged them with a volley and charge straight into a heavy body of infantry. Retiring and re-forming, dismounted, we were rapidly pushing forward to show them we were determined to fight, even against odds, when a bugle sound of "parley" was heard coming from the enemy's side, which we mistook for a charge, and were getting into position to receive them, when we discovered a white flag and a few mounted men approaching us. Halting, and demanding a halt, officers from both sides stepped forward, when it was found the enemy desired a cessation of hostilities and time to bury their dead. Word was sent back to our general commanding, who immediately sent word to the Confederates, "We will bury your dead. Move on."

They moved, and we were soon in hot pursuit again, but were ordered back to bivouac for the night near Chaplin creek. The smoke of battle had drawn together the lowering clouds, and all night we sat or reclined as best we could in mud and rain, with the windows of heaven open and a very deluge drenching us through and through.

In the morning, after pouring the water out of our cavalry boots, which we had not removed, and pouring down our throats a pint cup of boiling hot *raw coffee*, we took to the road and soon found evidences of a hasty retreat of Bragg's whole army, and we went galloping on through Harrodsburg, Lancaster, Crab Orchard, Wildcat, and nearly to Cumberland Gap— consuming about two days in our wild chase, and capturing a large number of prisoners, when we returned to Crab Orchard to intercept John Morgan with his raiders, whom we chased for fifty-six hours with only six hours' sleep, driving him out of Kentucky.

Kentucky was now well rid of all regular organized troops of the enemy, and for two months our regiment enjoyed the cream of soldier life; having our tents and camp equipage, well fed, and only moderate scouting duties to perform. Quartered near the pleasant towns of Lebanon, New Market, New Haven and Nicholasville, with one battalion detached to the Louisville & Nashville road, where they occasionally suffered from the ubiquitous John Morgan, who occasionally dashed upon them and on one occasion handled them pretty roughly, the battalion losing a part of their forces by capture (an account of which will be found further on), but the main part of the regiment continued in camp near Nicholasville, scouting a little, but mainly occupying their time in recruiting their horses and getting ready for the next move, which soon came in the form of a raid that was to eclipse all former efforts of the regiment, and for daring, combined with long continued hardships, is destined to take high rank as a successful cavalry raid, when future historians shall read up the events of the Great Rebellion.

While the first and third battalions were doing general scouting duty through Kentucky, from Lebanon to Nicholasville and on, during the Carter raid, the second battalion, under Major Frank Dickey, was operating against John Morgan and other marauders along the line of the Louisville & Nashville railroad. After camping a few days at Mumfordsville they marched to Glasgow and with an infantry brigade went to Gallatin, Tennessee, where they remained, under General Reynolds, scouting about until the 20th of December, when they started back towards Mumfordsville, and at Glasgow met some of Morgan's men, and had a sharp skirmish with them. Company C, being rear guard, had no knowledge of what had occurred, and marched into town after dark, and found they were getting mixed up with the enemy; could see them in every street. Hailing a citizen, they inquired which way the command had gone.

"Which command?"

"Second Michigan Cavalry."

"They took *that* road, and you'd better be getting out lively, for there's Morgan's men over there."

They were not slow in taking the advice, and on their way out of the town they captured two prisoners, overtaking the command after a brisk march of three or four miles. The battalion lost five or six men captured, and one wounded.

On arriving at Cave City, Major Dickey reported to Colonel Stokes, in command of a regiment of mounted infantry. Major Dickey said, "I am ordered by General Reynolds to report to General Hobson, at Mumfordsville, and to him I am going, but I would like to feed my horses, for we have rode all day and have had several brushes with Morgan and we are not in good shape to ride all night. John Morgan is coming and I would like to have you guard the road while I feed."

"O, you're scared. John Morgan ain't within twenty miles of you. I wish he would come, we've been aching for a chance to wipe him out."

Of course, Major Dickey was mad, but he smothered his wrath for the time, merely remarking, "I hope you may have a chance."

It came, much sooner than anticipated, for the horses had scarcely begun to eat, when a shot was heard, then another, then several—a volley, a rushing sound, and through the feeding grounds of the Second, came the whole of Colonel Stokes's command, half-saddled, half-dressed, but thoroughly demoralized. They had abandoned their tents and camp equipage and were fleeing for their lives. One company turned out, dismounted, from the Major's little command of about 175 men, fired a volley and the enemy stopped. There were probably not more than an advance guard of 50 or 100 men, and they retired for their command to come up.

Colonel Stokes, with his terrible annihilators, beat Major Dickey into Mumfordsville four hours, the latter reaching there about daylight, after nearly an all night's march.

Reporting to General Hobson, he found that a report had preceded him that the battalion had all been captured. One of the first to congratulate him on his escape was Colonel Stokes.

"Ah," says the major, "who's *scared now?*" and notwithstanding the difference in rank, the Major proceeded to dress the Colonel down in fine style, much to the amusement of General Hobson.

This was "Christmas," and the boxes from home were just in time, and were duly shared among the comrades.

Next day the battalion was sent to Bacon creek to notify the command there.

Men of greater military experience than Major Dickey have been surrounded, and therefore, it was no discredit to him that he should have fallen into a trap. But he fought his way out with the command, losing about 40 men by capture, including Captain Schuyler and Lieutenant McCormick. These men were stripped of outer clothing, watches, money and pocket-knives, and next day were parolled, after marching them to Elizabethtown, and treated about as might have been expected from some roving band of Indians.

Major Dickey retired to Mumfordsville and soon after joined the regiment in Tennessee.

CHAPTER X.

CARTER'S RAID—750 MILES IN TWENTY DAYS—MOUNTAIN PATHS AMONG THE CLOUDS—CAPTURING FORTS—BURNING BRIDGES.

December 20, 1862: The mild winter thus far had given us a grand opportunity to ride about the pleasant section of country surrounding Nicholasville, Kentucky, and become acquainted with the hospitable people (generally) of the village and neighborhood. Our comfortable quarters had become something like home to us. Railway communication via the Kentucky Central brought news from the North, and some had begun to indulge in visions of Christmas, when on the 20th of December, 1862, we set out with ten days' rations of coffee, sugar, hard bread and bacon, with instructions to leave behind everything except arms, blankets and rations. A degree of mystery surrounded our movements leading us to surmise that our ten days would probably be a score of very hard marching— where, we knew not, questioned not, nor cared.

At Mckeesville, Jackson county, on the second day out, General Samuel P. Carter (Admiral Carter) assumed command of the expedition, which consisted of two battalions of the second Michigan cavalry, one battalion of the seventh Ohio and the ninth Pennsylvania cavalry, a small brigade it is true, but they were tried men, well mounted, well armed and thoroughly disciplined.

Pack mules were loaded with provisions—the wagons turned back and we cut loose from the rest of the world, to march, and trust to a very poor country for the corn and fodder that must keep our horses on their feet while they trod the rough by-roads and mountain paths of that wild country.

Bragg had preceded us through that portion of Kentucky two months before and there was little left for us or our animals. Still we found a little and followed our guides up and over mountains, through torrents; crossing the head waters of the Cumberland river and camping late at night where there was the most corn to be had.

What a Christmas was that! Winding along a mountain road that sometimes described a semicircle halfway between summit and base. Looking backward or forward the entire command could be seen as it wound along the mountain side, the blue cavalry overcoats and the dark colored horses, marching by twos, gave the appearance of a long serpent creeping steadily onward until it disappears around a sharp curve in the mountain road.

The few Kentuckians remaining at home were out, with their sisters or sweethearts mounted up behind on their gentle fillies and mules, bound for the Christmas gatherings. But we plodded along, occasionally passing over higher mountains, along whose crest the gathering mists beat upon us in drifting sheets, and we began to realize what it was to be up among the clouds. At night these mists became colder and as we opened our eyes in the morning they were greeted by a mantle of snow, which soon disappeared, however, when the sun came, and we wended our way on to the foot of the Cumberland range. Here was a very sharp climb of nearly a mile, with no roads better than a narrow, steep path, along which the men, dismounted, found the horses had quite enough to do to clamber alone without carrying a man on their backs. To have taken an ambulance or a piece of artillery would have been an impossibility. And when we reached that summit, at Crank's Gap, panting and wet with perspiration, what a feeling of triumph possessed us as we cast our eyes back over the grand panorama of nature glowing with the setting sun's rays, bathed in the soft, hazy atmosphere of a Kentucky Christmas time. And again, as we crossed to the southeastern slope of the mountain (we were thirty-five miles northeast of Cumberland Gap) and halted for the setting sun to hasten on to rest, what a glorious sight burst upon our view! Standing a little in front, nearest the edge of the mountain, down whose side we knew we must soon go, stood General Carter, Colonel Campbell, Colonel Walker and the staffs of General Carter and Colonel Campbell. Behind them a thousand determined men who had taken their lives in their hands and set out to follow their leaders whithersoever they went. In front—ah! how language fails to describe the grandeur of that scene, made up of valleys and mountains, one range after another; fading in the distance as wave succeeding wave of ocean fades away into and forms a part of the blue ethereal dome of heaven, leaving no line to trace the division where earth leaves off and air begins; across the rugged Blue Ridge mountains of southwestern Virginia; over the dimly outlined ranges of northeastern Tennessee, and on to the nearly invisible Smoky range of North Carolina, twenty leagues away—and all this reflecting the glow of the setting sun!

Not a sound disturbed the ear, save that of a single ax, that fell in regular beats far down the mountain side at our feet. Not even a jingling spur or saber moved, and silence, almost oppressive, fell, as the light of day went out, and we moved, with whispered words of command, down into the enemy's country, where it was known Humphrey Marshall, with a division of rebel cavalry, was scouting about, occupying a country through which neither infantry nor artillery could be used.

As we moved down the rugged path, sliding, stumbling along in the darkness over rocks and logs as best we could, leading our horses, a staff officer was placed by the side of the moving column and a pass-word was given out. "If you are asked what command, say Nixon's Georgia Cavalry and Macklin's Tennessee," and as such we passed near Jonesville, Virginia, in our general southeast course, meeting occasional dwellers of that wild country, but meeting no serious resistance during the first night, as, hour after hour, we pressed on at a sharp walk, and an occasional trot in the rear, to close up the column. Once a shot was heard in advance and the column halted long enough to ascertain the cause.

The night was quite cold, and before the officers were aware of it the men had set fire to the corners of rail fences all along the road and we moved on with a bright track marking our course. This drew out the few scattering inhabitants and compelled a large amount of lying on our part to throw them off the track, for we had every reason to believe every inhabitant would turn bushwhacker if they knew the truth.

According to our yarns, the number of Yankees we had slain and captured was something marvelous. Our clothing was thus explained, and we passed on uninterrupted, finding good roads and few occasions for halting.

In the morning we came upon good corn-fields and allowed the horses to feed and refresh for an hour, when we were again in the saddle, and marched all day with scarcely a halt, fording the Clinch river and passing over the Blue Ridge by a good wagon road, and on into the night.

Who can forget the half sleeping, half waking horrors of that weary second all night's march, as we staggered, now into the fence corners, now against a tree? No moon, nor yet a star, to light our path. Darkness, pitchy darkness, enshrouding us, it was next to impossible to keep our command together. Often a sleeping man halts and all the command in his rear must halt until those in front, who were able to keep awake came back to arouse them, and the command again moves on. Officers, feeling the responsibility of their positions, rode back and forth along their commands, crowding back into the road the straggling men and keeping themselves awake by constant exertion. During the night our command came to a road where two roads became one, and here our expedition came near having an encounter that might have proved disastrous.

A scouting party from Humphrey Marshall's command marched into our column near our center and marched some distance before either was aware of the presence of the other. A few words passed between our men and theirs, which resulted in a mutual discovery and an exchange of shots at short range. One of our men fell dead and another wounded. What the results of our shots were we never knew, but we immediately separated, and they were apparently as glad to get away from us as we were from them. But this aroused our men; there was no more sleeping that night and our column was well closed up.

And so, on the morning of the 30th of December, 1862, we began to move more cautiously, and about ten o'clock a few companies, dismounted, were preparing to move forward to the crest of a hill over-looking the little station of Zollicoffer, wehn a solitary horseman came marching up the road, leisurely toward us. A few of our officers rode forward quietly, and after saluting, the horseman was found to be the major in command of the post. Our skirmishers were advanced to the crest of the hill and halted under cover of a fence and the officer was told it was useless for the garrison to resist. The bewildered major, out for a morning ride, seemed unable to reply, but without waiting for his decision a single staff officer was sent forward, with two mounted men in advance, and the three rode across the bridge at a walk, receiving a salute from the rebel guard stationed there, and passed on to the headquarters of the guard, near the railroad bridge and depot, then being formed into line to receive *some one*, they knew not whom. Our staff officer rode up, was saluted by the entire guard and their commander, when the staff officer coolly ordered "Order arms," "ground arms," backward march," and then informed the astonished officer of the guard that "along the crest of that hill a thousand rifles cover you. You are prisoners. Stand where you are until parolled."

The movement was watched by General Carter, and the command marched in before there was time to reflect, and not a shot was fired.

Then commenced the work of destruction and the entire command realized for the first that we were destroying railroad communications between Richmond and Bragg at Murfreesboro.

Here was the Holston river, spanned by a long wooden trestle bridge. Canteens of turpentine were emptied upon the timbers, the match applied, flames leaped across the network like flashes of lightning, and while the prisoners were being parolled the bridge fell with a crash upon the water and rocks below. The depot, filled with supplies, and the barracks met the same fate, while a portion of the command pushed on to Watauga. Here the enemy had received an intimation of our coming and were ready to receive us; but it was useless. Our revolving rifles were too much for them, and with a dash it was soon captured, though not without some loss on both sides. Here was another bridge, and while the flames leaped and crackled, a locomotive which we had captured, was run upon the tottering structure and with a loud crash our work was proclaimed "finished;" whether we got away alive or should be captured was a question of considerable doubt in our minds. These two bridges, ten miles apart, destroyed, told their own tale of disaster to any reinforcements attempting to move hurriedly through that great railway thoroughfare.

Soon after dark the two portions of our command were

concentrated, and after feeding the horses and resting them an hour we were again, at midnight, mounted and away through unfrequented roads, in the darkness that, if not Egyptian, was at least too black for a black horse to follow a white one even, except by sound or smell. This was now the third night of the third day that we had marched without sleep. It was a question of life or death; of physical endurance rather than strategy. Could we hold out? Could we keep awake? We could, and we would. But this darkness. This unbeaten path. No broad highway for us to-night. He must be a faithful guide, indeed, that brings us through this thicket. Then we are told that General Carter, himself, is familiar with this country.

"Well, that's a comfort, anyhow," says one.

"I'll bet my old shirt General Carter never rode through these woods of a dark night before in his life," says another.

"Look out!" and heads are ducked just in time to receive the full benefit of a swinging limb, square in the face.

This torment was continued with little interuption until near morning, when we stopped to breathe and rest our jaded horses. When daylight came we found we were in a small, rich valley, with a good cornfield near at hand. The horses were fed and groomed, and again we pushed rapidly forward. At Estellville our retreat was intercepted by a force of the enemy sent out in search of us, but we drove them off after a sharp little skirmish, and again took the best road we could find, pushing on with a determination not to be diverted by any ordinary force of scouts. But the numerous mountain passes afforded a splendid opportunity for bushwhackers, who kept up a constant guerrilla warfare on our flanks, in our rear and in our front. At our crossing of the Clinch river the shoalest place was up to our horses' sides; the current swift and the bottom filled with loose stones. It was getting quite dark and guerrillas fired upon us from every tree and hill, but our horses and men had just been well fed, and with a desperation that knew no checking we pushed on across safely, and entered upon our fourth all night march. But we now had a good road, and had caught an hour or two of sleep in the morning, so we had no delays of a serious nature, but kept steadily on, all night and all day; though our march by day was one of continued annoyance from long range Kentucky rifles. At Jonesville we were fired upon from the houses, overtaken by Marshall's scouts, and nothing but our haste saved the village from fire and destruction. Soon after dark, however, we reached the foot of the Cumberland mountain again, which we had left five days before, and now as the fifth night began to darken and we found our way over the mountain unobstructed we began to breathe more freely and talk of rest, which we all settled down to, at about ten o'clock, on the Kentucky side of the mountain, and so secure did we feel that little attention was paid to pickets or outposts, though they were doubtless posted. But whether they slept on their posts or not no one ever asked or cared. But as the night was spent by most of the command in cooking corn cakes and coffee there were always enough awake to prevent a surprise, and those whose nerve had kept them in the saddle, if they had one, or kept them up with the command, if on foot (for many had lost their horses), now gave away to tired nature's demands and slept.

During the 3d of January a detail of men went in search

of food for the command, for we had lost and consumed all we had taken with us and were thankful for a small ration of corn meal, burnt corn and any kind of coffee we could get, without questioning as to its ingredients. The few loyal women of the country gathered in and helped cook all night. On the 4th we reached Colonel Gilbert's, and received rations of beef and bacon. Marching by the most direct roads through Manchester we reached McKee's on the 7th, where we had sent our wagon trains. Our pack mule train had been used up and abandoned on the road, and our men whose horses had given out came scattering into McKee's all night. From thence our march was cut down to about twenty or twenty-five miles per day, through Richmond and back to Nicholasville, where most of the command went into camp, on the 9th of January.

This was the second great raid of the war that terminated successfully, and we only learned on our return that our instructions would have been, if hard pushed, to break into squads and scatter through to North Carolina, or anywhere, to get away. We also then learned that while we were burning the bridges and destroying the railroad in East Tennessee, Rosecrans was fighting the battle of Stone River, and our command received from him highly complimentary orders for direct service to his army in that great battle.

The following were the orders issued in connection with the Carter raid:

HEADQUARTERS ARMY OF KENTUCKY,
Lexington, Ky., December 17, 1862.

BRIGADIER-GENERAL S. P. CARTER,
United States Volunteers:

GENERAL:—You will at once assume command of the

cavalry brigade, composed of the ninth Pennsylvania *volunteer cavalry*; *two battalions of the second Michigan volunteer cavalry*; *and one battalion of the seventh Ohio volunteer cavalry*, and put it in complete condition for a long scout.

The command will march without baggage, or supplies, and will take only one hundred rounds of ammunition to each man, two axes to each company, one extra shoe, and spare nails for each horse and the necessary tools for shoeing, and such cooking utensils as are indispensable and can be carried on horseback.

     Respectfully, your Obedient Servant,
 [Signed]   G. GRANGER,
    Major-General Commanding Army of Kentucky.

      LEXINGTON, KENTUCKY, January 9, 1863.
MAJOR-GENERAL GORDON GRANGER,
 Commanding Army of Kentucky:

GENERAL:—I have the honor to submit the following report of the operations of the expeditionary force to East Tennessee which was intrusted to my command.

Although a movement on East Tennessee was proposed as early as the 25th of November last, it was not until the 19th of December that arrangements were completed and the necessary orders given for the movement of the troops. It was hoped that the force to be sent on this hazardous but most important expedition would have been much larger than that which the commander of the department felt could be detached for such service when the final arrangements were made.

My original design was to have divided the force into two columns, and strike the East Tennessee & Virginia railroad at two points at the same time, distant 100 miles apart, and, by moving towards the center, have destroyed the road for that distance; but on the junction of the different detachments I found that the number was too small to risk a division and I was, reluctantly, compelled to keep them united, or within easy supporting distance during the whole of my operations.

Having given orders for the junction of the forces—consisting of two battalions of the second Michigan cavalry, Colonel Campbell, the ninth Pennsylvania cavalry, Major Russell, and one battalion of the seventh Ohio cavalry, Major Rainy—near the mouth of Goose Creek, Clay county, Kentucky, I left this place with my staff on the afternoon of the 20th ult. for that point. By your order Colonel Charles J. Walker, of the tenth Kentucky cavalry, was placed in command of the cavalry brigade.

The troops were ordered to move without baggage, with ten days' rations and 100 rounds of ammunition, but as it was feared some difficulty would be met with in obtaining forage, a supply train was ordered to proceed some sixty miles on the route and there transfer forage and rations to a train of pack mules.

On the 22d ult. I came up with the two battalions of the second Michigan and the ninth Pennsylvania at McKee, Jackson county, Kentucky, where we were detained a day waiting for the supply train and pack saddles. On the 25th ult. we effected a junction with the remainder of the troops (first battalion, seventh Ohio cavalry), at Heard's, on Goose creek. I then found, to my surprise, that the whole force amounted to only about 980 men, and of that number a considerable portion were in the field for the first time. The marches, owing to the roughness and narrowness of the roads (being merely bridle paths along the banks of creeks, and over steep and rugged mountains), were of necessity slow and tedious, and their length had to be governed by the distance to the several points at which forage could be obtained. It was not until about meridian of the 28th that we reached the foot of the Cumberland mountain (on the north side), opposite Crank's Gap, twelve miles to the south and east of Harlan Court House. The horses were fed, a day's forage prepared and the pack train sent back under charge of a detachment of the Kentucky State Guard. A little before sunset we reached the summit of the Cumberland mountain and had the field of our operations with its mountains and valleys spread out before us. I then held a consultation with the officers of the command and it was the unanimous opinion that the force was entirely too small to venture on a division according to the original plan. This decision seemed to be the more necessary from the news we had received, through East Tennessee refugees, at the foot of the mountain, relative to the disposition of the rebel forces along the line of the railroad.

Soon after dark the advance commenced the descent of the mountain, hoping to make a long march before sunrise, but owing to the steepness, narrowness and roughness of the way, the rear column did not reach the foot of the mountain until 10 P. M. having consumed four hours in the descent. I was told there were some 400 rebel cavalry in the vicinity of Jonesville, five miles distant, and as it was important to move through Lee county, Virginia, without exciting suspicion, I moved down Cane Creek, passing through a gap in Poor valley ridge, and crossed Powell's valley, about five miles east of Jonesville. On leaving the valley road our guides were at fault and valuable time was lost in finding the way. The march was continued through the night, and at daylight we reached the top of Wallen's ridge, twenty-two miles distant from the foot of Cumberland mountain, and halted to feed the horses. Thus far we had advanced without giving any alarm, or even exciting any suspicion as to our character. The village of Stickleyville lay immediately below us and but for the imprudence of some of the officers, in allowing the men to visit the village, we could have passed on as rebel cavalry. A number of rebel soldiers, belonging to Trigg's battalion, came within our lines, supposing we were their friends, and were captured.

In a short time we were again in the saddle, passed through Stickleyville, across Powell's mountain, and through Pattonsville. Before sunset we crossed Clinch river, twelve miles from Estellville, Scott county, Virginia, and halted for a couple of hours to feed. News of our approach had gone before us, but few of the rebels were inclined to credit it, believing it impossible that a government force would venture so far within their territory. Upon arriving at Estellville, at 10 P. M., we were told that a considerable rebel force was in possession of Moccasin Gap, prepared to resist our passage. I could not afford to lose time. The Michigan battalions were dismounted, and, under command of Colonel Campbell, a portion deployed and moved through the gap. Being unacquainted with the ground, and having to guard against an ambuscade in this strong pass, which could have been held by a small force against greatly superior numbers, we advanced with great caution. It was midnight before the rear of the column had passed through. The enemy, deterred by the resolute advance of our brave men, fled toward Kingsport, East Tennessee, (as I afterwards learned), without firing a shot.

A rebel lieutenant and several soldiers, with their arms, were captured on the south side of the gap on the Blountville road. During the remainder of the night we moved forward as rapidly as was practicable, over unknown roads, picking up rebel soldiers by the way. Owing to the darkness of the night, a portion of the command lost their way and became separated from the main body. A small force of rebel cavalry, hovering about our rear, killed a sergeant of the second Michigan and captured two others who had wandered from the road. At daylight, on the morning of the 30th ult. we reached the town of Blountville, Sullivan county, East Tennessee, surprised and took possession of the place, captured some thirty soldiers belonging to the fourth Kentucky (rebel) cavalry and parolled them. We were here informed that at Bristol, some eight miles distant, there was a large amount of stores, besides the meat of a considerable number of hogs, belonging to the rebel authorities, but as the place was guarded, according to the best information we could receive, by a regiment of infantry, under Colonel Stemp, said to be 900 strong, a cavalry force under Colonel Giltner and a battery, we were reluctantly compelled to leave it on our left and move towards the railroad bridge at Union, six miles from Blountville. I accordingly sent forward Colonel Campbell with a portion of the second Michigan, under the direction of Colonel James P. T. Carter, of the second East Tennessee infantry, toward Union, with orders to take the place and destroy the railroad bridge across the Holston river. As soon as the rest of the troops, which got separated from us during the night, came up, I moved them rapidly forward in the same direction. When we reached Union, I found the town in our possession and the railroad bridge, a fine structure, some 600 feet in length, slowly burning. The rebel force, about 150 strong, consisting of two corps of the sixty-second North Carolina troops, under command of Major McDowell, had surrendered without resistance, the Major himself having been first captured by our advance, while endeavoring to learn if there was any truth in our reported approach. The prisoners were parolled and a large number of them were, that afternoon, on their way to the mountains of North Carolina, swearing they would never be exchanged. Their joy at being captured seemed to be unbounded.

The stores, barracks, tents, a large number of arms and equipments, a considerable amount of salt, nitre, a railroad car, the depot, etc., etc., were destroyed. As soon as the work of destruction was fairly under way, I dispatched Colonel Walker with detachments from the second Michigan, ninth Pennsylvania and seventh Ohio cavalry, in all 181 men, the whole under guidance of Colonel Carter, toward the Watauga bridge, at Carter's depot, ten miles west of Union. On their way, they captured a locomotive and tender, with Colonel Love, of the sixty-second North Carolina troops, who, having heard of the approach of the Yankees, had started, on the locomotive, to Union to ascertain the truth of the rumor. On reaching the station about sunset, they found the enemy, consisting of two companies of the sixty-second North Carolina troops, estimated by Colonel Walker at nearly 200 men, falling into line. Colonel Walker gallantly attacked them, and after a brief but warm resistance, they broke and fled to the woods. The gallant Major Raper, of the sixth Kentucky cavalry, with two companies of the ninth Pennsylvania regiment, under Captain

Jones, of that regiment, made a dashing charge and captured and destroyed many of their number. Our loss was one killed, one mortally and two slightly wounded. The rebel loss was twelve to sixteen killed. Dr. McMillan, of the first East Tennessee infantry, acting brigade surgeon, reports the wounds of thirteen, several of which were mortal. Owing to the darkness of the night it was impossible to learn with certainty the entire loss.

The railroad bridge across the Watauga river, some 300 feet in length, was soon in flames and entirely destroyed, also a large number of arms and valuable stores. The captured locomotive was run into the river and completely demolished, destroying in its passage one of the piers of the bridge.

The men and horses (especially the latter) were much worn and jaded from constant travel and loss of rest. The alarm had been given. The rebels had the road open to Knoxville, and could move up a strong force to resist us. I also learned that some 400 cavalry and four guns, under Colonel Folks, were within three miles of us; that an infantry force would be concentrated at Johnston's depot, six miles west of Carter's station, by daylight, and further, that Humphrey Marshall, who was at Abingdon, was moving his troops to occupy the passes in the mountains, and thus cut off our egress. It was deemed prudent, therefore, to return.

We left Watauga about midnight, and after a hard march reached Kingsport, at the mouth of the north fork of the Holston river, at sunset on the 31st ult. After feeding and resting a short time and issuing a ration of meat to the men we were again in the saddle. We passed eight miles south of Rogersville and reached Loony's Gap, on Clinch mountain, late in the afternoon; passed through without opposition, and about 11 P. M., January 1st, reached a place on the edge of Hancock county, Tennessee, where forage could be procured, and bivouacked for the night. This was the first night's rest we had been able to take since the night of the 27th ult. The command had been annoyed during the day and night by bushwhackers, but we providentially escaped with only two men slightly wounded. Soon after daylight on the morning of the 2d inst. we resumed our march toward Jonesville, Lee Co., Virginia, with the intention of reaching the foot of Cumberland mountain, on the Kentucky side before we halted. Our march was much impeded during the day by bushwhackers, who constantly annoyed our front and rear. Just before we reached Jonesville, they endeavored to check us, by occupying the hills in our front with two companies (supposed to be Larimore's and Staley's), but they were soon driven from their strong position by the skirmishers of the second Michigan. We reached Jonesville late in the afternoon, but before the rear guard had passed, it was attacked by about 200 rebels. The rear guard, company K, second Michigan cavalry, reinforced by two light companies, drove the rebels back to the woods. Several of them were killed, one in the village of Jonesville. Some twenty were captured during the day. We sustained no loss. From the prisoners we learned that the passes in Powell's and Clinch mountains, through which we marched in going to Union, had been blockaded and were occupied by three or four companies of infantry. [NOTE—The force encountered at Jonesville, it was afterward learned, was that of General Humphrey Marshall, and numbered some 1,900 men.]

We reached the foot of Cumberland mountain, passing through Crank's Gap, at 11 P. M. and bivouacked, men and horses completely jaded and worn, having been in the last five days and seventeen hours, out of the saddle but thirty hours.

On the 5th inst. the command reached Manchester, Clay county, Kentucky, and rested on the day following. The march was resumed on the morning of the 7th, and on the 8th I received your order directing the several detachments to be sent to their respective camps. After reaching Richmond, on the 9th, they separated, the first battalion seventh Ohio, moving on to Winchester and the two battalions of the second Michigan and the ninth Pennsylvania to Nicholasville.

Notwithstanding the inclemency of the weather, the severity of the marches and the scanty supply of rations for no inconsiderable portion of the time, both officers and men bore their hardships without a murmur or word of complaint. They returned, after a journey of 470 miles, 170 of which was in the enemy's country, in high spirits and in good condition, proud to think they had accomplished a feat, which for hazard and hardship, has no parallel in the history of the war. Where all were so ready and willing to do their duty and performed it with so much cheerfulness and alacrity, it is no easy matter to select a part for special commendation, but the two battalions of the second Michigan, under command of Colonel Campbell, deserve particular notice for their drill, discipline and efficiency. From the superiority of their arms and their skill in their use, they seemed to feel themselves invincible, and wherever there was an enemy to meet, they advanced against him with the coolness and steadiness of veterans.

I am General, respectfully, your obedient servant,

S. P. CARTER,
Brigadier-General Volunteers.

The force asked for by me, and promised, was some 3,000 men, and with that number the railroad running through East Tennessee could have been destroyed for more than 100 miles. Knoxville could also have been captured and the public stores of the enemy destroyed from Bristol to Loudon. No one but the commanding officer himself can know the disappointment he felt, when, on assembling the different detachments, it was found they numbered, all told, less than 1,000 men.

S. P. C.

CHAPTER XI.

RECUPERATING—PLEASANT HOURS SHORT LIVED—FAREWELL TO KENTUCKY—OFF FOR TENNESSEE—GREEN CLAY SMITH—THOMPSON'S STATION.

Our raid into East Tennessee had cost us very dear in horses and accoutrements, as well as costing the officers considerable personal loss in pack mules, blankets, private property which the government did not recognize as refundable, and, therefore, the next fifteen days of rest became a necessity; still it was none the less enjoyed in the various ways incident to a soldier's life in a friendly country. At the end of a little more than two weeks our horses and accoutrements were pronounced in condition for another move, and we set out for Louisville—passing through Frankfort on the 27th and Shelbyville on the 28th. We remained at Louisville from the 29th of January to the 3d of February, when the first and third battalions took the cars for Nashville, but did not arrive there until 3 P. M. of the 4th on account of obstructions. Here the second battalion joined us, on the 7th, after a separation of several months, and we remained in camp near Nashville until the 10th, with the town alive with soldiers, and the streets a perfect babel of noises—ambulances, army wagons, trucks, carriages and the clatter of hoofs combining to make this the noisiest and liveliest scene in all this land. On the 10th of February, 1863, the regiment broke camp at Nashville and moved out towards Murfreesboro, but the condition of the roads was such that our progress was slow, and we did not arrive there until next day at 4 P. M. The enemy was still lingering near, ready to pounce upon anyone venturing far from our main forces, but this did not deter our commander from sending out one of our battalions, the first, on a foraging expedition, on the 12th, taking the Bradyville pike and bringing in a good train of wagons well loaded with corn and fodder. This was repeated on the 15th, towards Liberty, the enemy's scouts watching our trains; but our scouts saw the tracks of horses going in an opposite direction. The enemy's pickets were driven in towards Liberty, and, turning about, their scouts were followed, resulting in a skirmish, the enemy retiring.

On the following day our battalion turned towards Nashville, by way of the Lebanon pike, fording Stone river, with the water well up on the horses' sides and the current running strong. Several days were occupied in swinging around to Murfreesboro, via Nashville and Cainsville, arriving back in camp on the 22d. The balance of the regiment had been kept busy, scouting and foraging in front of Murfreesboro, and on the 24th of February the entire regiment set out together for Franklin, where we arrived next day without incident of special note. Here began our memorable Tennessee campaign—reconnaissances, skirmishes and fights occurring almost daily. The first of these was made in company with the ninth Pennsylvania cavalry, February 27th, toward Springhill, where the enemy's pickets were driven in and the command returned to camp at Franklin. The country in front of Franklin was well adapted to the movement of troops, and our position was strengthened by the erection of Fort Granger on the banks of the Harpeth river, overlooking the town and surrounding country. We had here a strong force of infantry and artillery and one brigade of cavalry with three good turnpike roads extending southward from Franklin. This was the right wing of General Rosecrans's army, and was destined to receive a good deal of attention from the enemy, and therefore the cavalry was kept on the move almost constantly.

General Green Clay Smith was in command of the brigade, at that time known as the second brigade, second division, cavalry corps, army of the Cumberland, and during his short stay with us the engagement at Brentwood occurred. This was a very severe cavalry skirmish, between one of Forrest's divisions (Stearne's) and our brigade. The enemy attacked our block-house, placed to guard a railroad bridge in our rear, and we arrived in time to assist in repulsing them, a portion of the command gaining a strong position, dismounted behind a stone fence, and another portion charging on their flanks forced them to retire in confusion. For an hour or more it had every appearance of a general engagement, and the casualties were quite considerable for the numbers engaged.

I remember an incident at this time that illustrates what a man can endure. A large, fine looking young soldier from the

Second rode back to the rear with an ugly bullet wound through the mouth, passing out the back of his neck, and afterward we heard that he "died in hospital," but were astonished not many months after to see him walk into camp, apparently well, though part of his jaw was gone.

On the morning of March 4th, Colonel Campbell, in command of the cavalry brigade, was ordered to send out a part of the second Michigan and the ninth Pennsylvania cavalry, on a reconnaissance to Springhill, with Colonel Jordan, of the ninth Pennsylvania, in command of the cavalry and Colonel Coburn in command of the expedition. When five miles out we met the enemy in force. A sharp artillery duel ensued, followed by the enemy retiring, and our command bivouacked for the night, after driving them a mile.

On the morning of the 5th of March, our Colt rifles renewed the fight and, with the assistance of the ninth Pennsylvania, drove the enemy three miles.

Major L. S. Scranton, commanding the second Michigan, discovered indications of a trap, and checked his advance until Colonel Coburn with his infantry and artillery came up. Reporting to Colonel Coburn what he believed to be the position and strength of the enemy under General Forrest, the commander of our expedition seemed to think the major unnecessarily alarmed, in fact treating that officer and his two battalions of cavalrymen with something like contempt, or at least paying no attention to Major Scranton's words of caution, and without so much as bringing up his artillery, moved his infantry over the hill and down across an open field intending, no doubt, to drive Forrest across Duck river. As Colonel Coburn turned and followed his brigade over the hill, he appeared to have no staff officers, but in person directed the officer in command of one battalion of the Second to charge the enemy's battery. As that particular battalion had no sabers, but were really mounted rifles, the officer, a lieutenant, in his dilemma, reported to Major Scranton and asked for instructions; he directed that an orderly be dispatched to the ninth Pennsylvania, not far in the rear, with Colonel Coburn's order, and our two battalions immediately took positions on the left flank, where the enemy were appearing in force to turn Colonel Coburn's left. Nor was there any time to lose. The enemy were swarming into the bit of woods, apparently a whole brigade of them, and in five minutes would have had our defenseless ambulances and powerless artillery in their hands. The artillery was powerless, because they were in the road between two hills, *where Colonel Coburn had left them,* and were hemmed in and could neither move backward nor forward, nor could they turn out of the road by reason of the banks on either side. Worse than all, the commandant of the expedition had left the ninth Pennsylvania cavalry to look out for our rear, when they were the only mounted men in the command that were armed and equipped for a charge, and should have been at the front if such service was to be for a moment thought of. However, the Second had, in Major Scranton, a cool-headed officer, quick to grasp the situation, and the only thing that remained to be done at this stage of the blunder was to check the flank movement of the enemy, which was done in good style, both of our battalions being immediately dismounted and thrown under cover of the fence along the edge of the woods, a part of them lapping past the woods into the open field on the left. Major Scranton remained mounted, and rode fearlessly along the line, directing them and keeping the alignment perfect. Volley was met with

MAJOR L. S. SCRANTON.

volley, and the enemy soon discovered they had no easy task on hand. About this time loud cheers were heard in the direction of Coburn, and then the firing ceased. The road had now become clear and the artillery took up a position a short distance in the rear, expecting orders from Colonel Coburn, but none came nor could we see what was going on at Thompson's Station. Suddenly another flanking party attacked our rear, and Colonel Jordan, of the ninth Pennsylvania, turned his attention that way and attacking the enemy in our rear sent them flying into the woods and off around to our right to join their own forces. The Second then fell back and took position near our artillery, in plain sight of the enemy's flankers, but they appeared satisfied to let us alone, and returned to enjoy the fruits of their little game of strategy, which we now discovered was the capture of all of Colonel Coburn's infantry, except a part of one regiment he had left to support the battery. Colonel Coburn severely censured the cavalry, claiming that we run away and left him. He also criticised General Rosecrans for this disaster.

The least he has to say about that affair, the better.

Only his own blind rashness was at fault for the failure of his expedition. The cavalry was not *driven* from a single position, but fell back for a better one, and if he had been clear headed, he would never have gone with a brigade of infantry to attack 18,000 men in a strong position, without at least knowing that his flanks were clear and his artillery in position to cover his retreat, should it be necessary. Instead, he left his cavalry and artillery in an almost inextricable tangle with his wagons and ambulance train, which was apparently big enough to have brought back his whole command rolled up in blankets and bandages.

That Colonel Coburn was a brave man, and his brigade all good men, there can be no doubt—they proved that, by walking straight up to the cannon's mouth in the face of overwhelming numbers, but he should have listened to Major Scranton when warned by that officer that a trap was being set, and ascertained first whether the force he left behind was able to take care of his flanks. In short, he was unfit, at that time, for the independent command of an expedition, though he would, doubtless, have done his full duty as second in command.

It was said that General Gilbert, at that time in command at Franklin, underestimated the strength of the enemy and was at fault for Colonel Coburn's disaster. If that was true General Rosecrans did his whole duty by promptly removing him, and soon General Gordon Granger was in command, ably seconded by General Phil Sheridan.

On the 8th of March the right wing of our army (the Army of the Cumberland) moved out on the Columbia pike, with the Second in advance. Meeting the enemy's pickets, seven miles out, and sending out our skirmishers, we drove back the advance line of the enemy, and held our ground until the army should come up. But darkness coming on, we bivouacked for the night, our regiment forming the advance picket. Our lines were so near together that conversation could be heard from one camp fire to the other.

One of our pickets, Private Morris Fitch, distinguished himself that night by capturing two armed rebel scouts who were trying to steal across his beat. "Surrender, or I'll blow you through!" Their arms dropped and he marched them at the muzzle of his revolver back to headquarters.

Our line was maintained, and at daybreak we were again in the saddle; a mile further on we came up with the enemy's pickets strongly posted. Dismounting and forming a skirmish line we marched out of the little patch of woods, into an open field, and when half way across discovered the enemy in heavy force behind a stone wall, in the woods, with their cavalry forming strong flankers in full view. A murderous fire was poured into our ranks from behind the stone wall, when our commander, Major Ben Smith, shouted "Under cover," where we lay a few moments until the storm of bullets had slackened a little, when the voice of Major Ben was again heard, "Forward, second Michigan!" Over the stone wall we went, firing as we ran through the woods, and, in less time than it takes to tell it, we had either captured or driven out the last one of them, across the field and up the hill. Thompson's Station was ours and we continued our advance beyond Springhill, closely followed by the infantry and artillery. But not on foot all this while, for our movements were rapid at times, and rails flew like straws if in the way of our rapid advance mounted. Some of the most serious injuries sustained were caused by men crowding through gaps where there was not room; but nothing could stop the impetuosity of our men when they felt they had good backing. Night came on, however, and we were compelled to bivouac, with a cold rain drenching us to the skin, and the driest place we could find to rest upon was a few rails spread upon the ground, with mud and water all about us knee deep. A cup of coffee and a piece of hard bread seem thin fare for a tired and hungry man, but it was the best at hand and no use to murmur. But to lie down in wet clothing in a cold March wind was not calculated to bring much comfort or recuperation to worn and weary bodies. Yet there were no complaints, and morning found us again in the saddle, pushing, skirmishing and fighting all day, driving the enemy across Rutherford creek, where we found them in force as night came on. This stream, swollen by recent rains, was crossed and re-crossed after dark, our regimental commander, Major Ben Smith, nearly losing his life by being swept into deep water. But we gained the north bank of the creek and bivouacked for the night, occupying every house and the schoolhouse in our efforts to find shelter for our men, not hesitating to burn furniture, school desks or whatever we could find to dry our clothing. Was that vandalism? Who shall condemn?

In the morning we were as ready as ever to take the front, crossing Rutherford creek for the third time, driving in the enemy's skirmishers and following them along to Duck river, where the strong fortifications of Columbia stopped our further progress, and we retired leisurely to Franklin.

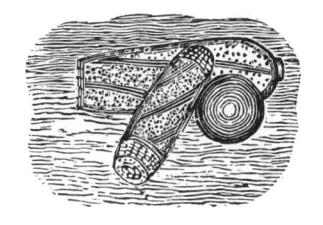

CHAPTER XII.

MIDDLE TENNESSEE—THREE MONTHS OF "POST" DUTY—BOOTS AND SADDLES—GRANGER—SHERIDAN—WATKINS—CAMPBELL.

To chronicle the movements of our regiment during the next three months would be to repeat much that is scarce worth our time, not to mention the question of interest at the hands of those whose attention we desire to claim. In another part of this volume will be found the dry details of daily movements as recorded by the adjutant of the regiment; also the losses, by killed, wounded and missing, in each engagement, which are purposely omitted from the *historical narrative* part here.

As we look back over the intervening twenty years it appears to us as in a dream—those pleasant valleys of middle Tennessee where the corn had ceased to wave, but the green hills were just as rich in verdure, the early bird-song just as enchanting, the marvelous beauty of flower and shrub and tree undimmed; but our duty was not all poetry and romance. The hard realities of life met us every hour, whether by night or day; at the bugle's shrill call every man "to horse" and away, meeting the enemy on their own grounds, and, if necessary, attacking them in their strongholds. Every foot of ground between Franklin and Columbia became as familiar to us as our neighborhood roads at home. We picketed every road and scouted over every plantation, and he who crept near our lonely videttes at midnight or early morning, when eyes were heaviest, found him as alert as at midday. No sleeping where the safety of the whole command depended on his watchful care, and for this our regiment soon became favorably known to our commanders and as frequently recognized. Nor did it matter to them whether it was the Lewisburg, the Columbia, Carter's creek, Nashville pike or Mathews road, they were always ready and equally at home.

At the same time it became necessary to study the people. There were the loyal, the professedly loyal, the conservative southerner and the bitter secessionist, and as our mission was against armed foes only, it often became a very difficult task to discriminate between the loyal and the professedly loyal; but all were watched alike and our dealings with them made as agreeable as possible under the circumstances.

As a rule, whatever was taken for food was paid for; yet as our army was the natural refuge of some of the worst elements of our northern society, as well as the same element from Canada, the better portions of our army—though largely in the majority—were often powerless to prevent outrages. Two worthless vagabonds to a single company would give to that company a very bad record—except for fighting—and while they often were found in the thickest of the fight they appeared bullet proof; in fact the devil seemed anxious to preserve them for some special job, when they were sure to be on hand. Yet the regiment made many warm friends at Franklin, and that friendship was appreciated.

On the 31st of March and April 1st we had skirmishes at the front, with Colonel Campbell in command of the brigade, and Major Ben. Smith in command of the regiment.

April 9th a part of the regiment were patrolling the road leading towards Murfreesboro when they were attacked by a strong scouting party near McGarrack's ford, but the detachment held their ground and defeated the enemy.

On the 13th our foragers went too near the enemy's lines and were driven in by a strong force, but not without loss to the enemy. General Granger's scouts reported an expected attack in force on the town and orders were issued that no fires be allowed near the picket lines. This was considerable of a hardship during the cool spring nights, but the order was strictly carried out.

Wherever Gordon Granger was in command there was little rest for soldiers; if not in the saddle, camp duties were numerous and inspections frequent. As a disciplinarian he had few equals, but as a downright aggressive *fighter* Phil Sheridan was considered at least his equal from the start.

Our commander at this time, Colonel Campbell, taken as he was from private life and advanced rápidly—too rapidly, perhaps, for his own good—had much to learn, but he was an apt scholar in certain ways and was, as far as he was able to comprehend, an imitator of every valued military officer with whom he came in contact. His management of a regiment or a brigade often commanded the admiration of his superiors, while he enjoyed the confidence of a majority of his own regiment, especially the men, and they would follow him anywhere and stay as long as he stayed. He often boasted that he could hold his own against five times his number, and whenever he had the choosing of his ground, he proved the truth of his assertions. Frequently, while at Franklin, the regiment went after forage with the entire train of wagons, and though often attacked on these occasions, it was very seldom the regiment failed to bring back the train well loaded with corn or fodder.

BREVET BRIG.-GEN. A. P. CAMPBELL.

On the 25th of April the bugles sounded "Boots and saddles" long before day, and we crossed the Harpeth to meet an attack, but it proved a false alarm, and the regiment returned to camp. Next day, at midnight, Colonel Campbell was ordered to march with his brigade and capture a regiment of rebel cavalry camping to the right of the Columbia pike, occupying an advanced position of the enemy's force in our front.

Out into the darkness with as little noise as possible, the brigade moved on, a mile or two, when it was reported to Colonel Campbell that the second Michigan had missed the road they should have taken to the right, and were marching straight forward on the pike into the enemy's lines. Grasping the situation at once, Campbell halted the column, directed his brigade adjutant to hold the command there until his return, put spurs to his horse and dashed across to the other part of his command, where he arrived just in time to prevent a collision. The delay caused by this misfortune brought the faintest streaks of morning light, and as the adjutant knew the objects of the expedition he communicated with Colonel Watkins, next in command, his fears if any further delay occurred, and advised him to assume command and strike while he could. Colonel Watkins received the order as coming from Campbell and immediately put his command at full speed and charged upon the enemy's camp, striking them just as they were beginning to arouse from their slumbers. Many of the rebels mounted their bare-back horses and scattered, but most of them were captured, with their equipments and horses, and brought back to Franklin. For this Colonel Watkins was made a brigadier, while Campbell, who should have been promoted but for his misfortune, was permanently assigned to the command of the brigade, in place of Green Clay Smith.

For several days after this dash at the enemy they were very active, threatening our lines at all hours of the day and night. To be aroused at midnight and hasten to the front, only to stand to horse till daylight, and repeat the same thing night after night, was not congenial sport for cavalrymen, and the language indulged in on such occasions was decidedly forcible if not elegant. On the 1st of May the regiment had an opportunity for venting some of their ill feeling, and in a skirmish with the enemy in front of Franklin used them roughly, capturing a number of prisoners. But, to their credit be it said, prisoners were always treated with military courtesy, if taken while in their regular line of of duty, but bushwhackers received little mercy—in fact few questions were asked as to what became of them, and no mistakes were ever made that we heard of.

During the month of May the usual routine of camp life was followed—including scouts, skirmishes, foragings and alarms, and we still had time left for the enjoyment of much that was pleasant in that beautiful valley around Franklin—its Roper's Knob, surmounted by fortifications, the headquarters of the signal corps, the clear running Harpeth, broad plantations dotted with pleasant Southern homes, surrounded by groves of fruit and forest trees. But this apparent inactivity was only a breathing spell to give the country roads a chance to thoroughly dry while the wet season was passing, and on the 2d of June, 1863, we marched out of Franklin, leaving only a small garrison there, while our lines were being contracted to our left, our right resting for a time on Triune, and our active campaign for the summer was begun.

CHAPTER XIII.

TENNESSEE CAMPAIGN—TRIUNE—A SINGLE-HANDED CHARGE—
A GALLOP TO FRANKLIN—GENERAL ARMSTRONG—GUY'S GAP—
A TEN THOUSAND CAVALRY CHARGE—STANLEY—MINTY—
CAMPBELL.

On the 4th of June, 1863, before we had fairly settled in camp at Triune, the signal corps reported Franklin attacked by a strong force of rebel cavalry and mounted infantry. Immediately our brigade was in the saddle dashing off towards Franklin. That was a long race. No place for worn out horses, or delicate, faint-hearted men. At four o'clock P. M. the artillery firing could be heard, distinctly, above the clatter of hoofs, sabers and spurs; and, plunging spurs into the sides of horses already white with foam, they madly dashed on, not knowing a word of the enemy they were to meet, and apparently caring little. Two hours later the second Michigan wheeled into line near Mathews house at Franklin, and, without waiting to dismount, opened their revolving rifles upon a brigade of rebel cavalry under General Armstrong, and in twenty minutes the enemy were fleeing in every direction, with twelve of the enemy killed, sixteen severely wounded and twenty prisoners, while our own loss was trifling.

The thorough military skill which seemed to possess every soldier of this command, whether officer or private, was sometimes remarkable. At this brilliant dash an incident occurred which will illustrate that fact. A private of company F, Tom Dixon, says: "I happened to be nearer company A than to my own company, and fell in with them at the time company A, who were in the advance, wheeled into the woods at the foot of a lane, filled with large loose rocks. A volley was fired at us from our flank and the Johnnies were so close we had no time to maneuver, but without command every man threw himself from the saddle and let the horses go to the rear. In less time than it takes to tell it we had given the enemy a volley and were following them up with another in quick succession. The regiment saw our horses, galloping riderless back across the field, and not seeing any of us, concluded the whole company had been annihilated, and for a few moments there was grief and consternation among them. But there was no time for that, and the boys came to the rescue on the gallop. About this time a Confederate officer said, 'Cut down the cowardly s―― b――!' but he did not finish the sentence. He fell with his horse and was pinned to the earth. 'O, boys,' yelled the reb, 'where's your ambulance? Help me out; I'm hurt.' 'We hain't got no ambulance,' says I; 'help yourself out and be d―― to you! We've got something else to do besides waiting on blow-heads like you. Learn to keep a civil tongue in your head, will you!' All this while our fellows were coming up rapidly and company A was holding the ground from behind every tree, stump or rock, and in ten minutes Armstrong's flag was ours and the lane and woods were full of dead and wounded. I got a dose in my foot that lasted me all summer."

The rest of our brigade were busy, and the enemy were entirely routed in an incredibly short space of time. This was the shortest and most decisive battle the regiment had been engaged in, and gave them renewed confidence in their strength.

The prisoners stated that had they known the second Michigan was there they would not have stayed to fight, for they knew what those revolving rifles would do, and declared they feared the regiment more than any other they had ever met.

Among the trophies of this engagement was a new and beautiful Texas flag that had recently been presented to the Confederate General Armstrong.

The wounded prisoners were removed to Mathews house and cared for, and the command bivouacked at Franklin until the night of the 6th, when they returned to Triune.

June 9th we were attacked in force; our pickets driven in and skirmishing continued all day with little loss on either side. On the 10th the enemy considerately gave us a rest long enough for the paymaster to discharge his obligations with the troops; but on the 11th we were again attacked and skirmished with the enemy all day, with now and then a dash by either side, the Second generally holding their ground sturdily at the front and our brigade band swinging into line occasionally to greet the flying enemy with, "Out of the Wilderness," and never was music more appropriate. On the 11th and 12th portions of the regiment had the disagreeable task of escorting a train to Franklin—disagreeable, because if there was a possibility of a fight, we wanted a clear field, not encumbered with a helpless wagon train; but we returned safely next day, and for ten days thereafter were drilled, inspected and put in fighting trim for a grand forward movement. At this time the cavalry was reorganized, and our regiment was assigned to the first brigade, first division of cavalry, army of the Cumberland, Colonel A. P. Campbell commanding the brigade, consisting of the second Michigan, ninth Pennsylvania, fourth Kentucky and first East Tennessee cavalry, General R. B. Mitchell commanding the division and General D. S. Stanley commanding the cavalry corps.

On the 23d of June tents were struck and our regiment proceeded along the Shelbyville pike, skirmishing with and driving the enemy till late in the afternoon, when our brigade was charged into by the enemy without breaking our lines, the enemy retiring in confusion. When the regiment moved through Eagleville, June 23d, artillery confronted them, and a portion of the regiment dismounted and routed them; mounting they drove the enemy three miles. In this movement the enemy's artillery continued to fire until the Second were within eighty rods, when they limbered up and galloped away. This was a very hot day and men were falling out continually, and soon a flank firing was heard, followed by a charge from the enemy. This was handsomely met by a counter charge from the first Tennessee and the flankers retired in confusion. At this moment a single horseman was seen to leave the enemy's ranks and charge down alone upon our brigade in front of the first Tennessee.

Nearly every man in that regiment and not a few from the Second fired at the charging figure, and at last stopped in blank amazement that the man was able to sit bolt upright in face of that shower of bullets. But he still came thundering on, while hostilities ceased on both sides to look and wonder if the man was made of iron, or, had he a charmed life. He soon rode in among the Federal troops and the mystery was explained. A bullet had cut both reins, and the horse refused to cease charging; all that the rider could do was grasp the horse's mane and pommel of the saddle and hang on. His clothes were riddled and the horse had many a scratch, but the man's skin was whole, though it may be doubted if he breathed during his ride.

Camping at Rover for the night the march was resumed, at 8 o'clock next morning, through Versailles and Middleton, where the enemy's cavalry made another stand, but the revolving rifles soon dislodged them, with severe punishment for the time engaged. Rains again set in and all roads except the macadamized turnpikes became next to impassable, while the discomfort of the troops was great; wagon trains could not keep up and our bivouacs were in the rain, no covering but our wet blankets and ponchos—and such rains as only Tennessee can boast of; while the red clay and black muck formed a barrier more serious than armed foe or frowning battlements. With such discouragements it was no wonder men should murmur, "Surely the Lord is not on our side—if He has anything to do with this weather."

General Rosecrans had evidently intended to throw his strong right arm around Bragg and crush him before he should cross the Tennessee. We were a part of that strong right arm.

But our trains and artillery were hopelessly stranded in the mud. Granger, Stanley and Mitchell were all here, but *push* we could not. However, as the cavalry corps came to Fosterville, and drove in the enemy's skirmishers, Stanley determined to abandon the mud-bound trains and artillery to their fate and strike with the cavalry alone.

Guy's Gap was before us, three-quarters of a mile away, and along its crest stretching out to the right and left were earthworks breast high; between us an open plain, ascending to the hill. The sun burst through the heavy clouds and shone full in the faces of 10,000 cavalry, in two lines, division fronts; banners flying, bands playing and the command marching in as perfect lines as if on a parade. Such a sight was rare in the history of the war—a corps of cavalry about to charge earthworks across an open field, and up a hill.

"Steady! steady!" was heard in low distinct tones along the line, though at every step the dreaded grape or canister was expected. A half mile, and yet no sign from the enemy; another quarter and still no curling smoke nor screeching shell. Casting our eyes for a moment to the earthworks not a man nor gun in sight. At this instant General Stanley ordered Colonel Minty, of the fourth Michigan cavalry, to lead the charge with his brigade, and right gallantly was the order executed, Colonel Campbell following next with his brigade, and the entire corps close in the rear in columns of fours and platoons.

The enemy had become frightened and fled precipitately, three pieces of artillery halting long enough on the hill at the entrance to Shelbyville to give us a few shots, then, wheeling again, dashed through the town, hotly followed by Minty and his brigade, while Campbell with his brigade, taking a street to the left, reached Duck river at the further edge of town in time to see hundreds of the enemy plunge in and endeavor to swim across, not half of whom ever gained the other shore, while Minty gained the bridge in time to cut off numerous prisoners from Wheeler's cavalry and capture one piece of artillery on the bridge. The roads were too heavy to follow the fleeing enemy far, and we returned to Guy's Gap for the night, having captured three pieces of artillery and 500 prisoners.

It was at Shelbyville that we were greeted by the pleasant sight of many flags bearing the "Stars and Stripes" suddenly flung out from chamber windows, and shouts of welcome from women and aged men who had lived like prisoners in their own homes; and colored women crying, "Bress de Lord, we knowed you'd come." And it was here, too, that we recaptured one of our female spies, the famous Major Belle Boyd, who had only saved herself from rebel prison pens or the gallows by feigning sickness, which she counterfeited admirably.

Though the Second took no part in the cutting and slashing at Shelbyville, they were among the first to reach Duck river and did their full share in helping to capture the prisoners and artillery. It was said that Frank Wheeler, "the gallant Frank Wheeler," as he was called, only escaped by swimming the river. Be this as it may, we had little trouble from him for weeks after.

On the 28th we returned to Shelbyville, through Fairfield, scouting the country to the right and left, and on the 30th marched through rain and mud toward Manchester; and on this march Governor Blair and Adjutant-General Robertson were with us, sharing our soldier's fare with apparent relish, though under most unfavorable circumstances. Passing through Manchester, on the 2d of July, we moved on through Winchester, fording Elk river and on to Decherd and Gowan, where we arrived at about the same time with General Sheridan, who had been hotly pressing Bragg, but now that individual had again slipped through our fingers and was over the mountains and practically out of Tennessee.

We had not seen our trains since leaving Triune, neither tents or baggage; no time to air or wash our clothing; therefore, it was not an unwelcome thought that possibly as we returned to Decherd we might remain until our wagons came swimming out of the mud; and so it proved, for near there we remained for two weeks, and while here we received the news of two great Union victories—Gettysburg, July 1st, 2d and 3d, and the surrender of Vicksburg, July 4th, for our telegraph operators had kept up with us and had a wire encased in rubber strung along the roadside and through the trees. We were able to celebrate our "Fourth" in a quiet way, with the sun once more smiling upon us and our "only shirt," hanging on the bush.

That Bragg had escaped without a general battle was a bitter disappointment to General Rosecrans and the officers and men under him, but we felt that only the elements were at fault. Streams were swollen, bridges gone, and supplies could not keep up with the movements of the army. We had been living on short rations, many of them nearly spoiled, and men were getting sick, while horses were abandoned by the roadside. That rain was a national calamity, yet the lesson was a needed one and was not without its good results later on.

After resting near Winchester until the 13th, foraging upon the country and recruiting our horses, we marched to Salem, Alabama, where the cavalry corps was concentrated, and moved on to New Market, passing on over a spur of the mountains, fording Flint river (very much swollen), and arrived at the beautiful city of Huntsville, Alabama, the heart of one of the richest sections of the south; with good roads, clear rivers, fertile plains, and, near by, fine mountain scenery with beautiful residences; and in the heart of the city a clear spring that is its own water power to convey to every home a bountiful supply of *aqua pura*. Our stay here was brief, when we marched to Fayetteville, camping for a few days near the Stone bridge, thence on to Salem and Winchester, and on the 31st of July returned to Fayetteville, camping on the same spot once occupied by General Jackson in 1813.

Crossing Elk river to Smith's farm, on the 4th of August, thousands of citizens from the surrounding country came in and took the oath of allegiance to the old flag.

On the 11th and 12th of August we again went to Huntsville and from there scoured the country toward Stevenson, Alabama, where we arrived on the 16th, having captured a number of rebel scouting parties that had recrossed the Tennessee river to watch our movements.

The rebel pickets are in plain view across the river.

CHAPTER XIV.

STEVENSON, ALABAMA—THE ARMY CONCENTRATING—HALF IN HOSPITALS—IMMENSE DEPOT OF SUPPLIES—OVER MOUNTAIN AND MOOR—SCOUTING THROUGH GEORGIA—CRAWFISH SPRING —"CHICAMAUGA."

During the latter half of August, 1863, the Army of the Cumberland drew together its main strength at and near Stevenson and Bridgeport, on the line of the railroad extending from Nashville to Chattanooga, with the nearly unfordable Tennessee River between us and the enemy, and no bridge, rail or otherwise. Here General Rosecrans amused himself and his officers one morning by coming down to the bank of the river and shouting back and forth inquiries and answers about "old Bragg" and "old Rosy." By common consent both sides had ceased firing upon the other so long as each remained on his own side and made no hostile demonstrations. The soldiers had learned to look upon picket firing as a species of murder which they had no heart to indulge in, and an armed silence was maintained. But as soon as our pontoons were ready our guns were placed to cover the opposite landing. With darkness came the cannonading at Bridgeport, and we knew they were laying the pontoon bridge, and that soon we must cross and grapple again with the enemy. On the 30th the Second went to Bridgeport, but was not needed there that day, and returned, going into camp at Bolivar.

September came—dry, hot, dusty. Nearly one-third the army were in hospitals. Half demented soldiers, straying from their beds, in coarse gowns, came wandering through the forest camps; sitting, uninvited, beside our camp fires; unfolding pitiful tales of imaginary wrongs, and shivering in the chill morning air; begging for a cup of water, and swallowing like a thirsty child.

"Bring out the stretcher, boys—more blankets; there, carry him back to the hospital."

And, as strong arms bear him gently away, eye meets eye, and we realize that rough soldiers sometimes have hearts of women. Sympathy chokes off conversation, and every man feels that there are greater enemies to human life than bullets.

The army had entire confidence in General Rosecrans, and they felt that when he moved again it would be to a sure victory, and it was understood that we were to be reinforced by a good strong corps from the Potomac, that was to join us by way of Knoxville, and that Generals Granger and Crittenden, with their corps, were to go up the river and cross at Chattanooga, while the main portion of the Army of the Cumberland drew the enemy out of their fortifications by attacking their rear. The plan was undoubtedly well laid, but Bragg had it figured differently, and came the nearest to carrying out his plans. He retired from the Tennessee, even to abandoning the fortifications of Chattanooga, before he was pressed. Could he have cooped up Rosecrans in Chattanooga, as he had hoped to do, with the aid of Longstreet's corps from the Potomac, he could, perhaps, have recrossed the Tennessee, with his cavalry, cut our communications and made it exceedingly interesting for Rosecrans, and possibly crushed him or sent him flying north and westward. This was undoubtedly his plan. How the two Generals' plans were both declared "off," the country has seen.

Bragg reported to Richmond that the Federals were attempting to cut his communications with Atlanta, his real base of supplies, and the movement of Federal cavalry to a point near Rome, Georgia, certainly had that look; therefore he was in a measure compelled to retire from Chattanooga.

General Rosecrans has never received that credit which was his due for that part of the great military move upon the national chess-board. By it he really out-generaled Bragg, but as the move continued events clearly showed that he had overreached his mark in permitting McCook and Crittenden to become too far removed from his center, "The Rock of Chicamauga"—General Thomas—around whom the fate of the nation hung trembling in the balance for forty-eight hours.

But let us not anticipate, but to our part in this very exciting campaign.

On the 1st day of September a part of our regiment and brigade forded the Tennessee river, near Stevenson, in the face of a scattering fire from the enemy. Another portion crossed on the pontoon bridge at Bridgeport, and marching down the river the regiment camped near Caperton's Spring, at the foot of Sand mountain, where we remained until the 3d, giving the army a chance to cross, when, everything being in readiness, we began the ascent of Sand mountain—half a mile high, and we found more rock than sand, with very steep roads—in fact, almost impassable for wagon trains. And while powerful mule teams drew themselves blind, big, burly drivers shouted themselves hoarse or bent their backs at the wheels. It seemed a wicked abuse of horse and mule flesh, and the oaths hurled out upon the mountain side did full justice to the M.-D.s' reputations, but were powerless to hurry along the creeping trains. As we reached the top and paused a moment for breath, we looked back, expecting to have a fine view of our late camping ground and the surrounding valley, with the river in the foreground; but a fog had arisen, and only its creamy white wave floated like a vast sea over the plain below; and from out its depths arose the faintest rattle and rumble of wagon or artillery wheels, and we knew our army was on the move and there was business ahead.

Turning our horses' heads we set out on the march across the mountain. A very hard march up hill and down, through heat and dust, and across Flat rock creek, 22 miles, brought us to Will's valley, where we bivouacked for the night, having only scant forage and little water, and the mountain air crisp, dry and sharp. Next day we passed over Winston's gap and into Little Will's valley, camping at night at Allen's farm.

We were still the right wing of Rosecrans's army, and on the 6th went scouting up Little Will's valley to the base of Lookout mountain, as far as Lebanon, Alabama. This we remember as a delightful valley, with clear mountain streams and a few rich plantations; but we found it necessary to charge upon rebel cavalry many times during the day, and the heat and dust were almost insufferable; but the enemy retired from every position, and we returned to camp at night, white with dust and streaked with sweat, scarcely able to distinguish one comrade from another.

September 9 we again ascended Lookout mountain at Valley Head, and crossing over, ten miles brought us to Alpine, in Broom town valley, Georgia, where we encamped. During the next three days the brigade scouted about Melville and towards Rome, Georgia, capturing small scouting parties and destroying the saltpeter works in the way, bringing up in camp near Summerville, on the 12th, and from that "deserted village" towards Lafayette, on the 13th, where we dashed upon the enemy's pickets, capturing and pursuing until brought up short by a park of artillery, stationed near a division of infantry which rapidly formed to meet us, and we discovered that we were near the headquarters of Bragg's army. Then, having accomplished the object of our mission, we countermarched in good order, with the enemy shelling the woods in our rear, but doing us no harm.

General Crook was temporarily in command of the cavalry and was with this expedition, though Colonel Campbell was in command of the brigade, and both those officers and their staffs were found at the head of the column and were at close range when the artillery opened upon them, with short range fuse shells, grape and canister. It was the evident intention of General Crook to dash in as near the center of the rebel army as possible, to learn something of their strength and position, and his plans were carried out most admirably. There was no stopping to deploy and skirmish, no time for throwing out flankers; but the brigade, led by the second Michigan with Colonel Campbell and staff at their head, grasping their rifles, revolvers or sabers in one hand, and reins in the other, dashed forward, on and over the pickets, yelling like wild Comanches, and continued their wild ride for more than a mile within the enemy's lines until halted by a stronger force.

There was not the slightest trace of fear on a single countenance as we countermarched, giving every trooper a chance to meet his comrades face to face, and all seemed to have enjoyed their little gallop amazingly.

Looking back to that scene, and remembering that the command was not large, and in an enemy's country, we can but admire (setting aside our own several parts) the cool boldness of the act. For, instead of wheeling to fly for their lives as many a command had done under anything like similar circumstances, every man grasped his arms with a firmer grasp and coolly wheeled his horse when his turn came, not sooner, and took up his return march at a walk—ready for a fight, if the enemy saw fit to pick up the gauntlet thrown at their feet.

Of course we were aware that we had stirred up a hornets' nest, and would doubtless be followed. But this did not worry us, for we had left a good road up the mountains in our rear and could reach there against odds, although the heat and dust were very disagreeable companions.

Returning to our former road down the mountains, we ascended. Looking back up the valley we had the satisfaction of seeing clouds of dust made by others than Yankees, and knew that we had not brought it *all* away with us. The enemy were looking for us and we were coolly perched on the mountain's brow, enjoying their over caution. It was very pleasant where we sat. Fanned by the gentle mountain zephyrs, we enjoyed the scene spread out miles away towards Chattanooga, and rather enjoyed seeing others take a hand at the dust and heat. But the enemy followed us only a mile or two in force, and we leisurely went into camp at Will's valley.

The 16th, at noon, found us again refreshed and in the saddle, passing through Winston's Gap, Little Will's valley and up Lookout mountain, crossing over to Dougherty's Gap, where we arrived late in the evening—very dark; there was no moon, and the stars, obscured by a hazy atmosphere, made our night work extremely hazardous should we suddenly come upon a well organized force of the enemy, but we believed our coast clear and found it so as we went sliding down the steep sides of a ravine into McLamore's cove, every step of a horse covering ten to fifteen feet, with the loose dirt and rocks crumbling and sliding along in front of us, behind us and all around us, and as we looked back to wonder if every horse and man was able to keep his feet, or would he come floundering on down the mountain side, the scene became one of intense excitement; but we arrived at the foot without serious accident, and then came a gallop of a mile or more to close up the column; but the road was good, and late in the evening we bivouacked for the night near Cave Spring in McLamore's cove, and were not long in finding an abundance of sweet potatoes to piece out our rations, which had been getting low since we cut loose from our trains and left them to make their way as best they could along the summit of the mountain out of the enemy's grasp. Here, too, we made our acquaintance with "goober peas," "goobers," or peanuts, and were glad to fill up with almost any kind of raw fodder if we could not get it cooked. But, thanks to a generous commissary, our coffee nearly always held out and we did not really suffer the pangs of hunger, for we had learned to live for days together on coffee, if bread and bacon both gave out. But here were sweet potatoes, to us as rich as rare, and we felt happy around our late camp fire over a steaming cup of coffee, a corn pone and a roasted yam, or sweet potato.

These bewildering moves, up and down valleys, over mountains, through coves and ravines, back and forth, losing our points of compass by night and regaining them with the next move by daylight, so completely turned our heads that we lost all desire to know where we were going or how we expected to reach there; our guides and our commander know and we settle down into passive obedience and the belief that we shall get "somewhere" in due time. It may be to the land "beyond the river," but we don't mean it shall be to a prison pen.

Our movements on the 17th and 18th of September were in the vicinity of Cedar Grove church and Bailey's, and we began to smell the battle "afar off." For, occasionally an artillery skirmish, away to the left towards Chattanooga, could be heard, and we afterwards learned that Colonel Minty with his brigade was there, disputing the passage of Chicamauga creek at Reed's bridge and Gordon's mill. We were still on the right, but our lines had not as yet had time to sufficiently concentrate to be of assistance to each other, and Bragg had intended to prevent such concentration by throwing Hood, Walker, Buckner and Polk's corps against our right, crushing and sweeping up the

BATTLE OF CHICAMAUGA.

Chicamauga to Gordon's mill. He had the men to have done so, but he also had the disadvantage of being the attacking party, and all along our line of scattered forces was heard some of the most desperate fighting of the war, when, on the 19th of September, the engagement became general.

Without attempting to enter into a detailed account of the great battle of Chicamauga, or Crawfish Spring, it is proper for a better understanding of the part taken by the cavalry to look at the position of our army on the morning of the 19th of September.

General Crittenden with his corps occupied a position toward the center, near the right, at Crawfish Spring, with the left stretching away up the valley, across Chicamauga creek, towards Chattanooga, with General Granger and his reserve corps in rear of the left near Rossville, with one brigade of cavalry, General Minty's, near the left, and the rest of the cavalry corps near the right wing. In our front was General Sheridan with his division (third division, twentieth army corps), who was gradually working his position towards the left, as were all the Generals, trying to contract the lines to be within supporting distance. This soon left the cavalry corps without infantry in their front, some little distance on the right; but as Bragg attempted to throw his cavalry on the right flank of our infantry they (the enemy) found a force they were ready to let alone, and we held our position all day, protecting our infantry on their right from being attacked on their flank while the enemy were unable to use their cavalry against our infantry in any other direction.

The rattle of musketry had increased to a roar in one continuous sound. The thundering artillery shook the earth, rolling, trembling, like an earthquake; smoke filled the air and shut out the combatants from each other's sight, and the hospital corps were soon busy bringing in the wounded around Crawfish Spring.

On the morning of the 20th it was quiet along the line until 9 o'clock, when the enemy began the engagement by a heavy assault on the left of our army, General Thomas's corps, and by 11 o'clock the engagement became general, and if possible more fierce than on the previous day. General Thomas was standing up to the main part of the rebel army at the center, while Sheridan and Wood were rapidly moving to the left to join him, when the enemy came up through an unoccupied space, cutting through General Davis's lines, of McCook's corps, when General Sheridan went to the rescue, and that part of the field was fought over for the third time, when each side stood looking sullenly across the sanguinary field without renewing the engagement.

It was then that General Sheridan confirmed his fears that he was cut off, but he succeeded at last in forming a junction with General Thomas. General Granger's important action at this juncture will be found in Part Second. During the morning struggle with the enemy's cavalry the Second lost some valuable men; among them Captain James G. Hawley, of company G, who was shot from his horse while assisting a Kentucky regiment in forming to make a charge. There were no better men in the service than Captain Hawley.

In the meantime the cavalry remained holding their position near Crawfish Spring until late in the afternoon, when the firing grew fainter, and, without knowing what had occurred or being able to communicate with the infantry to our left, Colonel

Campbell took his brigade to the left and rear, and to the left of the Dry valley road, marching rapidly about three miles from Crawfish Spring, when we came to an open piece of wood, and there burst upon our startled view a mass of officers, soldiers and camp followers in thousands, who were apparently fleeing from the "wrath to come." A look of worn-out, discouraged fear was upon nearly every countenance. Inquiring the cause of their panic they could give no definite account of what had happened, but all agreed that McCook's corps was "knocked into pi" and that McCook and others had joined Rosecrans and had gone towards Chattanooga.

There was a gap in the road just ahead where a regiment could hold their own against 10,000 men, and Campbell at once took advantage of it. Placing a straggling section of artillery in a commanding position, with his cavalry near at hand, across the road, he rapidly formed the disorganized fleeing troops into companies, properly officered, though made up of men from all the demoralized regiments, and with an oath declared there should be no "Bull Run" there, and before dark had a large command of the flower of McCook's army marching quietly along, guarding their rear and flanks, searching for General Thomas, whom Campbell knew to be second in command.

After dark we rode along the rebel front, close to their camp fires; could hear their conversation and see them getting their suppers as quietly as if nothing had happened. We followed their line until midnight, and though we could hear that General Thomas was near us, bivouacked near where he had been fighting all day, we did not find him, but lay down without food or fires, though the night was frosty.

It would have been some comfort for us to have known that our trains were safe, for we had left them on the mountains, fifteen miles away, unprotected. But they were looking down upon the terrible scenes of the past two days and were working toward Chattanooga. Next morning we set out for Chattanooga, where the army had preceded us, and, on getting within eight miles, skirmished with the enemy, remaining there until early on the morning of the 22d, when we again set out, with the enemy on our flanks in strong force; at one time driving us up the side

Point Lookout.

of the mountain, where we were fired upon from the valley by the artillery, solid shot being directed especially against Campbell and staff; but we came down again, and driving back a line of skirmishers by a charge, made our way inside the fortifications and across the river by a ford that led us three-quarters of a mile diagonally across the Tennessee, with the water breast high.

It has been claimed by Southern writers that the Confederates here fought the Union forces even-handed and whipped them. The facts were that Rosecrans had but 55,000 men on that field and that Bragg had, with Longstreet's reinforcements, nearly 70,000. It is true that Thomas, with his own and a part of Crittenden's corps, was on the defensive, but take from Rosecrans's army half of McCook's corps and the greater portion of the cavalry who were not within proper supporting distance, but were striving to get there, and we must admit that Thomas was contending against fearful odds. For while Bragg had several divisions that he could, from his concentrated position, throw into the balance against either wing of our army, McCook's corps was not in a commanding position, but must fight wherever he happened to be until such time as he should close up to the left upon General Thomas. In this closing up movement Generals Sheridan's, Davis's and Wood's divisions were twice caught in the whirling vortex and suffered terribly, but held their divisions well together and gave the enemy such terrific blows that even Bragg recoiled when asked by Longstreet to give him a division from their left and he would crush Thomas's left. "No," said Bragg, "they have been beaten back so badly they would be of no service to you."

Look at the cost in men:

	KILLED.	WOUNDED.	MISSING.	TOTAL.
Union forces	1,687	9,394	5,255	16,336
Confederate forces	2,673	16,274	2,003	20,950

We had been compelled to retire from the battle field, but we held the key to the South—Chattanooga.

More extended research shows that Crittenden had occupied a position as far east as Ringold, and that Minty had insisted, after Crittenden had joined Thomas, that a large body of Confederates were moving from the north and east to Bragg's support and that Rosecrans refused to give credit to the report even at the moment when Bragg's right was within striking distance between Lee and Gordon's mill and Reed's bridge. Minty had been reported captured beyond Reed's bridge, and that catastrophe was only averted by rapid movements and desperate fighting. At the moment of McCook's disaster Rosecrans was just in rear of McCook's right—a witness to that fierce assault by the enemy. While portions of Sheridan's and Davis's divisions had become disorganized and were seeking by a circuitous route to join Thomas or reach Chattanooga, the main portions of these divisions were moving in comparatively good order, by a nearer route to Thomas and Rossville, and that Thomas had a part only of his own corps, and parts of Crittenden's and McCook's corps in his immediate command. Divisions from one corps were at one time hurrying past divisions from another corps, eagerly searching for points where they were most needed.

CHAPTER XV.

VICTORY OUT OF DEFEAT—SOME REFLECTIONS, NOT DESIGNED AS CRITICAL.—GREAT SOLDIERS—WHEELER'S RAID—1,000 WAGONS BURNED—A WILD CHASE—CAMP LIFE—A FERRY DISASTER.

If we study carefully the lives of all great soldiers there is but one conclusion—no military genius ever received the plaudits of his countrymen without deserving them. Mistakes may occur, but the genius is there and will assert itself. If he is successful in one campaign and the victim of disaster afterwards, it is more than probable the fault could be traced to another's doings in part.

General Rosecrans's career shows him to have possessed many of these qualities which go to make up the great soldier. But his conduct of the battle of Chicamauga clearly showed him to be possessed of one element that amounted to weakness —hastily formed planning without positive assurance that the material in men and means would be at hand—to carry out his plans. He placed too great reliance upon his corps commanders, evidently thinking them all as good as Thomas, who stood with his men well in hand, his ground selected and studied carefully, and he was prepared to resist and did successfully withstand the assaults of many times his own numbers hurled against him.

Rosecrans ordered, and had a right to expect, that the several corps would close up to the left, provided the distance was not too great. There probably lay his fatal error; his army was covering too much front to be readily closed to the left.

General Sheridan's heroic efforts in that direction proved this; and after all the service the cavalry had done in discovering the enemy's position, their further service was considered of secondary importance. To guard the right flank was important, but they were ready and anxious to do more, and were kept further to the right than they were actually needed. Campbell's discovery in the afternoon proved that, and had Colonel Campbell with his brigade been ordered earlier to the assistance of McCook that general might have been spared the humiliation of so crushing a defeat. There was cavalry enough on the right without Campbell, and that good strong brigade of cavalry thrown into the fight at the proper moment must have had a telling effect.

Yet, after all, the prize which Rosecrans had in view— Chattanooga—was ours; though at what terrible cost—16,336 men, killed, wounded and missing, 50 pieces of artillery lost. Those were the figures, and the Confederate loss was probably more than 20,000, as they were the assailants; but their loss in artillery was less than ours.

Bragg had figured to crush Rosecrans's army and return to Chattanooga; he had failed, and by that failure had lost the key to the South. Who was the victor? The country will not

CHICAMAUGA.

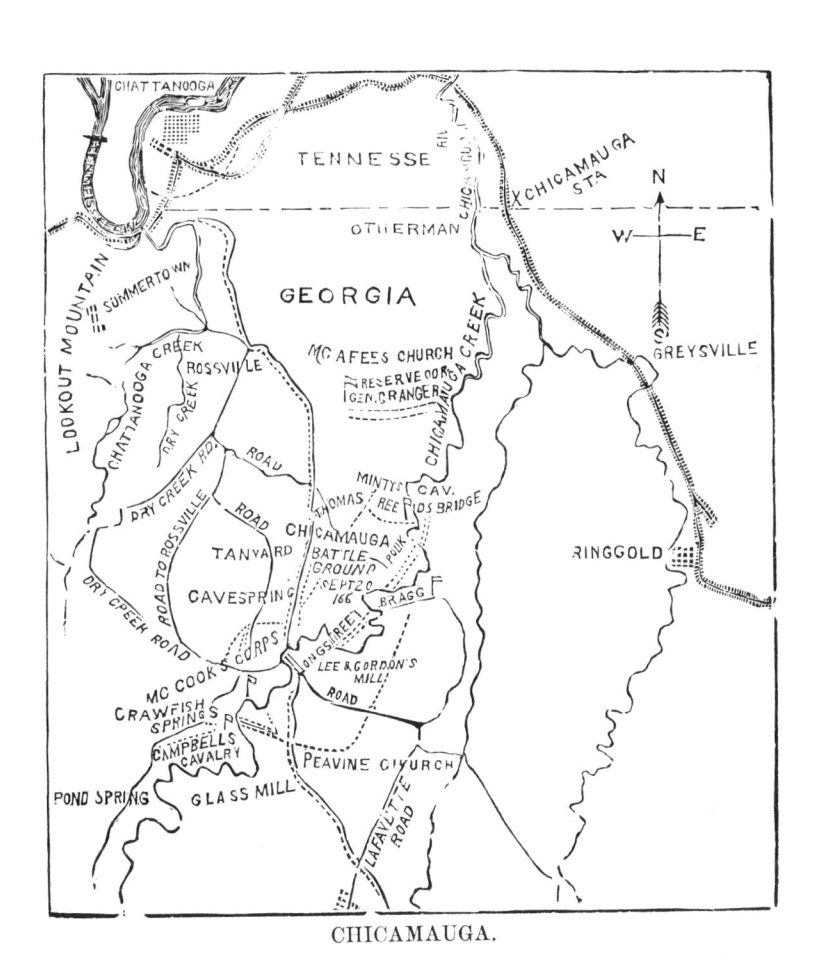

judge too harshly, but they cannot forget that Rosecrans left the field, at Garfield's suggestion, for Thomas and Granger to fight it out, and well did they do it, regardless of personal danger.

Granger lost his adjutant-general and wept, though bullets were rending his clothing and tore his hat from his head. That was his best fight of the war, and the reserve corps covered themselves with glory.

Sheridan's division of 4,000 men lost 1,492, including 96 officers, and the second Michigan again could point with pride to their old colonels, though the regiment's part in this great battle had not been a prominent one; still it had skirmished all day, and lost some valuable men and officers.

When our army were all within the fortifications of Chattanooga many soldiers appeared to think the rebels capable of retaking the place, but those who had seen the *heavy* fighting did not feel so. They knew the enemy had been severely punished, and they felt that with our army concentrated behind earthworks Bragg could never enter. He did not try seriously. He knew better, but made a show of attack by dropping a few harmless shells into our works and looked on sullenly.

Our first duty was the protection of our communications, and the regiment and brigade moved back a few miles on the north bank of the Tennessee to be in readiness to strike wherever needed, camping near Severly Springs a few days, finding a moderate amount of forage and recruiting our strength in horses and men for the next move, which we had no doubt would come soon enough; and it came, on the 26th. Moving down the river to Bridgeport, and to Stevenson on the 27th, passing on to Pump Spring, we remained until October 2d; the enemy trying to cross several times, and were driven back; but Frank Wheeler succeeded in getting across at some other point above, and on the afternoon of the 2d we were ordered to report to Colonel Ed. McCook, in Sequatchie valley, without delay. We started at once, passing through Bridgeport and Jasper, marching all night and until about ten o'clock next day, but were too late to prevent the disaster to our trains or even help stir them up while enjoying their short lived fun. The seventh Pennsylvania and second Indiana had started from Bridgeport and had that much the advantage of us, and came down upon Wheeler's cavalry while they were at their work of destruction. They had succeeded in setting fire to General Rosecrans's supply trains of nearly 1,000 wagons loaded with provisions and ammunition, when General Crook attacked them and routed them.

This was a heavy loss to the Army of the Cumberland (for they were on short rations) and Wheeler thought, no doubt, that it would be a serious blow; but, poor fool, he did not realize that we had wagons and mules by the thousands, in reserve at Nashville, with provisions and ammunition stacked up by the acre in sheds and ware-houses, and that within twenty-four hours after the burning of those trains, others were on the way. But Wheeler had no desire to stand and fight, but immediately got out, the only way open to him—up the mountain and away to the southward, with our cavalry pouring into the valley by three different roads, and General Crook pressing him hotly in the rear. On the morning of the 4th (October) we crossed the mountain at Kane Gap, and at ten A. M. of the 5th reached McMinnville, passing on through Woodbury, having made fifty-five miles in twenty-four hours, and, marching all night again, we reached Murfreesboro at eight o'clock on the morning of the 6th, where we drew rations and again joined in the chase toward Shelbyville, resting for a few hours at Guy's Gap.

General Crook had caught up with Wheeler on the 8th and captured several hundred prisoners, sending him flying south. The Second joined in the chase again, and passing on rapidly, often galloping for miles together, with the mud and water flying furiously, passed through Rainy Spring, Louisburg and Connersville, and on the 9th passed through Pulaski and on to Lamb's Ferry, twenty-four miles above Florence, where Wheeler was compelled to abandon his artillery and the wagons he was trying to carry away with him and also lost heavily in prisoners and deserters. On the whole the Wheeler raid was a losing game to the Confederates, without an equivalent. It was a daring act crossing the river, and had the cavalry been united earlier Wheeler could not have passed out of Sequatchie valley. Once out of there, he had us at a disadvantage, and kept it, on a wild chase of 300 miles in nine days, much of the distance being over rough, mountainous roads, and the usual "after the battle rains" having fallen, softening the valleys, made our progress difficult, not to mention the disagreeableness of Tennessee mud. Wheeler's cavalry must have suffered worse than ours, for our brigades took turns at the front attending to the "lively" business, while poor Wheeler's men dropped out, with broken down horses, all along the way.

These men were generally given an impromptu "iron-clad oath," often at the hands of some wag who was in too much of a hurry to attend to prisoners, and told to go home and enjoy themselves "till the war was over." Many of them were glad of the opportunity, while others probably found their way back into the Confederate army. But all larger bodies of them were cared for and sent to Nashville.

For more than a month, since the forward move on Chattanooga, the Second had been without tents, on short rations, marching night and day, much of the time over rough, mountainous roads, with dust and mud, heat, rain and cold alternating in quick succession, and both horses and men were in a worn-out condition. Therefore we were prepared to appreciate a leisurely march from Rodgersville, on the 10th, to Athens, Huntsville and New Market, by the 13th, where we learned that Roddy's brigade of cavalry had crossed the Tennessee below Huntsville, and away we went in pursuit of him; but he made no stand, was soon across the river again, and we were left in undisputed possession of that territory, camping first at Kelly's mill, on Barren fork of Flint river, but for nearly a month from the 20th of October we remained near Winchester, Tennessee, resting and recruiting for another campaign.

General Rosecrans was relieved about this time and went to Cincinnati, and many regrets were expressed at his misfortune, for we had become very much attached to him.

Our stay at Winchester was made quite agreeable to us, not only by the few Union people there, but Southern sympathizers often inviting officers and soldiers to their homes to dinner and tea, spreading their tables at such times with the best the land afforded.

We lived in our tents, and had time for wearing blacked boots and "boiled" shirts—almost forgotten luxuries. Neglected reports and unanswered letters were attended to, and the paymaster, Holloway, made his rounds. Fresh horses and new uniforms were added, and once more we "played" soldier at dress parade and inspection, General Grant calling to inspect us on his way to assume command of this army, now further strengthened by the addition of Hooker's corps.

It now became evident that a vigorous campaign was to be carried on all winter, and a part of this came to us by an order, November 16th, to swing through middle Tennessee, by way of Shelbyville and Murfreesboro, on our way to northern and eastern Tennessee. The country was nearly stripped of live stock, but our foragers brought in 400 bushels of wheat, 65 head of beef cattle, 500 to 600 head of sheep, besides horses and mules in one day, and we reached Murfreesboro on the 18th of November, 1863.

Here our division was placed in the hands of Brigadier-General Ed. McCook, and General Stanley, retiring from the cavalry, was superseded by General W. L. Elliott, who commanded us the year previous at Corinth and Blackland. These changes being completed the cavalry moved, on the 20th, halting for a night at Milton and five days at Liberty.

The weather was now cold and rainy, but did not prevent our forward movement, on the 28th, of twenty miles, and next day was made that memorable crossing of the Rainy fork of the Cumberland river, swollen to a rushing torrent.

Men will stand up and be shot without flinching, but to see comrades helplessly drown before their eyes moves the innermost heart. How pitiless that cold drizzling rain. How frail a craft for a division of cavalry to cross on. Only a flatboat, that ten horses would settle down to the water's edge, a craft which the least move would swamp; everything covered with ice and next to impossible for horses or men to keep their feet. If he lost his feet and went over—a splash, a cry, and he was gone. And so we lost eight men—a small number to have lost in battle, but a very large number to lose in such a manner. It was the saddest day of all our army experience. But at last the command was over, and went into camp at Sparta, near the Cumberland mountains, in middle Tennessee, directly east of Nashville.

CHAPTER XVI.

EAST TENNESSEE—CLIMBING THE CUMBERLAND—BUSHWHACKERS—"DANDRIDGE RACES"—A LIVELY CAMPAIGN AND MANY HARDSHIPS.

"Shall we ever get through with climbing mountains?" remained an unanswered question as the regiment set out at daylight on the 8th of December from Sparta to cross the Cumberland by a steep wagon road.

Next to rebel prison pens the meanest thing ever encouraged by the Confederates was guerrilla warfare. Many of their own officers were ashamed of it and stoutly denied any knowledge of the bands that infested the mountain countries of Tennessee. They were too cowardly to stand up shoulder to shoulder and face an honorable foe in common warfare, and were a disgrace to the army whose cause they pretended to espouse.

And on this march the command was terribly annoyed, on flank and rear, by parties they could not stop to fight, and we lost some good men while going over the mountain. It was murder, nothing but murder.

Our sutler, John F. Tinkham, who had just purchased a large stock, was unable to keep up with the regiment, and abandoning his wagon, with several thousand dollars' worth of stock, was glad to escape with his life. A rather decent sort of sutler was John, and the boys regretted their inability to render substantial assistance, forgetting that they had paid him a good share of their greenbacks from time to time for "truck" that they did not always need, at the usual sutler's "one and two per cent." prices. But his big wagon, full of shirts, knick-knacks, underwear, gloves, canned stuff and bottled "chain lightning," was soon riddled, and as John stood on the top of that mountain and looked back at the despoilers and their work, he waved his hand, telling them to help themselves, and turned sadly away.

The regiment crossed the Cumberland mountains, passing down the east side near Crossville, reaching Kingston on the 12th, camping for the night without food, or forage for the horses, but succeeded next day in finding both food and forage in the vicinity, and after a two days' rest moved on, through mud and cold rain, to Knoxville, arriving on the 15th, and on the 16th went on to Pryor's ferry into camp. The earthworks around Knoxville showed the fresh marks of Burnside's recent fight with Longstreet, who had been besieging Knoxville, but who had received some severe blows and was now at a respectful distance. Here, too, we met our old friend, General S. P. Carter, of "Carter's raid" fame; and resurrected Parson Brownlow, whose son Jim was a colonel of one of our regiments—the first East Tennessee cavalry, many of whom were at home here. The Parson came out and received a hearty, old-fashioned military salute with a "tiger."

On the 17th the brigade marched through Strawberry Plains, and, fording the Holston river, camped at Housley's. The fording of the Holston was a very cold bath; horses and men coming out of the water shaking as if caught in the death like grip of a Kansas ague. But the march to Richland creek and return warmed them up a bit and they went into camp to make themselves as comfortable as possible until the 23d, when they moved to New Market. Here some changes occurred in our division, being known thereafter as the first division, under General Ed McCook, with General S. D. Sturgis in command of all the cavalry of East Tennessee, Colonel Campbell continuing in command of the first brigade (second Michigan, ninth Pennsylvania and first East Tennessee) and Colonel Lagrange, of the first Wisconsin cavalry, commanding the second brigade (first Wisconsin, second and third Indiana cavalry), and they were all good fighting regiments.

And now began that memorable East Tennessee campaign, with Major L. S. Scranton in command of our regiment. On the 23d the brigade moved out of New Market, camping for the night at Broughton's, on the Dandridge road. By 3 o'clock next morning "Boots and saddles" brought every man and horse into line and soon on the road to Dandridge; skirmishing and driving the enemy through that place. At 9 A. M. our brigade was joined by Colonel Capron, of Ohio, with his brigade. The enemy were quite strong in front, but the second Michigan drove in their skirmishers, chasing them three miles. Colonel Capron took a left hand road which diverges from the main easterly road from Dandridge, Colonel Campbell taking the right hand road which passes near the French Broad river. It

162   HUNDRED BATTLES

was understood that should anything special occur they were to give each other notice. In fact Colonel Capron, being the ranking officer, sent to Colonel Campbell written instructions to press the enemy on the right hand road while he (Capron) would keep within supporting distance on the left. The enemy pre-

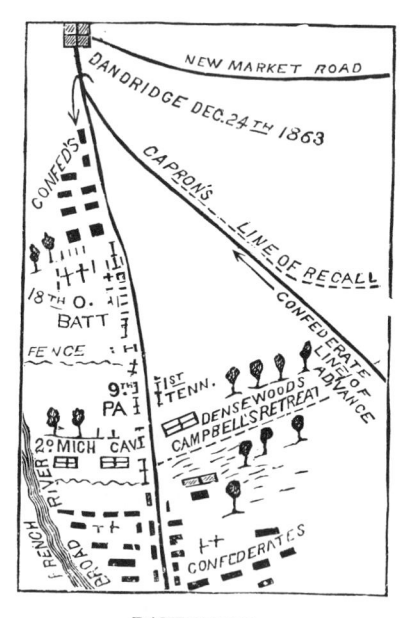

DANDRIDGE.

sented a strong skirmish line and the Second was immediately placed at the front, driving the enemy successfully, with the other regiments of the brigade, mounted, supporting the Second in the rear and on the flanks, and company D of the Second acting as rear guard; a part of the first battalion remained near the rear supporting a part of our artillery, while two pieces were taking position at the front. The Second had found the enemy in force and did not attempt to go further than a little ridge or range of hills, but gave place to the artillery to shell the enemy from the ridges, in front of which the enemy were beginning to show considerable strength, as if expecting a general engagement. When our mounted men charged the enemy they discovered the strength of the force at the front and knew that we must fall back soon. The Confederate artillery immediately opened, and their cavalry followed ours as ours retired.

Colonel Campbell had heard nothing from Colonel Capron, and began to feel anxious about his supporting force. He at once dispatched couriers across to Colonel Capron, supposed to be half a mile or a mile away to the left on the other road, but no word was returned, and he then sent a staff officer with escort, to find out if his support was all right. None of them returned, but, instead, a brigade of rebel cavalry charged down on our rear, driving in the rear guard, preceded by ambulances, led horses mules, cooks and camp followers in a badly demoralized condition. Pots and frying pans, coffee cups, tin dishes and all the rattle-traps of a company cook's paraphernalia flying in the air, as frightened black faces, mostly noticeable for the glaring expanse of white eyes, came tearing down upon the front—a position entirely new to most of them—provoking a roar of laughter at the first appearance, in spite of the grim surroundings.

The situation was truly appalling. A large force in our front and a force equal to if not larger than our own in rear. Charging on over the camp followers they captured the two pieces of artillery that had not been taken into action and were sabering the artillerymen and dragging away the guns. Then Major Smith with his battalion turned upon them and met them with a murderous fire, at the same time requesting a portion of the ninth Pennsylvania cavalry, mounted near by, to charge, which they did handsomely, the lieutenant in command losing his life by the charge, and the enemy were driven away from the artillery and back a half mile. In the meantime Major Scranton, with the main portion of the Second, dismounted, was stubbornly holding the enemy at the front in check, when he received an injury in the foot. Colonel Campbell directed the regiment to form a new line to the left and fall back in good order, assuring the major that he (Campbell) would soon find a position from which they could check the enemy, and give the dismounted men relief.

There was no road to the left, but Campbell, with the mounted portion of the brigade and his artillery, found a way, through hills, ridges and woods, but had scarcely succeeded in getting his column moving when the enemy came down upon that little band of dismounted cavalrymen before they had swung into their new line of march. The position was most desperate. Less than 1,500 men, one third of them dismounted, surrounded on three sides by brigades of cavalry, with mounted infantry coming to their assistance. Led horses, ambulances and camp followers were in the way, while continuous charges of cavalry were made upon right, left and rear. But every foot of ground was contested, and nobly did the revolving rifles respond to the work; retiring, fighting over all that mile or more until the woods were cleared, and across a field, over the creek, a bloody battle every inch, with most of our wounded in the hands of the enemy. One piece of artillery broke down here and was abandoned. This was recaptured at Fair Garden. It was a portion of the eighteenth Ohio.

When the Confederates came yelling out of the woods, expecting an easy victory in an open field, our own artillery, welcome sound, opened with grape and canister, and the slaughter was severe. Our cavalry then gave them a parting charge just as the darkness began to apprise us of the fact that we had been more than two hours in making that two miles; but the command retired to New Market without further molestation. We had lost heavily in officers and men, though our loss was probably

CAPTAIN J. H. SMITH.

trifling as compared with that of the enemy. Here Captain J. H. Smith received a fracture of the thigh by a musket ball, which left him on the field all night, in the hands of the enemy. Captain T. W. Johnston was also wounded in the leg, but was assisted away. In all forty-two men were killed, wounded or missing—just the number at Booneville, Mississippi, in an all day's fight.

The regiment had been in many tight places, but this was the nearest to a capture they had ever experienced.

It was here the rebels told the citizens they "did not like to fight the second Michigan. They loaded their guns all night and fired them all day."

It appears that no one was really at fault for this apparent blunder of leaving a brigade in the hands of the enemy to fight their way out. Colonel Capron received orders to come back from his expedition, certain knowledge having come to his superiors that made the further advance, or reconnaissance, both dangerous and unnecessary, and Colonel Capron was directed to notify Colonel Campbell to fall back, which he did, or supposed he did, by sending couriers to Campbell, but they did not reach him; neither did Colonel Campbell's couriers reach Capron; therefore it was simply a question of good generalship, whether it was the right thing to do—obey orders literally and return to New Market, or wait until he knew if his services would be needed in preventing the capture of Colonel Campbell's brigade. For no sooner had Capron left his route than the rebels passed in towards Dandridge, by the same road, and came up in Campbell's rear, before he had any intimation of their being there. For this stubborn fight, the officers and men were highly complimented in general orders. The following is an extract from a dispatch to General Foster, commanding the department:

December 24, 1863, 8:30 P. M.,
*   *   Colonel Campbell deserves great credit for the masterly manner in which he extricated himself.   *   *

S. D. STURGIS,
Brigadier-General, Commanding Cavalry Corps.

CHAPTER XVII.

MOSSY CREEK—A TRICK WHICH DID NOT PAY—A FIGHT, SHORT, SHARP, DECISIVE—AN ARTILLERY DUEL.

Merry Christmas was celebrated about as soldiers usually celebrate when there is business on hand—not by feasting and drinking, but by moving *towards* the enemy, to meet and take the chances of war. Camp was pitched at or near Mossy creek, and near here until the 29th of December a comparative rest was enjoyed.

Then the second brigade, under Colonel Lagrange, was ordered to move to Dandridge at 2 A. M. and surprise a Confederate force stationed there. The report proved false, having emanated from the enemy themselves, as a ruse to divide our cavalry force, and to that extent was successful, but no further. There was no enemy at Dandridge, but if they supposed the Second would be sent away they were to be disappointed. A full half mile in advance of all our troops the Second had been placed in camp—a most fortunate thing as it proved.

The morning sun came out clear and bright; the air cool and bracing, giving promise of a glorious winter's day. But little above the horizon had the sun climbed when our pickets sent in word that the enemy were advancing in force, with ten pieces of artillery, and the report was immediately followed by the retiring of our advanced guard, and close behind them the enemy, with flags waving, arms flashing in the sunlight, and the steady muffled tramp of horsemen—in numbers, apparently, a full division or more. Steadily on they came, as if a review was ordered, or perhaps by their numbers they thought to ride over an awed, insignificant force.

It was a gallant sight and provoked admiration from the little band drawn up to receive them; yet the feeling was not unmixed with pain and desperation. "If the enemy think to drive us from our position without a fight they are mistaken." Major Ben Smith was in command of the Second, and was about to open fire upon the enemy, when Colonel Campbell, commanding the brigade, ordered him to fall back upon Mossy Creek, covering both sides of the road, and notifying him that the ninth Pennsylvania cavalry would support the right and the first Tennessee the left. The order was obeyed quietly, yet promptly, realizing that Campbell proposed to choose his own ground this time, with *traps* barred out.

The Second had fallen back to a large brick house, at which the general commanding the division, McCook, had made his headquarters, when the Confederates began shelling fiercely. The air seemed filled with iron missiles, of all shapes and sizes —singing, whirling, whistling—with that peculiar blood-curdling, flesh-rending horror, calculated for the moment to chill the hearts of the oldest veterans. Then was realized the fact that the battle was sprung upon the brigade with half the division away on a "Tom Fool's errand." Couriers were dispatched in hot haste for the second brigade to return; but there was little hope of their doing so in time to be of assistance.

The evolutions of the enemy were rapid and precise. Before there was time for our first brigade to form in proper position to repel a charge of the enemy, their artillery ceased firing, the cloud of smoke lifted, and out from the white floating veil, at a mad gallop came a division of cavalry, with flanks well supported, sabers drawn, and a shout of expectant victory bursting from their throats. Every man of the Second cast a hasty look at his revolving rifle, and stood silent, firmly grasping his beloved weapon that had stood by him through so many a desperate onslaught.

Nearer, and nearer, until it seemed as if the little band of dismounted men would be swallowed in the wild whirlpool of horsemen. Not a shot was fired until the word was given, and when, at the moment of greatest excitement it seemed impossible to restrain the men longer, it came. "Ready, Fire!" rang simultaneously with a roar as if 500 men had been suddenly transformed into 3,000—before whose unerring volley the best horsemen the world ever saw could not stand. They halt, reel, tremble, break and fly in dire confusion, with a shower of lead cutting sad havoc in their ranks.

During this charge a portion of the enemy found themselves in a barnyard, and made a desperate effort to dislodge Captain Wells, with portions of companies L and H, partly concealed behind a fence. The range was short and few of the enemy escaped from that pen of horrors, but were piled thick upon the ground.

Here Major Smith's horse was shot under him, but our total casualties (according to the adjutant's report) was but eight, and only one of these was killed.

After their repulse, the enemy again opened a most terrific cannonade, every piece of artillery belching forth shot and shell that came square to the mark, and before which the Second fell back to a better position, half a mile in rear of the first, partly sheltered by a fence. Yes, a fence, for the Second never was ashamed to take an advantage that might save a life for future usefulness. "Stand out and fight if they must, but under cover when they might," was their motto.

Here they lay, "under cover," except for the exploding shells that dropped down upon them; though our captain approached the major commanding, with an excusable timidity, and suggested it was pretty warm at his position—"Shells are dropping pretty thick; I fear I can't hold my men much longer; too monotonous, lying there taking all their old iron and giving nothing in return."

In that measured tone, so well known to all of us, came the answer:

"The shells are falling pretty thick where I am, but I guess we will stay a little longer unless ordered to fall back."

The order soon came to fall back and form on the left of a regiment of infantry that had been sent to our support, and scarcely had the position been taken when one of the sharpest artillery duels opened that we had ever witnessed. Ten Confederate guns to three of ours, were brought up to within eighty rods of each other, and belched forth one continuous storm of shot, shell and grape.

A staff officer whose duties took him to every part of the field says: "Our battery stood while men and horses were mowed down. The commander, pale as death, issued his orders with the utmost military precision, and stood his ground against more than twice his own number of guns, backed and encouraged by repeated charges of the Confederate cavalry."

Captain Weatherwax received a dangerous wound in the shoulder from a mounted Confederate officer, who in turn fell from his horse riddled with bullets.

CAPT. J. M. WEATHERWAX.

One Confederate shot killed three of our men at their guns, but others took their places, and the game of give and take was carried on in dead earnest. But not for long. The enemy had reckoned upon an easy victory with their division against one brigade. Time was passing, and whatever was to be done must be done quickly. Grape shot went crashing through tree tops. Shells, exploding, filled the air again with their infernal music. Solid shot went plowing through the woods and fields, yet not a gun of ours was silenced; but, above this deafening roar and crash, that well-known rebel yell was heard again, and every man knew at once that a decisive moment was at hand.

Once more the enemy's artillery paused, as if for breath, and ere the smoke had cleared away they came, in such overwhelming numbers and such irresistible force, that for a time hope died and all seemed lost. Our lines wavered, fell back, firing. Then the enemy's lines moved more cautiously; slower and yet more slowly, and halted in doubt.

A sharp, angry voice was heard, and recognized. It was Campbell:

"You have fallen back far enough—forward!"

The men caught the spirit. Infantry and dismounted cavalry dashed upon the now wavering enemy, giving them fresh volley after volley, driving them into and through the woods, retaking the lost ground, and driving them beyond the first alignment.

During this repulse of the enemy Colonel Campbell showed himself in brighter colors than ever before, by leading in person the first Tennessee cavalry in a saber charge, an opportunity he had never before enjoyed, and the regiment proved conclusively that they were of the right material when properly officered.

The rout was complete and the enemy fled demoralized, though they had made a courageous strike; and had our men been in the open fields, on grounds not of their own choosing, the result—well, it is needless to speculate.

At this time the second brigade returned, and feeling chagrined at their having a second time been prevented from helping the first brigade in a hard struggle, they dashed away at the retreating foe with an energy that boded no good for laggards.

While the second cavalry does not claim to have done all the fighting of that day, there is no denying the fact that their position was in the thickest of it, and had their courage as a regiment been less, or their arms single barreled, the enemy could not have been repulsed; and their services were recognized handsomely in "General Orders."

After thé battle it was ascertained from citizens that General Martin commanded the Confederates and that his force consisted of ten regiments of cavalry and ten guns; and he was heard to boast that he would "drive the d—— Yankees out of Mossy Creek before breakfast, just for fun."

In view of the fact that he knew there would be but one brigade to oppose him, his conclusions, from his standpoint, were natural.

This closed the year 1863—one of the most eventful of the war—and summing up, we find that the second Michigan cavalry during the year was engaged in twenty-four battles, or battles and unimportant skirmishes where losses were sustained, besides numerous minor actions where no loss was met with on our side. They marched during the year nearly 2,500 miles, not including picket, scouting and foraging expeditions, which would add nearly or quite as many more. They received numerous recruits, yet the regiment was little more than half full.

CHAPTER XVIII.

SEVEREVILLE, OR FAIR GARDEN—A MIDNIGHT RETREAT—A MORNING ADVANCE—A "DEAD LINE"—STORMING BRIDGE AND BARRICADE.

Without entering minutely into the daily routine of camp life, picket and scouting duty and short marches, it will suffice the objects of this volume to note the fact of a quiet camp life from January 1st, 1864, until the latter part of the month, when the entire division moved to a camp near Dandridge; and it was generally understood that an advance was to be made on Longstreet, in winter quarters at Morristown, some twelve miles away.

General Gordon Granger with his corps and General Sheridan with his division met us there, having in all about 25,000 men. Some sharp skirmishing occurred on the way, but nothing serious, the enemy giving way, and the usual maneuvering took place on both sides to discover the strength, object or intention of each army.

On the second day of our arrival severe skirmishes occurred all along the line, in which numbers on either side were killed or wounded, several officers from our regiment being among the number. The Second was on the front line all day and held their position all night, fully expecting a general engagement in the morning, yet they lay down to rest with coolness, confident that there would be a place for them, and content to leave the events of the morrow to the God of battles.

At two o'clock A. M. orders came to fall back immediately; that Longstreet was preparing to advance.*

To fall back and we had not fired a gun. That was a new school of tactics, and a bitter pill to the Second. Evidently (we thought) some one has blundered. But the Second was given the rear. "Cover the retreat" came as a looked for order, and there was a kind of grim comfort in the reflection—a Michigan regiment of cavalry is thought enough of to be given the post of honor so often.

And so, back to Strawberry plains, leisurely, wearily, the army moved, and on to Knoxville, crossing the Holston river and closing up with the division at Severeville. Here the whole division participated in skirmishes until the 27th, when at daylight a line of battle was formed, and a general advance ordered, and the Second on the skirmish line, taking the main road, in the center of the army of the East Tennessee, with the first Tennessee cavalry on our right and the ninth Pennsylvania cavalry on our left.

The second brigade was ordered to make a detour to the

*It was not at the time known to subordinate officers, or, for that matter, to regimental commanders, even, but subsequent events led to the conclusion that it was part of a general plan to draw Longstreet into East Tennessee with as many troops as possible, that our forces operating against Bragg might, if possible, crush Longstreet, or failing to do that, drive Bragg south towards Atlanta; and the result was Mission Ridge and the the Atlanta campaign, in which Longstreet was needed and hurriedly left East Tennessee to join Bragg, soon after the events above narrated.

left in order to strike the enemy in flank while the first brigade pressed them in front.

Prompt at daylight the second Michigan was in position, behind Pigeon river, waiting for the fog to rise before advancing. Lieutenant-Colonel Benjamin Smith had just received his commission and, always ready for every emergency, was especially jubilant this morning, and his men saw blood in the eye, which seemed to reflect itself all along the line. Major Scranton had returned from his short rest since his injury at Dandridge, and the regiment seemed possessed of new confidence in their officers and themselves.

Soon the fog lifted and the order was given to advance. Without a moment's hesitation, in the face of a rattling fire of musketry and artillery, the men stepped rapidly into the river, holding aloft their arms and ammunition, crossing with the water up to their waists; and immediately dislodged the enemy from an orchard, giving them so sharp a fire that a whole brigade was supposed to be close in their rear, and the Second, following them closely across an open field, gave the artillery stationed there a volley, from which they "limbered up" and left on a wild gallop.

As the regiment had carried out their instructions, Colonel Smith halted them for orders. Generals Sturgis and McCook were soon up and complimented the regiment very highly on the brilliant manner in which they had driven the enemy with so small a force.

Again the command moved forward, soon arriving at a creek, crossed by a covered bridge. Dashing at the heavy line of skirmishers stationed there, the enemy was again put to flight, across the bridge and behind formidable barricades. But the Second was fairly wild this morning and nothing seemed likely to check them short of the uncovered lines of Longstreet's whole army. About sixty men had crossed with Colonel Smith and were looking for a weak spot in the barricade to attack, when they discovered that the main part of the regiment had not crossed. Here, too, the fleeing enemy met their reinforcements under General Martin, who turned upon our men, and, with overwhelming numbers, drove them back across the bridge, fighting every step. Here the Second halted, taking cover, waiting for the enemy to advance across the bridge, and for our own men to close up. They had only a few minutes to wait and the enemy filled the bridge, mounted, but as they emerged upon our side, the revolving rifles spoke—the dead line was drawn, and not a living soul crossed to our side. Reinforcements had arrived and again the regiment dashed at the now routed enemy, following them closely, occasionally meeting with stubborn resistance, but driving the lighter forces back upon the main army, now retreating, but in good order, ready to wheel and pour out their wrath in grape, canister and shell, whenever pressed too hard. In this manner the enemy were driven about five miles, before the second brigade had reached the striking point, when their final stand was made at Fair Garden, their artillery and infantry being apparently determined not to fall back further, but poured out volley after volley wherever our men showed themselves; also shelling the woods furiously. This gave us a temporary check, just the thing needed for the movements of the second brigade, who came dashing down upon the flanks of the enemy, while our regiment again pressed them in rear, and the rout was complete, several pieces of artillery, battle-flags, and about 200 prisoners falling into our hands.

This ended the battle of Severeville, or Fair Garden, begun at Pigeon river. And while it was not among the battles of heavy loss of life, it was none the less a heavy blow to the Confederates' hopes of obtaining a stand in East Tennessee.

The second cavalry were duly accorded their full share of praise by the members of other commands. The following complimentary letter from the general commanding explains itself:

HEADQUARTERS CAVALRY CORPS,
Marysville, Tennessee, February 2d, 1864.
COLONEL CAMPBELL,
Commanding first brigade, first division,
Cavalry department of the Cumberland:

General Sturgis, commanding the cavalry, directs me to inform you that it gives him great pleasure to thank you, in the name of General John G. Foster, commanding the department, for your gallantry in the engagement of the 27th ult., when your brigade drove the enemy from every position, finally driving him from the field with severe loss and in great confusion.

I have the honor to be, Colonel,
Very respectfully,
Your most obedient servant,
WILLIAM C. RANDKE,
Captain and A. D. C., U. S. A.

And right here it may not be out of place to remark that the Second, as a regiment, were never troubled by petty jealousies toward other regiments, but always rejoiced to see another regiment receive homage for worthy services rendered.

CHAPTER XIX.

VETERANS—SEVEREVILLE TO CLEVELAND—FLORENCE—SHOAL CREEK—FORREST AND RODDY—THE NON-VETERANS AND THE ATLANTA CAMPAIGN—LIEUTENANT DARROW—CAPTAIN FARGO'S FLAG OF TRUCE.

The 31st of January, 1864, found the regiment encamped near Marysville, East Tennessee, where they remained till the 9th of February, when they forded the Little Tennessee river and encamped on Four-mile creek, in Monroe county, and during the month no event of stirring interest occurred; moving camp often and working towards Cleveland, by way of Citaco, Madisonville and Calhoun. During this month the regiment was encamped amid some of the most romantic scenery of the South.

On the 29th of January, 1864, at 8 A. M., we marched through Severeville out on the Marysville road, and crossed the ridge into Weaer's cove, camping near Bryant's house. This cove seems a most wonderful place, for while many of the so-called coves in the mountains of Tennessee have a romantic and sometimes weird appearance, this seemed shut in from all the outer world, where a few families cultivate their farms. A beautiful valley, surrounded by lofty mountains, whose tops and sloping sides are covered with trees, having at this season many hues—an amphitheatre of beauty, with a clear blue sky for its canopy, and a mountain brook of crystal purity, meandering through the cove.

Next day we marched out of the cove along the bed of the stream, just wide enough for our wagons to pass; mountains rising almost perpendicularly on either side.

As we leave Weaer's we enter Tuckaleeche cove below, and thence along a little river, through some very wild scenery, and camp in a cedar grove near Marysville. These long marches and raids reveal to the observing cavalrymen some of the most pleasing of nature's works. Lofty mountains with their wonderful upheavals. Beautiful valleys, streams and forests with their many colored trees; dark green polished laurel leaves; the evergreen pines and cedars, the beautiful magnolias—beautiful whether in blossom or out of blossom—the live oaks and mistletoes—all, moistened by the spray of rushing cataract, adds charm to the landscape, perfected here and there by the dwellings of a Southern planter's home.

While encamped in these valleys one of our scouting expeditions brought in a company of Cherokee Indians, in full Confederate uniform. Using the prisoners with strictest military courtesy many of them expressed a desire to enter our army. They were not encouraged in this, but were provided for comfortably, and many of them permitted to return to their homes.

Here we had an example of doubtful loyal men seeking protection for slaves. One Scruggs, claiming to be a strong Union man, was extremely anxious about "my niggers." He hoped we would protect him and give him a guard to keep his slaves from running away. But he was not long in finding out that our troops "never guard niggers."

For a time Colonel Campbell commanded a division of cavalry here, and Lieutenant-Colonel Benjamin Smith commanded the brigade, but it was very difficult for a volunteer colonel to win his star, and Campbell returned home to Michigan as a veteran—and this trip cost him a wrecked ambition and his life.

On the 29th of March, at Cleveland, Tennessee, about 300 men were re-mustered into the service for three years more as "veteran volunteers," and expected soon to receive papers that would take them home for a thirty days' furlough. About this time Colonel Smith went to Loudon, Tennessee, where the fourth army corps was encamped under our old colonel, General Gordon Granger, and perfected arrangements for arming the regiment with the Spencer repeating rifle, at that time the newest and most effective weapon in the service.

On the 4th of April 315 men and nearly all the officers that went out as such, started for Michigan on veteran furlough, enough remaining behind, with the recruits, to keep up the organization of the regiment.

At Chattanooga the veterans got into trouble, through imperfect arrangements for quarters and rations, and were placed under arrest, but were released after twenty-four hours and went on their way. A history of this outrage will be found in Part Second of this volume. This furlough was one continuous round of ovations at different points in Michigan, and at the expiration of thirty days they again met at Jackson, and returned to Nashville, via Louisville, where Colonel Campbell, being taken sick, remained in hospital until returned home to St. Clair county, Michigan, to linger out an inglorious end in consumption, instead of returning to receive a "star," as he doubtless would, had he been more prudent of his health, which appeared, at the beginning of the war, of the most robust character; he was of almost gigantic stature and perfect physique. The death of Colonel Campbell left the regiment in command of Lieutenant-Colonel Benjamin Smith, who could not be promoted to colonel, as there were not men enough to muster one; but they returned to duty at Franklin, Tennessee, while the non-veterans, about 300 of them, under command of Major Scranton, were moving forward with the army under General Sherman toward Atlanta, and were engaged in skirmishes on the Dalton road to Mt. Pleasant church, Varnell's station and Buzzard's Roost and on through Tunnel Hill to Dug Gap where they were placed on duty in connection with the fortifications, and later took part in the movements of the army towards Atlanta.

The 300 non-veterans (mostly well tried soldiers) were very short of officers, most of them having gone home with the veterans. But Major Scranton held the confidence of his men by his cool-headed and general stubbornness in a fight. Their engagements began in the vicinity of Varnell's station, only a few miles east of Chicamauga and perhaps twenty-five miles south of Cleveland, Tennessee. Here it was that a new cavalry regiment, magnificently mounted, 1,200 strong, marched in so proudly, and looked down so contemptuously upon the little band of 300 with their tough, hardy, well cared for nags; not handsome; no superfluous flesh; rather raw-boned, but worth a whole brigade of "soft shells," and between whom there was affection almost human. A small brigade of infantry was making a demonstration upon our flank. The new cavalry regiment were sent to check them, and they rode away with a sort of look-at-me expression that provoked a broad smile from the older ones. They went in with a whirl, that, if properly managed would have swept the enemy from the field; but they could not stay, and the second Michigan 300 were immediately dismounted and ready to cover the retreat. They had but a few minutes to wait; back came the fleeing chargers, closely followed by the rebel infantry. When they came upon the 300 repeating rifles there was a crash that staggered them. The range was close and the firing rapid and unerring. It was the every day story, single shooters against repeating rifles, and the odds in numbers were not sufficient to dislodge them. The enemy retired, and the new cavalry, when they came up again, had a very different opinion of non-veterans in their old, faded blue; mounted on naggish looking steeds; caressingly toying with repeating rifles. Hanging upon the left flank of our army the cavalry moved on and again came upon heavy bodies of infantry massed behind earthworks bristing with artillery, at Tilton, a station not far from Resaca. The arrangement of the Confederate works was admirable, their center forming a crescent on the brow of a hill with flanking works thrown forward, giving them an enfilading fire upon our advance (the eighth Iowa), and the loss to that regiment was severe. They retired; the repeating rifles were dismounted and sent up and soon discovered that nothing short of very heavy bodies could carry the works, and then not without a severe engagement and heavy loss to the assailants. An infantry brigade came up and the commander rather contemptuously said, "I will send some of my infantry in there," intimating that dismounted cavalry had no business in front. General Stanley came up, and hearing what our men had discovered, immediately ordered up *all* the infantry at once. Before the order could be carried out the enemy opened, and the air was filled with bullets and shells, and the line was not advanced a rod, while the enfilading fire cut off our retreat across the open field and held our men there until after dark. But Thomas was thundering away on the right, and in a day or two the enemy's flanks were so hard pressed they withdrew from their stronghold and retired to Resaca. And thus pushing, and flanking, Resaca fell. Then Calhoun, and on to Burnt Hickory, where Tilton was repeated, and after that Ackworth and Lost Mountain. Here the non-veterans captured the earthworks on the flank and held them, while the main portion of our army swung around and drove the enemy toward Kenesaw mountains. From near this point the regiment made three raids to Powder Springs and points south of Lost Mountain. Some of the minor engagements between scouting parties and advanced pickets developed the strong fighting points of the "recruits." A gallant reconnaissance by a small handful of them *non-veterans* at Varnell's station, as related by an officer of General McCook's staff, will be found of interest in Part Second.

After this they were ordered to join the veteran portion of the regiment in middle Tennessee, where they were placed in charge of the railroad defenses towards Columbia.

These they held until September, having in that time comparatively little hard fighting, the enemy using all their forces in opposing General Sherman.

But it now became evident that the enemy were determined to draw off a part of our forces from around Atlanta, and three regiments joined us—the first Tennessee, fourth Kentucky and eighth Iowa, under command of General Croxton, a gallant young Kentuckian—to watch the movements of the enemy and prevent, if possible, depredations upon our railway communication. The move was none too quick. General Frank Wheeler, to whom we had given some lively compliments in times past, was again raiding, and the regiment, with the brigade and other forces which had come up immediately sent him whirling again towards the Tennessee river on a running fight, after a quite severe engagement near Franklin.

This raid of Wheeler's began near Nashville. Being driven back by our brigade, Wheeler swung around Franklin and attacked from the south, just as Croxton's brigade entered the town from the east. Wheeler was driven out, though not without a stubborn resistance, in which both sides lost quite severely. Among the severely wounded was Colonel Jim Brownlow, of the first Tennessee, and the Confederate General Kelly killed. After driving Wheeler back, Rousseau came across from the east, and being the senior officer, sent the cavalry on numerous wild expeditions, while he followed along slowly until the cavalry were getting disgusted with the stupidity of their movements, and none quite so much so as Croxton himself.

The last straw was added one evening just as the brigade had settled down for the night, without an enemy in a day's march of them. Rousseau sent word to Croxton to saddle up, and Croxton sent word to Rousseau by a trusted officer of the Second that "the brigade will not leave their present camp to night." Rousseau and several boon companions were gathered around a mess-chest, evidently about to discuss the merits of some liquid refreshments, and looking up, in well-feigned astonishment, ordered an officer to investigate what Croxton meant. But as nothing further was heard of it, the end is easily guessed —an incompetent or else demoralized commander defied with impunity. Rousseau had been a gallant division commander of infantry, but was strangely out of place with such a command as this.

During the first week of this month (October) the command had gone as far east as Winchester and back, Forrest dividing his forces there, to mislead us.

CAPT. DAN T. FARGO.

After escorting Wheeler out of the State for the third time, the brigade returned to Franklin, but had not settled down fairly in camp when word came that Forrest was on the way to pay his respects, and was tearing up the railroad, destroying block houses and bridges and raising sad havoc generally. During this rapid chasing of Wheeler's forces, Captain Dan Fargo, of Croxton's staff, was sent on in advance, with an escort of twenty-four men and a flag of truce, to ascertain if possible whether General Williams was with Wheeler, as it made considerable difference whether they were pushing a divided or a full force. This was a delicate mission—involving cool judgment, quick perception and a liberal amount of *sang froid*. The captain was given to understand that if his real mission was discovered he would probably be treated as a spy. "How do you think you would enjoy a little hanging bee?" "I think I'd rather go fishing," was the captain's reply, as he adjusted his collar and pulled down his belt. He was given a letter to General Wheeler asking if he had in his hands any prisoners which he could give in exchange for some we did not care to be burdened with, etc.—and instructed to get in among them as far as possible, and learn all he could.

They dashed away and rode on among them without firing a shot, neither heeding the commands to halt, backed by numerous shots. The dust hid their flag of truce, and the men's horses were apparently hard to stop, but at last they thought they had gone far enough, as they were all surrounded with Confederates, and pulling out by the side of the road, asked to see General Wheeler. His adjutant-general soon came back and in a few moments of conversation disclosed the fact unwittingly that Williams was off on another expedition. They had no prisoners to give up. A few pleasant words were spoken—mutual regrets at the death of the gallant young General Kelly were expressed and the Confederates moved on, with a pleasant "Good day, gentlemen," from both sides and respectful salutations.

Our command was up in five minutes, the Confederates had passed out of sight, and again the chase, the exchange of shots, and the charge of the stronger upon the weaker—so soon to be reversed.

Away the brigade went, with greatest haste, and arrived in Pulaski just in time to save that town and defenses from falling into Forrest's hands.

An all day fight ensued, and Forrest's men were finally driven back, but they were light and it made no difference to them which way they went; and their doings varied little from those of guerrillas—breaking in small squads when necessary, and dashing down upon posts, at weak points—burning, destroying and not always particular as to following the rules of civilized warfare, and no doubt, doing much to earn for the Confederates the reputation which that old tactician, Von Moltke, gave both armies. "An armed mob; I do not care to read their history," said the old war-dog.

When Forrest was repulsed at Pulaski, he swung around our rear and beat us in a race (he was always good at running) to Franklin, and destroyed many miles of railroad track, capturing and burning several block houses, and again breaking, fled for the Tennessee river. At Cypress creek, Alabama, he was brought to bay and disputed our crossing. This was on the 27th of October, 1864. Roddy had also been through Tennessee, destroying railroads between Athens and Pulaski, and between Duck river and Gaines, and here both of these ubiquitous freebooters joined forces of what was left (many had deserted or turned regular guerrillas), and these two, with their followers were striving to cross the Tennessee river, and, in order to do so, it was necessary to fight, and, if possible, keep our forces from crossing Cypress creek, a branch of the Tennessee, at a cotton mill, four miles from Florence. The eighth Iowa had been in advance while the running fight lasted, but their colonel, a good, old, unsoldierly sort of man, had not the confidence in himself neither had his men (though his men were among the best in the field), to press the fighting against odds; and that there were odds could be plainly seen, since it was learned Roddy had joined Forrest. Therefore, he told General Croxton of his inability to cross the creek, and the General sent for Colonel Smith and asked him if he could cross. The reply was promptly, "We can try."

The condition of affairs being communicated to the men of the Second, a shout went up that was enough of itself to demoralize *some* brigades, and they could hardly be restrained while the order to forward was being given; and before General Croxton had fairly realized what was taking place, the creek was crossed and the men were engaged at close quarters, mounted, and within twenty minutes the enemy were flying towards the Tennessee river. The other regiments supported handsomely, and in a very short time there was not a living Confederate this side of the Tennessee river except prisoners, Forrest himself having a very narrow escape from capture. The fight was too short for many losses, but among them was Lieutenant Darrow, a brave young officer, very much beloved by all who knew him, And what made this case especially sad was the fact that he had served his three years, had his discharge papers and was to have returned to his friends "after one more fight," as he expressed it. And this was the second time in a month the brigade had driven the enemy across the same stream.

LIEUT. RUSSELL T. DARROW.

It was evidently a deep humiliation to Forrest, who had once been able to hold at bay two divisions while he captured a brigade of our infantry at Thompson's station, that he could not hold so strong a position as that ford against a single brigade, and, in fact, was started on a run by one single regiment.

The regiment immediately returned to Pulaski, but were soon ordered to return to Shoal creek, near Florence, and watch the enemy, who were reported about to cross and invade Tennessee in force, as a counter movement against Sherman.

CHAPTER XX.

THE HOOD CAMPAIGN—FLORENCE—SHOAL CREEK—PONTOONS—
A FAITHFUL NEGRO—THE BEGINNING OF THE INVASION.

On the 8th of October, 1864, the regiment and brigade took up the search for Forrest and discovered that he had crossed the Tennessee, and the command returned to Lindsey's creek, and on to Rawhide and Hurricane creek. Here liberal supplies of chickens, hogs and cattle were found, and in our condition of short rations for days they were duly appreciated. Returning to Pulaski, on the 13th, we were made glad once more by the sight of our wagon trains, with regular rations, and during the rest of the month were employed in keeping watch of the territory south to the Tennessee river and north to Pulaski, maintaining courier lines under many discouragements; half the citizens along the route turning guerrillas, in their endeavor to break up our communications with General Thomas. For the fearless stand the regiment made in suppressing guerrilla warfare, they acquired a reputation along that line which, doubtless, will cling to them and all Michigan soldiers as the "worst lot of Yankees ever sent down here."

General Croxton was now picketing the Tennessee river for ten miles, and when Hood gathered his forces nearly opposite Florence, Croxton was watching him.

At midnight, on the 29th of October, an old negro crossed the Muscle shoals on the rocks and fish traps, wading, swimming and stumbling along—a perilous undertaking in broad daylight, in a favorable season, but at midnight, at such a season, who can doubt the courage required for such an adventure? Making his way to headquarters, and being halted by the guard pacing up and down, he asked to be shown the general's tent. A staff officer came, and, after questioning, led him to the General, to whom he recited his hardships in crossing the ford, and told him he had come from Hood's camp and that "the boys over the river had orders to cross at daylight, at Raccoon ford." His story was doubted, but after cross-questioning him closely, the general ordered the command to be at the crossing by daylight, only a picket remaining at our present encampment to protect our reserve supplies and tents.

The enemy appeared, *as advertised*, but our movements had been so quiet as to fail of observation, and their attempts to cross were in a manner which indicated their belief in profound ignorance on our part. They pushed out pontoons in close succession, but were met with volley after volley until they became uneasy, and wavering, fell back to their own bank. During the afternoon, however, they took advantage of an island, and, landing on the opposite side, under cover of timber, succeeded in crossing a sufficient force to be able to contend with more than ordinary cavalry brigades. But General Croxton left the protection of this (Raccoon ford) crossing to Colonel Benjamin Smith, with rifles, and they held the main landing until after dark, the brigade having other work on their hands.

General Thomas was informed of Hood's movements by courier line and telegraphed to hold the ford as long as possible. Hood crossed a division at Florence, and remained near there until November 5th.

The Second watched Hood's outposts daily, guarding the fords and advance pickets, and doing all that was possible to retard the progress of Hood. Here it was that a most daring venture was made by a small detail of men from the second Michigan cavalry. It is too long for place in this chapter. We refer to the story of Marshman Maxon, of company A. Of the truth of this romantic story there is not a doubt. It will be found in Part Second. Just here there is room only to say that two canoes, of three men each, went down to cut the bridges; succeeded only partially; were reported, "One canoe-load drowned, the other captured on the bridge." None were drowned, but three were captured on the bridge, and three, after nearly perishing with hunger, were captured, ordered shot, got mixed with other prisoners, sent to prison pens, afterwards to Memphis for exchange; were blown up on the Sultana, where 1,500 were burned to death or drowned and some were saved.

* * * * * * * *

The temporary delay caused by our partial cutting of their pontoons was over, and Hood crossed with all his army, driving in our little brigade on flanks and rear, though Croxton clung to them with a tenacity worthy of success, and the Second was ever at the rear on this retreat, but in this campaign every regiment of Croxton's brigade vied with each other for the post of honor. But the repeating rifles and the reputation of the men that bore them, won, and General Croxton—among the last to quit the field, amid a shower of bullets and a cyclone of shot and shell—said, "Fall back, Colonel. Look out for your flanks. Don't waste your ammunition, but give them a blast whenever it will count. I will send the first Tennessee and eighth Iowa to relieve your flankers." And so the brigade fell back, before the last forlorn hope of the Confederacy. Hood, with 40,000 men, was on his way to the capital of Tennessee, Tennessee the beautiful—the land of flowers and the land of enchanting valleys, the land whose every acre had been trodden 'neath the feet of contending armies, every brook had drunk of the best blood of our nation, and every hillside had gathered to its bosom the lifeless forms of our bravest sons— was now again to drink the bitter cup from war's devastating hand. The brigade fell back, but not until every foot of ground had been disputed and we had fought our way out of a trap formed by a large column of Confederate infantry crossing in our rear, and another force attacking the men with the led horses, and capturing about half of company E, that had gone too far toward the river, and killing or wounding a large number of our men and horses. But the regiment gathered themselves together and dealt death and destruction right and left, and the brigade, rallying to their support, were soon in a position to take care of themselves. And this battle was called Florence. That night, on arriving in camp, about ten o'clock, worn, hungry and dejected over the loss of many a comrade, orders came from General Croxton to burn all surplus baggage and be ready to fall back at midnight. Over the smoldering ruins of gathered mementoes, letters, superfluous clothing and what not, a hasty supper was prepared and eaten, and without sleep the command fell back, reaching Taylor Springs by daylight. Investigation proved that the reports which caused this hasty move were groundless, and Croxton returned with his brigade, and at night went into his old camping ground, where he remained in comparative quiet for several days. Hood was delayed in crossing two days by the episode of the pontoons referred to, and by this time General Hatch (he of the fighting second Iowa) joined us with his division of cavalry, going into camp three miles on the Waynesborough road.

In the morning it was reported that Hood had crossed in sufficient force to drive back all the forces we had to offer him, and the second Michigan was ordered to take up a position along Shoal creek, to hold in check, if possible, the enemy that might attempt to cross there. At ten A. M. the enemy, in strong force, were seen approaching the ford with flying colors—the hated "Stars and Bars." How could old Colonel Ben, or the men of the Second fall back without showing fight? Coming within close range the Second gave them so vigorous a continued volley that the advance was checked for a time. Then a flank movement was looked for and one company (all we could spare) was sent in the direction of the creek's mouth, where it emptied into the Tennessee river. Two ten pound howitzers supported our regiment, under Lieutenant Stephens, and all was quiet again until two o'clock, when firing was heard on our left, which, as it increased, showed that the enemy had crossed and our position was about to be assaulted or outflanked. Suddenly a masked battery that had crept up in our front, across the creek, opened with six guns, and their shots were well-directed. Lieutenant Stephens maintained the unequal contest until ordered by General Croxton to fall back. Colonel Smith had suggested to him that he ought to fall back, but No, said he, "General Croxton told me to stay until ordered to move, and I shall stay." The order came none too quick, and the section was saved by a hair's breadth. None of the Second were captured, but several were killed and wounded, and Hood's Invasion of Tennessee was marked at the very threshold with a cross of "fire and blood," for many were seen to fall as the command fell back, firing; and every officer and man felt that a long struggle was before him, for day nor night could we hope for rest until our main forces under Thomas were reached, or until such time as the sturdy old general was ready to fight.

CHAPTER XXI.

HOOD'S RACE WITH SCHOFIELD—"THE ADVANCE"—FROM THE TENNESSEE TO THE HARPETH — HALT! — BUTCHERY AT FRANKLIN—STANLEY—WILSON—COX—HATCH—CROXTON.

During Hood's crossing of the Tennessee, which really began on the 5th of November, and was not completed until the 20th, two of the most severe engagements in which the Second figured prominently had occurred, but every regiment in the vicinity had their skirmishes, and Hood was sometimes in apparent bewilderment as to the true strength of the forces opposed to him. He believed that the greater part of Sherman's army was with Sherman, in Georgia, and that it would be only a disorganized force that he had to contend with in Tennessee.*

In this he was not far wrong; but when he showed a disposition to ride over, with scarcely a halt, veterans of a

*General Thomas brought from Atlanta only himself and his staff—all that was left of the army of the Cumberland, aside from the scattered forces under Rousseau, Schofield and Wilson doing post duty at Murfreesboro, Franklin and Nashville and scouting the State. To re-form, equip and strengthen that army in time for the battle of Nashville was a herculean task that few generals would have accomplished. Chattanooga and Murfreesboro ought to be held, and were held; but at the expense of the army gathering at Nashville. When Hood cut loose from the main Confederate army at Atlanta, his objective point was supposed to be Chattanooga, and hence the scattering of the fragmentary army of the Cumberland, all over middle and southern Tennessee.

hundred battles, he exhibited a weak vanity in his own strength and the valor of his followers that soon developed into a succession of disasters for which he was not prepared. The boasts he indulged in to citizens along the route of his advance (if true), in the light of subsequent events, stamped him as among the most blatant braggarts as well as puerile (army) commanders. But it was a "forlorn hope," and as such the charitable historian may ever treat him.

When he had safely crossed his army and all things were ready, the race began, and on the 21st of November Croxton's brigade formed the rear guard again as the rear of our army entered Lawrenceburg. The eighth Iowa had been acting as rear guard, but Colonel Dorr recognized the inferiority of his regiment's armament and asked to be relieved, which was done, and the position cheerfully accepted by the second Michigan. Our line of march had been toward Pulaski, but on learning that evacuation had taken place there, our route was changed toward Columbia, the enemy pressing our rear guard furiously all the afternoon, the Second making some desperate stands, and falling back when outflanked or about to be swept over by superior numbers.

Thus fighting and falling back the afternoon of November 24 wore away; night came, and still the fighting continued, though with what result we could only guess; and at 10 o'clock the rear guard, waiting for further signs of the enemy and hearing or seeing none except the distant camp fires, bivouacked by the road side near Columbia. Here it was thought our troops would make a desperate attempt to hold the enemy in check for a time, but after a delay of two days, in which our forces were getting their trains and artillery across Duck river, it was ascertained that Hood was crossing on our right below Columbia and word was given to fall back. During this delay it was thought important to know if the enemy had sent a column through Pulaski. To ascertain regarding that point a volunteer detail of one officer and twelve men was called for, to pass out through our lines, on through the enemy's country, and go to Pulaski and back by daylight. Lieutenant Walter Whittemore went in charge of the scouting party and accomplished the perilous trip to the entire satisfaction of General Schofield. His story will be found in Part Second.

While Schofield was in doubt as to Hood's movements, and very much desired to check the enemy at Duck river, he had not sufficient force to guard the crossings above and below and hold Columbia at the same time. General Wilson suggested the immediate falling back of the infantry and trains, as he believed Hood could cross below and beat us to Franklin. Schofield was a much older man, and a most excellent general, but he erred in thinking Hood would not flank him so soon. Hood's reputation as a hard pusher, as well as a hard fighter, had been well established, and Schofield found he had delayed the evacuation of Columbia twenty-four hours too long. Our trains were in the way, and Hood's whole army was across Duck river almost as soon as Schofield's was, and the cavalry were necessarily too much scattered to form any serious barrier.

As Hood was evidently determined to push on to Nashville, regardless of our troops, who were taking the most direct route, it became a matter of some doubt as to which should reach Harpeth river first. General Schofield had about one good corps of infantry (parts of three) and three or four small brigades of cavalry—a small force, indeed, to contend with Hood's whole army, but we had the advantage of being a little ahead and could pick our own ground, we thought.

The command fell back in good order; skirmishing constantly until about five or six miles had been passed over, when camp was pitched for the night, and General Jas. Wilson, who had recently joined us, assumed command of all the cavalry. At three o'clock next morning General Wilson sent for Lieutenant-Colonel Smith and informed him that he desired the second Michigan cavalry to act as rear guard. The order to fall back was immediate and the regiment began to throw up barricades across the pike. Major Nicholson was left in command of one battalion, with orders to hold the position as long as possible, while the main part of the regiment fell back in column of fours on the left of the road to prevent a flank movement. In a very short time sharp firing was heard at the barricades, and the battalion began to give way. Hurrying up to supporting distance, Colonel Smith saw that Major Nicholson was being hard pushed. There was no time for forming a line across the pike, therefore the two battalions under Colonel Smith were formed in a line parallel to the road, and as Major Nicholson dashed past, with the enemy in hot pursuit, he was given time to pass to the rear, when the repeating rifles opened, and the enemy retired in confusion, believing they had been drawn into a trap. But the regiment took up their march unconcernedly, feeling well assured that future operations against the rear guard would not be of the "rush or hurrah" style. Yet the enemy followed closely for about three miles until we came up with our troops, formed in line of battle. But the enemy declined to fight, and each side retired a short distance, our command remaining in line of battle all night without camp fires, but the enemy's fires shone brightly, for they were apparently enjoying themselves. During the past two days our rear guard was frequently marching parallel to and even with the advance guard of the enemy, on another road, in plain sight, neither army stopping to fire, but apparently striving to reach Franklin first. When our regiment reached Springhill, Hood had thrown Cheatham's division against our infantry lines, and for a time our position was very desperate, but the infantry immediately showed fight, and our cavalry coming up at the time, Cheatham retired, with night coming on. Hood was very bitter against Cheatham for not taking and holding the road, but it would have been no easy task for him at that hour of the day to have brought his troops over the soft country, without roads, in time to have entirely checked so desperate a lot of men as formed the rear of Schofield's army, aided by the repeating rifles of the second Michigan cavalry. There was a short, sharp engagement, but the Confederates drew off. On the 29th of November, General Schofield determined to give Hood a warm reception at Franklin and at the same time rescue his trains and artillery, that were making all possible haste in crossing the Harpeth. There was no bridge except the railroad bridge and the ford was bad—the banks twenty feet high, cut deep, muddy, and the constant plowing through of army wagons made the crossing almost impossible. All day and all night the shout of mule drivers, the rattle and chuck of wheels, the burning of buildings, turned Franklin into a veritable pandemonium.

But out at the front there was work of a more serious character going on. Hood's troops could not move up in time to force the fighting during the forenoon, and little more than general skirmishing occurred. But this was done chiefly by the cavalry. The infantry were apparently determined not to be hurried out of Franklin nor lose any of the trains, and when shovels and picks were passed along the lines, dirt flew up in rows extending from river to river—a complete semi-circle environing the town, with laps and cuts at the roads, and here Schofield defied Hood with all his victorious army, and that memorable 30th of November (of which more later) stamped Schofield, Cox, Stanley and Wilson as among our ablest generals.

But let us follow the second cavalry a little further. Crossing the Harpeth on the night of the 29th, to be at hand should any raiders attempt to cut off our communications with Nashville, they again crossed the Harpeth to the south side on the morning of the 30th, and with one battalion of the first Tennessee were ordered to hold the Lewisburg pike to the very last. They were in position at daylight—their left resting on the Harpeth river, with a small creek running in our front. This position was unassailed until about eleven in the morning, when the enemy began to reconnoiter, soon forming a line of battle, and moved steadily forward, with the apparent determination of sweeping down the Harpeth and turning Schofield's left flank. Had they succeeded in this the result must have been most disastrous to General Schofield; but though the creek was easy to ford the Second did not permit them to cross. Our position was well chosen, and the enemy fell back at the second round.

But this was Forrest's cavalry, or a portion of it—the pride of Hood's army, and the boast of every individual member. They were not disposed to give way so easily, but came again with something like their Thompson's station vigor. Their ranks were shattered, but quickly re-formed, and moving steadily up to charging distance, burst forth, a perfect avalanche of horses and men, and in a moment more would surely sweep back across the Harpeth our little band of rifles. But there was the creek to cross—down and up—and the range was close. Again that row of rifles gleamed in strong, vigorous arms; along those barrels quick eyes caught the sights; the finger, true to the eye, fondles the trigger—for an instant only—and, one! two! three! times 500 bullets sped true to the mark, and not a soul crossed the stream.

This quieted the enemy in that quarter, and at one o'clock in the afternoon the regiment fell back about a mile (they had been holding a position two or three miles southeast of Franklin). The colonel had barricades thrown across the pike, extending from wood to wood, and there it was decided a final stand should be made previous to crossing the Harpeth, as we knew we must.

General Croxton came riding down the road—his brigade being not far away, ready to move as his help was needed—and remarked to Colonel Smith that everything seemed quiet. Not an enemy in sight nor a sound from the wooded depths in front. Our own men were under cover and quiet, and the General was evidently ruminating in his own mind whether to express an opinion as to the presence or absence of the enemy, when he was aroused by a shot dropped in front of his horse from an unseen foe. The spell was broken. The General "took cover" and had little to say, except to caution them about keeping their retreating route open, and hold the ground as long as possible. In this quiet position the regiment remained until three o'clock, when Captain Hodges, with company I, was ordered to reconnoiter, mounted, but not bring on an engagement.

The order was carried out, the advance of the enemy driven back a short distance, and, retiring, company I took up the position of advanced videttes.

Quieting down again, an orderly came from General Croxton, saying, "If you are whipping the rebels, go in!"

The Second well knew that only fifty rods away the enemy lurked in strong force, waiting for developments, or orders from Hood, yet there was an eagerness to break the spell. Company K was placed in a position to guard our retreat, and the regiment, mounting, moved forward without hesitation; first a walk, then a trot, and struck the enemy at a run. But the advance of the enemy was only a small force compared with their solid lines under cover of the woods and brush, and when these were reached, up rose two lines of infantry and poured a rattling fire into our regiment. But our movement was so sudden they had no time to aim, and fired wild, doing little damage; but the order was given to fall back, fighting, and carried out literally.

We had stirred them up and were prepared to take the consequences, and a very stubborn fall back fight continued past our former position—our reserve being also swept back with the others—the last to cross the river, some of the men being dragged across, clinging to a comrade's horse, and some of them captured; no time for mounting, the woods swarming with Confederates, and the air thick with bullets; but for some reason their firing was wild and comparatively few were hit. Our friends were ready to receive us and check the enemy, which they did at the banks of the Harpeth, and the left flank of our army was held firmly; while the firing in front of Franklin increased to a roar.

That our regiment of probably less than 500 men should have been able to charge into and fall back fighting so large a force that they were not all captured or shot before they could have retreated across that stream, was indeed a marvel—not an easy ford under any circumstances. But Croxton complimented them upon their tenacious disputing of the ground. "You have made the best cavalry fight I have seen during the war," said he, and the brigade felt they could hold their present position, if Schofield could only take care of himself. But the odds were fearfully against him in numbers, though the position of our infantry was greatly in our favor; and the continuous replies to volleys with volley told us that a terrible battle was being fought in the center, on Carter's creek and Columbia pikes. Here it was that two divisions met in deadly clash of bayonet, in the clear, broad highway. The charge was led by that gallant young officer, General Pat Cleburne, and when he and his horse fell, our men caught him over the earthworks and a hand to hand fight ensued for his body. All along the line desperate struggles were seen between big limbed men of the North and thin, catlike men of the South. Clubbing of muskets, thrusting of bayonets, casting about, cutting, slashing and grasping in a vice-like grip of death, the nearest foe, when arms failed them. See that big captain—his coat torn from his body, shirt sleeve in shreds, his brawny arm waving defiantly aloft and in his hand a sword, reeking with blood, and from half a dozen cuts and thrusts on his arm, small, red streams flow down to his elbow. He does not seem to know that he is wounded, nor care, for he has cleared a space about him and every man of his company is doing his full duty.

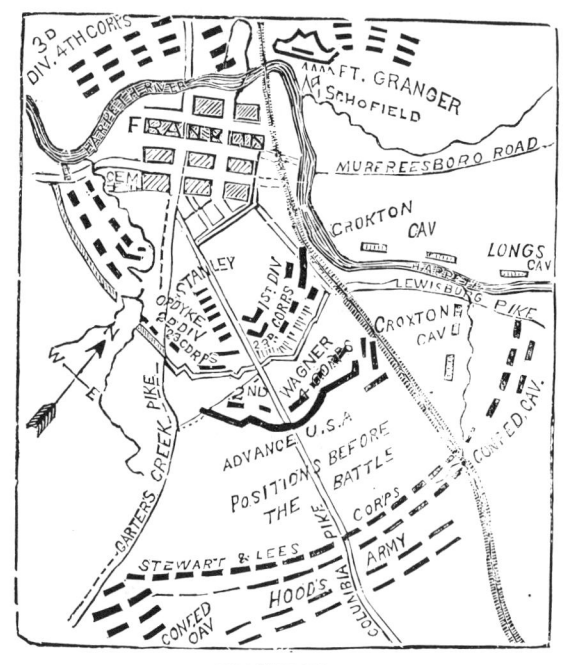

FRANKLIN.

Deeds of personal valor were too common to enumerate, even if the names were known to the writer (which they are not), but there was one desperate man from an Illinois regiment, whose name, were it known, would be cheerfully placed here. Skilled in the use of the bayonet, whole squads went down before his awful swinging thrusts, and to him more than to any one man was due the glory of checking that desperate charge of the enemy, which resulted in the cutting off and capture of a whole brigade of Confederates that had passed too far through our lines.

When the enemy appeared in force Wagner's division of Stanley's corps was out at the front on the Carter's creek pike, and the Confederates came with such impetuosity that the division was hurled back upon our earthworks, and many of the Confederates came over the works with our men; but few of them got away again, for as soon as the Federals had disentangled themselves and took up position behind the works, they turned upon the enemy, captured nearly a brigade, and probably during the next hour more men were killed and wounded as compared with the number engaged, than at any other period of the war.

An eye witness, Mr. S. B. Miller, a member of the one hundredth Ohio infantry, stood very near General Cleburne when he fell. He says: The awful roar, the whistling lead, the shouts, shrieks and groans checked many a strong man as if paralyzed at thought of the certain fate before him. I saw three Confederates standing within our lines, as if they had dropped down unseen from the sky. They stood there for an instant, guns in hand, neither offering to shoot nor surrender—dazed as in a dream. I raised my gun, but instinctively I felt as if about to commit murder—they were helpless, and I turned my face to the foe trying to clamber over our abatis. When I looked again the three were down—apparently dead; whether shot by their own men or ours, who could tell?

Colonel Wolf, commanding the fourth Ohio, was with the second and third brigades of Wagner's division, placed, by orders from General Stanley, commanding the fourth corps, about 1,100 yards in front of the breastworks, with instructions *not to be caught fighting out there*, but immediately fall back behind the earthworks, if Hood made a forward movement in force.

General Stanley had been more than half sick for a day or two, and was lying down in his tent near Fort Granger, where also General Schofield had his headquarters. A staff officer was sent a second time to see if Wagner understood the order, but the poorest charity we can extend him is that he (Wagner) must have been drunk (and Colonel Wolf says he was). Wagner said he understood his business, and the officer set out to return. Suddenly General Stanley hears musket firing. Springing to his feet, and seizing his field glass, he was horrified to see Wagner fighting Hood's whole army with two small brigades (less than a thousand men). Forgetting his illness, Stanley vaults into the saddle and dashes across the river in time to assist Opdyke with his brigade, the first (second division, fourth corps), in striking the Confederate column charging down the pike, on the enemy's left (from Opdyke's right) he, Opdyke, being on our right of the pike, just in rear of the works at Carter's house, and in this charge General Stanley, who rode in front of the left of Opdyke's brigade, was wounded and his horse killed. It was a most gallant deed, and ought long ago to have received better recognition from his country as well as enrolled him among the famous heroes of the war. But the deed would not have been possible with a less quick, clear-headed brigade commander or a less gallant fighting brigade.

In the meantime how fares it with General Cox and his twenty-third corps? Wagner had allowed the enemy to come right among our men by his foolish order to "hold the ground at *all hazards*," and they came over the earthworks together, and Cox could not for a few minutes tell friend from foe in the horrid din and thick smoke. But did they run? For a brief instant, only, did the right of the brigade next to the pike fall back as the enemy swung around the end of the breastworks, but as soon as the lines of blue and gray were drawn then came a crash of bayonets and clubbed muskets, axes, pickaxes, hatchets, and whatever was most convenient at close quarters, for they could not load to shoot, and here it was that the celebrated crossing of bayonets was witnessed, to which reference has been made earlier in these pages.

We are accustomed to treat illustrations of battle scenes as highly overdrawn, but Colonel Wolf says:* "It would be impossible to picture that scene in all its horrors. I saw a Confederate soldier, close to me, thrust one of our men through with the bayonet, and before he could draw his weapon from the ghastly wound his brains were scattered on all of us that stood near, by the butt of a musket swung with terrific force by some big fellow whom I could not recognize in the grim dirt and smoke that enveloped us. And as I glanced hurriedly around and heard the dull thuds, I turned from the sickening sight and was glad to hide the vision in work with a hatchet, for I had broken my sword. A rebel colonel came over the breastworks with me We raised at the same instant to strike; I had the advantage— we were close together; catching his sword near the butt, and raising my hatchet, I demanded his surrender. He did so and

*Since the interview with Colonel Wolf he has gone to his last muster. He died at Mansfield, Ohio, of injuries received twenty years ago, and the immense gathering at his funeral attested the popularity of this physically wrecked hero.

passed to the rear. Then our brigade was all mixed up with Cox's corps, and in all the enemy were repulsed eleven times."

General Cox in person directed his corps and they did valiant service. He and General Stanley should share the honors of that victory equally with Schofield.

Again, let us turn to our cavalry. Their part is an all-portant one to-day. General Schofield could never retreat across Harpeth river were it not for the aid his cavalry is giving him. Neither is the artillery idle. Far from it; but have been doing heroic service all day.

When the enemy in front of Croxton's brigade saw and heard what was taking place on the center they became stirred up to desperation. They succeeded in crossing a portion of their force further to our left, and, forming in line, were about to attack us. A company from some other regiment, armed with carbines, rode out, and, firing a volley, retired to load, returning to fire. The Second were at once sent to take their places, and moving quietly along without returning a shot until at close range, the brigade supporting on the flanks, a volley was given and only twice repeated, when the enemy broke and fled across the Harpeth, closely pursued by the Second; so closely, in fact, as to compel them to leave their ambulances, filled with wounded, in the middle of the river.

This closed the fighting on the left of that memorable battle of Franklin and was about the last firing at any point—a battle in which thirteen Confederate generals were either killed or wounded, and 5,000 Confederates placed *hors de combat*.

The Second was in the saddle from daylight until nine o'clock at night; they fired the first and last guns (except the straggling fire of the artillery) and were, probably, the only regiment that went into the same camp they left in the morning. The regimental losses were:

Killed—Wm. Price, Co. G.

Wounded—Co. A—C. Berg, left side; Robt. Armstrong, right side; Wm. Clark, arm. Co. C—Corp. Daniel C. Marsac, left thigh. Co. D—Sergt. John Vogle, right ankle; Corp. Martin DeGroot, left foot, slight; James Quant, abdomen, mortally; Mark Losso, lower lobe of left lung, mortally; Fred. Monsur, left shoulder. Co. F—Corp. Warren Green, left thigh; Wm. Sherwood, right leg. Co. G—Miles B. Hunt, back of neck; Charles Beckwith, leg, flesh wound; Jefferson N. Campbell, ankle. Co. H—Corp. Delos Rennell, right arm.

Missing in action—Frank Zahimger, Co. M; Richard Welch, L.

Taken prisoners—John Snyder, Co. K; Sanford Mill, K; Robert Gamble, K.

Thick darkness settled down over the scene. The deep bellowings of Fort Granger continued long into the night, provoking only spasmodic replies from the enemy's artillery, and these shots went screeching over the city, or, occasionally dropping low, went crashing into houses, whose inmates lay crouching in mortal terror in cellars and low places.

But at last our army, with all its trains, was across the Harpeth, and the enemy, creeping forward into the town, over the battle-field, were followed by their artillery planting a battery at twelve o'clock close to our deserted works, where the fighting had been hardest, and the ground was yet covered with dead, and where the shrieks of the dying were most horrible, as the horses went crushing and tearing along, heedless of all human cries. For this was war, with all pity buried; all sympathetic tears dried up; friendship dead.

And so the little squad of cavalry that remained to be the very last to cross, heard the sickening cries, silently preceded the scouting forces of the enemy, often standing within twenty feet of them without being seen; saw them enter our deserted supply depot and gather up abandoned food; followed them along the deserted streets, and down into the thick darkness and mud of the river bottom, and saw them when they paused to listen to our moving troops beyond the ford—then turning, escorted them, at a respectful distance, well up into the town, and, turning aside, recrossed the Harpeth and reported to General Croxton, "All are safely crossed and the rebels are apparently satisfied for to-night." This was done by three men of the second Michigan cavalry.

The fords of the river were picketed by our brigade, orders issued to be in the saddle by daylight, and comparative quiet reigned over this once peaceful valley, broken only by the shifting of artillery positions, and the low wail, mingled with occasional shrieks, that came floating on the morning air from that field of horrors—the plains of Franklin.

Hood's report on Springhill and Franklin will be found interesting, as giving his version of affairs. He says:

I left General Lee to menace General Schofield's front at Columbia, while I crossed Duck river below and pushed rapidly forward to Springhill to cut off Schofield. * * *

Arriving near the Franklin pike I saw the enemy passing their trains and part of their forces rapidly towards Franklin. Turning to General Cheatham, I said, "General, do you see the enemy retreating rapidly to escape us? Go, with your corps, take possession of and hold that pike,* and turn all those wagons over to our side of the house." * * * * *

*"Why Cheatham did not get there," see Part Second.

Little musketry firing was heard in this direction. By this hour twilight was upon us, and General Cheatham rode up in person.   *   *   *

Turning to Cheatham I exclaimed with deep emotion, as I felt the golden opportunity fast slipping from me: "General, why, in the name of God, have you not attacked the enemy and taken possession of that pike?" He replied that the line looked a little too long for him, and that Stewart should first form on his right.   *   *   *   It was reported to me after this hour that the enemy was marching along the road, almost under the light of the camp fires of the main body of the army.

The Federals, with immense wagon trains, were permitted to march by us the remainder of the night within gun shot of our lines. I could not succeed in arousing the troops to action, when one good division would have sufficed to do the same work and could have routed that portion of the enemy which were at Springhill and would have taken possession of and formed a line across the road, and thus made it an easy matter for Stewart's corps, Johnson's division and Lee's two divisions from Columbia, to have enveloped, routed and captured Schofield's army that afternoon and the ensuing day. General Forrest gallantly opposed the enemy further down to our right, to the full extent of his power; beyond this, nothing whatsoever was done, although never was a grander opportunity offered to utterly rout and destroy the Federal army.

General Hood thus lays the blame upon his subordinates for failure in crushing Schofield, and probably he was more than half right.

But next day Cheatham, Cleburne and other prominent generals redeemed themselves at Franklin (in Hood's eyes), though they did not succeed in driving Schofield into the Harpeth river, as Hood confidently asserted he would.

But it appears from General Cleburne's last words that he was not, as has been asserted, opposed to the movement on

Franklin. Said he to Hood, "General, I am ready, and have more hope in the final success of our cause, than I have had at any time since the first gun was fired."

"God grant it."

He turned and moved at once towards the head of his division; a few moments thereafter he was lost to my sight in the tumult of battle. * * * Within forty minutes he lay lifeless upon the breastworks of the foe.

General Schofield's official report of that sanguinary contest is given here that the reader may form some slight idea of the desperateness of that battle:

> HEADQUARTERS ARMY OF THE OHIO.
> Nashville, Tennessee, December 7th, 1864.

MAJOR-GENERAL GEORGE H. THOMAS,
    Commanding Department of the Cumberland
    and Military Division of the Mississippi:

GENERAL:—I arrived at Franklin with the head of the column, a little before daylight on the 30th, and found no wagon bridges for crossing the river, and the fords in very bad condition. I caused the railroad bridge to be prepared for crossing wagons, had a foot bridge built for infantry, which, fortunately, also proved available for wagons, and used the fords as much as possible. I hoped, in spite of the difficulties, to get all my material, including the public property and a large train at Franklin, across the river, and move the army over before the enemy could get up force enough to attack me. But I put the troops in position, as they arrived, on the south side, the twenty third corps on the left and center, covering Columbia and Lewisburg pikes, and General Kimball's division of the fourth corps on the right, both flanks resting on the river.

Two brigades of General Wagner's division were left in advance to retard the enemy's movements, and General Wood's division and some artillery were moved to the north bank of the river, to cover the flanks, should the enemy attempt to cross above or below.

The enemy followed close after our rear guard, brought up and deployed two full corps with astonishing celerity and moved rapidly forward to the attack. Our outposts, imprudently brave, held their ground too long and hence were compelled to come in at a run. In passing over the parapet, they carried with them the troops of the line for a short space, and thus permitted a few hundred of the enemy to get in. But the reserves, near by, sprang forward, regained the parapet, and captured those of the enemy who had passed in. The enemy assaulted persistently and continuously, with his whole force, from about half past three P. M., until after dark, and made numerous intermittent attacks at a few points until about ten o'clock P. M. He was splendidly repulsed along the whole line of attack. The enemy attacked on a front of about two miles, extending from our left to our right center, General Kimball's left brigade. Our two right brigades were only slightly engaged.

I believe the enemy's loss in killed and wounded cannot have been less than 5,000 and may have been much greater. We captured 702 prisoners and 33 stands of colors.

Our loss, as officially reported, was as follows:

COMMANDS.	KILLED.	WOUNDED.	MISSING.	AGGREGATE.
First Division, Fourth Corps.	5	37	18	60
Second Division, " "	52	519	670	1,241
Artillery " "	10	51	6	67
Second Division, Twenty-third Corps	30	142	135	307
Third " " " "	48	185	97	330
Seventy-second Regt., Ill. Vols.	10	62	86	158
Forty-fourth " Md. "	34	37	92	163
Total	189	1,033	1,104	2,326

On my arrival at Franklin, I gained the first intelligence from General Wilson since the enemy commenced his advance from Duck river. I learned that he had been driven rapidly back and had crossed the Harpeth above Franklin on the preceding day, leaving my left and rear entirely open to the enemy's cavalry.*

A short time before the infantry attack commenced, the enemy's cavalry found a crossing about three miles above Franklin, drove back our cavalry, for a time severely threatening our trains, which were accumulated on the north bank leading towards Nashville. I sent General Wilson orders, which he had, however, anticipated, to drive the enemy back at all hazards, and moved a brigade of General Wood's division to support him, if necessary. At the moment of the first decisive repulse of the enemy's infantry, I received the most gratifying intelligence that General Wilson had driven the rebel cavalry back across the river. This rendered my immediate left and rear secure for the time being.

My experience on the 29th had shown how utterly inferior in numbers my cavalry force was, to that of the enemy, and that even my immediate flanks and rear were quite insecure, while my communication with Nashville was entirely without protection. I could not even rely upon getting up the ammunition necessary for another battle. To remain at Franklin was to seriously hazard the loss of my army by giving the enemy another chance to cut me off from reinforcements, which he had made three desperate, though futile attempts, to accomplish.

I had detained the enemy long enough to enable you to concentrate your scattered troops at Nashville, which was the primary object, and had succeeded in inflicting upon him very heavy losses. I had found it impossible to detain him long enough to get reinforcements at Franklin. Only a small portion of the infantry and none of the cavalry could reach me in time to be of any service in the battle, which must have been fought on the 1st of December.

For these reasons, after consulting with the corps and division commanders and obtaining your approval, I determined

*This was unjust to General Wilson, as the careful student of history will see. Portions of Wilson's cavalry were on every flank, as well as guarding his retreating trains.

to retire during the night of the 30th towards Nashville. The artillery was withdrawn to the north bank during the early part of the night, and at twelve o'clock, the army withdrew from its trenches and crossed the river without loss. During the next day, December 1st, the whole army was placed in position in front of Nashville.

I have the honor to be
    Very respectfully,
      Your obedient servant,
(Signed)   J. M. SCHOFIELD,
        Major-General.

CHAPTER XXII.

BATTLE OF NASHVILLE—HOOD'S ARMY DEMORALIZED—HATCH'S CHARGE—CAVALRY CAPTURING EARTHWORKS—GENERAL THOMAS'S REPORT—CAPTURING PRISONERS—WHAT HOOD SAID—"THE RETREAT."

When on the morning of December 1st General Schofield had safely crosssd the Harpeth with all his trains, and was well under way for Nashville, the second Michigan cavalry, as a part of Croxton's brigade, formed the rear guard and leisurely made their way on to Nashville, passing through our lines of infantry, and with them lay in line of battle all night, five miles in front of Nashville.

At this time General Thomas's force at Nashville was comparatively small and he did not propose to contract his lines further than necessary until portions of his army had joined him from other directions than Franklin. General Thomas knew that Hood expected reinforcements from the southwest, and he supposed that the Confederate force was much greater than it really was.

General Grant, as commander-in-chief, urged Thomas to

drive Hood back before he had time to cross into Kentucky. But General Thomas understood the situation even better than Grant did, and took his own way to crush Hood. He knew he could drive Hood back, but that was not enough. He meant not only to crush, but to capture him and all his army, and his plans were as nearly carried out as it would have been possible to do with a foe that had become wary and ready to break cover and flee at the first serious attack upon his flanks.

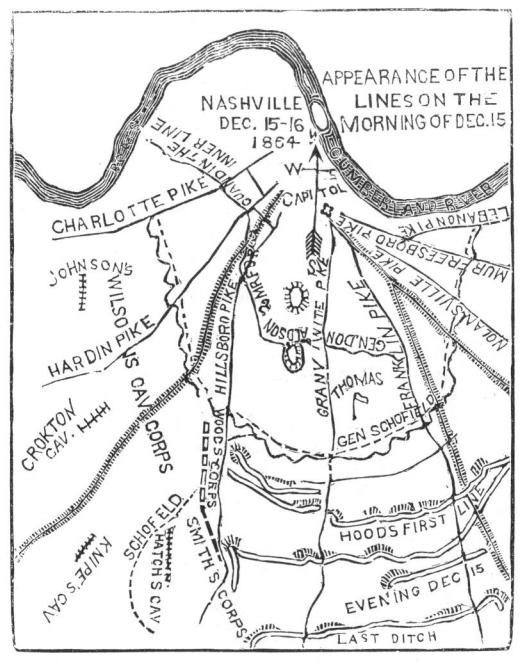

NASHVILLE.

To be upon the safe side, General Thomas sent the greater portion of his cavalry across the Cumberland (the cavalry were much too weak for the services before them) to guard the crossings above and below the city; but these were immediately recrossed to the south side when our army was about to move, and on the 12th of December the Second was placed upon the right, four miles out on the Charlotte pike, and during the first day (the 15th) the regiment swung forward and to the left about two miles, skirmishing and driving the enemy's skirmishers before them, but were restrained from pressing the enemy too far, lest the plans of the commanding general be disconcerted. But at night the regiment mounted and moved forward six miles further, making twelve miles from Nashville, on the morning of the second day of battle. Here the regiment and brigade were restrained from further advancing, while the infantry and artillery pressed the enemy's center and maneuvered for a position from which the final blow was to be struck. And soon it came. Never did infantry and cavalry vie with each other with more earnest vigor than on this occasion, to see which should be first over the earthworks of the enemy, with Hatch at their head. Where mounted cavalry could not go, dismounted did go, with a rush and determination that knew no checking, and repeating rifles, carbines and heavy revolvers struck terror into the hearts of the enemy that could not have guessed how so small a number kept up such a terrific fusilade. Many threw down their guns and surrendered. Hundreds threw themselves flat upon the ground, unharmed, to escape the thick blackness of the storm of lead. Other thousands ran, and but very few returned a parting shot after their ranks were once broken.

Away to the left, on our center, like a wave, rolled up and over that rocky mound, a blue sea of Federals, with a prolonged shout so full of victory that the dullest ear could interpret, if he could not see; and its echo was taken up and reverberated along the lines even to the farthest hill upon the left, where white and blacks were mingled in a death grapple for an earthwork that bristled with bayonets and shook beneath the incessant thunderings of Hood's artillery. And here the colored troops showed their discipline and fighting qualities in a most heroic manner— the saying of the commanding general passing into history— "The colored troops fought nobly;" and from the Southern officers the saying—"For a lot of cattle they did well."

When General Hatch saw, from his position on the right, that the forward movement was becoming general, his impetuosity knew no bounds. Hurling his entire division upon the enemy's wavering left, line after line was taken until the entire Confederate army was on the run. Then the brigade (General Croxton's), with the second Michigan on the extreme right, was drawn in toward the left, mounted, and joining in the rush, captured prisoners continuously, sending them to the rear, and passing on, crossed the Franklin pike and endeavored to reach Franklin and the enemy's front in time to cut off large portions of the Confederate army, but their reserve, though small, had enabled them to retreat in a less hasty manner than they began, though they made no stand of consequence until after crossing Duck river and gained some little distance beyond Columbia. But the cavalry drove them with little delay and dogged their tracks and harassed their flanks; having a sharp brush at Richland creek, and afterward, as they became desperate, turned "at bay" on every possible advantageous ground.

But the fighting regiments of our cavalry corps felt they had tramped up and down through Tennessee too often to leave the enemy any hope of ever crossing the Tennessee river again, and they charged upon every obstruction, firing at close range, using the saber whenever possible, and this continued daily, in all having about twenty sharp skirmishes—sometimes two or three daily. In fact they were too numerous to be remembered, except as a flying vision of fire, carnage, rapidly shifting horsemen—the one party bent on self-protection, fighting for life and personal liberty; the other, with angered, vengeful shouts and shots, determined to wipe out or crush their enemy.

Let us draw a curtain over this pitiful sight and turn to that grand old man, General Geo. H. ("Pap") Thomas. The nearly twenty years that have intervened since that memorable morning have not in the least dimmed the picture of human grandeur that riveted my attention as, when passing the St. Cloud Hotel at 8 o'clock A. M., December 15, 1864, I saw the familiar form of the General standing at the hotel desk, paying his bill as any ordinary traveler. His horse was at the door and a colored servant was bearing to the headquarters ambulance a small valise. A part of his staff stood to horse, awaiting the General's pleasure, and without a word he marched out, it seemed to me at that moment the most perfect soldier in his bearing that I had ever set admiring eyes upon. There was no haughtiness nor ostentatious parade, but a quiet dignity that well became his handsome face—with its short, smooth-cut, red and gray beard, that finished off his well rounded figure. And as he walked out grandly, modestly, and vaulted into his saddle, there was an unmistakable air of "business" about him which boded no good for Mr. Hood. He seemed to say, "Well, boys, we will go out and settle this little business now—it's about the right time to stop fooling."

I could plainly read in his face, "We are going to stay. We will not be back to-night, landlord." I turned to my comrades and remarked, "You will hear music to-day." And here is what happened, from the official report of General Thomas himself:

HEADQUARTERS DEPARTMENT OF THE CUMBERLAND,
Eastport, Mississippi, January 20th, 1865.

COLONEL:—I have the honor to report the operations of my command from the date of the occupation of Atlanta, Georgia, as follows:

*   *   *   *   *   *   *   *   *   *   *

[EXTRACT.]

General Schofield, by my advice and direction, fell back during the night to Nashville, in front of which city lines of battle were formed by noon of the 1st of December, on the hights immediately surrounding Nashville, with Major-General A. J. Smith's command occupying the right, his right resting on the Cumberland river, below the city, the fourth corps (Brigadier-General Wood temporarily in command) in the center, and General Schofield's troops (twenty-third corps) on the left, his left extending to the Nolensville pike. The cavalry, under General Wilson, was directed to take post on the left of General Schofield, which would make secure the interval between his left and the river above the city.

General Steadman's troops reached Nashville about dark on the evening of the 1st of December, taking up a position about a mile in advance of the left center of the main line, on the left of the Nolensville pike. This position, being regarded as too much exposed, was changed on the 3d, when the cavalry having been directed to take post on the north side of the river at Edgefield, General Steadman occupied the space on the left of the line vacated by its withdrawal. During the afternoon of the 2d the enemy's cavalry, in small parties, engaged our skirmishers, but it was only on the afternoon of the 3d that his infantry made its appearance, when crowding in our skirmishers, he commenced to establish his main line, which on the morning of the 4th we found he had succeeded in doing, with his salient on the summit of Montgomery hill, within 600 yards of our center; his main line occupying the high ground on the southeast side of Brown's creek, and extending from the Nolensville pike—his extreme right—across the Franklin and Granny White pikes, in a westerly direction to the hills south and southwest of Richland creek, and down that creek to the Hillsboro pike, with cavalry extending from both his flanks to the river. Artillery was opened on him from several points on the line without eliciting any response. The block house at the railroad crossing of Overalls creek, five miles north of Murfreesboro, was attacked by Bates's division of Cheatham's corps on the 4th, but held out until assistance reached it from the garrison at Murfreesboro. The enemy used artillery to reduce the block house, but although seventy-four shots were fired at it no material injury was done. General Milroy coming up with three regiments of infantry, four companies of the thirteenth Indiana cavalry and a section of artillery, attacked the enemy and drove him off. During the 5th, 6th and 7th Bates's division, reinforced by a division from Lee's corps, and 2,500 of Forrest's cavalry, demonstrated heavily against Fortress Rosecrans at Murfreesboro, garrisoned by about 8,000 men, under command of General Rousseau. The enemy showing an unwillingness to make a direct assault, General Milroy with seven regiments of infantry was sent out, on the 8th, to engage him. He was found a short distance from the place, on the Wilkerson pike, posted behind rail breastworks, was attacked and routed, our troops capturing 207 prisoners and two guns, with a loss of thirty killed and 175 wounded. On the same day Buford's cavalry entered the town of Murfreesboro, after having shelled it vigorously, but he was speedily driven out by a regiment of infantry and a section of artillery. On retiring from before Murfreesboro the enemy's cavalry moved northward to Lebanon and along the bank of the Cumberland in that vicinity, threatening to cross to the north side of the river and interrupt our railroad communication with Louisville, at that time our only source of supplies, the enemy having blockaded the river below Nashville by batteries along the shore. The Navy Department was requested to patrol the river above and below Nashville with the gunboats then in the river to prevent the enemy from crossing, which was cordially and effectually complied with by Lieutenant-Commander LeRoy Fitch, commanding the eleventh division, Mississippi squadron. At the same time General Wilson sent a cavalry force to Gallatin to guard the country in that vicinity. The position of Hood's army around Nashville remained unchanged, with the exception of occasional picket firing.

* * * * * * * * * * *

Both armies were ice bound for a week previous to the 14th of December, when the weather moderated. Being prepared to move I called a meeting of the corps commanders on the afternoon of that day, and having discussed the plan of attack until thoroughly understood, the following S. F. O. No. 342 was issued.

As soon as the state of the weather will admit of offensive operations the troops will move against the enemy's position in the following order:

Major-General A. J. Smith, commanding detachment of the army of Tennessee, after forming his troops on and near the Hardin pike, in front of his present position, will make a vigorous assault on the enemy's left. Major-General Wilson, commanding the cavalry corps, military division Mississippi, with three divisions, will move on and support General Smith's right, assisting as far as possible in carrying the left of the enemy's position, and be in readiness to throw his force upon the enemy the moment a favorable opportunity occurs. Major-General Wilson will also send one division on the Charlotte pike to clear that road of the enemy and observe in the direction of Bell's landing to protect our right rear until the enemy's position is fairly turned, when it will rejoin the main force. Brigadier-General T. J. Wood, commanding fourth army corps, after leaving a strong skirmish line in his works from Laurens hill to his extreme right, will form the remainder of the fourth corps on the Hillsboro pike, to support General Smith's left and operate on the left and rear of the enemy's advanced position on the Montgomery hill. Major-General Schofield, commanding twenty-third army corps, will replace Brigadier-General Kimball's division of the fourth corps with his troops and occupy the trenches from Fort Negley to Laurens hill with a strong skirmish line. He will move with the remainder of his force in front of the works and co-operate with General Wood, protecting the latter's left flank against an attack by the enemy.

Major-General Steadman, commanding district of the Etowah, will occupy the interior line in rear of his present position, stretching from the reservoir on the Cumberland river to Fort Negley, with a strong skirmish line, and mass the remainder of his force in its present position to act according to the exigencies which may arise during the operations.

Brigadier-General Miller, with the troops forming the garrison of Nashville, will occupy the interior line from the battery on hill 210 to the extreme right, including the inclosed works on the Hyde's ferry road.

The quartermaster's troops, under command of Brigadier-General Donaldson, will, if necessary, be posted on the interior line from Fort Morton to the battery on hill 210.

The troops occupying the interior line will be under the direction of Major-General Steadman, who is charged with the immediate defense of Nashville during the operations around the city. Should the weather permit, the troops will be formed to commence operations at six A. M. on the 15th, or as soon thereafter as practicable.

On the morning of the 15th of December, the weather being

favorable, the army was formed and ready at an early hour to carry out the plan of battle promulgated in the special field order of the 14th.

The formation of the troops was partially concealed from the enemy by the broken nature of the ground, as also by a dense fog which only lifted toward noon. The enemy was apparently totally unaware of any intention on our part to attack his position, and more especially did he seem not to expect any movement against his left flank.

To divert his attention still further from our real intentions Major-General Steadman, had on the evening of the 14th received orders to make a heavy demonstration with his command against the enemy's right, east of the Nolensville pike, which he accomplished with great success and some loss, succeeding, however, in attracting the enemy's attention to that part of his line and inducing him to draw reinforcements from towards his center and left. As soon as General Steadman had completed his movement, the commands of Generals Smith and Wilson moved out along the Hardin pike, and commenced the grand movement of the day, by wheeling to the left and advancing against the enemy's position across the Hardin and Hillsboro pikes.

A division of cavalry (Johnson's) was sent at the same time to look after a battery of the enemy's on the Cumberland river at Bell's landing, eight miles below Nashville. General Johnson did not get into position until late in the afternoon, when, in conjunction with the gunboats, under Lieutenant-Commander LeRoy Fitch, the enemy's battery was engaged until after nightfall, and the place was found evacuated in the morning.

The remainder of General Wilson's command, Hatch's division leading and Knipe's in reserve, moving on the right of General A. J. Smith's troops, first struck the enemy along Richland creek, near Hardin's house, and drove him back rapidly, capturing a number of prisoners, wagons, etc., and continuing to advance, while slightly swinging to the left, came upon a redoubt containing four guns, which was splendidly carried by assault at 1 P. M., by a portion of Hatch's division, dismounted, and the captured guns turned upon the enemy. A second redoubt stronger than the first was next assailed and carried by the same troops that captured the first position, taking four more guns and about 300 prisoners. The infantry, McArthur's division of General A. J. Smith's command, on the left of the cavalry, participated in both of the above assaults, and, indeed, the dismounted cavalry seemed to vie with the infantry who should first gain the works. As they reached the position nearly simultaneously, both lay claim to the artillery and prisoners captured.

Finding General Smith had not taken as much distance to the right as I expected he would have done I directed General Schofield to move his command (the twenty-third corps) from the position in reserve to which it had been assigned over to the right of General Smith, enabling the cavalry thereby to operate more freely in the enemy's rear. This was rapidly accomplished by General Schofield, and his troops participated in the closing operations of the day.

The fourth corps, Brigadier-General T. J. Wood commanding, formed on the left of General A. J. Smith's command, and as soon as the latter had struck the enemy's flank, assaulted the Montgomery hill, Hood's most advanced position, at 1 P. M., which was most gallantly executed by the third brigade, second division, Colonel P. Sidney Post, fifty-ninth Illinois, commanding, capturing a considerable number of prisoners. Connecting with the left of Smith's troops (Brigadier-General Garrard's division), the fourth corps continued to advance and carried the enemy's entire line in its front by assault, and captured several pieces of artillery, about 500 prisoners, some stands of colors and other material.

The enemy was driven out of his original line of works, and forced back to a new position along the base of Harpeth hill, still holding his line of retreat to Franklin, by the main pike through Brentwood and by the Granny White pike. Our line at nightfall was readjusted, running parallel to and east of the Hillsboro pike, Schofield's command on the right, Smith's in the center, and Wood's on the left, with the cavalry on the right of Schofield, Steadman holding the position he had gained early in the morning.

The total result of the day's operations was the capture of sixteen pieces of artillery and twelve hundred prisoners, besides several hundred stands of small arms and about forty wagons. The enemy had been forced back at all points with heavy loss, and our casualties were unusually light. The behavior of the troops was unsurpassed for steadiness and alacrity in every movement, and the original plan of battle, with but few alterations, strictly adhered to.

The whole command bivouacked in line of battle during the night on the ground occupied at dark, while preparations were made to renew the battle at an early hour on the morrow.

At 6 A. M., on the 16th, Wood's corps pressed back the enemy's skirmishers across the Franklin pike to the eastward of it, and then swinging slightly to the right advanced due south from Nashville, driving the enemy before him until he came upon his new main line of works, constructed during the night on what is called Overton hill, about five miles south of the city, and east of the Franklin pike. General Steadman moved out from Nashville by the Nolensville pike and formed his command on the left of General Wood, effectually securing the latter's left flank, and made preparations to co-operate in the operations of the day.

General A. J. Smith's command moved on the right of the fourth corps (Wood's) and establishing connection with General Wood's right, completed the rear line of battle.

General Schofield's troops remained in the position taken up by them at dark on the day previous, facing eastward and towards the enemy's left flank, the line of the corps running perpendicular to General Smith's troops.

General Wilson's cavalry, which had rested for the night

at the six mile post on the Hillsboro pike, was dismounted and formed on the right of Schofield's command, and by noon of the 16th had succeeded in gaining the enemy's rear, and stretched across the Granny White pike, one of his two outlets toward Franklin.

As soon as the above dispositions were completed, and having visited the different commands, I gave directions that the movement against the enemy's left flank should be continued. Our entire line approached to within 600 yards of the enemy, at all points. His center was weak, as compared to either his right at Overton hill, or his left on the hills bordering the Granny White pike, still I had hopes of gaining his rear and cutting off his retreat from (to?) Franklin. About three P. M. Post's brigade of Wood's corps, supported by Straight's brigade of the same command, was ordered by General Wood to assault Overton hill. This intention was communicated to General Steadman, who ordered the brigade of colored troops, commanded by Colonel Morgan, fourteenth U. S. C. T., to co-operate in the movement.

The ground on which the two assaulting columns formed, being open and exposed to the enemy's view, he, readily perceiving our intention, drew reinforcements from his left and center to the threatened point. This movement of troops on the part of the enemy was communicated along the line from left to right. The assault was made and received by the enemy with a tremendous fire of grape, canister and musketry, our men moving steadily onward up the hill until near the crest, when the reserves of the enemy rose and poured into the assaulting column a most destructive fire, causing the men first to waver, then to fall back, leaving their dead and wounded, black and white indiscriminately mingled, lying amidst the abatis, the gallant Colonel Post among the wounded.

General Wood readily re-formed his command in the position it had previously occupied, preparatory to a renewal of the assault. Immediately following the effort of the fourth corps, Generals Smith's and Schofield's commands moved against the enemy's works in their respective fronts, carrying all before them, irreparably breaking his lines in a dozen places and capturing all of his artillery and thousands of prisoners, among the latter, four general officers. Our loss was remarkably small, and scarcely mentionable. All of the enemy who did escape were pursued over the tops of Brentwood or Harpeth hills.

General Wilson's cavalry, dismounted, attacked the enemy simultaneously with Schofield and Smith, striking him in reverse, and, gaining firm possession of the Granny White pike, cut off his retreat by that route.

Wood's and Steadman's troops hearing the shouts of victory coming from the right rushed impetuously forward, renewing the assault on Overton hill, and, although meeting a very heavy fire, the onset was irresistible. Artillery and innumerable prisoners fell into our hands. The enemy, hopelessly broken, fled in confusion through the Brentwood pass, the fourth corps in close pursuit, which was continued for several miles, when darkness closed the scene and the troops rested from their labors.

As the fourth corps pursued the enemy on the Franklin pike, General Wilson hastily mounted Knipe's and Hatch's divisions of his command and directed them to pursue along the Granny White pike and endeavor to reach Franklin in advance of the enemy. After proceeding about a mile they came upon the enemy's cavalry, under Chalmers, posted across the road and behind barricades. The position was charged by the twelfth Tennessee cavalry, Colonel Spaulding commanding, and the enemy's lines broken, scattering him in all directions and capturing quite a number of prisoners, among them, Brigadier-General E. W. Rucher.

During the two days' operations there were 4,462 prisoners captured, including 287 officers of all grades from that of major-general, fifty-three pieces of artillery, and thousands of small arms. The enemy abandoned on the field all of his killed and wounded.

Very respectfully,
Your obedient servant,
(Signed) GEORGE H. THOMAS,
Major-General Commanding, U. S. A.

COLONEL R. M. SAWYER,
    A. A. General,
        Military Division Mississippi.

And here is what Hood said about it:

*   *   *   *   *   *   *   *   *   *   *

General Hood claimed that he had strong assurances from Isham G. Harris that his army would be reinforced by, at least, 15,000 men in Tennessee, and that he would be reinforced by 15,000 men from General Steele, from Mississippi, but that of his own force there were but 21,000 and 2,000 cavalry, the latter being away at Murfreesboro, confronting Rousseau.

Hood continues: "Finding that the main movement of the Federals was directed against our left, the chief engineer was instructed to carefully select a line in prolongation of the left flank. Cheatham's corps was withdrawn from the right during the night of the 15th and posted on the left of Stewart, Cheatham's left flank resting near the Brentwood hills. In this position, the men were ordered to construct breastworks during the same night.

"The morning of the 16th found us with Lee's right on Overton hill. At an early hour the enemy made a general attack along our front, and were again and again repulsed at all points, with heavy loss,* especially in Lee's front. About 3:30 P. M.

  *This is exaggerated.

the Federals concentrated a number of guns against a portion of our line, which passed over a mound on the left of our center, and which had been occupied during the night. This point was favorable for massing troops for an assault under cover of artillery. Accordingly, the enemy availed himself of the advantage presented, massed a body of men—apparently one division—at the base of the mound and, under the fire of artillery, which prevented our men from raising their heads above the breastworks, made a sudden and gallant charge up to and over our intrenchments. Our line, thus pierced, gave way; soon thereafter it broke at all points, and I beheld for the first and only time a Confederate army abandon the field in confusion. *

* * "I was seated upon my horse not far in rear when the breach was effected, and soon discovered that all hope to rally the troops was in vain. When our troops were in greatest confusion, a young lady of Tennessee, Miss Mary Bradford, rushed in their midst, regardless of the storm of bullets, and in the name of God and our country implored them to re-form and face the enemy. Her name deserves to be enrolled among the heroes of the war." * * *

With all his mistaken zeal, it must be admitted that Hood deserved well at the hands of his Confederate friends. For while his expedition was a hazardous one, and could not have succeeded, even had he demoralized Schofield's infantry (the cavalry were able to take care of themselves), in crossing the Tennessee with an army less than 50,000 men and an attempt to hold any portion of Tennessee, or Kentucky, was certainly a mark of great courage, worthy of success in a good cause (as he undoubtedly believed it) or a better cause (as we believe it).

It is, then, no wonder that, as he gathered his shattered ranks, constantly lessened by capture and desertion (or *scattering*), and moved quietly along that terrible "retreat," he felt that his work was over, and as he re-crossed the Tennessee, and retired to Tupelo, Mississippi, he turned over his command to General Beauregard, and telegraphed to his superior, the secretary of war: "I request to be relieved from the command of this army."

CHAPTER XXIII.

HOOD'S RETREAT—GENERAL FORREST NARROWLY ESCAPES CAPTURE—A BATTALION CHARGES A DIVISION.

After taking the left flank of our advancing army, and attempting to cut off as many as possible of the retreating Confederates, the Second swam the Harpeth to the east of Franklin and struck the enemy again at Spring Hill. This was on the 20th of December, 1864, and as soon as the division had closed up and our supply trains were provided for, we again took the first crossing, Duck river, December 23d. The rear guard of Hood's army was pressed all day, though not as vigorously as General Wilson thought they ought to be.

It was known that General Forrest commanded the rear guard with all his force, the remnants of what had been the flower of the Confederate cavalry. But their ranks had been greatly reduced by "straggling" and breaking into small bands, many of them seeking their homes, worn out and disgusted. Still there were enough brave spirits left to keep up a show of resistance, unless furiously pressed, as indeed they were liable to be by an army flushed with victory and tired of so long and apparently so useless a struggle.

As they neared Linnville General Wilson and staff rode up to the advance, where Captain Whittemore, of the Second, had three companies (the first battalion), and said, "The rebels are going too slow; can't you push them faster?"

"Yes, sir, I think I could start them on a run if I was sure of support when compelled to fall back by Forrest's main force."

"I will send the fourth regulars to support you."

Away they went on a gallop, scattering the lighter part of the rear guard, capturing many and sending them to the rear; others took to the fields and woods, and everything looked favorable for a general stampede of the Confederates, when, as they entered Linnville Captain Whittemore saw a number of soldiers, mounted; some of them sat resting, one leg thrown over the pommel of the saddle. Dashing into their midst, several of them were captured and others escaped in confusion.

General Forrest was there, surrounded by his staff and escort. One of his orderlies, standing within a few feet of the General, was caught by the shoulder by Captain Whittemore and sent to the rear. This escort laughingly told the Captain afterward that he had made a poor selection, as General Forrest stood next to him, and he might as well have been captured as an orderly.

Passing on through town it was discovered that the fourth regulars were not following. The enemy made the same discovery, and wheeling about in strong force checked what might have been a grand rout, if this little battalion had been backed by 1,000 men.

Returning, it was found our flanks had been threatened by artillery, with cavalry in support, and the fourth had been sent against them. And, as the rest of the brigade knew nothing of the charge they were not in supporting distance. General Croxton was greatly displeased in not being apprised of this movement sooner, for he looked upon that as the grandest opportunity he had known during the campaign for annihilating the best cavalry force the Confederacy had in the southwest—an opportunity of destroying or capturing in detail that was not often given by Forrest. In this charge two men were killed and six wounded. And this ended the third Christmas eve made memorable by a struggle, loss of life, and a shade of gloom settling down upon some portion of the regiment.

During the next six days ending the year 1864 the regiment closed the career of the Confederate army north of the Tennessee river, in mud, snow, rain and cold, and the regiment halted to "close up" at Waterloo, Alabama, having marched through Pulaski, Taylor Springs, Little Cypress camp and Richland Creek.

The affair at Richland Creek was for a time quite severe. The indefatigable Forrest made a desperate effort to give the worn out troops of Hood's command a little rest, and chose his ground well, making a show of resistance with artillery (which usually meant infantry support and a reserve force near), and as the Federal troops were also much jaded, it was some time before enough support was at hand to warrant a dash, with the possible resistance they might find.

The day was far spent before Croxton's brigade succeeded in dislodging them and went into camp on their grounds. In the morning a charge was ordered; the rear guard gave way; following them closely the cavalry was scattered and Croxton's men rushed on and followed the enemy to the creek, three miles, and there, upon the other side, the main force of the Confederate army was developed. For a time a general engagement seemed unavoidable and imminent, each side holding its own and the artillery opening up vigorously on both sides.

Troops were brought into position; shot and shell came and went crashing through the tree tops or bounding along the road, limbs of trees fell in all directions and that ominous silence of small arms spread its pall over the scene, and the gloom of night compelled "peace" between the combatants.

The Federals obeyed and went into camp, and the Confederates, retiring for a space, also sought the poor comfort from their camp fires.

A memorable year, in which vast armies had melted away, like the avalanche which sweeps all before it, until, in turn, it meets an unseen power and yields. On the one side the avalanche was already re-forming. How would it be on the other? Only a modest river between. The Federals could afford to rest. Could the Confederates?

Seventeen days of rest and the brigade was again in the saddle and across the river without opposition. Swinging around through Eastport, Iuka and Burnsville, capturing a few stragglers here and there, they entered, for the third time, the historic grounds of Corinth, and on to Farmington, Mississippi, and back to Iuka, the Saratoga of the south, where they rested for a day and again returned through Eastport to their old camp at Waterloo, remaining in comparative quiet a whole month; remounting the command with some of the best stock of Kentucky's far famed stables.

Soon the command recrossed the river and went into camp at Chickasaw bluffs, and from this point frequent short scouts were made into the surrounding country. Among them one, referred to in Part Second, made by the new commander of the regiment, Colonel Tom Johnston, will be found of interest. During the next ten days, the command marched south into Alabama, and their progress was very much delayed by their effort to keep with them their wagon trains; through mud, quicksand, slush and over bad hills. On this march efforts were made to prevent plundering, and officers were frequently ordered under arrest by the commanding general for violation of these orders.

Passing through Cherokee, Frankfort, Russellville, Jasper, crossing the Mulberry river, Black Warrior, and through Elyton, coming out on the Tuscaloosa road, on March 31, the command find a much richer country, with an abundance of forage for animals.

The brigade had cut loose from the division and was on a grand raid, General Wilson,* being farther east, also raiding.

General John T. Croxton, in his report on the raid through northern Alabama, says:

"At this time, as I afterwards learned, Forrest's entire train with his field artillery was at Tuscaloosa, and in apprehension of my approach was ordered to Northport. In view of this, Jack-

*For an account of General Wilson's life and services, in brief, see Part Second,

son, instead of following directly, took a road striking the Mud creek road, four miles nearer Tuscaloosa, and, moving rapidly, succeeded in throwing his forces there between me and that place. upon the only road east of the Black Warrior. He had two brigades, numbering, as I then supposed and have since learned, twenty-six hundred men. I could hardly hope to run over this force and take Tuscaloosa with 1,500 men (400 of which had not yet joined me), supported as he was by 400 militia and 350 cadets, who filled the trenches around the city. I determined, therefore, to effect by strategy what I could not hope to accomplish directly. I therefore turned north, marching ten miles on the Elyton road, halted and fed, while the fourth Kentucky joined me. From this point we moved directly west to Johnson's ferry, forty miles above Tuscaloosa, which point we reached at sundown, having marched during the day over forty miles. I ordered the eighth Iowa to begin crossing at once, and at sundown, April 2d, the whole command was west of the Black Warrior, the men, with their equipments, crossing in a single flatboat and the horses swimming, losing only two or three. April 3d, moved at daylight toward Tuscaloosa, the advance guard capturing all the scouts and citizens, thus preventing any knowledge of our approach. At nine o'clock at night we reached the suburbs of Northport, massed the brigade in Cedar Grove, and with 150 men of the second Michigan cavalry moved up near the bridge. I intended to put this picket force in ambush as near the bridge as I could get, quietly await daybreak, then seize the bridge by a dash, and throw the whole brigade over, mounted, and envelop the city before the cadets and militia could be assembled.

"As I approached the bridge, however, I could distinctly hear the rebels removing the flooring, and apprehending they had received notice of our approach, and knowing the difficulty of success should they have time to assemble their troops, I gave the order, and Colonel Johnston, of the second Michigan, dashed ahead on the guards, who fired and retreated into the bridge, in the center of which the reserve was stationed behind cotton bales and in front of which twenty feet of bridge had been torn up. The detachment of the Second, led by Colonel Johnston in person, rushed into the bridge, halting for nothing until they had killed and captured the entire guard and had possession. These were moved ahead to cover the approaches to the bridge, and fifty men sent double-quick to seize the two pieces of artillery, the location of which I had learned, and which were soon in our possession. In the meantime the floor of the bridge was relaid so that footmen could pass, and the balance of the second Michigan, the sixth Kentucky and eighth Iowa thrown across, dismounted, and put in position to cover the bridge against an attack from the militia and cadets which were assembling. They made several unsuccessful attempts to dislodge us, but failed, and morning found us in peaceful possession of the premises with 600 prisoners and three pieces of artillery."

After the brigade had destroyed the foundry, factory, two nitre works, the military university and immense quantities of stores, to cripple the southern army as much as possible and give that portion of the south a taste of war, with all its devastating horrors, General Croxton began to look out for a way to rejoin the cavalry corps under General Wilson. Going southeast, he learned that Forrest with 3,000 mounted men was in his front. It was useless to attempt a fight against such odds, and even could he have driven Forrest, it was not desirable, but rather his policy to draw Forrest away from Wilson, which he did by returning to Northport. "On the way," Croxton continues, "the rearguard was attacked by Wirt Adams with 2,800 men. The sixth Kentucky cavalry, in the rear, was driven in, past the second Michigan, which was immediately thrown across the road and repulsed the enemy three times as they charged against my little band of Michigan men. We were not molested further, but gathering up our wounded, thirty-two and one killed, they were brought away in ambulances, though two of our ambulances were broken down and abandoned." Without giving all of General Croxton's report, which follows the movements of the brigade across the Black Warrior into Elyton valley, to Jasper, Arkadephia, Trussville and Talladega, we note:

"On the 23d of April (fifteen days after Lee had surrendered, though the brigade had not yet heard of it,) we attacked General Hill between Talladega and Blue mountain at Mumford's station and routed him, capturing the works, the artillery and a number of prisoners and scattered the rest in the woods."

On the first of May the brigade joined the corps at Macon, after an absence of one month, during which time Croxton had no communication with any Federal forces. Had marched 653 miles through a mountainous country, swimming numerous rivers, capturing many prisoners and losing few, aside from stragglers out of their line of duty, and destroying large quantities of stores and munitions of war.

Among others of the brigade, General Croxton, in his

reports, recommends for promotion for meritorious services, Lieutenant-Colonel Thomas W. Johnston to be colonel of the second Michigan cavalry, also Captain Walter H. Whittemore to be major by brevet. The General did not mention severe skirmishing which lasted all day April 1st, in which forty-five men of the sixth Kentucky and a few of other regiments were lost, and neglects to mention the stirring events of forcing the horses into the Black Warrior and driving them across, while the men crossed in a few miserable dug-outs. It was not only a very hazardous undertaking but very laborious and exciting, and occupied a whole day.

The affair with Hill was started by a brilliant dash of two companies, led by Lieutenant Woodruff, of company M, second Michigan cavalry. Two pieces of artillery opened on our command. Colonel Johnston ordered the advance to charge and followed them rapidly with the regiment. The advance had possession of the artillery within five minutes and the brigade did not overtake the Second until night.

On April 26th and 27th Lee's army came marching home in squads, with flags of truce flying, and our troops began to settle down to the fact that the war had ended. And now—what? Was this to be the end?

The troops of General Hill scattered like men who had become demoralized, or had risked their lives as often as they cared to in a bad cause. Yet in their breaking up and scattering they carried with them several of our men, who, by their headlong course had become detached from the regiment, and there was an apparent disposition to spare lives. Our men were immediately parolled.

Here properly ends the record of this remarkable regiment, though their marches and camp duties continued on through Georgia, across the Tallapoosa river, the Chattahoochee and on, back and forth, settling finally at Macon, but sending detachments to Thomaston, Barnesville, Forsyth and Milledgeville, and maintaining military posts at those points until finally mustered out in August, 1865, having kept up its organization for about four years, and in that time borne upon its rolls 2,400 men, including recruits, and mustered out less than one fifth of them at the final muster.

END OF PART FIRST.

ADJUTANT EDWIN HOYT,
A. A. A. G. 1st Brigade, 1st Div. Cav.

ADJUTANT H. C. AKELEY.

SURGEON WM. BROWNEL.

QUARTERMASTER S. BROWNELL,
Lieut. Col. and Com. Sub. Army of W. Va.

COMISSARY E. W. LAWRENCE

PART SECOND

PART SECOND.

LETTERS FROM PROMINENT GENERALS.

A LETTER FROM GENERAL POPE.

HEADQUARTERS DEPARTMENT OF THE MISSOURI,
Fort Leavenworth, Kansas, October 12, 1882.

MY DEAR CAPTAIN:—I am very glad indeed to hear that you are writing a history of your regiment. Certainly there was no better regiment in the service, so far as I knew, and I remember very well its gallant and soldierly appearance at all times.

The raid in which it was engaged south of Corinth, in 1862, was, I think, the very first military operation of that character ever made by our troops, and deserves a much fuller recital than ever has been made. I am sure there is no one who feels more interest in the history of your regiment or who looks back, to it with more affection than I do.

Sincerely yours,

JNO. POPE.

CAPTAIN M. P. THATCHER, Detroit.

The following is from General Elliott, colonel of the second Iowa:

SAN FRANCISCO, June 17, 1883.

MY DEAR CAPTAIN:—I was glad to receive your favor of the 9th. I regret that I have not a copy of my report of the Mossy Creek fight to send you. * * * * *

The National Tribune published an account of that fight, but the troops I had the honor to command and my own services were entirely ignored. * * * * *

If I remember correctly, the battery attached to the first division of cavalry was Lilley's, the eighteenth *Indiana*. One gun was abandoned as disabled (a broken axle at the Dandridge fight, under Colonel Campbell). That left us but three pieces for the Mossy Creek fight. * * * * * *

You ought to be able to make up a fine record for the second Michigan cavalry. My first acquaintance with the regiment was at St Louis, and soon after I joined it with my regiment in Grant's army of the Tennessee, near Corinth. Then Sheridan joined your regiment and his first service was with me on the celebrated Booneville raid—the first of the war; in which I had the honor of being the senior colonel in command.

I do not think history has given the importance to this raid which it is entitled to. We really supplied Halleck's army with railroad rolling stock, besides what we destroyed and the prisoners we parolled—more than twice our own numbers, and that, too, in the teeth of General Beauregard, with his whole army. * * As a general thing I don't think the result obtained compensates for the demoralization of the troops on a cavalry raid. * * * * * * *

I am sorry to hear that Colonel Campbell lived so short a time to enjoy the reward in this world for his valuable services during the rebellion.

I don't think the whole army could boast of a finer brigade of two regiments than the second Iowa and second Michigan cavalry.

Very truly yours,
W. L. ELLIOTT,
Brevet Major-General, U. S. A.

GENERAL STANLEY'S LETTER.

FORT LEWIS, COLORADO, May 31, 1883.

DEAR CAPTAIN:—Your letter came after some delay. I have read your sketch of the battle of Franklin, and it is, according to my recollection, so correct I could not make any alteration.

Yes, it is true that I was in front of the left of Opdyke's brigade when they made that charge and it was there I got my dose of lead.

Yes, Wagner was, to say the least, "full" of whisky, if not drunk, and told Corsair's aid to "tell Corsair to fight the *rebs* till h—l freezes over." That was directly contrary to my instructions. But he was in a vainglorious condition, though it was not known at the time to General Schofield or myself.

I am sorry I can not give you additional light on Chicamauga. Ten days before that battle I was attacked by acute dysentery and was lying prostrate at Stevenson during the great battle. Perhaps I ought not to express an opinion under the circumstances, but I think you are right in your suggestion that the cavalry was not handled as a whole as skillfully as it should have been. A few brigade commanders, as near as I can learn, acted independently and conducted the cavalry in a great battle that might, it seems to me, have been changed to the discomfiture of the Confederates. I have always regretted the sickness which kept me from Chicamauga.

Yours truly,
D. S. STANLEY.

To CAPTAIN M. P. THATCHER, Detroit.

P. S. You appear to have had so good success in getting correct information, that I don't think I can add anything to the sketch you sent me. D. S. S.

FROM GENERAL EDWARD HATCH.

FORT RILEY, KANSAS, January 4, 1884.

CAPTAIN:—I regret that your letter was so long in reaching me. * * *

The cavalry did not receive that credit which was their due for the part they took in the Hood invasion. With 4,200 cavalry we were constantly fighting with Hood's advance from Florence to Nashville; and that, too, against a force of cavalry under Forrest that equaled all of Schofield's army. Had it not been for the stubborn fight of our cavalry at Columbia and Franklin, on Schofield's flanks, that officer would have been lucky had he reached Nashville with his staff only, and the battle of Nashville would have been fought at Louisville or somewhere in Kentucky.

From Franklin to Nashville, Croxton's and my commands had the rear, and in the forward movement from Nashville it is well known that we crushed the enemy's left, over a line of breastworks, consisting of four, six and four guns, respectively. General Wilson credited our division with capturing seventeen guns, and as many prisoners as we had men.

You can not say too much of the fighting qualities of the second Michigan cavalry. I was with your regiment in action at Booneville, Mississippi, certainly one of the hardest fought cavalry affairs of the war. The two regiments went into action with about 1,000 men all told. The Confederates acknowledged a force of 5,000. The fight lasted all day.

That the second Michigan had for its colonel General Sheridan, the commanding general of the United States Army, and to-day the most remarkable cavalry officer in the world, is sufficient glory for you all. I know of no regiment that ever equaled the fighting qualities of the second Michigan cavalry.

Probably I witnessed two of its most trying moments, Booneville and Shoal Creek. I have not forgotten at Booneville, when Campbell, fighting with desperation against fearful odds, passed the word along to his men, "Hold on a moment longer, the second Iowa are coming." Neither, when at Shoal Creek, the second Iowa, nearly two years after, was again received with the same old cheer.

The regiments seemed to have perfect faith in each other.

I am glad you are writing your regiment's history. Michigan should know that every man of the second cavalry was a hero.

     Very truly yours,
       EDWARD HATCH,
       Brevet Major-General, U. S. A.

ARMY OF THE CUMBERLAND.

THE STATES REPRESENTED—WHO WERE OUR COMMANDERS.

The following were the troops that served in the Army of the Cumberland, compiled from the official rosters and arranged with reference to the states to which they belonged, as shown by the report of April 10th, 1864:

Connecticut, Infantry, 5th and 20th regiments.

Illinois, Infantry, 10th, 16th, 19th, 21st, 22d, 24th, 25th, 27th, 34th, 35th, 36th, 38th, 42d, 44th, 51st, 59th, 60th, 73d, 74th, 75th, 78th, 79th, 80th, 82d, 83d, 84th, 85th, 86th, 88th, 89th, 92d, 96th, 98th, 100th, 101st, 102d, 104th, 105th, 110th, 115th, 123d, 125th and 129th regiments; Cavalry, Co. K, 15th regiment; Artillery, Batteries C and M, 1st artillery, C, H and I, 2d artillery, Bridge's battery and Chicago Board of Trade Battery.

Indiana, Infantry, 6th, 9th, 10th, 15th, 17th, 22d, 27th, 29th, 30th, 31st, 32d, 33d, 35th, 36th, 37th, 38th, 40th, 42d, 44th, 51st, 57th, 58th, 68th, 70th, 72d, 73d, 74th, 75th, 79th, 81st, 82d, 84th, 85th, 86th, 87th, 88th and 101st regiments; Cavalry,

2d, Cos. G, H, I, K, 3d, 4th, 8th, 9th, 10th, 11th, 12th and 13th regiments; Artillery, 4th, 5th, 7th, 8th, 10th, 11th, 12th, 13th, 18th, 19th, 20th and 21st batteries.

Iowa, Cavalry, 5th and 8th regiments.

Kansas, Infantry, 8th regiment; Artillery, 1st battery.

Kentucky, Infantry, 1st, 2d, 3d, 4th, 5th, 6th, 8th, 9th, 10th, 15th, 17th, 18th, 21st, 23d and 28th regiments; Cavalry, 1st, 2d, 3d, 4th, 5th, 6th and 7th regiments; Artillery, 1st and 2d batteries.

Maryland, Infantry, 3d regiment.

Massachusetts, Infantry, 2d and 33d regiments.

Michigan, Engineers and Mechanics, 1st regiment; Infantry, 9th, 10th, 11th, 13th, 14th, 18th, 19th, 21st and 22d regiments; Cavalry, 2d and 4th regiments; Artillery, Batteries A, D, E, I and K, 1st regiment.

Minnesota, Infantry, 2d regiment; Artillery, 2d battery.

Missouri, Infantry, 2d, 15th and 23d regiments; Engineers, 1st regiment; Artillery, Battery G, 1st regiment.

New Jersey, Infantry, 13th and 33d regiments; Artillery, Battery I, 1st regiment, and 13th battery.

New York, Infantry, 45th, 58th, 60th, 68th, 78th, 102d, 107th, 119th, 123d, 134th, 136th, 137th, 141st, 143d, 149th, 150th and 154th regiments; Artillery, Batteries I and M, 1st regiment, and 13th battery.

Ohio, Infantry, 1st, 2d, 3d, 5th, 6th, 7th, 9th, 10th, 11th, 13th, 14th, 15th, 17th, 18th, 19th, 21st, 24th, 26th, 29th, 31st, 33d, 35th, 36th, 38th, 40th, 41st, 49th, 51st, 52d, 55th, 59th, 61st, 64th, 65th, 66th, 69th, 71st, 73d, 74th, 79th, 82d, 89th, 90th, 92d, 93d, 94th, 97th, 98th, 99th, 101st, 102d, 105th, 106th,

108th, 113th, 115th, 121st, 124th and 125th regiments; Cavalry, 1st, 3d, 4th and 10th regiments; Artillery, Batteries A, B, C, E, F, G, I, K and M, 1st regiment, and 6th, 9th, 12th, 18th and 20th batteries.

Pennsylvania, Infantry, 27th, 28th, 29th, 46th, 73d, 75th, 77th, 78th, 79th, 109th, 111th and 147th regiments; Cavalry, 7th, 9th and 15th regiments: Artillery, Batteries B and E (independent).

Tennessee, Infantry, 1st, 2d, and 10th regiments; Cavalry, 1st, 2d, 3d, 4th, 5th, 8th, 9th, 10th, 12th and 13th regiments; Artillery, Batteries A, C, D and F, 1st regiment.

Wisconsin, Infantry, 1st, 3d, 10th, 13th, 15th, 21st, 22d, 24th, 26th and 31st regiments; Cavalry, 1st regiment; Artillery, 3d, 5th, 8th and 10th batteries, and Battery C, 1st heavy artillery.

To these organizations were added four regiments of infantry, one regiment of cavalry, and seven batteries of artillery, of the regular United States troops, making the grand total, present and absent, of the Army of the Cumberland, at the opening of the Atlanta campaign, one hundred and seventy-one thousand four hundred and fifty, officers and enlisted men.

WHO WERE OUR COMMANDERS.

Major-General D. S. Stanley—commanding cavalry corps, Army of the Cumberland.

General J. B. Turchin, first division.

General S. C. Smith, second division.

Colonel R. H. G. Minty, first brigade, first division.

Colonel Paramore, second brigade, first division.

Colonel E. M. McCook, first brigade, second division.

Colonel A. P. Campbell, second brigade, second division.

These were our cavalry commanders on the 1st of May, 1863. Soon after there was a change in the numbering of the brigades and divisions, and our own brigade was known as the first brigade, first division, and this position was maintained until the end of the war.

At Stevenson, Alabama, General Stanley was taken sick, and the cavalry corps suffered by his absence at the battle of Chicamauga.

During the winter of 1863-4 Generals Elliott and Sturgis alternated in the command of the cavalry. Generals Mitchell, Crook and McCook successively commanded the first division, and later General Hatch.

General Wilson was in command of the cavalry corps from October, 1864, to the end of the war.

Brigadier-General Croxton commanded our brigade during the Hood invasion and until the close of the war.

Previous to the organization of the Army of the Cumberland, under General Rosecrans, the cavalry was poorly organized; the regiments serving independently or attached to some division of infantry. This was why we lost General Sheridan, by promotion—he was promoted out of the regiment, and there were no brigades of cavalry to command. Had General P. H. Sheridan been in command of all our cavalry at Chicamauga, and used them as at the East, there would have been a thorn in the side of Braxton Bragg that would have worried him.

Had Thomas had at Nashville Rosecrans's cavalry from Chicamauga, with plenty of commanders like Hatch and Croxton for the brigades and divisions, Hood would never have recrossed the Harpeth.

The real strength of cavalry was always underestimated.

STONE RIVER.

"WE SHALL WIN THIS FIGHT!"—GENERAL ROSECRANS AND THIS MEMORABLE BATTLE.

Of all the heroes brought out by the events of the great rebellion, none has suffered so much from the vacillating minds of a great people as William S. Rosecrans.

Although the writer of this volume does not profess to be giving the tenth part of the stirring events that were being enacted near or within signal distance of his immediate command, but has followed closely to the original intention of narrating only events in which his regiment, or at most his brigade, was directly interested, a slight digression is here deemed admissible, from the fact that, while 200 miles or more separated us from Stone River, yet we were assisting Rosecrans's army, and were passing through scenes as trying and hazardous as were any other troops and were in fact cutting off reinforcements by destroying railroads leading from Richmond to Bragg.

"Carter's raid," an account of which appears earlier in these pages, was that duty, and that, if excuse is needed, is ours for giving a brief summary of the terrific battle of Stone River, near Murfreesboro.

General Rosecrans came to us at a time when the army of the Ohio, as it was then called, surely needed a great soldier to lead it. The material of that army had proven itself of the finest quality. Twenty-three thousand soldiers, half of them raw troops, had withstood the demoralizing effects of a surprise, rout and slaughter, at Perryville, and rallying had beaten back as fine a corps of spirited soldiers as ever wore the gray, under one of their hardest fighters, Hardee, backed by 35,000 men.

Had it happened where newspaper correspondents were courted and numerous, the country would have been thrilled by the brilliant victory out of defeat.

But Rosecrans saw the record, and Lincoln saw it, and had his eye upon that army and Rosecrans at the same time. There had been another record—away down in Mississippi. Abraham Lincoln had a very long head, and a way of quietly asserting his authority when he knew he was right.

Buell had lost a grand opportunity. Bragg had escaped out of Kentucky. Rosecrans dropped into the place, knowing little of the territory or men, and embarrassed by great expectations on the part of the nation.

Buell was said to have gone out of Louisville on that memorable 1st of October with 100,000 men and flying colors. The colors were flying, but alas for that army! the siege of Corinth and a Mississippi campaign had spread desolation in its ranks, and every green hill from Booneville, Mississippi, to Cincinnati was dotted with newly made graves, and the rolls showed the deplorable fact that there were but 68,000 men within five miles of Perryville and only one third of these engaged, and hence the barren victory.

The army was thought well equipped and disciplined, but their actual fighting strength was greatly overrated—probably not less than forty per cent.

But General Rosecrans was known to most of his men, and had from the first their confidence. He saw with alarm that nearly one-third his infantry were unfit for duty, either from sickness or imperfect arms. He also saw that his cavalry consisted of three or four regiments that might be called cavalry, yet were not fully up to the standard as compared with the dashing horsemen of the South, and as to numbers the Confederate cavalry so greatly outnumbered his that he scarcely dared send his own cavalry out to operate alone unaccompanied by artillery and infantry, unless it was some dashing expedition where small numbers stood a better chance than a multitude.

And such was the army when General Rosecrans came to it at Louisville, October 30, 1862, and issued his general order No. 1, assuming command of the fourteenth army corps, henceforth to be known as the army of the Cumberland, and announcing his staff—mostly brought with him from Mississippi.

Bowling Green was at the time the southern terminus of railroad communication, but General Negley held Nashville with one good division, and here the Confederate cavalry were constantly threatening that important post, harassing the lines and keeping them constantly on the alert, while Breckenridge held Murfreesboro, and Bragg was moving as rapidly as possible from his circuitous retreat from Kentucky through east Tennessee, to assist in forming a strong barrier against our further advance into the South.

One of Rosecrans's first acts was to ask for General D. S. Stanley as chief of cavalry, and the rapid reconstruction of the Louisville & Nashville road.

Very soon, headquarters were established at Bowling Green and here General George H. Thomas joined Rosecrans, and from the first was recognized as the real chief of staff upon whom "old Rosy" loved to lean, for counsel and support. "Old Rosy" and "Pap Thomas" became at once names to be spoken in the same breath, with loving confidence, and that confidence grew as it became known that frequent consultations were held by them.

General McCook and corps were on the way to Nashville by November 4th, and next day artillery firing was heard in the direction of Nashville, over forty miles away. Couriers met them soon and announced that the Confederates had been driven back from an attempt to burn the railroad bridge across the Cumberland at Nashville. Here John Morgan established his record for dishonorable warfare, taking advantage of a flag of truce to form troops near the works and dash into the town.

But they were driven off, the bridge saved and Nashville let alone.

Within ten days from the time of assuming command Rosecrans had reconstructed the railway and established headquarters at Nashville, and had formed his army into three wings—Major-General Aleck McDowell McCook commanding the right, Major-General Geo. H. Thomas the center, and Major-General Thomas L. Crittenden the left.

For the next forty days all were busy perfecting arrangements for a forward movement. Supplies of all kinds were hurried from the north and the few recruits ready were pushed on, thrust into blue clothes, given a musket, and informed they were soldiers of Uncle Sam's army—"Prepare to be shot."

Upon the sloping hills south and east of Nashville the rows of white tents gave one of the most spirited of military pictures, and with brothers, husbands and lovers all driven away to the war, the women of Nashville had nothing to do but make it interesting for the "Yankee army"—and the arts and wiles of those keen-witted females kept provost marshals and clerks busy with passes, or more frequently *refusals* of passes.

And so the time passed rapidly, General Stanley meantime showing his mettle by a reconnaissance to Triune and Franklin with a small force of cavalry, capturing both of those places by a dash and establishing the fact that the enemy's forces were mainly concentrated at Murfreesboro.

Then began the query among outside parties, "Why don't Rosecrans move?"—the same old "on to Richmond" cry forever ringing in the ears of commanding generals.

Rosecrans's invariable reply was, "I'll move when I get a good ready. I believe I know my own business best, and will not allow public clamor to guide or influence me."

On the 5th of December there were but five days' rations at Nashville. By Christmas, enough had accumulated to last until about the 1st of February. At this time the muster rolls showed but 46,910 men, with only about 3,000 cavalry and 2,000 artillery included.

To oppose these, Braxton Bragg was reported to have an

army of 75,000 men, well disciplined, and, for them, well equipped. Bragg relied upon the superiority of his troops in point of discipline and dash, and fully expected to keep Rosecrans busy at Nashville with one division while, with the remainder, he crossed the Cumberland and again invaded Kentucky.

Making due allowance for sick and desertions, Bragg had probably not less than 60,000 men. For Rosecrans to confront these with any less numbers looks, at this distance, like foolishness, with men so nearly equal in fighting qualities. But he had confidence in the staying qualities of his troops. He used to say, "Bragg is a good dog, but Holdfast is a better;" and so he proved.

On Christmas night Rosecrans and his generals met for consultation and—"orders." That consultation ended in the chief giving them all to understand that he was ready to move, and proposed to "show Bragg, to-morrow, that the Federal army had *not* gone into winter quarters;" and after a vigorous speech to them, closed by saying, substantially, "Fight, keep fighting. Push, push ahead. Spread your skirmishers far and near. Keep fighting and pushing. They will not stand it. Good night, gentlemen."

This was past midnight. The indefatigable Garesché was deep in his papers, never weary, never out of humor, and, like his master, the General, was conscientiously devotional.

The morning of Friday, December 26, was dreary enough; black clouds hung over the hills and thick mists climbed up from the damp, dark valleys. Soon the rain had filled the little streams to small rushing torrents, and as reveille rattled from hill to hill, blue coats came swarming out of snow white tents like ants, shouting, crowing, and responding cheerfully, all unmindful of the surroundings. They were ordered to break camp and fall in, and within the hour, breakfast was off, trains packed and the army moved.

Thomas, with his center wing, swung out upon the right to Brentwood and found nothing.

McCook moved towards Nolensville and Jeff. C. Davis's division found the enemy ready to dispute Knob's Gap.

Stanley was everywhere along the front, uncovering every nest and covering the movements of the infantry as much as possible with his small force.

Crittenden, with his 13,300, moved down the main pike towards Murfreesboro, with Colonel Minty, of the fourth Michigan, and his brigade covering the front and left. The Confederates made a strong stand at Lavergne towards night, but Colonel Enyart's brigade charged and drove the enemy across Stony Creek.

Awaiting at Nashville to give the different wings time to gain their points, Rosecrans moved out with his escort, and midnight found him still in the saddle, retiring from McCook's position, at or near Nolensville, to a position near the left, nor did he retire until fourteen hours had been spent in the saddle.

On Saturday the left wheel of the army began sweeping around Triune, Hardee retiring, and General Wood's division pushing vigorously through Lavergne, capturing a few at the bridge over Stewart's Creek, and saving the bridge by a dash of our artillery to a covering point, and Rosecrans established his headquarters near Lavergne, observing Sunday by religious exercises under Father Tracy.

On Monday headquarters were moved to Stewartsboro, and at three o'clock in the afternoon General Palmer signaled from the front that he was in sight of Murfreesboro, and the enemy were running. General Crittenden was ordered to send a division to occupy Murfreesboro. But in attempting to carry out this move Generals Wood and Palmer found Breckenridge in a strong position, from which it was concluded best not to attempt a dislodgment until further orders. Orders were withheld until evening, when the General examined the situation along the front, and night settled down, with a feeling in the minds of all that to-morrow would bring stirring events. Tuesday, the 30th, dawned, dark and dreary. Mud everywhere, in which the soldiers had lain all night, with rain drenching them, and long before daylight they were glad to stand to arms. At seven o'clock Crittenden's lines moved through the heavy cedar thickets on the left. The enemy had discovered Rosecrans's headquarters, and dropping a few shells among them, killing one of his orderlies (McDonald), their position was changed.

Then the maneuvering of troops began, and as line after line formed out to the left, heavy mutterings were heard away on the right.

Around the General staff officers were busy writing dispatches, beneath outspread rubber ponchos.

At noon reports came of strong attacks upon McCook's right by the enemy's cavalry. Later the enemy cut our trains on the Murfreesboro pike.

General Thomas was pushing successfully on the center and was directed to press the enemy according to his own discretion.

McCook reports Sheridan successful on the right and Rosecrans said things looked brighter, and night came down with rain and cold; strong picket lines well posted all along the lines, and the utmost precaution taken to prevent surprise.

McCook was directed to press the right and hold as long as possible. Thomas and Palmer were to press the center, Crittenden to advance on Breckenridge, and Wood to push forward by the upper ford and if possible take Murfreesboro.

Rosecrans's intentions were evidently to swing Wood around by the left—and if possible strike the enemy on their right and weaken their strength, opposed to Thomas in the center and McCook on the right.

To McCook he said: "Can you hold your position three hours?"

"I think I can," said Aleck McD.

"Well, you know the ground; change your position if you think necessary."

And then followed orders, and before they had been delivered to all, in the morning the thunderbolt had been hurled against McCook. Though he was driven back he was not surprised. It struck the divisions of Rousseau, Negley and Sheridan and found them standing to arms. But, as it proved, nearly all of Bragg's army had concentrated against McCook. Naturally they were driven. Stragglers said: "The right wing is broken, General Sill killed, two batteries captured."

The roar of artillery showed a sullen disputing of the ground, but McCook had undertaken more than he thought. He could not hold the right three hours.

It was an anxious moment for Rosecrans. To a staff officer from McCook: "Tell him to hold every inch." He had not heard of the capture of two brigades.

The plan of battle was disconcerted, but the commander was not discouraged. Mounting with his staff he rode to the rescue. Ordering a brigade here, a battery there and a division yonder—every point was taken in at a glance. Hastening to the right, amid a shower of bullets and shells, he saw quiet Phil Sheridan disentangling himself from a cedar thicket; short of ammunition, but with perfect ranks, and Negley was still in the fiery furnace, in front of Thomas. Rousseau went to his relief. Gallant old Loomis planted batteries here and there and a temporary check was made.

Sheridan replenished his empty cartridge boxes and wheeled promptly into line. But the right wing was unquestionably doubled back nearly upon the left.

It was the grandest. moment of Rosecrans's life.

Although divisions were broken—brigades and sections of artillery captured, still the old hero could exclaim, "We shall win this fight!" Nineteen guns were a severe loss, but the day was not lost.

Massing his batteries in the center, never having a thought for his own personal safety, though frequently admonished not to expose himself so much, he said, after correcting his lines and issuing orders, in person:

"Forward! The whole line forward! Fire *low;* then charge them! They can't stand cold steel!"

And with a crash from the throats of every gun upon that crest, before which the Confederate army quailed, forward sprung the undaunted heroes of Sheridan, Rousseau, and Negley.

O! to what extent will human nerves stand tuning with such wild, hellish music and not break! Forward they go, volley following so close upon volley that not a musket shot was heard—it was as if a thousand locomotives were thundering over as many bridges, and the roar was simply awful.

"Shoot low!" Yes, so low that it seemed as if scarce an ounce of lead went astray. No; they could *not* stand it. Nor did they wait for "cold steel." They ran.

"Ah-h!" and shouts drown all other sounds, as Rosecrans himself leads the charge in person, and the enemy retired in confusion amid an avalanche of shot, shell, bullets and shouts of victory.

Turning slightly to the left, attention was turned to a weak point, in front of Thomas, being assailed furiously by the enemy. Leading the way, fresh batteries rushed to the rescue, and turning the tide of battle at that point solid positions were being established along our right, and the enemy were rapidly forming on our left center, though feinting the extreme right.

Rosecrans understood them and prepared Crittenden for the struggle, and Hazen was discovered a trifle too far to the left, and was compelled to stand repeated assaults against his brigade, but Parsons's battery came up and responded sharply, soon relieving him.

Thomas was busy in the center; it had become quiet on the right, and the ominous silence along towards the left plainly indicated a decisive struggle.

Rosecrans first prepared for defensive operations, hoping the enemy would force the fight, estimating that the Confederates outnumbered him about 6,000 for the final struggle.

Bragg had found out his great mistake in supposing the Confederate army the best fighters, man for man, and he realized his only hope lay in the impetuosity of his men. He hurled a corps against Crittenden. They were hurled back with about equal loss. Then came every available man, thrown with all the grandeur in which human fiends can possibly assume the heroic form, but they met solid phalanx upon phalanx, and the crash was simply horribly grand and terrible. It was discipline against discipline. * * * * * *

It was the last day of the year; the sun was smiling upon this scene of carnage, as it went sailing away to the west, but it warmed the hearts of those Northmen, cut off, as they believed themselves to be, by the enemy's cavalry at Lavergne. Grasping their guns with a firmer grip, lightly weighing the cartridge pouch at their sides, and casting a hasty glance at the sun as a sight they never might see again, they met the onslaught unflinchingly. Above and around them five score cannon belched forth iron and smoke. Great furrows flew up amid the racked and bleeding masses. Gaps filled mechanically.

To face such a storm, mounted, one must surely lead a charmed life. Out of all those generals and staffs, with their escorts, it was remarkable so few lost their lives. Garesché, chief of staff, ever by the side of his general, lost his head, snuffed out as suddenly as a candle, and he was the second of Rosecrans's followers to whom "death came quick and pangless" on that field, and in the same horrible manner, but many others of the staff were hit and a few others were killed; while among the general officers, very few escaped unscathed.

It is not my purpose to dwell upon the horrors of that or any other battle field. It could not be pictured by pen or brush in all its realism.

The day waned slowly. Bragg again concentrated on the center. Again the artillery from their commanding position opened upon them, and the enemy's infantry would not come. Again upon the left, and the left stood firm; and the battle died away, as night, slowly, silently, pityingly, rung down her curtain upon the bloody scene, and Rosecrans was master of the field; yet the army retired to rest, as rest they might, with the fullest expectation of renewing the engagement upon the morrow. Troops had been thrown like a shuttlecock, from right to left, and from left to right, regardless of rear communications. "We will die right here, or we will win this battle," said Rosecrans, and his generals echoed, "Like men!" and there were no laggards. Many of our troops were short of rations; but there was never a murmur.

"We may have to eat parched corn, but we will stay by them," said Rosy. "We have enough ammunition for another battle," and preparations were made for the morrow. It was cold and very dismal; but they slept on their arms where they had fought. Some cut and broiled *horse* steaks, and others parched corn, and after midnight rain fell again. Long before day the troops were in line, ready for the onslaught. New lines were formed, and new plans adopted, but the day wore away with only demonstrations, and January 1st closed down with the two armies holding their own.

On the 2d the maneuvering continued, until Breckenridge with a strong corps moved solidly against the left. They were met with a terrific cannonade.

The lines break, and Davis, Carlin and Morton dash upon them, and the enemy are routed—leaving 2,000 upon the field, and again the old hero says, "We shall beat them!" Sunday passed with few demonstrations from the enemy, met promptly and with disaster to the Confederates, and before daylight Monday morning burial parties brought intelligence that the enemy had fled.

High mass was held that morning, and so, after seven days of heroic struggles and self denial, the army could rest. Our losses were:

KILLED.		WOUNDED.	
Officers......................	92	Officers..................	384
Enlisted men.................	1,441	Enlisted men.............	6,861
Prisoners...			3,000
Total loss...			11,778

The enemy's loss was not known, but as they were the assailants, it must have been much heavier than ours. They left only those they were compelled to and left *nothing* for them to eat. They buried many, but not all, and took with them all that were but slightly wounded.

Rosecrans marched in, and the fate of Bragg's army was sealed. It had been a fair, stand up fight in the open field, and Northern steadfastness had won the first victory of the war where neither numbers nor position were in our favor.

BIOGRAPHIES OF A FEW PROMINENT OFFICERS.

GORDON GRANGER.

The civil war in America developed few brighter military geniuses than General Gordon Granger, yet we have not, as a nation, begun to look upon him as among our heroes. He graduated from West Point in 1845, being sent there from New York, near Geneva, where he was born. He was about thirty-five or thirty-six at the breaking out of the war (the date of his birth is not at hand). He entered the army under General Scott, in Mexico, and served with honors at the battles of Vera Cruz, Cerro Gordo, Contreras, Cherubusco, Chapultepec and the City of Mexico, and was breveted first lieutenant for gallantry at Contreras and Cherubusco, and at Chapultepec was breveted captain for meritorious services.

At the breaking out of the rebellion he was mustering officer at Cincinnati, and soon after was with General Lyon at Wilson's Creek, Missouri, where Lyon was killed, and for courageous conduct was breveted major. At this time he was sent to St. Louis on some special duty and, while there, was appointed, by Governor Blair, of Michigan, colonel of the second Michigan cavalry, and his military genius soon asserted itself by many severe lessons to the volunteer officers and men of this regiment. He brought them up to the full standard of regulars within a period of three months.

Men of his stamp were needed then, and he never had the opportunity to take the regiment into a fight, but was given a star and placed in command of a brigade, then a division, and won the respect and admiration of nearly every man with whom he came in contact. Big, rough fellows, soldiers in the Second, who had carried logs and rode wooden horses, under the discipline of "Old Granger," as they called him, stood in silent awe as they first saw him under fire at New Madrid, giving his personal attention to the field pieces, shaking the dirt from his whiskers as a cannon ball buried him in a cloud of dust, and moving along the line unconcernedly. One of these same wooden horse heroes from the pine woods of Michigan was heard to exclaim, admiringly, "Bully for old Granger!"

He was Pope's right hand man and chief counselor during that short and brilliant campaign, and, with Pope, took the center of Halleck's army in front of Corinth.

After the evacuation and demoralization of Beauregard's army at that place, Granger was ordered to Cincinnati to command the department and the army of Kentucky, where he remained until after the battle of Stone River, when he joined Rosecrans, merging his army into the Army of the Cumberland, and held command of the right wing, which occupied, as an outpost, Franklin, until the grand forward movement to the southeast, through Tennessee, began, in 1863, and the right wing swung around the center, bearing the scattering fragments of Bragg's army back upon Chattanooga.

This corps was known there as the "reserve corps," consisting of three divisions—General Stanley (who had been transferred from the cavalry), General Steadman and General ———

Bragg withdrew from Chattanooga, and Granger slipped in, and with Steadman's division moved down to the front.

Rosecrans placed him on the left, ordering him to hold Thomas's extreme left, to look after Reed's bridge over the west fork of Chicamauga creek, and prevent any force from coming in on that flank that might attempt to get in our rear through Lafayette gap. That was Saturday. Taking up a position on a little ridge in front of McAfee's church, overlooking the valley and bridge in plain sight, they burned the bridge and lay there all night, expecting a severe engagement in their front next day. But, instead, Bragg hurled his best troops, with the veterans of Longstreet's army, from Richmond, against Thomas, expecting to crush him in the center and destroy the wings afterward.

Granger heard the fierce assaults and knew that Thomas needed him. He sent an aid to General Rosecrans and asked if he might not go to Thomas's assistance. The aid returned and could not find Rosecrans; his headquarters had been moved and the enemy was there. Granger sent again and again the third time; meantime he was chafing like a caged lion. At last he sent all his staff away and they dashed here and there, often riding to the thickest of the fight, knowing Rosecrans's disregard of personal safety. They returned to Granger at half past eleven in the morning, and all reported failure.

He was pacing up and down in front of the little church. His orders were imperative to hold the bridge at all hazards.

Should he disobey? He listened a moment, then paced, and looked, and the storm gathering upon his face was something terrible to behold. At last, turning to his chief of artillery, Colonel Thompson, he said, "I can't stand this any longer; we are needed over there," and immediately sent his staff in different directions. Soon General Steadman had two of his brigades, Whittaker's and Mitchell's, hurrying forward in the direction of the awful roar which they feared meant destruction to General Thomas.

Ed McCook's brigade remained to guard the passage of the bridge. The march to Thomas was made in short time, and they reached there none too soon. The enemy were pressing nearer and nearer in heavy lines, and the ridge which Thomas had held all day was apparently within the grasp of the enemy, when Granger, with Steadman, Whittaker and Mitchell, hurled their two brigades of fresh troops against the flanks of the enemy, and they recoiled with a shake like a discomfited bloodhound pack, and rallying again, the next onslaught was weaker, the defense stronger. The Confederates break; the Federals charge, and "that red field was won."

Reporting to General Thomas he was welcomed by a warm shake of the hand and—"Well, General, fifteen minutes more would have been too late."

General Granger is dead, but his staff (many of them) live to honor him and love his memory.

After Chicamauga he was placed in command of the fourth army corps, and as he was misrepresented by certain army officers, he was glad to be relieved and enter some other army, where the spirit of jealousy did not so seriously exist.

He went to Canby, at New Orleans, and took charge of the land forces co-operating with General Farragut against Mobile. Later he commanded the reorganized thirteenth army corps.

After the war closed and we had too many generals, Gordon Granger found himself Colonel of the twenty-fifth United States infantry, stationed at Santa Fe, New Mexico, where he died, and was removed to Lexington, Kentucky. There a handsome monument has been erected by his widow. He was breveted for meritorious services, at Mobile, as brigadier, and at Forts Gaines and Morgan as major-general, but he lacked the necessary influence at Washington, and, obedient to the last (a duty which amounted to religion with him), he dropped back to his rank of Colonel.

Taken all in all, Gordon Granger died with a good big account to his credit from his country.

An eye witness at Chicamauga says: "If Gordon Granger had never fought in another battle than Chicamauga, that one heroic act—disobeying orders (to stay at Rossville, or McAfee's church, until ordered up), at the risk of his military head and reputation, should stamp his name forever indelibly upon the hearts of a grateful people." Thomas was being surrounded. He could and did repel the assaults of Bragg's whole army, but his lion heart almost sunk within him as he saw the enemy pouring around his right under cover of a gorge. Every man and every gun was bathed in fire, smoke and blood, and must stand or fall where they stood—none could be spared to meet this new emergency—and then, O, Heaven! where was his commander, Rosecrans, and all the troops that ought to be within call? Must he surrender, or, continue the butchery?

Away to the left a cloud of dust, streaming banners, hurrying troops. Was it the enemy? Think of the suppressed agony of that grand old man as he nervously handed his glass to a staff officer and said: "My horse is unsteady—here, what do you see?" He could not make it out. Turning sharply to an officer, in a tone very unusual to him, he almost shouted; "What troops are those? Find out!" and he never took his eye from the point, though the roar on his right was as if the heavens were rent asunder and the earth trembled with earthquake shocks. At last he drops his arm, breathes a sigh as if the whole nation breathed through him, and his countenance changes, as lightning changes, from darkness to light. He saw and recognized the battle flag of Granger.

O, glorious Thomas and glorious Granger! His heart told him there was need of help, though the summons did not come, and he was there none too quick. Never waiting for orders he hurls his fresh troops upon the flanks of the assaulting foe, and Thomas is saved.

With all his gruff ways, Gordon Granger at times revealed a strong character for justice, truth and mercy.

A company commander, thinking himself and his men aggrieved, appealed to Colonel Granger. "All I ask is simple justice." And the reply came prompt and vigorous, "I will do what is right, though the heavens fall." An officer who deceived him, disregarding truth and promises, was put under arrest, charges preferred against him, and he would have been dismissed from the service promptly but for his humble apologies and appeals for mercy. Then the officer was released, and placed on duty again—a faithful and truthful subaltern ever after. Another, who disregarded the rules of the service as to sobriety, was promptly dismissed. A citizen who had been arrested on suspicion of prowling about camp at Franklin, Tennessee, to gain information useful to the enemy, was interceded for by a Union man, who represented that the man was mentally irresponsible, a victim of epilepsy. While the prisoner was being discussed, he sat not far away, leaning against a tree.

"Look, General!"

The man had fallen over, his arms flying wildly in spasms.

"Take him away, quick, I don't want him dying on my hands," and he got up and moved into his tent, out of sight. It has been hinted that it was, as the saying goes, "a put up job." But the General was undoubtedly glad of an excuse to send the man through the lines.

When Gordon Granger was assigned to the command of the second Michigan cavalry at Benton Barracks, St Louis, there was not much love for the man at first among the officers or privates. A strict disciplinarian, he had no patience with careless infringement of strict military orders, and his way of bringing volunteers to the same level with regulars was often made the subject of unfavorable comment. Our little Lieutenant-Colonel, as gallant an officer as ever "mounted a horse," was compelled to resign for the too common offense of intoxication, though he was an old soldier in the Crimea, and later in our war did good service as a lieutenant or captain in some other regiment.

But the Colonel met his match just once. A rough character (of company—Q—let us say) was taking care of his horse in the stable in his own peculiar way (good care enough, only *peculiar*) when the Colonel came "smelling around," without shoulder straps or other insignia of rank, and called out to "Charley" roughly, "What are you doing there?"

"None your d—— business."

"Do you know who I am?"

"No! nor I don't care a d——"

Without replying, Colonel Granger seized a piece of board and was about to "break up camp," when a fork was caught up and rushing at the Colonel, Charley drove him out of the stable. For a wonder the fellow was not arrested, and though Charley manifested no uneasiness about the matter, he insisted that he did not know who it was, but would have done the same in any event. "Let old Granger put on his shoulder straps if he wants to give any orders around here," was his only comment.

But later in the war the regiment thought much of him; in fact were proud of him.

LIEUTENANT-GENERAL P. H. SHERIDAN.

The stone that the builders reject not infrequently becomes the head of the corner, and Captain Phil Sheridan is an example in point. When the second and third regiments of Michigan cavalry were at Benton Barracks, St Louis, the Second chose Captain Gordon Granger for their Colonel from the regular army. Not to be outdone, the Third sent out a committee of officers to hunt up a regular army officer that in their judgment would *do* for their colonel. In their *smelling* around they found Captain Sheridan, of the quartermaster's department. He was of the opinion that the war would be over before he had a chance to get above a captaincy. His first appearance did not seem to impress the committee favorably, for they came back and reported, as their first day's work: "We found a little *red faced* Irishman down there that some of those regular officers would like to saddle on to us; but we don't think we want him." They selected a genteel, strict, band-box disciplinarian from West Point, with a good record as an organizer, and a better record for insisting upon all the details of drill, bright buttons and blacked shoes, than for *exceeding* his orders in the field. But the material of the Third was equal to any regiment in the field.

Colonel Phil Sheridan was not one of your cringing sort of men, and was ever ready to assert his rights, under every circumstance.

One day the regiment had occasion to halt by the roadside, and the Colonel was busy looking after certain affairs connected with the movement of the troops from Mississippi to Kentucky, when an officer came out of a house and, speaking from the veranda told some of the men to "Tell the commander of this cavalry to move on away from the front of my headquarters." The soldier reported the fact to Colonel Sheridan.

"Who is it?" says the Colonel.

"General Grant, I believe."

"Tell General Grant this is Sheridan's cavalry, and he says he will move when he gets a d— good ready!"

The soldier obeyed to the letter, but as nothing more was heard of it, it is presumed the General rather liked him for it, as he highly complimented Sheridan not long afterwards for certain military operations.

A horse pistol, even if it was a Colt revolver was not always supposed to be an accurate shooter; but Colonel Sheridan taught the boys one day that good shooting could be done with it, if they tried. A rattlesnake lay coiled up in a brush heap, with his head raised as if about to strike, when the Colonel decapitated him as slick as if cut with a knife.

At the outset Sheridan won the hearts of his soldiers by his thoughtful care of them. At the struggle with Chalmers, Booneville, Mississippi, July 1st, 1862, about forty had been wounded, more or less seriously (a large number for so small a handful engaged), and a number of the enemy wounded had also fallen into our hands and had received equal attention with our own men. It was near midnight when the surgeons had made all as comfortable as circumstances would permit, and were wrapping themselves in their blankets for a few hours of rest, when Colonel Sheridan came to the surgeons' quarters and inquired, in his quiet way, as to the condition and number of the wounded. "Can they be moved without injury to the men?"

"They can."

"It is quite possible that we may be attacked again in the morning, and it would be better for them to be away from the excitement, and if you think they can endure it have the ambulances at work at once, and take them to Rienzi. An escort will be ready to accompany you."

This was accomplished before morning, and the poor fellows breathed more freely as they felt they were not to be left to the tender mercies of an enemy.

Among the "immortal names that were not born to die" the present century has furnished none brighter for the pages of history than that of Sheridan.

This can be said without detracting, in the least, from the glorious records of other illustrious captains of the age. General Grant won fame by possessing a broad, comprehensive mind, coupled with stubborn tenacity, and cool executive ability, though lacking in that concentrative, quick, dashing force that characterized the great Napoleon. Grant's opinion of Sheridan was "one of the ablest generals of the day," and this, too at a time when Sheridan had scarce shed his regimental clothes. And before the country had begun to recognize him as anything more than a good division commander, he electrified all Christendom by his masterly achievements with whole army corps, wheeling into line as methodically as a small band of scouts might do, and crushing the finest Confederate army that had occupied the Shenandoah valley.

Not waiting for the results of an all day stand up slaughter, strategy and dash combined enabled him to hurl a fighting corps upon a vulnerable point in the rear and flank, and demoralization seized the enemy as victory followed fast upon the banners of the assailants.

The ability to command an army, and not forget the smaller details of flank movements, meeting surprises with surprise, is given to but few, and among that few General P. H. Sheridan will ever occupy a prominent place in history.

When the war begun, the subject of this sketch was only a little past the period of boyhood. He was born September 6th, 1831, in Perry county, Ohio, and was therefore not quite thirty years old in 1861. But he looked, every inch, the soldier that he was, with his broad shoulders, long, heavily set arms and trunk, though a little below the medium in hight, not so much so as he jokingly made himself appear sometimes.

As we watch his movements, quick, alert, decided, he suggests to the swordsman "a dangerous antagonist," and to the pistol shot a man of quick eye, steady nerve, and—well, look out! But when greeting friends his face wears a natural pleasant look that is very gratifying to his admirers, none of whom have yet been able to turn his head with their flattery, a very strong point.

Admiration for bravery is instinctive in the human breast. While no one doubted Sheridan's courage, he very seldom, while colonel of the Second, had opportunity for showing disregard of personal safety. We must therefore look to other qualities for his popularity among his officers and men. He was above any vain desire of exhibiting his courage to win esteem, but if he could win a battle by dividing his men and using strategy he looked upon it as saving his men and gaining time, and to think was to act—no "all summer" business about him. We see this strategy first developing itself at Booneville, Mississippi, where he defeated Chalmers, having 5,000 men, with less than 1,000, by sending a part to attack suddenly in the rear. And again, on a larger scale, when he made a feint in front of Early, at Fisher's Hill, firing away with musketry at "nothing" for half a day in front, while a strong force by a circuitous route struck him in the rear and "sent him whirling up the valley." And yet at each of those engagements we find him very careful of his men, his losses being comparatively trifling. He looked upon every officer, soldier and horse as holding certain important positions in the great problem of war, and his first duty to his country demanded the greatest possible return for the men and material intrusted to him; and first the officers and men were treated as human beings, possessed of like feelings and instincts as himself, and were never called upon to expose themselves needlessly, but avail themselves of every protection which nature threw in their way—a tree, fence, log, or, if neither presented itself, then load and fire from the ground. He could see nothing cowardly in that, nor anything especially deserving of commendation if a command stood up and fired in the open field where their comrades were falling all around them; better lie down, advance or retreat. And, so, men have learned to look upon him, not as a butcher, but as a man, a comrade, a soldier.

To a staff officer who had been riding hard all day: "Mr. ———, you're pretty tired, I expect, but I should like to know how Captain ——— is getting on in his scouting over on the right. Take a fresh horse if you go again." And again, as an aid came into his tent late at night, to report, he finds the General rolled in his blankets, but wide awake, a light burning and ready for business. He hears the report, and remarks simply: "That's good. Reach that bottle and a couple of glasses over there," his usual toast, "How;" the glasses clink, and the General joins the least of his staff in a social "night-cap."

His care for the faithful animals that bore him and his followers over many a hard trip and through many a victory was proverbial. If on the midnight march the horses needed easing up a bit, the men were dismounted and led their horses until ordered to mount; and if any crept into their saddles before the General did, they were sure to receive a shot from the General's vigorous English that brought them to their feet, at their horses' heads, tramping along in cowed silence. Yet, next day, if the humblest private sought the General's tent for some favor, his request was listened to with gravest consideration. And ever, when greeted by any member of his old regiment, after he had won a star, his hat was lifted with as much courtesy as if addressing an equal in rank. And always when cheered by the command he received their adulation with as much modesty as a woman.

In personal appearance he was not unlike President Lincoln's description of him. "A little brown fellow, with a large body, short legs, not enough neck to hang him, and arms long enough to scratch his ankles without stooping," yet no one who has seen him casually would remark anything unusual in his form. That he has an iron frame and a strong constitution that ought to prolong his days to a good old age is very plain to be seen; and in the minds of those who have studied his military genius most there rests a satisfied conviction that this nation has nothing to fear in having General Philip Henry Sheridan at the head of the United States army. "Long may he live to remain there," is the fervent wish of all his old comrades, and may he escape the hands of politicians that would make him President. We would sooner see him where he is.

MILITARY HISTORY. Cadet at the United States Military Academy, from July 1, 1848, to July 1, 1853, when he was graduated and promoted in the Army to Brevet Second Lieutenant of Infantry, July 1, 1853. Served: In garrison at Newport Barracks, Kentucky, from September 1853, to March, 1854; on frontier duty at Fort Duncan, La Pena and Turkey Creek, Texas, March, 1854, to March, 1855; in garrison at Fort Columbus, N. Y., June and July, 1855; Second Lieutenant, fourth infantry, November 22, 1854; on frontier duty duty escorting topographical party from Sacramento Valley, California, to Columbia River, Oregon, in August and September, 1855. Commanding detachment of dragoons in the Yakima expedition, October to December, 1855,—stationed at Fort Vancouver, Washington Territory, December, 1855, to March, 1856,—scouting against Indians in March, 1856,—engagement with Indians while defending the Cascades of the Columbia River, Washington Territory, April 28, 1856, (complimented for gallantry in this engagement by Lieutenant-General Scott, in Army Orders No. 14, of 1857,)—stationed at Grande Ronde Indian Reservation, Oregon, from April to July, 1856,—at Fort Hoskins, Oregon, August, 1856, to May, 1857, and at Fort Yamhill, Oregon, June, 1857, to September, 1861. First lieutenant, fourth infantry, March 1, 1861. Served during the rebellion of the seceding states, as captain thirteenth infantry, May 14, 1861. President of board for auditing claims at St. Louis, Missouri, in November and December, 1861. Served as chief quartermaster and chief commissary of the army of the southwest in the Pea Ridge campaign, from December 26, 1861, to March 12, 1862,—served in the Mississippi campaign from

April to September, 1862, as follows: Quartermaster of Major-General Halleck's headquarters on the advance to Corinth, Mississippi, in April and May, 1862.

Colonel second Michigan cavalry volunteers, May 25, 1862. Commanding second Michigan cavalry in the following operations: Expedition to and capture of Booneville, Mississippi, May 28th and 29th, 1862,—pursuit of rebels from Corinth to Baldwin, Mississippi, May 30th to June 8th, 1862; commanding regiment in engagements with the enemy at Booneville, Blackland, Donaldson's Cross-Roads and Baldwin. Commanding second brigade, cavalry division, army of the Mississippi, from June 11th, in the following operations: Battle of Booneville, Mississippi, July 1, 1862; expedition to Guntown, with flag of truce, July 10, 1862; expedition to and capture of Ripley, Mississippi, July 28, 1862; forced reconnaissance on enemy's lines, with engagement near Guntown, Mississippi, capturing prisoners and 300 animals, August 15, 1862, and engagement near Rienzi, Mississippi, August 26, 1862. Brigadier-General United States Volunteers, July 1, 1862, for battle of Booneville. Commanding third division, army of Kentucky, on the advance into Kentucky, in September 1862; commanding eleventh division third corps, army of the Ohio, in the battle of Chaplin Hills or Perryville, Kentucky, October 8, 1862, and on the march to the relief of Nashville, in October and November, 1862. Commanding the eleventh division, fourteenth army corps, the third division, right wing, fourteenth army corps, and the third division, twentieth army corps, army of the Cumberland, successively, in the Tennessee campaign from November, 1862, to September, 1863. Commanding the third division, twentieth army corps, in the battle of Stone River, or Murfreesboro, Tennessee, December 31, 1862, to January 3, 1863, (Major-General United States Volunteers, December 1862, to November 8, 1864, for battle of Murfreesboro) and in the following operations: Engagement at Eagleville, Tennessee, capturing train and prisoners, March, 1863,—in pursuit of rebels under General Van Dorn, from Franklin to Columbia, March, 1863; in the advance on Tullahoma, Tennessee, June 24th to July 4th, 1863, crossing the Cumberland mountains and Tennessee river, with engagements at Fairfield, Tennessee, June 27, 1863; capture of Winchester, Tennessee, July 3, 1863; engagement at Cowan station, July 3, 1863, and engagement at University (on the mountain top), July 4, 1863. In command of the third division, twentieth army corps, in the battle of Chicamauga, Tennessee, September 19 and 20, 1863; commanding the second division, fourth army corps, in the battle of Missionary Ridge, Tennessee, November 23d to 25th, 1863; in the operations around Chattanooga, Tennessee, September to December, 1863; and in the operations in east Tennessee, from December 1863, to March, 1864, and the action at Dandridge, Tennessee, January 17, 1864.

In general command of the cavalry corps, of the army of the Potomac, from April, 1864, to April, 1865. In immediate command of the cavalry corps, army of the Potomac, in the following battles and operations in the Richmond campaign, from April to August, 1864: The battles of the Wilderness, May 5th to 8th, 1864; the battle of Todd's Tavern, May 5, 1864; battle of the Furnaces, May 6, 1864; battle of Todd's Tavern, No. 2, May 7, 1864; capture of Spottsylvania court house

(Spottsylvania court house was captured on May 8, 1864, by General Wilson's division of cavalry, and held for two hours), May 8, 1864; expedition in rear of the rebel army, cutting the Virginia Central and Richmond & Fredericksburg railroads; action at Beaver Dam, May 10, 1864; battle of Yellow Tavern, May 11, 1864; battle of Meadow Bridges and Richmond, May 12, 1864; actions of Hanovertown and Tolopotomy creek, May 27, 1864; battle of Hawe's Shop, May 28, 1864; battle of Metadequin Creek, May 30, 1864; battle of Cold Harbor, May 31, and June 1, 1864; raid to Charlottesville and return to Jordan's point on the James river, June 7th to 28th, 1864, cutting the Virginia Central and Richmond & Fredericksburg railroads; battle of Trevillian Station, June 11, 1864; action of Mallory's ford cross-roads, June 12, 1864; action of Tunstall station, June 21, 1864; skirmish at St. Mary's church, June 24, 1864; action of Darbytown, July 28, 1864; and action of Lee's Mills, July 30, 1864. In command of the middle military division from August 7, 1864, to May 22, 1865, and in immediate command of the army of the Shenandoah, from August 4, 1864, to February 27, 1865, in the following battles and operations: Actions of Kernstown and Toll Gate, August 11, 1864; action of Kabletown, August 26, 1864; Smithfield crossing of the Opequan, August 29, 1864; action of Berryville, September 3, 1864; action of Opequan Creek, September 15, 1864; battle of the Opequan September 19, 1864; Brigadier-General U. S. Army, September 20, 1864, for battle of the Opequan; battle of Fisher's Hill, September 22, 1864; battle of Tom's Brook, October 9, 1864;

battle of Cedar Creek* (called Winchester), October 19, 1864, and engagement at Middletown, November 12, 1864; Major-General U. S. Army, November 8, 1864, for Shenandoah campaign. In command of the cavalry expedition from Winchester to Petersburg, February 27 to March 24, 1865, (known as "The Winchester Raid.") Destroying the James river and Kanawha canal, and cutting the Gordonsville & Lynchburg, Virginia Central and Richmond & Fredericksburg railroads and destroying many railroads, canal and river bridges and trestle-work, and capturing and destroying sixty canal boats, containing large quantities of rebel government property, consisting of ordnance and ordnance stores, clothing, camp and garrison equipage, commissary stores and medical supplies, and destroying hundreds of army wagons and ambulances and several factories, warehouses, tanneries, forges and workshops, used for the manufacture of and filled with military supplies of the description above enumerated, and capturing eighteen battle flags, sixteen hundred prisoners, and two thousand one hundred and forty-three horses and mules, and engaged with the enemy as follows: Action at Mount Crawford, March 1, 1865; battle of Waynesborough, March 2, 1865; engagements at North Anna Bridges and Ashland, March 14th and 15th, 1865. In general command of the cavalry, in the Richmond campaign of 1865, called also the Appomattox campaign, from March 25th to April 9th, 1865, with the following battles and operations: Commanding the cavalry corps, and in com-

---

*The thanks of Congress were tendered, February 9, 1865, to General Sheridan for the gallantry, military skill and courage, displayed in the brilliant series of victories achieved by his army in the valley of the Shenandoah, especially at Cedar Creek. Resolutions of thanks similar to that of Congress were also tendered to General Sheridan by the legislatures of New York, Rhode Island and other states.

mand in the battle of Dinwiddie court house, Virginia, March 31, 1865; commanding the forces (cavalry and infantry) in the battle of Five Forks, Virginia, April 1, 1865; and commanding the cavalry in the following engagements: Action at Scott's Corners, April 2, 1865; action at Amelia court house, April 4, 1864, and Jettersville, April 5, 1865, and commanding the forces (cavalry and infantry) in the battle of Sailor's Creek, April 6, 1865, and the cavalry in the combat of Farmville, April 7, 1865; battle of Appomattox depot, April 8th, and engagement in front of Appomattox court house, April 9, 1865,[†] and in numerous minor actions between February 27th and April 9th, 1865, and present in command of all the cavalry at the capitulation of the insurgent army (known as the army of Northern Virginia) under General Robert E. Lee, at Appomattox court house, Virginia, April 6, 1865. Marched in command of forces (cavalry and infantry) against the army of General Joseph E. Johnston, as far as South Boston, North Carolina, on the Dan river, April 24th to May 3d, 1865. In general command of the forces west of the Mississippi, May 17th to June 3d, 1865, and of the army organized for contemplated operations against the army of General E. Kirby Smith, who surrendered on the 28th of May, 1865. In command of the military division of the southwest, June 3d to July 17th, 1865, and of the army in Louisiana, Texas,

[†]During this engagement a white flag from the rebel lines arrived in front of the cavalry, the bearer requesting a suspension of hostilities pending negotiations with General Grant for the surrender of General Lee's forces. General Sheridan immediately rode to Appomattox court house, and there met General Gordon, who repeated the same request. General Sheridan replied that he thought it very strange that while General Lee was negotiating with General Grant for the surrender of his army, it should have made, that very morning, an attempt to break through his lines and make its escape, and therefore demanded some authorized assurance before he would suspend hostilities. This assurance was given by General Gordon, who said "there was no doubt of the surrender of General Lee's army." Hostilities were soon afterward suspended, and the surrender took place on the arrival of General Grant.

Florida, and Mississippi, and the army of observation on the Rio Grande until the troops composing these armies were mustered out of service.

In command of the military division of the Gulf, July 17, 1865, to August 15, 1866; in command of the department of the Gulf, August 15, 1866, to March 11, 1867; in command of the fifth military district (Louisiana and Texas), March 11th to September 5th, 1867; in command of the department of the Missouri, September 12, 1867, to March 16, 1869; conducting the winter campaign of 1868 and 1869, against hostile Indians, resulting in their defeat and surrender. Lieutenant-General U. S. Army March 4, 1869. Commanding military division of the Missouri (headquarters in Chicago), since March 16, 1869, Lieutenant-General of the Army, headquarters at Washington, D. C., since December 1, 1883. During the Franco-Prussian war of 1870, General Sheridan was in Europe, at the headquarters of the King of Prussia, and present at the battles of Gravelotte, Beaumont and Sedan, and afterwards at the headquarters of the German armies at Versailles, witnessing many engagements around Paris, during the siege.

SHERIDAN'S HORSE.

There have been so many statements made respecting "Sheridan's horse" that considerable time, and no little trouble and expense have been given to looking up the history of that remarkable animal. It is a matter of history that of all the staff and orderlies that set out with General Sheridan on his celebrated ride "from Winchester down" not one was able to keep up with him, and perhaps there may have entered, already, into the minds of some a wonder that the General should have been so favored in high bred horse-flesh.

"Here is the steed that saved the day
By carrying Sheridan into the fight
From Winchester—twenty miles away!"

The history of the horse as given by neighbors of the owner, is that a Canadian mare was brought into St Clair county, Michigan, *with foal*, and when foaled proved to be a thin, *rangy* black stud colt. The sire was known to be a full blooded fox-hunter and the dam was *three-quarters* fox-hunter, therefore the colt was near enough for all practical purposes a thoroughbred.

Captain Archibald P. Campbell raised a company of cavalry (K) for the Second, and the citizens of Port Huron presented him with a horse—the black colt, then three years past (1861). Captain Campbell was not accustomed to horseback riding, and the colt was too fiery for him. In fact, Campbell was afraid of him, and very seldom rode him, but turned him over to the company farrier, who, on Colonel Sheridan's taking command of the regiment, had the old farrier—John Ashley—detailed as his headquarters farrier. Ashley took the black colt with him, and about the time of Colonel Sheridan's winning his first star, the horse began to develop into a well rounded out, magnificent animal. Sheridan liked the horse, and Campbell, then a Colonel, liked Sheridan, and so the horse was given to the General, and was the pride of the division, corps or army over whose destinies the master so fearlessly wielded rein, spurs and saber.

If we stop to reflect upon "what might have been," had the horse lagged or fallen by the wayside, who shall say that this country does not owe that animal a big debt of gratitude?

GENERAL STANLEY.

"Gay old Stanley," as his associates loved to call him, was a young man. His record began at Corinth, under Grant, where he commanded a division in that severe engagement, the Second Corinth, and won distinction by the brilliancy of his movements.

He was considered by many as the best cavalry officer of his day. He graduated from West Point in 1852, and served with the second United States dragoons.

General David S. Stanley was immensely popular with all who were intimately acquainted with him, but his nature was retired, and he was not given to crowding himself forward nor mingling with his troops in that familiar way, sometimes common with officers who courted popularity; consequently he was not well known, and his continued ill health during the last year of the war was a great disappointment to him. When he took command of Rosecrans's cavalry, in October, 1862, there were but about 3,000 mounted men in that army and of these there were not to exceed 1,500 well disciplined cavalrymen. But, under his management he had the satisfaction of commanding 16,000 as good cavalry as the army could boast when the forward movement from Murfreesboro began in June, 1863. It was often remarked at the time, that, had Stanley been at the head of his command at Chicamauga, the cavalry would have had other duty than guarding flanks—a very important and hazardous duty, but they were not all needed for that service. Had Stanley been there to have sent half of them to the enemy's rear, as he undoubtedly would have done, when Thomas was in such sore straits, or to have attacked the enemy in front of Thomas, in the flanks, that General would not have lost so heavily, nor have been so terribly pressed on all sides. But, unfortunately for Stanley and the country, each brigade of cavalry was thrown on its own resources, and was not kept informed of the movements of the infantry, and poor Stanley, flat upon his back at Stevenson, Alabama, lost the grandest opportunity of his life.

And, so, discouraged from undertaking further the arduous duties of a chief of cavalry, he accepted an infantry corps, and passed the remaining days of his active service as best he could with the fourth corps, and at the end of the war dropped back to his colonelcy in the regular army. But he has the best wishes of every officer and private who ever knew him. He earned his star in the regular army long ago.

GENERAL WILSON.

Major-General James H. Wilson, of cavalry fame, came upon the military horizon of the Western army at a time when (no matter how brilliantly flashed the career before the eyes of a grateful, yet exacting nation), he was constantly hampered by a lack of appreciation of that branch of service, even among military men. If a commander of infantry suddenly found himself surrounded with more men than he knew what to do with, and a few supporting regiments of cavalry chanced to be hanging on his rear or brushing away the *obstructions* from his front, he treated them about as the railroad contractor treats his pioneer corps—gives them an ax and a bundle of hay and sends them on.

General Stanley had the real military genius for handling cavalry, but unfortunately for him and his country he was a sufferer from ill health and dropped back to the less arduous duties of an infantry corps commander.

General Wilson had filled every position assigned to him with credit, and his abilities had attracted the attention of General Geo. H. Thomas, during the Tennessee campaign, and he enjoyed the confidence of that distinguished general to a degree that was alone sufficient guarantee of General Wilson's ability. Yet General Wilson was never left free to act as he thought proper when with infantry commanders, whose commission happened to bear an older date, but was ordered to send a brigade here and there--in fact, was expected to be omnipresent, yet never allowed to strike in full force where the nature of the country permitted such action, and if mistakes occurred Wilson and his cavalry were made the scapegoats, not by General Thomas, but by generals who had no confidence in cavalry.

This is not written as an apology for General Wilson. He needs none. But as an urgent reminder that General Wilson and his cavalry should long ago have received at the hands of the truthful historian a more careful hearing and a more generous appreciation.

While it is true the cavalry force of the army of the Cumberland was small in numbers, and mostly thrown together in brigades not always well balanced in point of discipline and thorough organization, yet the hard duties and heroic struggles at different periods of that campaign, compel the acknowledgment that Wilson's management of the cavalry corps was masterly, and that the results obtained were all that could have been expected. His placing of Croxton's brigade at a point where the enemy had the greatest hope of forcing a breach, at Franklin, and doubling back upon the center, Schofield's left wing, was a wise move, and his disposition of the other brigades upon the extreme flanks, fully justified General Thomas's reliance in the ability of his chief of cavalry.

General Wilson has been censured by General Schofield for crossing his entire force to the north bank of the Harpeth. But without orders from Schofield it is difficult to see what other course he should have pursued just at that moment when the infantry were behind earthworks and the rear was—who could say whether or not?—open to the enemy, whose cavalry at that moment had been retired from the front and might naturally be expected in our rear, as at Columbia and Florence. The rear was picketed and scouted, and reporting for orders Wilson was sent back across the Harpeth; but Wilson knew his duties quite as well as his superior, and sending his best known brigade to hold the approaches to the left flank on the Harpeth, the rest of the corps was placed at the weakest points up and down the river, and their positions proved not merely points of observation but battle grounds over which some of the fiercest struggles of the day were witnessed. And again at Nashville, what more could have been expected? The left flank of Hood's army was turned by Wilson's cavalry, and when the final blow came, half of Wilson's cavalry, under dashing Edward Hatch, were among the first to clear the earthworks, and, joined by the other half from the extreme right, were by General Hatch hurled upon the broken ranks of the enemy and captured more prisoners than Hatch's own numbers.

From that time on, whatever was done, was for the most part the work of the cavalry, and Wilson was the head. The raid through Alabama was a death blow to the Confederate hopes in that quarter, and the last battles of the war were fought by Wilson's troops. Forrest, Wirt Adams, Hill and Jeff Davis himself received their quietus from "Wilson's raiders," and Hatch, Long, Lagrange and Croxton were his able lieutenants.

The following is the military record of James H. Wilson, and it will be seen that he was among the youngest of our officers. In fact, he was so young that his age was looked upon by some of the older heads as an objection to his being appointed to so important a command as the cavalry corps, army of the Cumberland. But General George H. Thomas was not given to making mistakes:

James H. Wilson, born September 2, 1837, in Gallatin county, Illinois.

MILITARY HISTORY. Cadet at the United States Military Academy from July 1, 1855, to July 1, 1860, when he was graduated and promoted in the army to brevet second lieutenant topographical engineers, July 1, 1860, served as assistant topographical engineer at the headquarters of the department of Oregon, October 3d, 1860, to July 14, 1861.

Served during the rebellion of the seceding states, 1861–66: On recruiting second lieutenant topographical engineers, June 10, 1861, service for topographical engineer company, September 3 to October 14, 1861; as chief topographical (first lieutenant, topographical engineers, September 9, 1861,) engineer of the Port Royal expeditionary corps, October 14, 1861, to March 15, 1862, and of the department of the south, March 15 to

August 19, 1862, being engaged in various reconnaissances and explorations, and siege of Fort Pulaski, Georgia, February-April, 1862, including its bombardment and surrender, April 10-11, 1862; in the Maryland campaign as acting aid-de-camp to (brevet major, April 11, 1862, for gallant and meritorious services at the capture of Fort Pulaski, Georgia,) Major-General McClellan, commanding the army of the Potomac, September-October, 1862, being engaged in the battle of South Mountain, September 14, 1862; and battle of Antietam, September 16, 1862; as chief topographical engineer of the army of the Tennessee, October 17, 1862, to March 3, 1863, being engaged in Major-General Grant's flank movement to Oxford, Mississippi, November-December, 1862; as assistant engineer (lieutenant colonel staff, United States volunteers, November 8, 1862, to October 31, 1863,) and inspector-general of the army of the Tennessee in the Vicksburg campaign, March 3 to October 31, 1863, being engaged in the attempt to turn Vicksburg by Moon Lake and the Yazoo Pass, March 25-April 20, 1863; advance to Bruinsburg, April, 1863; battle of Port Gibson, May 1, 1863; in bridging the Bayou Pierre, May 3, 1863; action of Jackson, May 14, 1863; battle of Champion Hill (captain corps of engineers, May 7, 1863), May 16, 1863; combat of the Big Black, May 17, 1863, and siege of Vicksburg, May 22-July 4, 1863; in engineer operations about Chattanooga and on expedition to East Tennessee, October 31, 1863, to February 1, 1864, (brigadier-general United States volunteers, October 31, 1863,) being engaged in the battle of Missionary Ridge, November 23-25, 1863, (brevet lieutenant-colonel, November 24, 1863, for gallant and meritorious services at the battle of Chattanooga, Tennessee); pursuit of the enemy November 26-27, 1863, and march to the relief of Knoxville, November 28 to December 4th, 1863; constructing several bridges, particularly a trestle over the Little Tennessee, made in thirty-two hours from dismantled houses; in charge of the cavalry bureau at Washington, D. C., February 17, to April 7, 1864; in the Richmond campaign, in command of third cavalry division, army of the Potomac, May 4 to August 1, 1864, being engaged in the action of Craig's meeting house, May 5, 1864; capture of Spottsylvania C. H., May 8, 1864; (brevet colonel May 5, 1864, for gallant and meritorious services at the battle of the Wilderness), "Sheridan's raid" to Haxall's Landing and returning to New Castle, May 9-29, 1864, cutting the Virginia Central railroad; action of Beaver Dam, May 9-10, 1864; battle of Yellow Tavern, May 11, 1864; combat of Meadow Bridge, May 12, 1864; action of Mechump's Creek, May 31, 1864; action of Hawe's Shop, June 2, 1864; action of Tolopotomy, June 2, 1864; skirmish of Long Bridge, June 12, 1864, and of White Oak Swamp June 13, 1864; raid to destroy the Danville & South Side railroad, June 20-30, 1864; participating in the action of Nottoway court house, June 23, and Roanoke Station, June 25, and combat of Stony Creek, June 29, 1864; and cavalry operations about Petersburg, July, 1864; in command of third cavalry division in the Shenandoah campaign, August 4 to September 30, 1864; engaged in the action of Summit Point August 21, 1864; battle of Opequan, September 19, 1864; and pursuit of the enemy, September 20-27, 1864; in command of cavalry corps of the military division of the Mississippi, October 24, 1864, to (brevet major-general, United States volunteers, October 5, 1864, for gallant and meritorious services during the rebellion) July 28, 1865; in Major-General Thomas's Tennessee campaign, November–December, 1864, being engaged in driving the rebel cavalry across the Harpeth river during the battle of Franklin, November 30, 1864; battle of Nashville, December 15–16, 1864, and pursuit of General Hood to the Tennessee river, December, 1864; (brevet brigadier-general United States army, March 13, 1865, for gallant and meritorious services at the battle of Nashville, Tennessee,) in command of cavalry expedition into Alabama and Georgia, March 2–22 to April 20, 1865, being engaged in the action of Ebenezer Church, April 1, 1865; assault and capture of Selma, with large numbers of prisoners and stores (brevet major-general, United States army, March 13, 1865, for gallant and meritorious services in the capture of Selma, Alabama), April 2, 1865; surrender of Montgomery, April 12, 1865; capture of Columbus, with great supplies and military establishments, April 16, 1865; capitulation of Macon, April 20, 1865, having in this brief campaign of twenty-eight days (major-general United States volunteers, April 20, 1865,) captured five fortified cities, twenty-three stand of colors, 288 guns, and 6,820 prisoners, and finally on May 10, 1865, adding Jefferson Davis, the rebel president, to the captures made by a detachment of his forces; in command of the department of Georgia, July 28 to October 7, 1865; and of district of Columbus, October 7, 1865, to January 8, 1866; on leave of absence, December 19, 1865, to (mustered out of volunteer service, January 8, 1866,) April 26, 1866; as assistant engineer on the defenses of the Delaware river and bay, April 26 to July 31, 1866; as superintending engineer of the survey of (lieutenant-colonel, thirty-fifth infantry, July 28, 1866,) Rock and

Illinois rivers, July 31, 1866, to December 31, 1870, and of improvement of Des Moines and Illinois rapids of the Mississippi, August 3, 1866, to December 31, 1870.

GENERAL ROBERT H. G. MINTY.

Although General Minty was better known as colonel of the fourth Michigan cavalry, the fact that he was, during the period of our organization, senior major of the second Michigan cavalry, and still refers with pride to his connection with the Second, warrants us in claiming him as a member of the Second.

He was a popular officer, wherever he served, and though his stars were won long before he was breveted major-general of volunteers, recognition of his valuable services came very tardily. Had it not been so, the movements of the cavalry belonging to the army of the Cumberland would undoubtedly have attracted more attention, and the blows struck by that arm of the service would have been more decided in their effect. Until the last six months of the war, the moment an officer developed any special fitness as a cavalry commander he was wanted elsewhere.

Had Colonel Minty been made a brigadier from the moment of his first success as a brigade commander in the Tennessee campaign, he would have been in a position at Chicamauga, by his rank, to have struck a blow with the cavalry that would have changed the map of that fierce struggle, from a position of defense and dread uncertainty to one of bold offensiveness, unless deprived of power by too much interference from his superiors.

Whatever may have been the abilities of the corps and division commanders of cavalry, it was evident that Rosecrans lacked confidence in his acting chief of cavalry, and he was practically ignored.

Without following Colonel Minty in his career as senior major of the Second, lieutenant-colonel of the Third, and colonel of the Fourth, it is not saying too much to assert that in whatever position he was placed, every duty was discharged with ability, courage and fidelity.

At Stone River, Shelbyville, and the movements in Tennessee, he was everywhere the active leader, prompt in carrying out the orders of his superiors, and always struck the enemy in their weakest points.

At Chicamauga his services on our left gave timely warning of Bragg's plans against Chattanooga, and without his services in the vicinity of Reed's Bridge and towards Ringgold, Rosecrans's army would never have had the road to Chattanooga open to him after the morning of the 19th of September.

And more than that ; officers of Minty's brigade have asserted, that, had Rosecrans listened to Minty when first the news of large bodies of troops concentrating on the left was brought to his notice, Rosecrans's army would have had plenty of time to concentrate nearer Chattanooga, and fought at a greater advantage, with less loss to our army.

And that statement was undoubtedly true. For two days previous to the battle of the 19th and 20th, Minty and Wilder, each with a brigade of as good men as were ever seen in any army, had had frequent severe skirmishes with the enemy, thirty to forty miles from Rosecrans's right, and the opportunities for observation were certainly better than any other which Rosecrans had at his command, and yet the reports that were frequently sent in to headquarters of large numbers of the enemy "moving from the northeast, east and southeast towards Chattanooga" were apparently ignored.

Though Minty lived to see his statements borne out by later developments, it was poor satisfaction for him, and did not atone for the blunders of that campaign, or the lives that might have been saved.

In the movements which followed to the close of the war Minty figured actively, and at last was breveted brigadier-general, and at the taking of Selma was among the first to scale the works, and was then breveted major-general. He figured conspicuously in the grand closing up scenes of the rebellion with Wilson, Hatch, Croxton and Long.

Since the war General Minty has been prominently connected with railroad affairs, and is at this writing with the Union Pacific.

INCIDENTS CONNECTED WITH OUR IMMEDIATE SERVICE.

CROXTON'S BRIGADE.

[*Correspondence Chicago Paper, November*, 1864.]

I have witnessed many fields of desperate strife during the rebellion, but among these sanguinary contests, I have never seen anything that would compare with the cool, stubborn and unflinching stand made by the second Michigan cavalry, on the 30th of November, in the beechwood forest, about four miles from the town of Franklin. This regiment is armed with the Spencer carbine, a seven-shooter, regarded as being the most effective cavalry arm in the service, and the regiment is known as a part of the dashing brigade of General Croxton, of Kentucky. Along the Lewisburg pike-road, leading to Franklin, it was learned that three brigades of the enemy's cavalry were moving with the view of striking the town of Franklin upon the left, at the moment that Hood, with his entire army, should be engaged in an attack on our front and right, and it was across this road that the second Michigan, with instructions to hold the enemy in check, formed.

its line of battle. The regiment numbered about 450 men. The Confederate cavalry was composed of Texas, Georgia and Louisiana cavalry, under the command of General Forrest, who was recognized as the ablest Confederate cavalry officer in the service. We were standing on an elevation, a little to the rear and left of this Michigan regiment, which gave us a full and complete view of the battle. We saw them slide from their saddles and rush forward a few rods to the acclivity of a gentle slope that shielded their horses from the fire of the enemy, and here they fell upon their faces, hugging the ground so closely that it was almost impossible for the enemy to see them, while their commander, Lieutenant-Colonel Smith, seated

LIEUTENANT-COLONEL BENJAMIN SMITH.

upon a log in close proximity to his crouching line, with his bridle rein strung upon his arm, seemed to be engaged in trying to light his pipe. Through the woods, along their front, as far as the eye could reach, nothing was to be seen but the heavy gray columns of the enemy moving slowly but confidently forward. Presently they halted, when a column of Louisiana cavalry, apparently about 2,000 strong, swung round by the left, dismounted, and forming in line of battle, came rushing forward, pouring from their Enfield rifles volley after volley, while the woods resounded with the wild scream of the Texas ranger. Turning our face for a moment to the right we discovered General Croxton sitting upon his horse a few feet from us, with one leg thrown over the pommel of his saddle, looking at the scene. Thinking that he had not seen the heavy line of the enemy that was now moving up, and partially hid from view by an undulating swell of the ground, we exclaimed, "General, those men will be annihilated." Turning his head slowly toward us and taking us to be a resident of the country, he observed, "Don't be alarmed, my Tennessee friend, those are my whitefish boys; you'll hear them speak in a minute or two." He had scarcely finished speaking when Michigan arose to her knees, and, in that praying position poured into the enemy a sheet of fire which could be hurled from no other arm than the Spencer carbine. For a full minute an incessant stream of fire poured from the muzzles of those carbines, drifting upon the heavy columns of the enemy a sheety spray of lead, such as no human power could resist, halting, then staggering the advance. The line wavered for a moment, and then, under a rallying shout, it bounded forward a few feet against the storm of leaden hail. Again it halted, broke and fled. For nearly two hours column after column was hurled upon that Michigan regiment, and each in its turn was driven back with terrible slaughter. At length there was a pause; silence broken only by the fitful rustling of the forest leaf. In the distance the enemy could be seen dismounting and massing columns for another charge—one that would trample beneath its feet the power that had so stubbornly resisted their advance. We turned to point them out to General Croxton, but he was gone. Onward came that black mass of the enemy, flaunting their banners with maddened desperation, and again did Michigan empty her carbines. Then came the ringing shout of their commander: "Up, Michigan, right about, double quick, mount." Now was the moment of peril—the moment of danger. Not less than four thousand rifles were ready to sweep away the line when it rose from its leafy couch, but at the very instant that the command was given to fall back, the eighth Iowa cavalry, under the command of Colonel Dorr, dashed through a thicket and struck the enemy upon the right flank with an enfilading fire that rolled it up into a mass of confusion. Amazed and bewildered, the rebels directed their glance for a moment in the direction of this unexpected attack, and in that moment Michigan was in the saddle and all was safe.

AT FRANKLIN—MRS. SNYDER'S ACCOUNT.

One of the most interesting accounts of the desperate battle of Franklin that has been given the writer was related after eighteen years by a lady who was present—the young wife of a railroad engineer—a Mrs. Carrie Snyder, at this writing a resident of Indianapolis.

When it is remembered that the battle did not begin until after three o'clock of the afternoon of November 30, and therefore could not have lasted more than three or four hours, and in that time nearly 8,000 men were placed *hors de combat*, many of them having fought their last battle, it will at once be seen that its desperateness was unexcelled by any other battle of the war.

General Hood, in his "Advance and Retreat," takes occasion to anathematize General Sherman for firing upon Atlanta, ordering the people out of the city, etc., and says, in speaking of the battle of Franklin, in substance: "The enemy took refuge in the town where he knew we could not or *would not* use our artillery against him," intimating thereby that he (Hood) did not use any artillery in that engagement.

Every Federal soldier knows this is absurd, and anyone visiting the town after the battle could plainly trace the course of solid shot and shell through dwellings, cutting wooden pillars, with the slivers plainly showing that the shots came from the south, and were fired *at* our army, *at* the town. And it is well known that Fort Granger was high enough above the town to enable our gunners to fire over, and that what little field of artillery the Federals used stood either on the bluff overlooking the city, or at the front, south of the city, and could not therefore have been *toward* the city.

General Schofield would not have taken up his position at the south of Franklin had he not been compelled to or abandon all his trains, ambulances, sick, etc., together with all his artillery, and probably the greater part of his army would have been captured before they could have crossed the Harpeth if they had not turned at bay; therefore Schofield did the only thing he could have done, fight, without regard to the possible destruction of a little city of three or four thousand—mostly of very doubtful loyalty.

Mrs. Snyder heard the first shot, and as it came crashing through the town near where she stood on the porch, and killed a Federal on the common near the house, she could not be mistaken.

"I had been sitting on the back porch playing at backgammon with Mrs. Rainney, as was our custom after dinner. A few shots from the infantry had been heard; then, as it became quiet, I began to think there would be no fight after all. Young and foolish thing that I was, I began to *fear* there would be no fight. I wanted to see a battle, or hear one; but I got enough of it, sooner than I expected. We kept on playing backgammon until about three o'clock, then the firing began to get thicker and sounded more like a snapping roar than anything I could otherwise describe. We got up and walked about the house and yard; bullets occasionally whistled over our heads, We did not fear them much if we had the brick house between us, but presently a cannon ball or shell came screeching over the house from the Confederate side. I think I *grew short* quicker than anything you ever saw. Oh—my! but I just thought I was hit sure. What did I do? Well you'd better believe I got down low and wasn't long in following the old folks into the cellar. Then the noise began in dead earnest. I hadn't *seen* anything, but I had heard more than I wanted to. I wanted them to quit right off, but they wouldn't; they just kept up a roar, and rumble, and screeching that fairly stopped my heart from beating. We thought, down there in that cellar, that a shell would come through those walls, explode inside of the house and blow us all into 'Kingdom come,' the next minute. Just think of us three women and one old man curled up on that coal bin, in that dark cellar, from four o'clock in the afternoon until four o'clock in the morning—no light, no fire, no sleep, and the old lady bewailing the fact that we had not caught up some bedding and brought down with us. She thought more of those old quilts than she appeared to think of our lives and wanted us to go up stairs and get them. Not much. There had been rumors among the special friends of the Confederates that if the Federals fell back they had said they would burn Franklin. There was a young lady of our party whose friends were in the Southern army and she had given this report circulation. Suddenly a bright light turned darkness into day and her fears were apparently about to be realized. 'Fire!' she screamed. There, what did I tell you? Now we've escaped the battle to be burned alive in this horrid old cellar. Oh, my God, what will become of us!'

"It seems the Federal army had thought best to keep up the appearance of fright or great haste in their evacuation (for Schofield evidently intended to draw Hood on to Nashville), and had set fire to the government stables, in which there was nothing left but a few tons of hay and some worthless saddles, harness, etc. That was the only building destroyed, unless by accident, or if in the way.

"Then the firing had entirely ceased and steps were heard over head, and Mr. R., lifting the trap door, calls out 'Who's there—friends?' We went up out of our dismal prison, with limbs cramped, and fairly shaking, as in fact we had been all night, and Confederate soldiers told us they 'had the town, and the *Yanks* are gone.' So we began to move about more freely, but what do you suppose were my feelings as I thought I was among the enemy, cut off; did not know where my husband was nor how long I must remain where I felt that I must keep my mouth shut and no sympathizing ear to pour my troubles into?

"Well, in the morning we went out upon the battle field, and O, horror upon horrors! what a sight. God forgive me for ever wishing to see or hear a battle. They said that beside the wounded the Federals had carried away in their ambulances, there were over 6,000 dead and wounded soldiers—blue and gray—all mixed up together; you had to look twice as you picked your way among the bodies to see which were dead and which were alive and often a dead man would be lying partly on a live one, or the reverse—and the groans; the sickening smell of blood! That sight and the sounds I then heard were with me in my dreams for months, startling me with their horrid nightmare vision. I noticed while wandering along the earthworks that all or nearly all of the Union soldiers were shot in the foreheads, and I think any general that would order men to march across such an open field to drive men, protected by such an earthwork as that, must have been a heartless wretch. They came up in the very worst place they could have come, for them (the Confederates) and ought to have known what the result would have been. There were twelve or thirteen of Hood's best generals dead on the Union breastworks, and in front the ground was covered with bodies, and pools of blood that it was no fiction to call 'fields of gore.' The cotton in the old cotton gin was shot out all over the ground and looked as if it had been scattered there by some designing hand, and the small grove of locusts to the right of the Carter's creek pike was cut off by bullets as clean as if cut by a knife. Mr. Carter's son (a Confederate soldier) was found dead in his own father's yard next morning. The family had stayed in the cellar all through the fight, and all night. Our soldiers had all been stripped of everything but their shirts and drawers; but the Confederate soldiers could not be blamed much for that, for they were half clothed, half barefoot and many of them bareheaded; but I saw one thing I thought contemptible. A fine looking Union soldier had been stripped of all but his shirt and drawers. He was lying off by himself at the roadside near the depot. He was apparently an officer. His shirt was fine flannel. 'H'yar,' says a big Confederate, calling to some of his men—'boys, h'yar's a mighty fine shut on this ere dead Yank' (giving him a kick). I thought it was bad enough to strip him of hat, coat, pants, boots and socks; they might at least give him a single garment to bury him in. When I went past one of their hospitals there were several wagon loads of limbs in a pile that had been amputated.

"It was several days before they knew that I was a northern woman, but when they did they seemed to respect my helpless condition and treated me kindly. And I shall never forget one of the men, a nurse and cook for the wounded—a Mr. Hicks, from Mississippi. He had no confidence in Hood's forward movement, and tried to comfort me as we walked among the flowers, and talked in whispered words. 'Be comforted,' said he; 'it is only for a few days, and you will be among your friends again. This cannot last.' And sure enough, sooner than I thought, the fierce cannonading eighteen miles away, at Nashville, told me that something would happen soon. I overheard an officer say, 'We are going to cut the bridge.' Then I knew that the Confederates were falling back. And there they came. Barefoot; bareheaded; half of them without guns; running; and as the rear guard of the Confederates passed through and scattering shots were heard, I jumped to my feet and went out. I could stand it no longer. Among the first men to enter town were some railroad men that I knew, and I rushed out and caught them in my arms. I was a prisoner no longer. I expect I acted like a crazy woman. But do you wonder at it?"

WHAT SERGEANT MOODY SAYS.

Sergeant W. D. Moody, of company E, remembers vividly the battle of Franklin and corrects a statement made elsewhere that our forces abandoned Franklin and its approaches by twelve or even three o'clock A. M. He says: "Our company, E, second Michigan cavalry, was stationed along the bank of the river from Fort Granger, south to the stone abutments of the old burnt bridge, east of the city. The banks along on the east side, you remember, were high—perhaps thirty feet, and the opposite banks between the river and the railroad were low, rising gradually from the water's edge. As we stood there or marched quietly up and down along the bank, the Johnnies came down on the other side, built fires, got water from the river, gathered around the fires, cooked, chatted and talked about the 'Yanks,' polishing them off occasionally in good style, and the wags of the crowds making some good hits, and some expressions that sounded very droll to us northerners. We could have pitched a biscuit among them or "murdered" numbers of them, for the stream was narrow just there, though deep, forming a barrier that no one cared to cross. But they were not apparently aware of our presence, though we made no special effort to conceal the fact. During the night we heard a noise at our left and a few of us went to reconnoiter. We came down to the ford where we had such a warm brush in the afternoon, and stopping on low ground, we could count against the sky until fifty mounted men had passed down the bank and over the ford to the Confederate side. What did this mean? Surely there should be no Confederates on our side at that hour; and where were our pickets that should be further to the left? We reported to General Croxton. Inquiry revealed the fact that a company of cavalry from a comparatively new regiment had been sent to our left; but where were they? A search was made and the bold soldiers were found at least a quarter of a mile back of the ford, in camp, asleep, and no pickets out. The captain was put under arrest (he might have been shot according to strict military rules), and the company, after a sharp reprimand and fright, were sent to the ford, and a sergeant's squad of some older regiment sent to assist them. The company of Confederates were supposed to belong to a party that were driven back and cut off by General Long, on the extreme left, in the afternoon. At sunrise I was standing by the stone abutments when some Confederates again came down to the water to wash and make coffee, when they discovered us for the first time. They were staggered a little at first, but as they saw we sat on the stones with our guns in our laps, not offering to shoot, they took in the situation, cooled down and said—'Hello, boys!'

"'Hello!'

"'What you doing there? thought you had skedaddled.'

"'O no, we are guarding this ford and stream.'

"'Been there all night?'

"'Yes; our command is close by, just over the hill.'

"But in less than five minutes we were ordered away and as we joined the rear guard, a quarter of a mile back, we saw the Confederate advance guard, mounted, come up where we had stood, and watch our movements, but not apparently caring to push us."

A DYING CONFEDERATE'S STORY.

A pitiful voice was heard outside the breastworks after dark at Franklin, calling: "For the love of God help me; roll this horse off me." Our men had their hands full with calls upon their sympathy, but at last one said, "I can't stand that any longer, I am going out there and see if I can help that poor devil." He found him badly wounded, a Major Knox, of the eighth Tennessee (Confederate), and he was pinioned to the earth by his fallen horse. The horse was rolled off, regardless of the desultory firing all along the line, and the Major brought inside our line and made as comfortable as possible, with stray blankets, of which there were many. A cup of water revived him and he became communicative. He said, "I can't live till morning, and I don't mind saying to you that our boys have been greatly deceived as to the kind of forces here. There has been some kind of a quarrel or division among our officers. Last night General Hood called in all the regimental commanders to headquarters. I was one of them, and he said, 'There are eight or ten thousand Yankee conscripts down there by the river. Go, take them; they are yours, and after that we have only to walk into Nashville and take possession of all the vast stores that have been accumulating so long.' * * * * "My God!" said the dying Major, "if Yankee conscripts fight like this, what may we expect from Thomas's veterans?"

A HORRID SCENE.

Under the above heading a southern paper, *The Meridian Clarion*, published an account of the night of horrors on the battle field of Franklin, written by a Confederate artilleryman. If true, it certainly does not speak well for Mr. Hood's humanity; for no good general would ever permit so grave an offense to escape his notice and immediate disapproval. There was plenty of time for the removal of all helpless heroes of both armies that had offered up their lives for a principle.

"That was a horrid scene, on the night of the battle of Franklin, at ten o'clock, when our battery came upon the field and was ordered to a point near the enemy's (the Federal) works. With horses at full speed, the twelve pounder Napoleons, with their heavy carriages, were hurried over the bodies of the wounded and slain. Skulls and bones were crushed and horses' hoofs planted in faces and breasts of the helpless fallen and dead. Agonizing shrieks came up on every hand. The poor wretches shrieked in vain; and then, when the trenches were reached, what a scene! The dead and wounded filled the ditch and wounded soldiers were strangled and drowned in the blood of those who had fallen upon them."

The fallen, in front of the earthworks, were nearly all Confederates. Those behind the earthworks, or "in the trenches" were Federals.

Although the second Michigan cavalry was at New Madrid when the battle of Pittsburgh Landing was fought, our battery, the second battery, as it was first known, and later battery B, raised at the same time, and designed by the governor to accompany us, had been dispatched to the Tennessee and arrived just in time to participate in the desperate fighting between Shiloh church and Pittsburgh Landing.

For some unaccountable reason our troops had settled with a feeling of security that was not warranted by their surroundings. Grant had, indeed, won the two battles, Forts Donelson and Henry, and had reinforcements under Buell approaching rapidly from the east; but, with Albert Sydney Johnston and Beauregard at Corinth, twenty miles away, and an impassable river in his (Grant's) rear, the feeling of security on the part of Grant, Sherman, Prentiss and McClernand was unaccountable. Their three divisions were pushed out on the Corinth road nearly to the Shiloh church, two miles, and there for three weeks they lay, without so much as surrounding their camp with intrenchments or abatis. Even their chain guard was not strong, and the wonder is that the whole line of raw troops at the front were not captured along with Prentiss and his division.

Grant's headquarters were at Savannah, three miles down the river. He arrived on the scene at ten o'clock in the morning, and set to work repairing the blunders of the previous three weeks. Fortunately for our cause, the material of Sherman's and McClernand's divisions was of the stubborn sort, and though greatly outnumbered, every inch of the ground was contested, though Stuart was cut off and fought without communicating with Grant.

318   THE GLASGOW COLLISION.

In front of Sherman's division Captain W. H. Ross, battery B, was sweeping down the well formed and skillfully handled troops of Johnston, but they were soon compelled to take up a new position in rear of Sherman's lines. With commendable forethought Captain Ross sent one portion of his battery, under Lieutenant Laing, to take up a more secure position still in the rear of Sherman's lines, when the enemy's cavalry charged in overwhelming numbers and the greater portion of the battery was captured, including Captain Ross, Lieutenant Bliss and Lieutenant Arndt. General Hurlbut gave the battery great praise for the vigorous support given him during the severest trials of the day.

During the remainder of the engagement Lieutenant Laing, with his section of artillery, gave a good account of himself and was mentioned favorably in general orders.

THE GLASGOW COLLISION.

When John Morgan was on his raid into Kentucky, the second battalion of the second Michigan cavalry had been sent by Colonel Hall from Gallatin, via Glasgow, to Mumfordsville. As the advance guard entered Glasgow it was just after dark. A sergeant with six men was on the extreme advance, with orders not to bring on an engagement. As they reached the public square they saw, entering from a road nearly parallel with theirs, a column partly mounted, partly dismounted, stretched across the street, greeting their friends. The battalion halted, and the first impulse was to fire. Then they thought of the numerous citizens standing about, and determined to push on without firing unless fired upon. At that moment a Confederate officer rode up to the column and with a drawn revolver demanded: "Who the h—— are you?" but immediately cold steel was pressed against the back of his ear and a voice whispered: "Keep still, d—— you, or I'll blow the top of your head off. Disarm and move him back." It was the sergeant that whispered (Sergeant Hempstead, of company M,) and the advance moved on. The only lights on the streets were from the poorly lighted store windows, and the men were evidently well filled with Kentucky whiskey. Saloons were seen open and well filled, and in one of them a crowd of Confederate officers were seen treating a captured Union officer. Our advance moved on. The Confederates, in line across the road, parted, giving room as the column moved through.

Soon our foraging trains and other wagons were heard thundering up. Then a shot was fired and indiscriminate firing was heard all around the square. But the advance of the enemy becoming alarmed, fled back to their main command.

The enemy had sent out a picket on the road our advance took towards Cave City, and there, hearing the shots, returned.

The horse of one of our men fell, hurting him, and the sergeant dismounted to help him. At that instant two mounted men rode up noiselessly on the sod at the side of the road and commanded the sergeant to surrender and give up his revolver. Thoughts of rebel prisons flashed through his mind, and, though his hand was on his revolver at his side, the darkness shielded him and he said, "I have no revolver; that man lying there has a revolver." Turning upon him, they demanded his revolver. In that instant the sergeant's revolver was whipped out—two shots in quick succession—two groans and two horsemen went reeling away. Then other shots were passed between the rebel picket and the Federal advance, and the sergeant joined his advance, but the Confederates were routed, returning by the flanks to their command.

A shot was heard between the advance and the command under Major Dickey, and returning, Sergeant Hempstead found that the prostrate man, Alexander, had been murdered in his helplessness, probably by some lawless drunken fellow. Let us hope it was not by any Confederate soldier in his right senses.

LEFT ON THE FIELD.

To be left on the field, wounded, dying, was bad enough; but with a belief in recovery and a lingering death in prison, half fed, half cared for, was worse. At such a time few officers would think of their men, and give the order by signs to leave him to his fate, rather than strew the field with his followers. Such an instance occurred at Dandridge. A few companies, dismounted, not exceeding 200 men, had been stubbornly resisting charges and flank movements; falling back as rapidly as possible yet determined to save their (then) useless artillery and ambulances until the artillery could get a position where the mounted cavalry could support them by counter charges. An open field was in their rear, and the enemy, three lines deep, were rapidly advancing to crush them, when the dismounted men changed their position across that dreaded open field. Among the last men across was Captain J. H. Smith, of company G. It was a narrow field; a high lane fence, barn and corn crib offered temporary cover at the other side. Away they rush, knowing well that a volley would follow them and many might go down. Yet most of them escaped with slight wounds. But in the middle of the field Captain Smith felt as if hit by a hundred bullets, and went down. Examining himself he found his thigh broken, his leg lying limp and useless, in an unnatural position, his hat and coat full of holes, but he thought at once, "If I don't bleed to death I am all right yet." His men had gained shelter and were pouring a destructive fire back upon the Confederates. He could hear his men say, "Who's missing?" Then a few hasty words and—"Rally, boys, the Captain's wounded. Rally, let's never leave without him. See, he is trying to turn over. He is only wounded." He did turn over; and as he thought of their devotion hot tears filled his eyes, and he shouted, "No, go back." But his voice was drowned in the enemy's firing close to his ears, and as he saw his men and others of the regiment about to climb the fence to charge in the face of twenty times their number he raised his hand and waved then back. They hesitated, but obeyed, and left him to his fate. But those were a stubborn lot of men that fell back from that fence, and every shot was made to count. But the enemy halted and passed around by the flanks and compelled them again to retreat. The stragglers of the enemy appeared to have plenty of time. And when they came to him, the first thing was his watch, ring, knife and boots.

They looked over his hat and coat, but threw them down in disgust, as not worth having. He had put his money inside his shirt and that was saved. He asked the fellow that had his watch what time it was, "Twenty minutes past four." Then they asked questions and he talked with them, good naturedly, and wound up by saying: "Boys, I am a solid Yank, and the best feeling fellow you ever saw when I am at home and well, but you Johnnies have knocked my pins from under me, and now one good turn deserves another; you have shot me, now carry me to that house." I was getting cold. They went and got a fruit ladder; got me on, very carefully, too, and carried me to the house. It was locked, so they put me in a weaving room, and laid me down, rack and all, in a corner (not the "northeast corner").

The family returned about nine o'clock. I heard some one outside and called out, "Hello!" A young woman came in, groping in the darkness, and said, "Who's there?" "A friend." "Confederate or Yankee?" "Yankee." Then she stooped down and said how glad father will be, not that you are wounded but that you are a Yankee, and, in a whisper, "Pa is a Union man, and I have a brother in the Union army." Then I said, "Can I trust you?" "Yes." "Here, then, is my pocket-book; the rebs may search me again. The doctor says I must have my leg off. Go tell your father to come here. Mr. Blackburn came in and I told him I had heard the rebs searching the fence corners for the officer that fell in the meadow. I had removed my shoulder straps before they first got me, and since then they had supposed me a private. They had lanterns and I could hear them. He went and got a neighbor and between them they carried me in and laid me in front of the fire. It was freezing cold outside and the reaction, after our exciting exercise, had set in; and, I tell you, you may believe that fire felt good. Soon Generals Jenkins and Corse came in, and began to question me about what officer fell on the meadow. I evaded them. Finally General Jenkins asked if I was not an officer. "Sir, I am a poor wounded Yankee, in the hands of the enemy."

"Were you not an officer when with your command?"

"I had the pleasure of being a sergeant—they wanted better men for officers, and generally had them in the second Michigan cavalry."

"Where's your coat?"

"Under my head. It's a jacket." He looked it over, and said, "Was all this done to-day?"

"Yes and more, my hat has lost half its rim, and part of the top."

"A close call, my boy."

"And now, General, it's my turn. I want to ask that you allow me to remain here until I die or get better." He instructed his adjutant to make an order to that effect. Then he returned to his questioning again. "What officer fell here in front of the house?"

"I saw no officer fall."

"Didn't you fall here in front of the house?"

"Yes, sir."

"Why didn't you say so, then?"

"You didn't ask me." Then he laughed, but Corse got mad and was very abusive, but General Jenkins checked him, and turning to his own surgeon said: "Do all you can for this man."

He probed and pushed and shook his head. "It must come off or you can't live three days."

"Clean it and get that bullet and loose bone out and I'll take the chances."

He did so, and time, careful nursing and a strong constitution did the rest. "But do you see that leg, two inches shorter than the other, but a good deal of a leg yet?—and I tell you, old man, I'll never forget that Blackburn family. Our troops recaptured me when I was well enough to be moved and I was sent to Nashville."

Captain Smith has a history back of the last war that would make an interesting chapter, but we will only intrude upon these pages sufficient space to say that at the age of fourteen he entered a company of soldiers at Detroit in 1847, and joined Scott in Mexico. Although but a child in years he was large of his age, and carried a musket; was believed to be nineteen years old. He was in the principal engagements up to the battle of Chapultepec, where he was wounded, and afterwards served as a nurse in the hospital. He says: "There was a Lieutenant Wilkins in my company [probably the late Colonel William D. Wilkins, of Detroit,] he was a *good fellow*, and *bully* on a fight."

Without entering more into the history of Captain Smith it is perhaps little enough to say that very few have the record as hard fighters which he enjoyed among his superiors, and especially from Sheridan.

A DARING SCOUT.

A most daring expedition by a small scouting party

was that of Lieutenant W. H. Whittemore and twelve men, during the falling back of our army, under Schofield, before Hood, in 1864, from Athens to Nashville.

General Schofield was making desperate efforts to save all of his trains and artillery as well as men, and he knew that Hood largely outnumbered him. Therefore, while his trains were being rapidly pushed across Duck river at Columbia, Tennessee, he held Columbia as long as possible, but it was quite important that he should know whether Hood was effecting a crossing at Lewisburg or not. The last of our army would be over the river by morning and to ascertain whether or no he had a flanking party to contend with, he called for a volunteer of twelve mounted men and an officer, to go to Lewisburg and return in time to join the army in the morning. The distance was about sixteen to eighteen miles by the road they were obliged to take, through a country supposed to be infested with rebel cavalry. Said the general: "This is a very hazardous undertaking, and you may not be permitted to come back the way you went, if you get back at all."

As the little squad passed out through our chain of pickets an officer said to them:

"You can not get out here; there is a chain of rebel pickets all along there, across the road."

"Well, if we have to come back flying, don't fire on us," and they rode out into the darkness. Taking a road leading off to the southeast, as much as possible away from the main portion of the rebel army, they soon saw their camp fires. The lieutenant instructed his men and soon they were riding boldly along the road, talking as indifferently as if going on picket.

"Hello, boys," said the Johnnies, "going on picket?"

"Yes, and we were on last night, too; you fellows haven't been on in a month," and to avoid further conversation they trotted their horses on, and soon came to another fire. They were now between two fires and could not turn back, and at this moment they heard a volley of shots in their rear, whether at them or not they never knew, but, dashing on, they soon discovered a deserted camp, with fires still smoldering, and resolved then to push on at all hazards. This reckless riding was kept up to the full endurance of the horses until three o'clock in the morning, when they came near Lewisburg. Seeing a house near the road they shouted to the occupants and a man came out.

"Have you seen any Yankees about here?"

"No," says the citizen, "until I saw you." Then he continued: "You need not be afraid of my blowing; I am as good a Yankee as you are; what you looking for?"

"We belong to the ——— Georgia cavalry, and are looking for our command; did any of them cross here?"

"No."

Their secret was understood and the desired information given, and, also, telling them the best road by which to return. They saw other citizens who confirmed the intelligence received; and immediately set out on the return by another route.

It was not only very dark but rainy, and the streams were rising, and where they had been told there were fords, the water had risen and they could not cross. Every mile now brought them nearer the rebel army. They would try one more ford if they could get there, and if not they must swim. By the time they had reached the last possible ford it was broad daylight, and if the rebels had learned of the little scouting party they were probably being sought for.

"Now for it, boys," and a dash of half an hour brought them to the river. As they had feared, they must swim, and to add interest to their situation, horsemen were seen up the road coming towards them on the gallop. They plunged in, giving the horses the rein, throwing themselves from, but clinging to saddles, and every one of them safely reached the other shore, climbing up the steep bank as the enemy dashed down to the opposite side and gave them a volley. But their bullets were harmless, and giving the rebels a parting salute the little band returned in time to join the command as the last of them had left Columbia.

General Schofield had given them up as captured or scattered, perhaps to be bushwhacked, or scattered before reaching our lines, and his pleasure at seeing them all safe can only be imagined. He complimented them highly on the success of their daring expedition.

THE ROMANCE OF WAR.

When an army is lying in camp, waiting for a forward movement, and that camp chances to be amid pleasant surroundings, then often occur scenes around which "memory loves to linger." There were many such in the south, and Franklin, Tennessee, during the spring of 1863 comes back fresh as a pleasant dream after these twenty years.

I was an early riser those days, and occasionally when the sun began to streak the east, about four o'clock in the morning, and not a sound from human voice disturbed the slumbering camp, I have wandered away to the hills or "knobs," as they were called, to be where I could hear and take in the first awakening of the camp.

If this article falls under the eye of any who are not "moved by the harmony of sweet sounds," they need not read it. But come with me, you lovers of Nature, and I will try and paint you a picture. Walking briskly along the path, the modest sensitive plant droops and lies prostrate until you have passed on out of sight. The mocking bird—prince of vocalists—flits from bush to bush, singing as he goes in circles around a certain tree, and you know the mother bird is near brooding a nest. You have heard the song all night, perhaps, yet it is just as sweet and strong as when first you heard it. The twitter of other birds is there, but they sink into insignificance beside our favorite. We climb the hill, perhaps 200 feet, and find a tempting boulder on the hillside. Now sit here and listen and look. Half a mile to the south the Harpeth winds through the valley, and beyond, the early rising citizens are sending heavenward wreaths of smoke from nearly every chimney in the town of Franklin. Between us and the river, spread out in bird's-eye view, are the tents, wagons, horses and mules of 25,000 troops. Around each regiment, in measured tread, along a well beaten path mechanically tramps the stiffly alert soldier. Suddenly from the headquarters grounds, near the tent of General Gordon Granger, a long haired Indian bugler stands out before the flag-staff. The air is clear, and his proud bearing is noted, even at this distance, as he raises that old copper bugle, different from all others in the army, and, poising it for an instant only, with its mouth pointing above the distant hills, he sends forth an ear-piercing, elephantine blast that might serve well at the judgment day. How rich, at this distance! like the Alpine horns echoing across the valley and against the hillside, back and forth, the last drawn cadence serving to bring to his feet the sleepiest laggard among the regimental and company buglers.

Then the cavalry and artillery repeat the call and the infantry drums roll and rattle tr-r-r-r-r-rat, tr-r-r-rat-tat! and now, listen—a horse neighs; a mule brays! listen again, there they go. Ye-haw, ye-haw, e-haw, haw, from 5,000 mulish throats in horrid discord, yet musical when distance lends enchantment. And now the sleepy teamsters are seen moving from under the wagons, out of the wagons, from tents and from every quarter to feed and "stop that racket." There are acres and acres of them; rows of wagons a half mile long parked in wheel to wheel. And now, as the mules' reveille is cut short by rations of oats, corn or hay, we can hear the roll calls from the parade grounds and the answers, Here! here!! here!!!

Suddenly we discover smoke or dust away south on the Columbia pike, two miles away. Then a horseman comes tearing over the hill out of the dust and disappears behind the trees and houses nearer town. Then a line of horses, in groups of fours moving back rapidly, but not in very good order; evidently being led by one man out of four, and just behind them a line of dismounted men, running for cover. They reach a stone wall and are immediately over and faced about. Then we see a line of smoke from the guns of the dismounted men, and a rushing up and scattering of mounted men. Then the dismounted men fall back as a party of mounted flankers are seen swinging around the right. The next instant our long roll is sounded, and "boots and saddles" immediately after. There is shouting and hurrying and we have seen enough for this morning. Tumbling, jumping, running, down the hill we go, and find our horses saddled by our faithful negro and ready for an all day's fight or a foot race along the front line of our advance pickets.

This is no fancy picture, but a real copy of scenes that were witnessed almost any morning in May or June, 1863, along that lovely valley of the Harpeth.

SURGEON CHARLES L. HENDERSON.

This officer was sick during the entire period of my labor on this work, and therefore I only have his official record from which to write. He joined the great band beyond the river about January 15th, 1884, and we can but say he was a faithful officer and friend.

What greater praise needs any man?

SURGEON WM. BROWNELL.

Surgeon Brownell entered the service in 1861 as assistant surgeon and served as such until Surgeon Henderson was mustered out in October, 1862, when he assumed the duties of surgeon and filled them with great success and acceptability.

While surgeon of the regiment he was frequently called upon to take charge of brigade and division hospitals and at the close of the war was in charge of the post hospital at Nashville.

The knowledge he added to his store during the war placed him in a high rank as a physician and surgeon in civil life and he has enjoyed the reputation of being one of the first in his profession in the state. He has resided since at Utica, Michigan, and his reputation has extended far beyond his local practice, and so arduous have been his duties that he has of late been much shattered in health.

SURGEON W. F. GREEN.

This officer came to the regiment as acting assistant surgeon at Pine Hills, Mississippi, from the ranks of the seventy-first Ohio, at a time when surgeons were in demand. We were well officered as to surgeons, Drs. Charles Henderson and William Brownell, but sickness did not let the doctors alone more than others, and, in that Mississippi country, the surgeons were sorely tried, by overwork and a bad climate. Hospital steward Ranney was sick, and Dr. Henderson scarcely equal, physically, to the task, and, at such a time, a cheerful word, such as Dr. Green always had, went far among the boys, and he was welcomed with open arms. His papers, a certificate from the examining board of surgeons, were satisfactory, and he went to work in real earnest. From this time on he was ever at his post, by night or day. On the front line, if need be, or wherever duty called him, there the tall, lank form of Dr. Green loomed up like the ghost of old Hippocrates himself; and while the regiment slept after the battle of Perryville, he, with the other surgeons, works, cutting, slashing, sawing, binding, and bathing during the long hours of that horrible night, and had for a morning appetizer the sight and smell of cartloads of arms and legs. What a dissecting table that! But we felt that "old saw-bones," as we affectionately called him, would make no useless sacrifice of limb.

His reputation was now firmly established, and, at the first opportunity, he was promoted, and we saw him assistant surgeon, surgeon of the first East Tennessee and brigade surgeon, and had charge of forty ambulances filled with wounded on the retreat from that slaughter pen around Crawfish Springs traveling all night and arriving at Chattanooga on the morning of September 21.

He continued as brigade surgeon through the Wheeler raid, the East Tennessee campaign, and was division surgeon with General E. M. McCook in the Atlanta campaign until the regiment returned and the Hood campaign began, when he again joined the brigade under General John T. Croxton and served with it to the end of the war.

NOTES BY DR. GREEN.

A few weeks after the battle of Perryville, in crossing over the field a party was seen digging among the new made graves. It proved to be an old gentleman from Indiana. He had brought a rude coffin in the wagon with him, and when the body was reached, he gave it a hasty, heart-broken look, and, shaking his head, declared this was not his son.

We asked to see his letters and soon discovered he had come to the wrong part of the field. The letter said the son was color bearer of the regiment and was the third man who had fallen that day while bearing the colors. The letter gave directions where to find the body, "near a large white oak tree—a burnt log," etc. On the breast was a piece of the colors of the regiment, and a piece of paper, with writing, which enabled them to identify the body.

He picked up a cannon ball and, saying that was the first he had ever seen, declared he would take it home, and, with the money the son had sent home to assist in paying for their farm he would erect a monument.

He also took up a small cedar standing near and wrapped the roots carefully.

That scene at the identification, deep, yet simple, demonstrations of affection, was very touching, and the sorrowing old man moved quietly away, as if leading a solemn but grand funeral cortege.

SURGEON GEO. E. RANNEY.

George E. Ranney comes from a family well known in history, for military and naval achievements. He is a direct lineal descendant of Samuel Champlain, the French naval officer and explorer, the founder of Quebec and the French colony in Canada. There has been a crossing of Scotch blood, but the family characteristics remain.

When the war begun, Geo. E. Ranney, at the age of 22, entered company B, second Michigan cavalry, as a private.

He had been studying medicine, but was not a graduate. His knowledge of medicine, however, made his services in demand, and he was assigned to the hospital department as steward, where he served until overwork and sickness drove him home, in the summer of 1862. During his convalescence he entered the medical department of Michigan University, and graduating in 1863, was immediately sent by Governor Blair to the regiment as second assistant surgeon.

A surgeon's duties with a cavalry regiment, if he is with his regiment, as he should be, on all raids, night or day, are not of "elegant leisure," and the assistant surgeons are usually expected to do the bulk of the *work*, and young Ranney found himself immediately in business. Joining the regiment at Triune, on the very first day's advance he assisted the medical director in amputating a soldier's arm to the music of whistling bullets during the sharp engagement at Rover. His coolness of nerve at once established him in the highest esteem with the medical director.

Surgeon Ranney remained constantly at his post during that campaign, which culminated in the battle of Chicamauga, September 20, 1863, where he was captured. He was sent to Libby prison soon after and held there till November 24 following, as a hostage. Returning to duty with his regiment, he was soon after called upon to operate for the brigade at Pulaski until the retreat, when he joined the regiment, serving as the only medical officer of the regiment, also acting as brigade surgeon. He served with them through the Tennessee campaign—the advance and retreat of Hood—and soon after Ranney was made full surgeon and placed in charge of the division hospital, and made its chief operator. As the cavalry moved south and liberated the prisoners, Surgeon Ranney was the first to report on the brutality of Captain Wirz, which resulted in the arrest and final hanging of that brute.

The hospital departments of the three divisions of the cavalry corps being consolidated at Macon Surgeon Ranney was ordered to receipt to the surgeons in charge of the second and third divisions and establish and take charge of the corps hospital, where all the sick and wounded of the command were treated

When the second Michigan cavalry was mustered out Surgeon Ranney was assigned to the one hundred and thirty-sixth United States colored infantry, and remained in the service until January, 1866.

Since the war Dr. Ranney has lived and practiced his profession at Lansing, and his experience and natural and acquired abilities have won for him a reputation that has made him well and favorably known, even beyond the confines of his own state.

CHICAMAUGA AND ATLANTA—NOTES FROM SURGEON RANNEY.

An Irishman had his haversack strap cut by a bullet. "Bedad, they're cutting off my supplies"—came quick and fresh, though lead and iron filled the air like swarming bees.

Some three weeks after the battle of Chicamauga the wounded were parolled and sent to Chattanooga under a flag of truce. Surgeon Ranney (a prisoner on duty at Crawfish Springs) assisted General Bragg's provost marshal in parolling the wounded under Dr. Ranney's charge. An able bodied man placed himself among the wounded, and as the doctor came to him he gave a meaning and anxious look which plainly said: "I have had all I want of prisoner's life; *get me out.*" So his name was entered among the wounded and he went away with a light heart.

The Federal surgeon in charge of the hospital asked soon after. "Where is Wright?"

"He is parolled."

"How did he come to be parolled? He was not wounded."

"Yes, he was; severely wounded."

"Why," said the Federal surgeon, "I did not know that before; where was he wounded?"

"His feelings were terribly lacerated, and I recommended a change of climate."

Just before the battle of Resaca, General Stanley, who had previously commanded our cavalry corps, but was then in command of an infantry corps, was informed that he would have the advance in the morning, and that probably there would be sharp work; and was asked what cavalry regiment he wanted in the advance to open the fight or skirmish, as the case might be. He replied: "Give me the second Michigan cavalry."

And his choice, though not generally known at the time, proved a wise one, for the regiment drove the enemy's skirmish lines of cavalry behind their infantry and following them up fiercely drove the first line of infantry, also, from behind their intrenchments. But as they anticipated, they were then met by large bodies of infantry and driven from the captured works. As we were falling back we met a brigadier-general who asked: "What is the trouble?"

"We have met the enemy in force and can advance no further."

"Oh," said the brigadier, "I will send a company or two of infantry in there and give them a volley and I guess we will start them."

Just then General Stanley came up. "Well, you found them. How is it?"

He was told the situation and the infantry brigadier repeated his remarks, with not a little sarcasm in his tone.

"Put your whole brigade into line at once," said Stanley, and before the brigade was in position, the enemy opened upon them, with a part of our regiment Dr. Ranney, (who had gone back to get a wounded man) among the number, between the two lines.

The second Michigan took the left, and the battle raged fiercely all day, the Confederates breaking our lines at the point where the cavalry was replaced by infantry, and when night came, our infantry lines having been driven back, and the cavalry still remaining out on the left, were supposed to be captured. Coming into camp at midnight we were fired upon by our infantry pickets.

COMMISSARIES.

There were few men in the army whose positions were more arduous and whose labors were less appreciated, when faithfully discharging their duties, than the commissaries. Dependent upon the quartermaster, generally, for transportation, it mattered little to the hungry soldier whether the hard bread had become wet and mouldy en route or not. The commissary was more often greeted with: "Say, old hard-tack, what sort of stuff is this you're givin' us?" Or, if rations of fresh beef were being issued, he was more than likely to be greeted with, "Hello, when did that old bull die?" If it was bacon, "sow-belly" was the euphonious name indulged in. If the boys happened to be "dry" and they knew the commissary was well fixed, there was no *taffy* good enough for the commissary.

Amid all these trials E. W. Lauranse, whose gray hair and whiskers made him a conspicuous figure in the regiment, and extended even through the brigade and army, made many friends and won for himself a reputation for faithful services second to none. His portrait will be found among the staff officers. He is, at this writing, still living, though well advanced in years, in comparatively good health, at Utica, Michigan.

IN THE HOSPITAL.

There was heroism among the women of the south on both sides of the Union question that women of the north as a whole have known little about. It was necessarily so. The war, whatever the cause, was upon them, among them, destroying home circles by dividing families, destroying homes as well, and often, very often, bringing gaunt hunger to the door. In times when men's and women's souls are tried, heroic characters are made all the more conspicuous by their throwing aside all considerations of personal safety and social ostracism.

The true heroes were not two faced, "all things to all men," but they dared, in the face of a thousand to one, to shout, on the streets or housetops "Hurrah! hurrah! for the Stars and Stripes," and wave their dainty kerchiefs as that starry emblem passed by, even though they knew that behind every window screen sharp eyes were watching them.

Such a woman was Miss F. O. Courtney, of Franklin, Tennessee, and this feeling, though less fearless, her mother and sister shared with her. It is related of her that she was first brought to the notice of Federal officers and soldiers by waving her handkerchief to a regiment on their way to the battle at Shiloh. A major was in command, and he gallantly dismounted and deftly slipping his diamond scarf pin from his throat, placed it upon the necktie of Miss Courtney; mounting his horse, he passed on without so much as knowing the young lady's name. As regiment after regiment marched onward the story was wafted to the passing army, and cheer after cheer rent the air for the patriotic girl of Tennessee.

But it is of her part in the hospital that I would write. It was known from the time that Sherman cut loose for his march to the sea that Hood would invade Tennessee, and those who could, at once began to prepare for the crisis. A secret cellar was made ready, the entrance to which was by a trap door under a carpet, in the house of Mrs. Courtney, and this underground room was filled with substantial provisions—bacon sugar, coffee, etc.

That terrible 30th of November, 1864, (the battle of Franklin) came, and at once every house was a hospital, and every yard was filled with dead and dying, while the surgeons were busily fitting up churches and school houses for more permanent and roomy quarters.

In the largest school building there were, among others, 120 Federal officers and soldiers, most of whom ought, under favorable treatment, to recover, and over these an assistant surgeon had been detailed to watch, but the importance of his position seemed to turn his head, and he at once became so overbearing as to attract the attention of the few Unionists who visited there. The Misses Courtney, with their mother, at once made it their special business to be at the hospital, some, or all, of them constantly, and not only to nurse the suffering fellows, but to prepare, from their own storehouse, such provisions as they had (which were much better than the Confederates had for their men) in such a palatable manner that their presence was hailed like angels' visits. Every piece of white cotton, even to their skirts, was torn up for bandages, not even a change of under linen was preserved. Confederates were nursed by their hosts of friends and Federals by these three and, perhaps, in all, a half dozen women of Union sympathies.

The Federal surgeon in charge was very negligent and, sometimes willfully indifferent to some of his men, and the pleading looks and words the boys gave, "Don't leave me to that scoundrel, or I shall die," were heart-rending.

Unceasingly those women labored, cooking and nursing, and the thundering artillery of Nashville was heard on the fifteeth and sixteenth day after the Franklin butchery.

The last bit of bacon and coffee, flour and sugar had been eaten. The nurses had become, in their garments, nearly as filthy as the soldiers had been on entering the hospital. What should they do now for food? The seventeenth day had come, and no signs of the Federal army. The heavy artillery firing had ceased. Which way had the battle gone? If the Confederates knew they were silent.

Fainting, sick and wounded soldiers began to clamor for something to eat, but the Confederates appeared not to hear them, and the day wore on.

Women of the North, can you picture to yourselves the horrors which oppressed the minds of those 120 neglected "boys in blue?" Can you wonder that those loyal hearts turned silently away to hide the fast welling tears, at their powerless condition?

A distant shot is heard. "There!" another, and another. "They are coming!" in faint murmurs ran through the room. Straggling soldiers, ragged, unarmed, hurried through the streets and then, in broken squads, companies and regiments they came, closely pressed by the Federal soldiers. Hunger was forgotten in their great joy, and soon the hospital supply train followed. Then there were hastily prepared dishes, and once more faces grew bright, and a quiet, peaceful night settled down over those hospital cots.

If the services of those devoted women have ever been recognized by the government we have not heard of it.

LIEUTENANT RUSSELL A. DARROW.

It was a notorious fact that few men who entered the army with ordinary pretensions to morality or religion withstood the powerful influences for evil that surrounded them. Lieutenant Darrow was one of that few who kept themselves pure and spotless, and his heroic devotion to his country, extending as it did beyond all just claims upon his service, was the subject of admiration. His time had expired and his muster out had been ordered but was only awaiting his presence at the muster out officer's. He had thought the war about over and was about to return and enter upon his study for the ministry.

Forrest's men were trying to escape out of Tennessee and were nearing the river between Cypress creek and the Tennessee, when three companies of the second Michigan, under Major Dickinson, were ordered down a by-road to intercept them. They gained the front of the enemy by a charge of three miles to a point near the ford, with a piece of woods on one side and a field on the other. Twenty dismounted men of company M occupied the road and to the left of it. The others of the battalion were deployed in the woods.

Lieutenant Darrow remained mounted, though partly under cover of the woods. The enemy pressed upon them, apparently a whole division, mounted. Many of the Confederates wore the Federal uniform, and deceived Lieutenant Darrow into thinking perhaps he was firing upon our own men of some other regiment. He asked, "What regiment is that?" The enemy were close at hand—short pistol range. The reply was a volley of bullets, and poor Darrow reeled in his saddle. But the twenty men at the road sides replied with a volley that more than trebly avenged (so far as numbers were concerned) the death of their young commander, and compelled the enemy to abandon that line of retreat and pass around by the flank.

"Oh, my God! My poor old mother," said he, as he passed into an unconscious state, and quietly breathed out his life, a victim to treachery.

TURNING THE TIDE—JIM BROWNLOW CAPTURED.

At one time during the sharp engagement at Fair Garden, East Tennessee, the second Michigan cavalry were driven back from the edge of a wood they were approaching across an open field and up the steep bank of a creek, by the enemy's cavalry, mounted in strong force. But there they took up a position and held it. The first Tennessee, seeing the second driven back, became panic stricken and breaking wildly, fled. Colonel Campbell seeing what had happened hurried a staff officer after Colonel Brownlow with his regiment of Tennesseeans. He found them and soon returned. Meantime the enemy had apparently run the other way, and following with a small force in advance for about two miles, they were discovered in the woods The enemy seeing only a small force, contented themselves with keeping them in check by a few shots, and Colonel Campbell brought up his artillery, and showing the commander the position, very close to the enemy's lines, asked if he dare place his guns in the edge of the woods—so close to the enemy's line that as Colonel Campbell expressed it, I could see the whites of their eyes." The artillery captain's reply was: "I dare place it wherever you say, if it's in hell."

"All right," said the colonel, I will go with you, and take

the second Michigan cavalry as support; and before the enemy were aware of the presence of our main force, the artillery opened upon them at short range.

Campbell ordered a charge and the rebels broke in confusion. They made a desperate attempt to get their guns away, but Colonel Lagrange, with his brigade, charged them on the left and captured three pieces of artillery and 150 prisoners. killing and wounding many and scattering the rest.

This was Colonel Jim Brownlow's opportunity, and he rushed after them with the utmost recklessness until far within the enemy's lines. The regiment mostly got away, but Colonel Jim was captured, though unrecognized, having a plain jacket on, and by a little strategy succeeded in making his escape in the night and return to camp next day, amid the wild cheers of his men, as well as the whole brigade, with whom he was a general favorite, notwithstanding his recklessness.

"FIVE DOLLARS FOR THAT REBEL."

It was at Fair Garden, East Tennessee. The second Michigan cavalry was deployed, dismounted, in front of the brigade, and for want of better cover, both armies were lying flat upon the ground and pouring a deadly hail of lead at each other. This continued for a short time, when a soldier on the Confederate side arose to his feet and boldly dashed back to cover of the woods. Lieutenant-Colonel Ben Smith shouted at the top of his voice. "Five dollars for that rebel!" When the whole regiment sprang to their feet and dashing forward drove the advance of the enemy from the field.

"WALK ROUND."

The negro's love of amusement was always a source of delight to the soldiers of the Union army that found opportunities for indulgence under the most gloomy surroundings. The hot July sun beat pitilessly upon the Federal soldiers in Mississippi, filling camp and hospital with fever racked patients, and kept burial parties busy, but the down trodden blacks were happy. They felt that the presence of an army of slavery-hating soldiers meant something, though no promises of protection or escape were held out. Male and female, young and old, flocked to camp, asking nothing; expecting nothing; half clothed and always barefoot, they gathered around camp fires, and indulged their overflowing spirits in songs of freedom and plantation breakdowns, or "walk 'round." The end-board to an army wagon, with the smooth side up, afforded them just the thing for a platform, and around they go, in a circle, one behind the other, pausing as their feet touched the end-board to shuffle and jig to the time of spatting hands against hands, knees and hand again; patting of feet and a genuine plantation melody—a jumble of meaningless words and sentences, and perhaps the tum-tum of a home-made banjo, all in the most perfect time; changing off as each new dancer struck the rattling end board, and the puffing, tired ones dart off with a boisterous yah! yah!

And this was often kept up until taps were sounded and the dusky dancers disappeared, as mysteriously as they came—no one knew where.

It was a scene that professional minstrels have tried hard, but unsuccessfully, to imitate, yet will never be forgotten by the soldier.

BURNT HIS FINGERS.

Major Scranton sat in front of his little band of 325 non-veterans at Resaca, his leg thrown over the saddle, his men all mounted close in his rear, thirty feet, perhaps. They were awaiting orders. Shells were flying pretty thick, and often uncomfortably close. Inaction was nervous work. His short stub of an Indian stone pipe was between his teeth; his hand sought the depths of his pocket and brought up a handful of loose tobacco. Then a match, briskly applied to his pants, and, holding it aloft in his sheltering hands, while the sulphur spluttered and sizzed—a shell buried itself in the earth, between him and the men, fifteen feet away. Casting his eye askance, he never moved a muscle, but kept his eye on the smoking hole in the ground, while the match burned away, and suddenly, instead of being blown from his horse, the blazing match reached his fingers, and took hold sharp. The shell was forgotten in his efforts to shake the pain from his fingers, and the roar of laughter that broke the spell would have drowned the noise of the exploding shell. It was a mean thing to laugh at, but the boys couldn't help it, and the major was too good-natured to make any remarks.

While Hood's rear guard (Forrest's cavalry) and Croxton's brigade were confronting each other at Richland Creek, December, 1864, a little of the grim humor of war occurred.

The troops were under cover of the trees, but the artillery was having a savage duel. Captain T. W. Johnston, then of Croxton's staff, was near the creek, and, with Lieutenant-Colonel Ben. Smith, was taking observations. A cannon ball cut off the limb of a tree, which fell directly upon Captain Johnston. A sharp bud struck the Captain in the corner of his eye, breaking his glasses and causing the blood to flow quite freely. The sharp, pricking sensation led him to believe, for a moment, that he had been hit by a bullet. Clapping his hand to the back of his head, he felt sure he should find a hole where it had come out, and, at the same time he sat down by a tree with the fullest expectation of expiring in a few minutes. But he very soon discovered he was not much hurt, and, jumping to his feet, said: "I reckon I hadn't better die yet; I'll put it off a week; changed my mind."

A few minutes later a staff officer from General Wilson came riding down. He looked around, talked a little and set out on an easy gallop back to headquarters, down the open woods road. Just then a long shell came whirling end over end from the enemy's artillery, making that peculiar music so often heard at such times, and passed very near Colonel Ben and Captain Tom. Quick witted but deliberate spoken old Ben speaks out: "*By crimus*, if-the-Cap'n-don't-hurry-up-that-ball-'ll overtake-him."

At Perryville the command had been short of rations of fresh meat until after the battle, and during the night preceding sharp foragers only had been able to provide themselves with meat.

Going over to company M, I found Captain Tom had preceded me, probably following the same scent.

"Hello Tom! what you got?"

"Oh, the boys have been out skirmishing; found an old sheep that *couldn't get away;* sit down and have some."

It smelt good, and I sat down. But somehow that "couldn't get away" haunted me, and, with its dry, leathery appearance, my appetite was quickly appeased.

Other companies, more fortunate, had captured a number of grasshopper fed turkeys, that neglected to "roost high" and the smell of burnt feathers, roast turkey and things reminded one of a premature Thanksgiving; and the quiet but voracious circles around those camp-fires all night told plainly how men would rather eat than sleep.

But, oh! that horrid muddy water. What wouldn't we give for a pail of clear water for our coffee, and to moisten our lips and throats.

"We'll have it to-morrow, or die trying," was our comment.

"HERE'S YOUR MULE."

Soldiers who were through the East Tennessee campaign of 1863-4, November to February, used to admire the handsome mule teams connected with General Elliott's headquarters and wondered where he got them. They were of good size, round as a barrel, white as snow or black as ink, and as playful, when at rest, as a lot of kittens.

With General McCook's scouts were twenty-four men from the second Michigan cavalry. Sixteen of them under Sergeant Brooks, were sent off on a scout below Fair Garden, to ascertain the plans of the enemy, the location, or any other intelligence. Very early in the morning they came on to the trail of a scouting foraging party, and, following on cautiously, came suddenly upon them feeding five teams of mules, six in each team. The foragers were dismounted men from Longstreet's Richmond soldiers. Looking them over our boys saw there were twenty of them.

"That's not enough odds to talk about," said the sergeant, and they dashed among them, capturing with out hurting anyone. The Richmond soldiers felt terribly chagrined at being caught napping by western Yankees; but they were loaded into the wagons and hurried out of the country, the object of the scout having been accomplished through information gathered from loyal citizens and negroes living in that territory.

The Confederates had loaded the wagons with hams, bacon, and meal and were ready to leave, little dreaming there were Yankees within fifty miles of them. The provisions were dumped in a pile beside the road and the citizens told to go and get their "truck."

Returning to Fair Garden, General Elliott was met with all the cavalry, on their way to that battle. Riding up to the General, "Here's your mule," said the sergeant, and from the thirty mules General Elliott, through his quartermaster, selected a team of six that were noted all through the army for their beauty.

DESTROYING PONTOONS.

The following reminiscence was related by Marshman Maxon, of company A, second Michigan cavalry, at their reunion February 22, 1883, and had it not been, in part, already familiar to us, we fear the story would have seemed too much like fiction to have been received as proper matter for a volume which we have studied faithfully to keep within the bounds of truth:

"On the 6th of October, 1864, while we were encamped near Florence, Alabama," began Mr. Maxon, "watching Hood's movements, General Croxton requested Colonel Smith to ask for volunteers to go down the river in canoes to cut the pontoons. Only six men were needed, but half the regiment were ready to go. Besides me there were Joseph Jones, Alfred Foy, Joseph Gage, James Dodard and Jerry Mahoney who were accepted, and at midnight we were on the way and had pressed a citizen into the service as guide. Whether the old fellow knew better or not we never knew, but he took us down on one side of an island, of which we had no previous intimation. Our party went in two log canoes that were little more than square sticks of timber, sharpened at each end and dug out inside enough to admit of a board about twelve or fifteen inches wide, which was kept in the bottom, generally to keep you dry, but, in our case, it proved quite a convenience in bailing the canoe when it tipped over, as we frequently did in going down the rapids. At such times we frequently stood up against the strong current of cold water, and, righting our craft, lifted the boards from one end, and, presto! the water rushed out at the other end and in we clambered again. This was probably repeated five or six times before we had passed Muscle Shoals, with its sharp breaks, whirling eddies and projecting rocks. When we had passed that terrible ordeal and shot out into the dark current, of about seven miles an hour, I think every man of us would rather have gone through a sharp battle than attempted such a trip again. To add to our discomfort the rain was pouring down piteously, and we were becoming chilled from our baths.

"We were to strike the bridge at three o'clock a. m., and judging of time by what we had passed through we concluded it must be near that now; so, paddling up to land, we climbed out and, striking a match, found we were too early by an hour, and probably not far from the bridge. Rebel camp fires could be seen reflected against the sky, not far below.

"Waiting another half hour we headed down the river and soon discovered that instead of a pontoon bridge we had a trestle to encounter; and then for the first time realized that we had been passing along between an island and the main land, on the Confederate side of the river. We shot under the bridge without noise and passing below about two miles landed, turning loose our old 'Secesh' friend, wishing him good-night, and set out for camp, where we reported next night after a long, weary, hungry march, dodging the enemy's scouts.

"Then a second detail was asked for, but not so readily filled since the actual hazards of the undertaking were better known. But, as I did not like to leave a job until I had done something, I volunteered the second time, with most of the men who had gone with me on the first trip, one or two backing out and others taking their places. The same shooting the rapids, half the time in the water, was repeated, and we neared the bridge on the pontoon side of the island and kept the two canoes side by side until within sight of the bridge. Then, separating, each canoe darted towards either end of the bridge, and with one man standing in the bow, with a sharp hatchet, we expected to cut the lines and float the greater part down the river. There was a strong light glaring from the banks at either end and a small train of army wagons were crossing. It was an exciting moment. Capture meant death, as marauders. Swiftly glide the frail boats, nearer, and it seemed as if this time our eyes must surely catch sight of the lines, when, a sudden shock, a splash, and, I saw my two comrades plunged into the rushing torrent, and felt the boat giving way beneath my feet, swing round, and, as I felt myself going, I caught sight of a big line and struck it with my hatchet. The next instant I found myself swimming, and heard our canoe roll beneath one of the pontoons, rolling as a square piece of timber would naturally roll when swept broadside to the current underneath a flat bottomed boat. The noise could be heard a long distance, and we felt that the pickets would be down upon us in no time. Swinging quietly to the canoe we all caught hold and floated silently down the stream with camp fires and burning buildings lighting up the bank, glaring out on to the river and casting weird flitting shadows on the dark clouds above—all for our benefit (?).

"It appeared that the man in the bow of the boat, Jos. Gage, did not see the line. It was not where he was looking for it and it caught him under the chin, lifting him clear of the canoe as it swung around and was carried under. My stroke cut the line about half off so that it sagged a little, and the men in the other canoe cut the line entirely off, but lost their boat and climbed on to one of the pontoons.

"Although the bridge sagged it was found to be anchored with chains, as well as ropes, so that our expedition, after all, was little better than a failure, delaying Hood only two days.

"The three men were captured on the pontoon next morning when the planks were being replaced to cover the gaps caused by the sag.

"When the pickets came on to the bridge to see what had happened, one cried out, 'The line's broke—no, cut! that's another d— Yankee trick.'

"The boys were placed in a log prison by themselves, with strict orders to the guards not to allow other prisoners to be put with them, but this order was broken in the night, and the three prisoners, by disguising themselves, helped by the escape of three other prisoners through the roof, succeeded in saving their necks for the prison pen. But as for us three poor devils floating down that cold stream, for two or three miles, clinging to the canoe, we felt that we were getting more baths than we had bargained for. At last we drifted on to an island and righted our canoe. Then we moved cautiously on down the stream, until the fires along the river were all left behind and we moved noiselessly toward shore. Seeing something white, like a snow bank, we determined to investigate, hoping to find a place to crawl in until morning. Creeping by the bank, and on our hands and knees cautiously, when within ten feet of us we saw a man, stooping over a smoldering fire, from which a white bank of smoke was floating away, and the man was trying to fan it to a flame with his breath. We saw that he was a soldier, and evidently an outpost, and probably not alone. Touching my comrades, I signaled them to back out, and back we went, feet foremost, like three great crawfish, into the water and down we floated until we were about eight miles below the bridge. Here we were to have been met by an escort of our own men, but we waited about in the woods until three o'clock next day when we set out, alone, without rations, without arms, in an enemy's country, and no maps or guides. We had not gone far when we discovered a camp of Confederates, and captured a man with a basket of provisions for General S. D. Lee. This we took back into the swamp and soon put it where it would do the most good—the first food we had eaten since we left camp.

"That evening we approached some scattering houses, and found one of them occupied by a negro. While there we saw some rebel soldiers go into one of the houses for supper, and we concluded it was not safe to remain, so we crept along by the fence and when near the houses heard some one say 'whoa.' We had only seen horses there and the voice was like one from the grave. I was in the advance and dropped among the weeds, close beside the road. Presently the voice said, 'Come on, boys, and the soldiers came out, put spurs to their horses and passed within fifteen feet of me, and as it was not yet dark, I felt my time had surely come, but they were looking down the road and passed me by.

"We crept back to the negro's quarters and stayed with him until twelve midnight, when he faithfully led us out on our way, for ten miles, then, directing us as best he could, returned, to be at home by daylight, fearing to be absent afterward. Wearily that day wore on, as we dodged about from clearing to wood, and from wood across clearing, taking the road when we could see for long distances, and avoiding it in suspicious looking places; often crossing fresh tracks, but meeting no one until night, when we suddenly came upon half a dozen infantry resting in an old deserted house. Our clothing was turned wrong side out, and we began to pass ourselves off as Georgia cavalry, when one of the boys weakened, and to a direct question answered: 'Second Michigan cavalry.'

"Like a flash six rifles came to the shoulder and—'surrender.'

"What else could we do? Our hands went up, and then we all sat down together, and they shared with us the best they had, remarking, 'We have heard the second Michigan always treat their prisoners well; we'll do the best we can by you, boys,' and soon we set out for Florence, and were taken before General Stovall, provost-marshal. His first question was:

"'Where've you been?'

"'Down the lower ford, where we got cut off and were trying to make our way back to camp.'

"'That's a lie. How far will Hood get north?'

"'About to Duck river.'

"'Ha! He will drive you d— Yankees across the Ohio.'

"'Perhaps.'

"'Do you know who it was tried to cut our pontoons?'

"'I do not.'

"'Well, if it's any satisfaction to you, we've got three of them, and the other three were drowned. Sergeant, bring them to me again in the morning.'

"Next day we saw the old citizen whom we had compelled to guide us down the river and he recognized us. This was a new danger. He was a prisoner, on suspicion, and wanted us to go with him to clear him of the accusation of being a Union spy.

"'You are mistaken, sir; we did not come down the river.'

"'I knew if he told his story to the general our game would be up, so I got acquainted with one of my guards, a kind hearted fellow, and throwing myself on his mercy, told him all, and begged him to go and tell the old fool to keep still—he would get clear in a few days. The guard hesitated a moment, and said, 'I believe I will do it'—and he did.

"From Florence we were taken to Corinth, and on to Meridian, and here we got our first glimpse of that perfect hell upon earth—a prison pen.

"It was dark when we arrived. The old gate that opened into the stockade pen squeaked on its hinges as it opened for our admission, and there, huddled together in little groups, in the open air, mud knee deep, crouched 1,200 miserable beings in human form, clothing in shreds; legs and arms half bare; coatless, hatless; leaning forward over little miserable fires, their hands shading their eyes, they glared at us like fiends from the infernal regions, and I shuddered as I thought—must I, too, be one of those? Then the gate closed with a bang, and the startling cry of 'Fresh fish!' rang close in our ears. Next we knew a piece of clothing was cut away from our scanty garments; then another, and another, until we were arrayed as nearly like the others as possible. Then a voice whispered. 'You must defend yourselves, or they will strip you,' and we soon learned what was expected of 'Fresh fish.' After a day or two we were considered *initiated*, and left alone.

"To tell the horrors of that place would fill a book, and I don't care to recall them, and will skip the fare, the filth and the famine; the deaths by hundreds and the living deaths in heaps, trying to keep each other warm; only referring to the miserable, drunken brute in command, as a coward, who never dared to meet men in the open field of battle, but trembled at every unusual noise, fearing a revolt.

"After being shifted to Cahaba, Alabama, and several other places, some of them not so bad, some worse, we at last were sent on our way to be exchanged at Memphis.

"The scene of that explosion, on the steamer Sultana, where 1,700 prisoners were either burned to death or drowned, will ever be a living nightmare from which I would gladly close my eyes, and I will not attempt to describe it; but I was saved among the very few, and exchanged, just as the rebellion was in its last throes, and until to-day, February 22, 1883, I have never met one of my comrades who were with me during that terrible imprisonment."

COMPLIMENTS TO WIRT ADAMS.

When Croxton's brigade was on its way from Tuscaloosa General Wirt Adams came up, on another road, from Pickensville, and ran into Croxton's rear guard accidentally, neither party knowing previously of the whereabouts of the other. Adams had a force of two divisions (four brigades), and was therefore as strong as Croxton. The rear guard was, unfortunately, a light cavalry regiment, not armed with repeating rifles, and therefore, lacking in that self-reliance which characterized the second Michigan. They gave way rapidly until driven in upon the brigade. Croxton would not believe it was anything but bushwhackers. He ordered four companies of the Second, under Captain Walter Whittemore, back as rear guard, and

CAPTAIN WALTER H. WHITTEMORE.

moved on. Two companies dismounted, and two remained mounted. These checked the advance three times, though the enemy made a gallant charge each time. The men of Adams's division had evidently never met these troops before. One Confederate officer, near enough to be heard, shouted, "Come on, the d— Yankee cowards won't fight; they'll run!" "But," said a correspondent of the *Louisville Journal*, "they stood like statues, and that murderous fire it was almost impossible to face. And they would have stood there all day had not the enemy become satisfied and withdrawn."

A southern paper spoke of it as "a desperate battle in which 300 were killed," but they did not mention the wounded.

Soon the rear guard moved on. Then it began to grow dark, and they halted for the enemy to come up to check them once more, that they might have the night undisturbed. Two companies dismounted, and forming behind the brow of a hill waited. Soon the Confederates appeared again in full force; Opening a heavy volley the enemy again retreated rapidly, and the rear guard moved on, through mud, quicksand and water. Passing on until after dark it was thought prudent to ascertain if the enemy were following, and again the rear guard halted, and soon they came, and by their conversation it was apparent they were hard hit, for they were telling of one and another that had gone down. They were halted by a random volley in the darkness, and abandoned the chase for the night.

LEAVES FROM A DIARY.

COLONEL THOS. W. JOHNSTON.

The following clippings, abbreviated from the diary of Colonel Thomas W. Johnston, will doubtless prove interesting to the general reader for the insight they give to the rough life of a cavalryman, especially from an officer who was too little self-seeking for his own good:

CHICKASAW, ALABAMA, March 17, 1865—Was relieved from duty at headquarters first brigade, first division cavalry, army of the Cumberland, to accept command of the regiment at the request of Majors Dickinson and Nicholson. * * *

March 18—Assumed command of the regiment. Received circular directing the command to be in readiness to move. One mule allowed for each twenty-five men to pack rations and ammunition. Six days' rations of coffee, sugar and salt packed in haversacks. Two days' rations salt meat, three days' rations of hard bread. On the mules nine days' rations of coffee, five days rations of sugar and salt; four days' rations of hard bread. Drew 10,000 rounds of ammunition from Colonel Dorr, eigth Iowa, all worthless, wet.

March 20—Weather changed to wind and rain. Forage has given out and can take nothing but hay. Detailed a sergeant and eight men to be relieved from all duty but *pioneer* and *fighting*. Turned over all surplus stores, ordnance, quartermasters', etc., to be to be sent back to storehouse at Edgefield.

March 22—Began to move (the division) àt 5:30 A. M. The Second, taking the rear, got off at 6:30. Lost most ot our forage, through neglect of the commander at the front, who made no allowance for closing up after passing obstacles; the front continuing to move on compels the rear to gallop to close up. Passed through Cherokee—two splendid residences and about forty cabins for "niggers and poor white trash."

March 23—Worked all the afternoon to get our trains over a bad hill.

March 24—Passed through Frankfort and had better roads and more forage. Passed through Russelville. Pat ———, of company C, threatened the life of Lieutenant Woodruff.

April 25—Bonner's Plantation, Georgia, two miles northwest of Carrolton. Received papers containing the news of Lee's surrender, and an armistice between Sherman and Johnston. Numbers of Lee's parolled soldiers returning to their homes.

April 26—Crossed the Chattahooche river and arrived at Henderson's plantation, Georgia, five miles northwest of Newman. This planter claims the benefit of the armistice; respected the same and slept on his stoop.

April 27—Griffin's plantation, eighteen miles from Newman, on the Greenville road. Passed through Newman at seven o'clock A. M. Band playing, flags (what's left of them) flying; citizens came out in their Sunday best, 1,500 Confederate soldiers came into town while we were passing through and we passed on, through Hughesville and Rocky mountains.

April 28—Roads and weather better. Passed through a portion of country quite like western New York. Went into camp near the plantation of the Rev. Mr. Maddox, an Episcopal minister.

April 29—Marched to Barnesville, Georgia; town full of ex-Confederates returning to their homes. Went into camp near Forsyth, a pretty little town. This town is also filled with "Johnnies."

April 30—March to camp near Macon, Georgia.

And here follows the routine of camp life, interspersed

with the "trial of Pat ———" for insubordination, the conviction, sentence to the guard house and camp police duty, the expiration of sentence and later the attempt of Pat to "muster out" the officers who sat upon his court martial, and the final tragic death at the hands of Captain Vance, in self-defense.

The details of colored troops' organization, and their rush to the camps of the "Yankee sojers" to breathe the new air of freedom would fill a volume.

The difficulty of attending the proper restraint of marauding bummers, the outrages, robberies and general cussedness of outlaws from both armies would fill another volume, but does not properly belong in these pages.

Captain Tom's method of disposing of a disagreeable subject is well illustrated by his memoranda, made while a Captain, at Dandridge:

December 24, 1863—The regiment was ordered to move at two A. M., without the sound of bugles; we go in advance. About worn out with previous duties, and not appreciating that kind of nonsense *for fun*, there was a general listlessness, and it was next to impossible to arouse the men, and some little delay to all the command ensued, causing some confusion. The major commanding the regiment was blowed up by the Colonel in command of the brigade; the commander of the second battalion in turn was blowed up, and in turn made a scapegoat of me. I was put under arrest. But about nine o'clock A. M., just as arrangements were being made for a fight, and I had begun to congratulate myself on being out of one scrape, I was relieved from arrest, ordered to take command of my company and soon after found things getting interesting on the skirmish line.

Drove the enemy's lines back and while waiting for orders made coffee, but orders came and we began skirmishing again and drove the enemy back about four miles from Dandridge, when we were suddenly attacked in the rear, the force in front having entirely disappeared. We wheeled to the rear, and found the enemy among our led horses, and holding possession of three pieces of our artillery, which we immediately recaptured.

Finding ourselves attacked in front and rear, with forces double our own, retreat towards New Market through the woods was all that was open to us. After fighting slowly through the woods for some miles I was wounded in the back of my calf. The brigade lost eighty men and one piece of artillery *disabled.*

December 25, 1863—Was brought to New Market last night; moved back balance of the wounded to Strawberry Plains this afternoon; stopped at the house of Mrs. Thomas.

December 27—Knoxville; arrived here at four o'clock A. M. Have been all night coming from the Plains, fifteen miles. This is a new hospital with no conveniences whatever.

January 4, 1864—Going home on wounded leave of absence, came to Loudon, thirty miles.

January 7—Got a boat from Loudon at seven A. M.; forty-first Ohio on board, going home; 150 rebel prisoners on board. Stopped along the river several times for the crew to go and get rails; very cold. The cabin of the boat is loaded so heavily there is scarcely standing room.

January 8—Arrived at Chattanooga at twelve noon. One rebel prisoner died on board. Stopped the boat and buried him —gave him five minutes. Passed on down the river from Bridgeport. In passing through the rapids the boat bounded like a cork. After getting off the boat at Bridgeport came near freezing. Could not walk and there were no fires.

January 9—Stevenson; came here at three A. M., just in time to see the Nashville train leave. Weather very cold. No stove in the car. Several men perished here from cold and exposure. I shall always be under obligations to Captains Runtan, A. Q. M., and Rickets, Kelly and Spencer.

January 11—Arrived at Nashville. Kelly was robbed last night of $300.

January 14—Left Nashville for Louisville. Was not allowed in first class cars. These were reserved for brigadier-generals, Jew peddlers and harlots.

January 15—Missed connections at Louisville.

January 16—Missed connections at Indianapolis. Started for Michigan City at eleven A. M. Freight train off the track at Brookston; waited ten hours.

January 17—Arrived at Michigan City in the morning. Had my wound dressed; changed my clothes, etc.

January 18—Home (Marshall, Michigan,) at two o'clock A. M.

From this it will be seen that it took fourteen days after receiving his furlough, and getting on the way, to accomplish a journey which can be made now in two or three days, and that during this time he, with many others, was suffering not only from his wound but from imperfect sanitary accommodations and the rigors of a severe winter, and treated by railroad men and guards like a lot of cattle.

A SCOUT ON FOOT.

In February, 1864, while the regiment was stationed at

Waterloo, Alabama, a detachment under Captain T. W. Johnston with Lieutenants Shaw and Woodruff started out on foot to Chickasaw Bluffs to capture a company said to be encamped near there. A negro guide led them to the spot, but they learned their game was nine miles further on. Not to be discouraged they set out through the darkness, with mud knee deep and rain falling. The rebel scouts were found near Price's tanyard. First they captured two mounted men riding along the road, who tried to put Captain Johnston on the wrong track, but they pressed on and when the rebel camp fire was discovered our boys crept near and made a dash. Captain Johnston proved the best runner, though he stumbled over a log, but he sprung to his feet and dashed up, shouting with all the breath left in him. His glasses were wet and blurred, and the objects before him scarcely distinguishable, but he brandished his revolver and shouted, "Surrender!"—standing all alone over a full company of now thoroughly cowed rebels. But he was soon joined by his men, panting for breath, and the pretended sleepers were made to uncover their faces and get up.

Throwing the captured arms and saddles upon the fire, our men locked arms with their captives and marched them back to camp, only one escaping as they stumbled along in the darkness.

Why some of our infantry, camped there, should not have been sent on such a dismounted expedition was not explained, but no duty, however disagreeable or unreasonable, was ever shirked by men of the Second. It was an all night tramp, and as they trudged wearily along the captured horses were made to do double duty in carrying the "lame ducks," and keeping the stragglers closed up. It is safe to conclude that no more scouting was done on foot by any of that party.

"DID THEY STING?"

Among the absurd things that were daily occurring along the line of march of our army, not the least were the requests for protection to private property. There was a strong desire among our officers to protect citizens who were *strictly* non-combatants, but these, unless outspoken Union men, were not so easy to find.

To suppose that a general could turn his attention from the weighty affairs that were crowding upon his brain, during a pending engagement, to attend to the loss of a chicken or a hive of bees was extremely absurd; yet just such things were expected, and almost invariably from people who had no sympathy with the northern army. Our generals who were taken from the border states saw these absurdities more readily than the more extreme northern men. During the battle of Franklin, or just as it was about to begin, a citizen who had never been distinguished to any alarming extent for his extreme loyalty to the Union cause came to General Croxton and said:

"I am looking for General Croxton."

"Well, I reckon you are about as near him as you need to get," turning his head indifferently and looking him over dryly, recognized him.

"Well, your men are carrying off all my beehives."

Turning his head again and looking up at the man out of the corner of his eye, he drawled out in that peculiar inimitable manner of his, "Did they sting?" and mounting his horse rode away to attend to his own affairs.

AN INTERRUPTED WEDDING.

When a detachment of Croxton's brigade, from the second Michigan cavalry, charged across the bridge in the night at Tuscaloosa, captured the artillery, scattered the cadets and regular Confederate troops stationed there, a squad of men hunting up Confederate officers came upon a house full, with hacks standing about the door. They surrounded the house and a small squad entered, and without attempting to frighten the ladies present told the officers they must leave the untasted banquet and report to General Croxton. The ladies threw their arms about the soldiers' necks and begged them not to take the officers away. It is said that there were in this squad two or three rough fellows who were always looking out for plunder and relieved the ladies of their gold watches while these appealing demonstrations were being made. If this was true it was much regretted by General Croxton and the officers and the best portion of the men of the Second, but it was not known until too late, and the guilty ones could not be brought to justice.

The officers were removed, and the captain, who had just been married, requested to be shown to General Croxton's tent.

The meeting between these two officers was most affecting. It appears they had been friends in Kentucky before the war.

"Captain," said the general, "I am very sorry to meet you again under these most peculiar circumstances."

"Yes, general, it is to me most trying, I assure you; and without asking anything because of our former friendship I simply appeal to you as a gentleman and an officer, to hear my story and if possible parole me. The lady to whom I have just been married is sinking into her grave with consumption. She requested this marriage before she dies and I have hoped I might prolong her life by the comfort she might gain in being my wife if only for a few months. Of course the excitement of this evening has prostrated her and I only ask to be allowed to return and assure her that I will not be sent to a northern prison, but can remain near her. I belong to the staff of General Forrest, and I think under the circumstances you need have no fears of my violating my parole."

"You can go; send an escort with him, major."

And the captain reported promptly at nine in the morning according to promise and was given an indefinite parole, although it was not then known that Lee had surrendered nor that Lincoln had been assassinated.

HORSE SENSE.

Instances of the animal intelligence of the horse were almost too common in the army to be commented upon, yet memory lingers around the deed of that noble friend of man, and brings with it the recollection of long weary days and nights, plodding through mud, rain, snow, cold, or summer's heat—sweltering, bruised, and hungry, yet faithful and uncomplaining. Do you wonder that there was a degree of affection and sympathy between soldier and horse that was often touching in the extreme; and as horse and man were often compelled by the exigencies of war to part company, is it any wonder that manly tears dimmed the eye and the voice choked as hand stroked head or neck of the suffering brute? "Poor fellow, must I leave you here?"

"Put him out of his misery."

"I can't, boys."

And so the poor animal was abandoned by the roadside to die of his wounds—died for his country!—perhaps alone, but more probably upon the battlefield, with thousands of human beings to mingle their blood with his.

If the rider was unhorsed, then the feelings of the horse manifested themselves. If it was during a charge, the horse, true to his education and instincts, kept his place in the ranks till they were broken. Then if left to himself, he was often seen looking, in his mute, appealing way, as if in search of his master. If swept along by the whirling mass of horsemen he kept his place as long as permitted and proved stubborn if his removal was attempted by anyone he had never seen before.

An instance of this came under my observation at Booneville, Mississippi. The enemy had charged upon the dismounted men of the second Michigan cavalry for the fourth or fifth time, when a Confederate officer (said to have been a colonel), mounted upon a fine blooded animal, fell from his horse and the horse was borne along by his impetuosity through the ranks of our men. Passing near at the time, in my line of duty as aid-de-camp, mounted, I reached out my hand and caught the loose rein. So long as I rode along or near the front I had no difficulty in leading him on a sharp gallop, but when I turned towards the rear, that was another affair. I had to abandon him to some one who had more time to fool with him than I had. He was taken to camp, however, presented to me by Colonel Sheridan, and proved a fleet-footed, valuable animal, but was stolen at Rienzi by some lover of horseflesh, probably for racing purposes.

LUCKY ESCAPES.

When the rebel General Frank Wheeler attempted to cross into Tennessee on his big raid after the battle of Chicamauga, he found it quite difficult to find a crossing. Our cavalry was scattered along in detachments of one company or a battalion, according to the weakness of the position, and whenever Wheeler presented himself he was met with a sharp resistance. Without attempting to force a passage he passed on up the river until he got beyond our men, and so passed around our extreme left. About twenty miles up the river was company K, under Captain Baker. Two citizens came into camp and reported a company organizing across the river, and Lieutenant Sanborn, with ten men and the two citizens, was sent to break them up.

It was a foolhardy piece of business and would not, probably, at that time have received the sanction of the officers higher in command, but that company never seemed to tire of fighting and were ready to volunteer for anything, especially if there was a chance for plunder on the way. Crossing over, they had not passed out of sight but a short time when Captain Baker and his reserves were fired upon; and, looking across the river, there appeared a large force of rebel cavalry. The fire was returned with spirit, and the enemy passed on up the river in search of an easier ford. The little scouting party was of course at once given up as captured, and Baker passed many hours of unpleasant suspense, cursing his folly in sending them, and expecting certain court-martial and disgrace. But the scouts had taken another road, and were far enough away from the river to miss even the sound of firing in their rear. Passing down the valley about ten miles they came upon the headquarters of the organizing rebels, and dashed upon them, capturing ten, but were not quick enough to prevent seven from escaping, firing over their shoulders as they ran. The horses of the whole party were captured and, taking another route, they set out hastily for camp, expecting every moment to be followed by some new force, but they reached the ford in safety long after dark and were beginning to recross, when they were fired upon by their own men and it was some minutes before Captain Baker could be persuaded they were his scouts. At last he asked, "Is that you, Sanborn?" and the reply, "Yes, you d—fool, what you firing at!" came echoing across the river with a distinctness truly marvelous. As the scouts had not heard of Wheeler, and the reserves had long since given them up as captured, that meeting on the river bank can only be partly imagined. It is safe to conclude that Captain Baker never sent out scouts again without consulting those higher in authority.

Among the earliest receipts of recruits in 1862 was a young boy soldier. His reception by his brother, a lieutenant in the regiment (Darrow), was not of the most welcome character. The elder brother felt that one out of the family was enough, and, with the utmost kindness of heart, he regretted the step taken by the younger brother, but endeavored to make the best of it, and kept a watchful restraint over him.

John Morgan came into Kentucky in December, 1862, and found the State comparatively free from Union forces. Sweeping north he entered Glasgow, and his doings there and at Bacon Creek have been noted elsewhere in this volume. Among Morgan's captures at Glasgow was young Darrow. The prisoners were marched up the street and halted by the curbstone to await orders. Whiskey had been flowing freely among the officers and men of Morgan's command, and while some were disposed to be facetious others were ugly, and went swaggering and swearing up and down. It was now dark and Darrow noticed with keen eyes his guards were becoming indifferent and reckless. Watching his opportunity he quietly slipped from the ranks. No one appeared to notice him. He backed away a step or two. No one said halt, and putting on a business like air he walked away, jumped over a fence and found himself free. Then came the trouble. The enemy had pickets upon every road. Which way the command had gone he could only guess. At two o'clook in the morning he had made a successful escape through their picket lines and found a hiding place in the chamber of a good Union man by the name of Ellington Beck, some four miles out of Glasgow, where he remained till Morgan's forces had marched from that section, then young Darrow made his *single handed* march on foot and joined his own company at Mumsfordville, Kentucky, unharmed except some bruises by the fall of his horse during the skirmish, where his coat was shot through the right side and right sleeve, one ball passing through the side, cutting off a part of the suspender. He had been reported among the missing and as he crept into camp at midnight after three days' absence, and made himself known to his brother, that meeting in the dark can easier be imagined than described.

WEAER'S COVE.

Early in January, 1864, when part of our forces (cavalry) were stationed on the Little Tennessee and the enemy were holding Marysville and Severeville, sixteen scouts belonging to General Ed McCook's headquarters, left camp in the afternoon and set out by a circuitous route for Tuckaleeche Cove, which they reached a little before the mountains shut out the sunlight. Passing rapidly up the little stream that ripples through this quiet nook, the early twilight found them at the head of the cove; and, alighting from their horses, a breathing spell was taken and a consultation was held. They were in among the

Union men of East Tennessee, men who knew what it cost to be known as "loyal"—a plain, hardy set of mountaineers, who lost no opportunity of gathering about their Yankee friends and offer aid whenever needed. And this time they had exciting news to tell. The Confederates had sent a squad of twenty men into Weaer's Cove and that afternoon they had gone in, "just a bit above," and were foraging upon the poor settlers.

The good wives and daughters prepared a hearty supper for our boys, served out upon the jutting rocks near their dwelling.

The scouts were mostly second Michigan men, in charge of a non-commissioned officer, and they were mostly young men, mere boys some of them. Robert McDougall was looked upon as a leader among them, and to him two of the boys came, and in a whispered consultation asked to be allowed to go over into Weaer's Cove and ascertain as to the truth of the rumor. These were Robert Crotty and a boy from the second Iowa cavalry named Farnsworth. The latter was an effeminate looking boy, with fair face, blue eyes and an altogether too delicate look for so daring an undertaking.

"It is getting very dark," said McDougall, "and the horses are too much jaded for more work to-night than is absolutely necessary."

But they concluded to go, and taking with them eight of the home guards they set out on foot.

"Remember, now, boys, we are nearly in rear of the enemy, and a mistake might be fatal to us all," said Mack. "If you discover them, return at once that we may all act together."

"All right," and away they went out silently into the mountain passes.

The fires were put out (all but one, that was thought sufficiently obscured by the overhanging rocks), and folding themselves in their blankets, and hugging their guns in their arms they reclined against rocks and trees to await the return of their scouts.

Says McDougall: "Some hours had passed, during which I had slept with one eye and an ear open, when I felt a gentle touch, and looking up saw the anxious face of a woman, as the faintly glimmering camp fire shone upon her. Bending over me she whispered: 'Isn't it time they were back? It is now past midnight.'

" 'Yes, they should be here; have you heard any firing?'

" 'No.'

" 'The air is very clear; we could hear it if there had been.'

" 'I think so.'

"Presently a noise was heard. The men sprang to sheltered points. A clatter of hoofs was heard on the rocks above.

" 'The men took no horses with them.'

" 'No,' she faintly whispered.

"Louder came the clatter.

" 'Halt!' 'Friends,' rang out the cheery voice of Crotty and before we had time to say more they were among us, with seventeen unarmed Johnnies and twenty good mules and horses.

" 'Any one hurt?'

" 'No. You see, Mack, we did intend to come back, as we said, but when we reached the top of the mountain we saw a fire, down in the cove, and we crawled along on our hands and knees, expecting every moment to come upon their guard, but when we got near the house of Mr. ——, we came suddenly upon those chaps all snoozing around a comfortable fire, and a little to one side were all these mules and horses. We looked again, hardly believing they had no sentinel out in such an open place.

"'Presently I crawled up to the nearest one and touched him. He opened his eyes and looked into my navy. He knew what to expect and quietly got up. I touched the next. The same surprise and the same result, and the next, until every one of them stood up like a row of cobs and not a word was spoken.

"'No more in sight, so we drew the wagons together, broke the guns and set fire to the heap. Then we started back, bringing the horses and men with us. As we passed the house Farnsworth asked me if any one had been to the house. "No." "Then I am going back." "Don't; we have got all we can attend to now, besides, you may get hurt." But he was bound to go; so he hitched his horses under a tree and that's the last we have seen of him.

"After waiting some little time, we got anxious and were about to go in search of him, when we again heard the clatter of hoofs, and Farnsworth dashed among us.

"'There,' said he, 'that's what I got,' and he threw down a large revolver, and an old wallet.

"'I killed the cuss, and took these from him. Let's see, what's this?—some Confed—what's *this?*—an order to Sergeant ——, to take twenty men and go into Weaer's Cove. By order brigadier-general.'

"'Now, Farnsworth tell us what you did.'

"'Well, when I got to the house I looked through the window and saw an old woman, elbows on her knees, face in her hands, bending over a dimly burning fire of pine knots. Just back of her I thought I saw a pair of boots and what looked like two men under a blanket. I tapped on the window. The woman straightened up and said, "What's wanted?" "Tell those men to come out;" and I stepped from the window so as not to be seen. Two men got up and came to the door. As one of them stepped on to the stoop I could just see his outlines; his hand was down by his side. I brought up my old Spencer and said Surrender. He raised his arm and fired into my face. The ball just grazed my temple. I guess you can see the burnt mark there. It staggered me, but, before he could fire again, I fired. He fell on the floor. Then I heard the other man rush for the back door and I hurried around and headed him off. Back he came to the front door and before I could get a chance at him he was gone, out in the dark. Then I searched my man. Only one shot out of his revolver. A brave soldier, and he deserved a better fate, but I had to do it. Why didn't he surrender?'

"Well, Farnsworth, you have done well, but you took too many chances. And now, boys, this detail calls for twenty men. We have but seventeen here. The others probably heard the firing, and detachments will be sent from Marysville and Severeville to head us off. We must be away from here by sun up. Woman, can you get us some breakfast?"

"Yes, yes,"—and before the sun was peeping over the hills we were well down the cove.

"To continue the main road through the foot hills, as we

came, was dangerous, so we turn to the left, pass over the mountain into Cade's Cove, to follow the summit of Chilhowie mountain and strike the Little Tennessee about twenty-six miles above our forces. We had scarcely left the main road when our rear guard came up and said: 'The rebs are coming up from Marysville, about 200 strong.'

"Up, up, the zigzag path we toil and were scarcely at the top when the rebels reached the base of the mountain.

"A citizen stood watching the enemy from a projecting rock at the roadside near the summit. He gave a shrill blast from his horn and was answered back from every dwelling in the cove. Then the inhabitants were seen in every direction climbing the mountain side where horses could not go. We were not yet at the top of old Chilhowie when we looked back and saw the Johnnies on the ridge between Tuckaleeche and Cade's Cove —the one we had just left.

"They heard the horns, saw us down in Cade's Cove; stood a few moments as if bewildered then turned to the left and passed over into Weaer's Cove, leaving us to quietly return to camp with our prisoners and booty, to the no little surprise and gratification of our commander."

A BULL RUN HERO.

Among our officers was one who, it was said, had shown skill and bravery as an officer in a Michigan regiment at Bull Run; but the memory of that demoralizing race for life clung to him. He never could stand; but his legs, or those of his horse were always sure to bear him away whether his men followed him or not, and at last he left the gory field to those who did not know enough to run.

A LIVELY PRISONER.

When the regiment was within about three miles of Elizabethtown, Kentucky, on its scout, October, 1862, it was reported that a company of Confederate recruits were in camp near a road leading to the left, and Captain Smith, with company D, was sent to capture them. Away they went on the gallop, and sooner than they expected came upon the "doughty warriors" fast asleep under a beech tree, with their arms inconveniently stacked a short distance away. As our men came near them, a few awoke in time to shout, "The Yankees are coming," and all succeeded in getting away to the bush without their arms, except their captain, who sprang up, and seizing a double-barreled shot gun, cocked it and leveled it at Captain Ben Smith, who cried out to him, "Surrender or you're a dead man," and seeing too many against him the rebel concluded "discretion was the better part of valor" and threw down his gun.

Placing Lieutenant Buddington in charge of the prisoner, Captain Smith, with his company, pursued the scattering Johnnies and had the satisfaction of securing about twenty of them.

In the meantime Lieutenant Buddington had become a little uneasy with his one prisoner, and began to move around towards the arms to get between them and his captive, holding in his hand the while a revolver, ready for service. Taking advantage of an unguarded moment the prisoner sprang upon the Lieutenant, and with a death like grip caught the muzzle of the revolver, but the Lieutenant held firm and in the struggle the piece was discharged, carrying away two of the prisoner's fingers. That scheme was at once abandoned, and another put as rapidly into execution, showing the fellow to be a man of pluck in an emergency. He jumped away from his Yankee antagonist (still mounted), and running behind a wagon, dodged hither and thither from expected bullets, when, to his infinite satisfaction, a rampageous hog came to the rescue, dodging between the legs of the horse, neatly dismounting the Lieutenant, landing horse and man in a promiscuous heap, from which the Lieutenant arose, no little chagrined to find himself minus a prisoner, and the Captain, with his company, returning just in time to join in the laugh, which even the rebel prisoners enjoyed.

The Lieutenant's only remark was, "By thunder! if that feller will send me his card, I'll give him this d— old pistol, to pay for the fingers he left behind."

A FLAG OF TRUCE.

In the latter part of July, 1862, while we were encamped near Rienzi, Mississippi, the necessity for an exchange of prisoners was acknowledged, and General Granger, with part of his staff, accompanied by Colonel Sheridan, and a part of his staff (Colonel Sheridan having been recommended for promotion to brigadier-general, and acting as such), set out with an escort of thirty mounted men, bearing the white flag of peace, in search of the Confederate headquarters. The most strict order was maintained throughout that long day, and not a sign of scout or picket was met with until the sun was nearly set and we brought up at a little burg thirty miles south, known as Guntown. The column was halted at the outpost and a courier dispatched to headquarters announcing Yankee visitors. Without much delay orders were returned to escort the officers to headquarters, the men being shown a pleasant camping ground near by, with a clear spring of cool water at hand and an abundance of food for horses. Such a quiet little nook among the hills and trees was rarely met with, and our men were not slow to settle themselves down to a night of perfect rest and enjoyment; and though a guard of Confederates was detailed to remain with them, the most courteous hospitality was extended and received in good faith.

The officers were invited to private houses near by and tables were spread with the best the land afforded.

Piano music and songs—including "Star Spangled Banner" and "The Bonny Blue Flag"—were given with zest, and to the sharp raillery of the young ladies good natured responses were given by the gentlemen in blue, and the evening wore away very pleasantly and we were given the "best beds" and wished a pleasant good night.

Where Generals Granger and Sheridan passed their evening and what official acts were consummated was not for us subalterns to know; but we retired in such perfect peace of mind that we were sorry to awaken on the morrow and dispel this pleasant dream. But with the morning, after a hearty breakfast, our escort was at the door, and mounting, our adieus were spoken to the ladies, while the blue and gray paired off and moved away side by side, chatting, not gaily, but with a subdued feeling of mingled sadness and pleasure. For were we not—to-day friends and brothers, yesterday and to-morrow enemies, whom to shoot on sight was our sworn aim and intent?

At their outpost a short halt was made, brief words of hope for another and more lasting peaceful meeting were expressed; hands were pressed in warm and earnest friendship; hats were lifted in courteous salute, and we filed out with our backs to our foe.

Out of respect to this friendly meeting not a scout was made on either side for many days, and soon after thousands of prisoners from both sides were exchanged at Memphis.

SCOUTING IN NORTH CAROLINA.

While the cavalry division under General Ed McCook lay at Severeville, East Tennessee, frequent scouting expeditions were made by his picked scouts, and one day in January, 1864, a glorious bright winter's day, eight of this little band of scouts mostly second Michigan cavalry, with some from the eighth Iowa, first Wisconsin or third Indiana, went over the mountains, watching for roving bands of the enemy. Passing over into North Carolina they looked back from one of the peaks and could plainly see Knoxville, Dandridge and Mossy Creek, thirty-five miles away. Below them, sweeping across the valleys, were occasional white clouds that looked very harmless and very beautiful, but as they swept up and over the face of the mountains, these lowland scouts were given the new sensation of a cloud bath, a wet experience, but quickly passed; and as the sun burst through again they moved on down into the enemy's country.

Keenly alert to every sound or sign of an ambush from bushwhackers or more formidable bands of the enemy they pick their way through that broken country, and finding nothing set out on their return. Suddenly a lagging scout comes rushing up from the rear and shouts, "A whole company of cavalry are after us." The odds were against them and they dash away to gain a more sheltered position. A horse stumbles, throwing his rider heavily, and the others check their speed to give their unfortunate comrade time to mount and come up. He was unable to mount, but hobbles along at a painful step, and seeing they must make a stand or lose a man they turn fiercely at bay. Fortunately they had entered a gorge, high rocks towering on either hand and a bend of the road in their rear.

As quick as thought those rifles are brought to the shoulder and the foremost of the pursuers brought to the ground, men and horses all in a confused mass. A sergeant and one man (a recognized bushwhacker), unable to check their speed, but missing the first discharge are among them. A continuous volley from the seven shooters warns the Confederates that they have no faint hearted boys to deal with, and all that could get back were not slow in doing so, leaving our scouts to retire at their leisure without losing a man or horse.

Among the number was a mere boy, who had no other weapon than a cavalry saber.

"Shall I charge them?" said he.

384   DODGING SHELLS.

The absurdity of the proposition was too much for the sergeant in command.

"Yes," said he, laughing, and at it he went; riding fiercely down upon an officer he cut and slashed at the Confederate's neck until they all fled, the man's head appearing squarely on his shoulders not much the worse for his encounter; but he was seen a few days after with his throat bound up, and our boy had the satisfaction of knowing that he had at least made a saber-charge and drawn blood.

The scouts soon returned to camp without further adventure, but such deeds of daring were not uncommon to them in that wild disputed territory.

DODGING SHELLS.

It rarely occurred that shot from a cannon in any form could be dodged; yet such incidents did occur, and no doubt oftener than would be thought possible. It must be done when the shot or shell is coming directly towards you, otherwise it could not be seen. Stand directly behind a piece of artillery when it is fired, the smoke of battle not yet so thick as to cloud the vision, and there is no trouble in following the flying missile through the air if the eye is quick. And some have asserted their ability to follow even a musket ball in its flight if the range is not too short. A case of dodging was witnessed at Thompson's station that was peculiarly exciting for a few moments. The firing had just began to wax warm, when a shell that would have been "too high," struck the large branch of a tree and glancing downward was seen a hundred yards away, coming end over end, with that peculiar whir-r-r which plainly indicates it is not flying "point blank." An officer standing a short distance in front of his squadron, and seeing at once that his legs and the body of his horse would be hit, slashed his horse with the spur and shouted to the officer in his rear and the men near him:

"Look out!"

Those who were at "attention" did move slightly, and escaped, but one horse, slower than the rest, caught it on the knee, breaking his leg; but so many obstructions proved too much for the shell and it stopped.

Knowing it to be a conical or long shell, from its peculiar noise, an explosion was expected, and those nearest held their breath while they stood in that peculiar attitude a person would naturally assume if he saw a lighted match fall into a powder magazine, ten feet away.

It is useless to speculate as to men's bravery and what they would do in trying moments like that. No man, in his right mind, but looks upon this world as preferable to a world of which he knows nothing except by an eye of faith, and so with that first law of nature uppermost in his mind, he steps aside, if by so doing he can save his life and continue in the line of duty.

One man, Captain H——, more foolhardy than the rest, without stopping to think whether the fuse was still burning or not, picked up the shell with the remark, "Why the darned thing *hain't* bust," and held it in his hand until warned that it might possibly "bust" yet, when he threw it away, and in a few minutes thereafter we had something else to do besides "dodging shells."

UNEXPLODED SHELLS.

Frightful accidents sometimes occurred in camp by the careless handling of old shells picked up on the battle field. At New Madrid some infantrymen had removed the fuse from a thirty-two pounder and allowed the powder to be scattered along on the ground; this became ignited by a cigar dropped from the hand of a comrade and the trail of powder flashed, extending to the shell, and blowed two men into eternity.

WHO HIT CHALMERS AT BOONEVILLE?

At the eleventh hour an interview with members of the second battalion has given some additional light upon the routing of Chalmers at Booneville, Mississippi, July 1, 1862.

Twenty-four men of company L, with about the same numbers from companies M, H and one company from the second Iowa cavalry, all under the command of Major Alger, gained the rear of the left wing of Chalmers's forces. Captain Wells, of company L, led the charge and they were soon among the

Confederates, cutting, slashing and shouting, and the enemy were immediately thrown into confusion and began a stampede. Then the Confederates' main forces charged back upon the little battalion of one hundred men and all moved back, firing promiscuously at close range and in a confused mass. The enemy made no special effort to capture, but each party seemed anxious to leave the other, and our battalion, taking the first road leading off to the right, soon found themselves free from the enemy, the woods concealing the real strength or weakness of our force. But it was a free fight from the start, and many were either killed or wounded on both sides. Company L lost six men by capture (their horses were shot), one man was killed and fifteen wounded.

Lieutenant Hutton's horse was killed and he was wounded, but escaped with the aid of a lieutenant of the second Iowa.

Major Alger was injured, but escaped.

The few prisoners captured thought the movement on their rear was to draw them into a trap and thought our force was very much larger than they had at first supposed. They continued their rapid retreat for ten miles before going into camp.

Our little battalion returned leisurely.

RUNNING THE GAUNTLET.

While the second battalion, under Major Dickey, was retiring before John Morgan, with his 4,000 mounted men, from Glasgow to Mumfordsville, Kentucky, Sergeant Henry Woodruff, with six men forming the extreme rear guard, was cut off by a party of scouting flankers. Telling the men to follow him he put spurs to his horse and dashed down the road. Throwing down his reins he drew his revolver in one hand and an old single barreled horse pistol in the other and not a shot was fired until he was fairly among the rebels, when he fired right and left. The scouts appearently mistook him for one of their own men and not until he had passed them did they recover from their astonishment and opened fire upon him with carbines, pistols, muskets, shot guns loaded with buckshot, but he dashed away unscathed and was received on the next hill by his own men with loud cheers. The other six men lacked the nerve to attempt the perilous ride and were all captured.

A regiment of such men as Sergeant Woodruff would have rode through an army without hesitation.

A CORPORAL'S GUARD MAKES A RECONNAISSANCE.

Were it not that war is a serious business the following account of a reconnaissance by a mere handful of men would sound ridiculous, but so far from that being the fact it was as important in its results as though the whole division had gone:

A small detachment of company F was sent out in charge of private Bradford (corporals were too scarce to throw away on small affairs) to ascertain the position of the enemy at Varnell's station. The advance was rapid, mounted, firing as they neared the advanced skirmishers, and driving them behind the first line of infantry, who, in turn, fell behind their earthworks as the little squad dashed across the field, through the woods and up to the very cannon's mouth, and a row of muskets poured forth a sheet of fire and lead that ought if properly directed to have swept them from the earth, but strange to say not a man was killed, though some were more or less injured. The enemy came out, and following on, back through the town, drove our little squad doggedly from cover to cover until the crest of a hill was reached; a few of the regiment came up; rocks, rails and logs were hastily thrown up as a breastwork; the horses sent to the rear and on comes a brigade of Confederate infantry.

The order was given to "fire low and give it to 'em lively," and at six rods' distance the slaughter begun. The Confederates broke and run, demoralized by a handful of green troops, although it would be difficult to make them believe there was not a brigade of Yankees behind that temporary breastwork. A citizen reported five of the enemy killed and twenty wounded.

UNDER ARREST.

When the veterans of the Second reached Chattanooga, on a wet, disagreeable afternoon of April, 1864, they were sent by Colonel Smith to a point most convenient to the depot, under command of an officer, to select the most available quarters that could be found, while the Colonel went to look after necessary papers for transportation home, and if possible, procure a temporary shelter from the rain.

No preparations had been made, and the outlook was gloomy enough. Their tents and camp equipage had been left behind, and there seemed only one alternative—to "skirmish" for boards or anything that could cover them. They happened to be near the headquarters of a colonel of colored troops. Without knowing or caring who the comfortably quartered officer was they commenced to gather in all the boards, fencing, pickets, etc., within reach. A company A man was picking up a board near the colonel's quarters, when the colonel rushed out, and jumping with all his weight upon the board, crushed the man's fingers. This was more than company A could stand, and without recognizing, in the darkness, that it was an officer with whom they had to deal, the valiant colonel was felled by a single blow of the fist, and they went on with their construction corps; a few of the men and most of the officers finding quarters in houses and hotels. Soon Colonel Smith received an order to report to General Thomas's headquarters, which was promptly complied with, when General Whipple informed him that his regiment had been guilty of unheard of outrages, depredations, etc., besides seriously injuring the "colored colonel," and that his regiment would be put under arrest in the morning, their furlough taken from them and the regiment otherwise punished.

Colonel Smith used his best arguments to change the decree, but all in vain. One side of the story had been heard and there appeared to be no extenuating circumstances. The Colonel said he would be responsible for all damages, but that would not do. The Colonel was suffered to return to his quarters for the night, with instructions to be at headquarters in the morning.

The news that the second Michigan cavalry were to be disarmed and put under arrest had created quite a stir in camp. Their fame as a fighting regiment was widely known, and it was hinted throughout the camp that there would be a fight. General Steadman, in command of the post, was ordered to make the arrest. It was evidently a disagreeable duty for the old soldier, for he was a hard fighter himself. But he ordered out a regiment of infantry and two pieces of artillery, placing them in a position commanding the camp of the Second. He then ordered the Second into line, arms in hand; and though a brave soldier, he turned pale as he looked into the eyes of those 315 scar worn veterans standing before him. Stating to the men, in a few words, his duty, in a voice full of emotion, he ordered them to stack their arms.

Only for a moment the turbulent, rebellious spirit welled up in their hearts, and promptly the arms were stacked, the long agony over, though there was many an eye moist with indignation on the one side and sympathy on the other. Every man felt that he could afford to leave the redress for their wrongs to their record in the past, and sure justice in the future.

They took their disgrace lightly, almost indifferently, and in twenty-four hours were released and on their way home.

The damages were assessed at $5, and paid, so ending the first and only unpleasantness with our own troops.

ONE DAY NEARER ATLANTA.

The following memorandum copied from the diary of a private soldier of company F, second Michigan cavalry, gives us a glimpse into the every day life of the soldier during that memorable campaign:

June 4—A detail of fifteen picked men under private Bradford was sent to take a rebel picket post on our left. It proved a strong position and we had a hard struggle to dislodge them. La Bean, Vliet, Helmer and Blackmer bore themselves like heroes, forcing the fighting from the start. This was a hard day's work and we were without rations. Relieved about 7 P. M. Rebel loss, three killed and wounded and three prisoners.

WHY CHEATHAM DID NOT GET THERE.

General Hood, in his book, "Advance and Retreat," bears down heavily upon Cheatham for not taking possession of the turnpike and cutting off Schofield's retreat from Columbia to Franklin.

The following from a member of company M, second Michigan cavalry, has but recently come to hand, in fact after the MS. was in the hands of the printer, and it could not, therefore, appear in the proper place. He says:

"Company M had been left the night before on picket at the crossing of Duck river, and was ordered to stay as long as possible and then follow the regiment towards Franklin. They stayed until the enemy's cavalry was on three sides of them in strong force, and the enemy's infantry was in sight, when they made their way (skirmishing along and keeping the rebel cavalry at a comfortable distance) back to Columbia and gave the alarm and then moved out east of the town, where the enemy were also appearing in strong force. We repulsed their advance skirmishers several times, but fell back before their main lines, fighting as long as possible, until some of our infantry came to our relief; and we checked the enemy until the trains got a little start. A very stubborn fight was kept up until dark, when the enemy bivouacked for the night, and our trains passed along the pike towards Franklin, with a small force of our infantry and our one company of cavalry ready to dispute the road until the last wagon had gone on, not long before daylight."

While it is more than probable that Cheatham would have forced his way to that pike it is also evident that he had a few desperate men to contend against, who fully understood and appreciated the dangers that threatened our trains, and had Cheatham taken possession of the pike he would have found it necessary to indulge in something more than an ordinary little skirmish, and that, too, with darkness coming on to aid the troops on the defensive.

GENERAL CHEATHAM'S STORY OF THE BATTLE OF FRANKLIN—
"THE MOST DESPERATE HAND TO HAND CONTEST OF THE WAR."

A correspondent of the Cincinnati Enquirer recently visited the battle field of Franklin, Tennessee, in company with General Cheatham, who commanded a Confederate corps in the action of November 30th, 1864. General Cheatham said:

"I had the largest corps in that army—something less than 9,000 men. Hood's disposition of his forces for that fight was:

The corps I was directing on the left and center, Stewart's corps on my right, and Stephen D. Lee's corps in reserve. My disposition was: General Bate on the extreme left, General J. C. Brown with my old division on the left of the Columbia pike, with his right resting on that road, Cleburne on the right of the same pike, with his left resting on it. As General Bate had a long road around to the left, I waited some time after he started before giving the order to advance. Finally the line moved forward. Brown and Cleburne were to stop as they reached the open field at the foot of Winstead's hill. I rode forward to its summit as they moved, and established my headquarters there, and waited for the troops to pass over."

"It was the grandest sight I ever saw when our army marched over the hill and reached the open field at its base. Each division unfolded itself into a single line of battle with as much steadiness as if forming for dress parade," said ex-Governor Porter, who was in those days General Cheatham's chief of staff. He was looking over the hill from Winstead's hill as he spoke, and seemed to recall the events of the day, and again pass them in review before his mind's eye. "As I look over this field to-day," he continued, "it seems as though I can almost witness the pageant over again. The men were tired, hungry, footsore, ragged, and many of them barefooted, but their spirit was admirable. Bear in mind that it was the first time the two divisions of Cheatham's corps—Cleburne's and Brown's—had met side by side in full view of each other in an open field, with the advantages for desperate work equally balanced between them. For years each had contended for the right to wear the name of the crack division of that army, and the faces of both men and officers seemed to say: 'Here is a field upon which the right shall be decided.'"

"Yes," broke in General Cheatham, "fight was not only in those two divisions, but in the whole army that day. Don't you remember, Porter, that as they wheeled into the line of battle, in full view of the enemy, their precision and military bearing were as beautiful a sight as was ever witnessed in war? I could see that the Federal line was short and curved and I knew that we could easily cover it by going forward in line of battle by brigades. So this information was made before the time to charge came.

"Before moving our troops from Winstead's hill I had arranged with both Cleburne and Brown, the two divisions under my eye, to give them the word with a flag when to move. When their lines swung into position they corrected their alignment and then faced toward me, waiting for the signal to advance. A moment of suspense to see that everything was ready, then the flag dropped, and the line moved forward as steady as a clock. It was two miles and a quarter from the starting point to the main Federal line, and our advancing column was in full view from General Schofield's position and from the intrenched line of the Union troops at the Carter house nearly every foot of the way. My twenty-four pieces of artillery followed the advancing troops, and occasionally dropped a shell into the Federal lines. There was no halt from the time our force started until it struck the Federal breastworks. A regiment was thrown out as skirmishers in advance of each of my divisions. They struck Wagner's two brigades posted a half mile in advance of the main position, and as they gave way our main line followed them right in on to the Federal breastworks. I lost hardly a man until within fifty yards of the intrenchments. The fleeing men from the two brigades posted in their front kept the fire off from our troops until after their men got behind the main line. Our line of battle followed them in. The Federals could not fire upon it until it was within very close range. Our advancing line must have been visible, not only to the Federal commanders, but to all of their troops in the fortifications for nearly an hour before it struck Wagner. Had it not been for the protection the two brigades that were in advance gave our men, Cox would have mowed my line with artillery from the moment I started until I reached his main works. As it was, our troops marched for an hour in full view of the enemy without any molestation to speak of, except a little harmless artillery fire from the fort where Schofield had his headquarters. The same may be said of Stewart's corps that was on my right, and also in full view. I followed and watched my line closely, and then took up my headquarters on Merrill's hill, a sharp knob within musket range of the fight. Hood was just back of me on the pike.

"It would be impossible to describe the operations on this field after the men got together. It was the bloodiest battle of the war. I lost six general officers killed and two wounded. Cleburne was our greatest loss. He was a capital soldier. He had some unpleasantness about Spring Hill with Hood, and I think was a little more daring than usual that day. It was reported to me that he had some words with the commander of the army just before going into battle. The charge of the two divisions of my corps, my old division commanded by General J. C. Brown, and Cleburne's, commanded by himself, was one of the most desperate and gallant of the war. Arms were trailed until time to give the steel came, when the order to charge was given simultaneously by Cleburne and Brown.

"The men marched to the terrible work with perfect precision and great spirit and determination. Cleburne's horse was killed under him just after the charge begun. With sword in hand he sprang to the front of his men, encouraging them with his words and example. Just before he reached the Federal works he was shot dead. Poor fellow. He never reached the enemy's earthworks toward which he was leading his men. He fell right here," said the old general, as he pointed to a spot not far from the old gin-house. "Here one of the best soldiers that ever drew a sword, gave up his life." The veteran's eyes moistened as he looked at the place in the open field where his friend was slain, but Mr. Carter, who owns the farm, has marked the spot, as every one who visits this field asks: "Where did Pat Cleburne die?" It is now obscured by the footprints of peace. After a moment General Cheatham turned from the field toward the road, and running his eye along the line said: "A little further to the right, looking toward Franklin, and around on the other side of the gin-house, General John Adams, of Stewart's corps, was killed on his horse astride the Federal breastworks. Scott, of the same corps, was also slain near there. General Cockrell, now United States senator from Missouri, and General Quarles were also wounded there. Stewart's corps did desperate work that day, and fully divided the honors with my own troops. Brown, who commanded my old division, was wounded early in the fight, after Cleburne was killed; and of my brigade commanders Gordon was captured, Granberry, Gist, Strahl and Carter were killed—a greater mortality of general officers than was ever known during the war when an equal number of tropps were engaged? The corps I commanded lost eight generals, killed and wounded, and Stewart lost five. About dark Ed John's division of Stephen D. Lee's corps, that was in reserve, was sent to the support of Brown and did some hard fighting. General Manigault, of that division, was wounded. General Bate, who went to the left, had a long and rough road to travel to reach his position, but he went into battle on the left just about dark and had a sharp engagement.

"Artillery played but a small part in this battle. We had very little chance to use ours, except during the advance, and the Federals had very little chance to use theirs. The artillery in the fort on the opposite bank of the river did a little damage to Stewart, but that was about all.

"It would be impossible to describe this battle, for it was fought in such close quarters, and the work was so exacting upon both armies, that there was not a second for hesitation and thought. From the moment Wagner's two brigades got behind the main line, so that they could shoot without killing their own men, the Union troops poured a most destructive fire into our ranks. General Brown, on the left of the pike, from the direction in which we were advancing, carried a portion of the first line of earthworks in the first charge, and held his advantage to the last. He also pushed the whole of his line right up against the Federal works, and so intrenched himself that the fighting men were so close together that they could reach across from one line to the other. Brown's division suffered terribly. He gained position and held it under the most trying circumstances.

"Cox's position was naturally a strong one, and he added to its strength by taking advantage of every point in building his earthworks. The line which Brown struck sloped quite sharply to the left from the cotton gin around beyond the Carter house. The earthworks on the right hand side of the pike, as he approached, were so built the force in it could enfilade his whole line as it reached the Federal position on the left of the pike. As Brown charged it a terrible enfilading fire from these works was poured into his men. It was very destructive, and to save themselves as much as possible his troops made breastworks of the dead bodies of their fallen comrades until they could throw up earth to protect themselves.

"The battle was short, but desperate. I lost a greater number of men, according to the number engaged, than in any battle of the war, except Murfreesboro. The real fight only lasted about two hours, but there were sharp assaults on both sides until ten o'clock. About eleven the Federals withdrew, and about two o'clock I made into the town and got something to eat, the first I had tasted that day. Just at daybreak I rode upon the field, and such a sight I never saw and can never expect to see again. The dead were piled up like shocks of wheat, or scattered about like sheaves of grain. The fierce flame of battle had nearly all been confined within a range of fifty yards, except the cavalry fight on the other side of the river. Almost under your eye, nearly all the dead, wounded and dying lay. In front of the Carter house the bodies lay in heaps, and to the right of it a locust thicket had been mowed off by bullets, as if by a scythe. It was a wonder that any man escaped alive from that storm of iron missiles. A man who counted the dead told me that there were over fifteen hundred bodies in the narrow space on the right and left of the pike; 900 Confederates and something over six hundred Union. I spent two years in the Mexican war and four years in the late conflict. I never saw anything like that field, and never want to again.

"It is all over now, and these are only reflections upon a sad subject. I did not come here to talk of them, but to show you the position of our troops and point out where we began and ended. This is the first time I have visited this battle-field since the fight took place, and I have talked more of the events of the war to-day than during all the past fifteen years. I have never read a true story of this battle. It will be hard to write one. I should have added to what I said about a visit to the field next morning at daybreak that we buried the dead, cared for the wounded men of both sides as best we could, and then moved on to the battle at Nashville."

CAVALRY AND GUNBOATS.

It was at New Madrid, in those "verdant" days, when volunteers knew no more fear than the average youth knows of the dangers of Fourth of July pyrotechnics. A battalion of the Second was sent to reconnoiter towards the river where the Confederates were known to have forts, gunboats and troops. The battalion charged upon the pickets, driving them in and following them down a lane, which led them into a pen surrounded by a strong fence, from which there was no escape except by the way they came. The lane brought them up short in a yard strongly inclosed by a high fence and here they found themselves in close proximity to a gunboat which immediately proceeded to "unload," and would, doubtless, soon have annihilated the major with his foolhardy battalion, had not the general commanding sent word: "What in blankety blank are you doing down there? Charging gunboats? Git out!"

The major returned, with a much less exalted opinion of his own valor, and possibly with a grain or two of wisdom stored away for future use.

CAPTURING OUTPOSTS.

That was a *nervous* sort of a place to put a handful of men —two miles southwest of Rienzi, Mississippi, during the summer of 1862.

Beauregard's cavalry outposts seemed anxious only to give as much annoyance as possible with as little real fighting or other important service.

A road that continued straight in one direction for half a mile was unusual. If there were less than five forks leading in as many directions to each plantation it was a mistake of the old pioneer who surveyed it with a mule. Then the woods, too, were not the most beautiful groves in the world, but they were capital places for bushwhacking operations. Some of the boys think our friend (?) Street, across the way here, is none to loyal; even suggesting that he would not hesitate to ride a blind mule fifteen miles on a dark night to get the Johnnies here and show them our vidette posts and guard headquarters. As I came here frequently as commander of this outpost, I resolved to get acquainted with and watch him.

The third Michigan cavalry had lost several men here by capture and I resolved that they should not find me napping. And this was my plan for the night: One man at the principal forks on the main road, eighty rods in rear of the day posts, dismounted, his horse back with the main guards, concealed in the woods near the road. One man mounted to patrol the main road, and one vidette upon each fork.

Now, boys, no fires, no noise. One half watch while the others sleep, with your bridles in your hands. Patrols and guards, if you are attacked, fire and fall back out of the way. We will do the rest. There is no sleep for me to-night. Rub your eyes. Keep awake, outposts, for I shall visit you often, all night. The safety of our whole army may depend upon our vigilance. Egyptian darkness would not more effectually hide the approach of an enemy. A slight noise is heard in the bush. It is coming nearer—hst! wait, let us see if there is one or more. Silence! then, creeping on, he comes—"woof," it's only a hog. Run him off.

And so the hours drag slowly on, and soon the cocks will crow. This is the hour we may look for a dash from the enemy's scouts.

Hark! There, a shot, then half a dozen, and our patrol comes in, firing. He passes on to the rear. Ready! there they come. Fire! Crack, crack—crash, from every revolving rifle.

A few wild shots are returned; they break, and retire in confusion.

Come on, boys, let's follow them. Give them a parting blast.

And hurrying after them, firing as we run, their clattering hoofs are soon heard faintly in the distance.

Halt! let us see if they will return in force.

Daylight streaks the east, broadening into the brighter day, and we return to our horses, conscious that our army has not been disturbed by the pickets being driven in, and none of us have been captured or hurt.

That was the last night attack upon our outposts at that point.

STRAINING A POINT TO SAVE A LIFE.

There was a time when my conscience troubled me about the following incident as I reflected upon the thought, "A neglect of duty is the highest military crime;" but as no harm came of it I have long since ceased to upbraid myself.

We were on picket in Mississippi. The enemy's cavalry had sometimes crept up, and dismounting had captured the outposts stationed there. As yet our regiment had been spared that humiliation, and as I went out that morning, looking over the positions of the videttes, the responsibility seemed very weighty. I, a mere boy, in charge of a half mile of line—far in advance of the infantry and the enemy's videttes within speaking distance, while their lines of infantry were much nearer than ours. To see that the guards were relieved every two hours was the sergeant's duty. To see that the position was slightly changed every hour was my especial care, accompanied by a sergeant or corporal of the guard.

Was there ever darkness more intense than those cloudy, moonless nights in the south? To ride or walk along that gloomy path with low hanging boughs catching at your eyes and nose at every step and not make *some* noise, was impossible. To stand in one position and not fall asleep, required a nerve of iron, unless, as it sometimes happened, the man was sleepless.

There was one soldier in my company—a tall, fine looking young fellow, upon whom, as I afterwards learned, the miasma of that mid-summer Mississippi climate had begun to have some effect, yet from whom there had been no word of complaint, and it fell to his lot at two in the morning to take up a position by a tree, dismounted, and move as little and as noiselessly as possible, while he listened for creeping noises, distant jingling spurs and sabers, and peered down the two roads which here became one. At half past two I approached him stealthily from the rear and found him alert, but leaning for rest against the tree.

He halted me, and immediately recognized my low whispered reply.

"All quiet in front?" "Yes, sir, but there was a slight rustling just to the left of the right hand road. It moved off, and I suppose it was only a hog."

"Don't fire unless absolutely necessary."

At half-past three I moved that way again. He was sitting down with his back to the tree; his gun leaning carefully against his shoulder, his head drooped—asleep.

"My God! asleep upon his post and the penalty is death!" flashed with crushing force upon me.

I will give him one chance. "*George!*" I whispered near enough to have been heard if not asleep.

Bursting with suppressed emotion I seized his gun with one hand and his shoulder in the other and threw him full length upon the ground.

Springing to his feet he drew his revolver, thinking me an enemy. "George," said I.

"Lieutenant, is that you? What's the matter!"

"The *matter?* Do you know what you have done?"

"What! was I asleep? Lieutenant, I ought not to have gone on duty to-night. I haven't felt just right for several days. Shall you report me to the Colonel?"

There was a slight tremor in his voice and I could not reply, and I cursed myself as I turned away, handing him his gun in silence. "Am I a man or a boy? A soldier or a poltroon? What have I to do with sympathy?" and I leaned against the nearest tree and struggled with myself in silence. This comrade's life is in my hands. The life of many a comrade was in his. What *shall* I do? Perhaps he was sick. Why did he not say so?"

It was a moment of intense agony. I felt called upon to act as judge advocate and members of court, and act at once. "He *may* be sick. The danger is past at all events. I must have a *little* time to think," and returning to my guards I sent a corporal to stay with him his watch out, and I kept on thinking, until, glad of an excuse, I sent the man to the doctor for *treatment*, and never before mentioned it to a living soul that I remember of. He was afterwards murdered by bushwhackers, and that settles his part of it. As for me I am not proud of my overwhelming sympathy at that time, but perhaps there may be those who can appreciate my position on that occasion and be generous to him who strained a point to save a comrade's life.

AN OMEN.

While Pope's army was drawing the lines closer on the left before Corinth, it became necessary to open and keep up communication with our right under Buell. The afternoon of the fierce engagement at Farmington, which came so near resulting in a general conflict between all the forces, was one which taxed the cavalry severely in maintaining their communications and in charging the enemy wherever a vulnerable point was shown. The "twin Seconds," the second Iowa and second Michigan cavalry, distinguished themselves alike on special service, nor stopped to ask whether some other would get the credit for it. While a part of the second Michigan was used on the left in protecting that flank, and the second Iowa made a bold and successful charge on the center, a squadron of the second Michigan, under Captain L. S. Scranton (mostly company F men), were sent to the right to give notice of any attempt at a flank movement in that direction. For two or three hours the cannonading and musketry firing were terrific, and as the detachment moved cautiously along through wood or brush they would occasionally come out upon a small clearing. Most of us were not familiar with the fowls of the air in that country and when one cries out, "Look, boys, see that eagle flapping his wings over us; that's a good omen," it was a little too bad for Captain Scranton to spoil their pretty little superstitious sentiment by replying, "That! why that's a turkey buzzard looking for dead Yankees or rebs." And true enough, there they sat, great lazy, filthy looking creatures, on limbs of old dead trees, with wings wide distended, moving as if about to crow, but in reality airing their filth bedrabbled plumage.

ALLEGED OUTRAGES.

That there were many outrages perpetrated upon peaceable citizens in the south during the war there is little doubt. Yet the most intelligent were disposed to make due allowance if there was the least excuse.

Among the many closing incidents of that great tragedy one is remembered that might have been construed as inexcusable, wanton, or something terrible.

When the veterans of Lee's army came tramping along towards their homes, they were a motley crowd and their pitiable condition evoked feelings of genuine sympathy among the soldiers of the Union army. If a squad was met that were short of rations, the boys of the second Michigan cavalry were always ready to divide, and it was no uncommon thing to see one of our soldiers skirmish around for a pair of shoes, to wear which would be better than "hoofing it" barefoot all the way home; and some even went so far as to take the shoes from their own feet, and say, "Here, Johnny, I can get a new pair when I get to camp; take these." and so ride on in his stocking feet.

We were riding along from Tuscaloosa towards Talladega, and had not heard of the cessation of hostilities, and seeing a squad of perhaps twenty-five or thirty Confederates feeding their animals by the roadside, and supposing them to be the advance guard of some cavalry force, we dashed among them as brave as a lot of sheep, shooting wildly, with the object of creating a panic and causing them to surrender without firing. The Johnnies scattered, dodging behind mules, fence corners, trees, bushes, or anything that would afford a temporary shelter; others throwing up their hands in token of surrender. By this time we discovered an old white rag tied to a stick, in a not very prominent place, and ceased firing. We then began to see the blunder we had made and were really excited by the fear that we had hurt some one. But on looking around we discovered that aside from killing a few mules and wounding a few we had, fortunately, done some very poor shooting.

To make matters all pleasant we divided up with the boys, who had simply stopped there to feed their mules. They had gathered up the worthless tag ends of the army mules abandoned along the roads, and were giving them their time. They each had a parole from the army of the Potomac, and at this particular moment had found an abandoned camp, with corn scattered about where other troops had been feeding their animals.

We expected to see this chronicled in some of the light caliber papers of that section as an "outrage," but were agreeably disappointed. Yet it was just such incidents as this that gave color to many of the so-called "outrages."

CAPTAIN AVERY.

Beauregard had one officer that could go back to his friends and say a good word for the Yankees.

It was on June 10th, 1862, below Booneville, Mississippi, that the Second, with company K in advance, pressing the near guard of the Confederates, saw a single horseman in gray pants, but coatless, his light calico shirt sleeves flapping in the breeze, gallop gracefully down towards us. At first we thought him the advance of a squadron about to charge upon us. We were dismounted, deployed across the road, and every man meant six shots from an unerring rifle.

There were just trees enough to conceal about half our men; and before they had time to think what it meant, the young officer, speaking in a low but distinct voice, said, "Come on, boys," evidently supposing them to be his own men. His horse stopped and he was just in the act of turning the other way when forty rifles were leveled at him, and "Halt," "halt," rang out from as many throats.

There was agony in the voice of that young lieutenant, as he shouted "Don't shoot," and rushed between the line of rifles and the young Confederate officer. Who will say it was mistaken zeal that prompted him to save the life of one whose hand was raised against us? Was it not, rather, admiration for the cool bravery of the man under trying circumstances?

He instantly saw his mistake and moved up to our lines, and was our prisoner. It proved to be Captain (afterwards Colonel) Avery, of a Georgia cavalry regiment; and during his stay of two or three days with us captor and captive shared the same blanket and mess, and an attachment sprang up between them that has been remembered since the war, by a correspondence and mutual expressions of good feeling.

The Booneville fight of July 1st was probably a sequel to Captain Avery's visit to our camp.

It has been a wonder to many how Loomis's battery did so much valuable service and so much accurate shooting. Loomis was not a West Pointer, but received his first military education under Captain Lewis, who commanded the Coldwater artillery in the three months' service. Captain Lewis did not feel like sacrificing his business for three years, and so Lieutenant Loomis was made captain, and soon the fame of the Loomis battery became national, and was probably dreaded more by the Confederates than any other battery in the service.

One of the gunners of that battery says: "We belonged to General O. M. Mitchell's brigade, and that officer took great pride when we were at Bacon Creek, Kentucky, in taking us out to guess on distances, and soon we thought it a poor guess if we did not explode our first shell within fifty yards of the object fired at, and the second shot almost invariably struck just where we wanted it to."

At Perryville, the second shot fired by this battery exploded beneath the guns of the celebrated Washington battery (Confederate), three-quarters of a mile away, and drove the best battery of the south from their position.

At Stone River, Loomis's battery dismounted the guns of half a dozen batteries of the enemy, and rendered them almost powerless in their operations against that part of the field.

At Athens, Alabama, when the troops under General O. M. Mitchell approached that place, Loomis's battery took up a position over-looking the railroad. A train of cars was pulling out rapidly in their evacuation of that place. "Stop that train," said Mitchell. The first shot struck the top of the cab. The second struck beneath the engine, entirely demolishing the drive-wheels and bringing the train up short, all of a heap. The staid old atlas maker spatted his hands like a school boy. "Well done, boys;" and from that time forward the reputation of the battery kept steadily onward in favor with all whose fortune brought them snugly beneath their protecting wings.

At Chicamauga Loomis's battery was cut off by a flanking force of the enemy and lost four of her six guns. At the moment of their greatest peril the gunners of those four guns were heroically working their pieces, rapidly firing canister at the front, when the officer in command shouted to them, "Limber up!" but he might as well have shouted in the face of the mighty Niagara; and only until shots from their rear gave them warning did they discover that the flank was turned. Then they "limbered up," but it was too late. Horses were shot at the guns and there was nothing left but to save themselves. They turned to fly and run into the arms of the enemy, where but a few moments before our own infantry had stood resolutely firing.

A LONELY GRAVE.

Every soldier hoped for a respectable burial, yet it is doubtful if all would not have chosen the trench with hundreds or thousands of others hurriedly thrown along side of them, rather than a grave by the roadside, in a lonely wood, without the soldier's glory of dying on the battlefield.

Yet thousands were stricken by camp fevers or kindred complaints, and if they recovered were perhaps left with a lingering weakness that drove them to the pension office with its humiliations, and are perhaps to-day but physical wrecks with one foot in the grave.

A sudden death and burial under peculiarly sad circumstances, occurred below Corinth, while the regiment was on the march from Rienzi to Pine Hills. Leo Cook, a private detailed on account of his small stature and youthful appearance to the charge of a wagon, was discovered crawling into an old cotton gin, as the regiment went into an early camp near Corinth. On being questioned it was discovered he had rode all day but was quite sick. The information being brought to the lieutenant commanding the company, an ambulance was sent, and the poor boy brought to camp. The surgeons were busy elsewhere and not knowing what else to do, a bath was ordered until the surgeons should come up. He was placed on a cot covered nicely with clean blankets, and as he settled down apparently comfortable he seemed quite worried for a moment lest he should be thought trying to shirk his duties, saying, "I kept up as long as I could, Lieutenant."

"Yes, too long, I fear," was the sympathetic reply.

It was the last he spoke, but sank away to a quiet sleep, and while the warm June sun dropped lower and lower among the trees his breath grew shorter, shorter, and ceased, before we had even thought him dangerously ill. It seemed cruel to lay him away in the ground within the same hour, but more cruel still would it have been to have kept him till morning and perhaps have been compelled to leave him hurriedly for an enemy to bury or for carrion fowls to tear and rend piecemeal. And so, the roadside lonely grave was dug, and, wrapped in his martial blanket, the body was laid to rest, the company volley fired, and many a tear moistened the grave of this our favorite boy soldier.

DIED GAME.

It is not often that a coward is transformed into a hero and dies game inside of five minutes. Colonel Ben Smith, at Dandridge, saw one of his new recruits that had never been under fire, start to slink away. "Come here; let me see your gun; I see you have it loaded with six good bullets. You are equal to six men. We need you. Take your position by that tree; keep cool and let's see what you can do." The man obeyed; fired his six shots as if he had been shooting ducks, and fell riddled with bullets.

A YOUTHFUL SOLDIER.

We were approaching Corinth. The Confederates under Beauregard made a sortie upon our advance, and a severe engagement was heard in the vicinity of Farmington.

Troops were hurrying forward rapidly to the support of our imperiled center. Among the regiments under General Payne was the eighth Wisconsin, with the famous eagle, Old Abe, screaming and flapping his wings in apparent glee.

A boy, not more than 14, and small of his age, was seen following along in rear of the eighth, with a musket on his shoulder, twice as long as himself, crying as if his heart would break.

"What's the matter, boy?"

"They don't want me to go; said I must stay and help take care of the camp; I want to go-o-o, I can shoot jess as well as any of 'em," and on he trudged, with shell screeching and whirring; bullets zipping and hissing uncomfortably close overhead.

They were soon lost in the smoke and tumult of battle. The enemy having accomplished their object (apparently an armed reconnaissance) they retired to Corinth, and soon the eighth Wisconsin were again seen retiring to their camp. As they halted by the roadside we were again attracted to "Old Abe" and the youthful soldier, as he stood with a group talking over the events of the hour. Having a little curiosity to hear how the boy had stood the trial, we drew nearer. He had his say with the rest, as cool as any of them, when we discovered what appeared to be a small hole through the visor of his cap, cocked back upon his head. Reaching down we took his cap from his head, remarking, "What is that hole in your cap?"

He took it; looked at it for an instant; turned pale as death; reflected a few moments, and philosophically remarked: "Gosh, boys! I wished I was bigger a while ago, but if I had been, where'd I be now?"

His interest in the conversation was gone, but that old cap had a new value to him.

COURTING DEATH.

Occasionally men were found too stubborn to yield, and would rather die than turn their backs upon the enemy, even when wiser men thought "discretion the better part of valor." Such a man was Harvey Olmstead, of Company C, who at Severeville, East Tennessee, during a temporary reverse (the three companies in advance falling back before a whole division of the enemy), remained unflinchingly behind his tree, firing with death dealing precision, and in his kneeling attitude coolly drew a bead so long as he could raise the gun or pull a trigger, though he was known to be wounded long before his last shot was fired, and probably his life's blood was oozing away. When his body was afterward recovered, it was found to be literally riddled with bullets.

TOO MUCH GOLD.

It would probably have remained a secret who committed the robberies at Tuscaloosa had it not been discovered by an accident.

Crossing a stream, one of our men was thrown into deep water from his horse and sank without coming to the surface, as a drowning man usually does. This led to inquiry as to the cause, when it was ascertained the man was heavily loaded with gold, in belts about his body. If there were others in the same condition, it was known to but few.

DISCIPLINE.

Officers of volunteer regiments often committed egregious

blunders in matters of discipline, and were sometimes "brought up short."

A major of the Second was placed on duty as "officer of the day," and while on his rounds among the pickets, would stop to chat and joke with the boys. Arriving at guard headquarters he saw some hogs in a pen, and the thought occurred to him that some fresh pork might not be amiss. His hint, "Boys, don't let those hogs jump over the fence and bite you," was acted upon, and one company of the regiment had fresh pork for a day or two; but the major was arrested, "disciplined," and soon after left the service "in poor health."

THE LAST BATTLE.

Numerous battles have been written up as "the last fight of the rebellion." Without disputing in regard to the matter it is a fact, not generally known, that a battalion (the saber battalion) of the second Michigan cavalry, under brevet Major Whittemore, charged the force (1,000 men) under General Hill, near Talladega, Alabama, on the 23d of April, 1865, and was supported by the regiment and brigade, scattering the entire Confederate force and capturing the artillery, and many prisoners. This was fourteen days after the surrender at Appomattox, and therefore quite late enough after a cessation of hostilities. The next day the country was filled with small parties returning home—a sadly broken down people.

THE ROSTER.

PART THIRD.

ENGAGEMENTS PARTICIPATED IN BY THE SECOND MICHIGAN CAVALRY—ROLL OF HONOR—THE ADJUTANT'S REMARKS—THE ROSTER.

ENGAGEMENTS.

During its four years of service the Second Michigan Cavalry had engaged the enemy at the following places :
Point Pleasant, Mo., March 9, 1862 ; Tiptonville, Mo., March, 1862; New Madrid and Island No. 10, Mo., March 13 to April 7, 1862 ; Pine Hill, Mississippi, May 2, 1862 ; Monterey, Mississippi, May 3, 1862 ; Farmington, Mississippi, May 5, 1862; Siege of Corinth, Mississippi, May 10 to 30, 1862; Booneville, Mississippi, June 1, 1862; Blackland, Mississippi, June 5, 1862 ; Baldwin, Mississippi, June 7, 1862 ; Booneville, Mississippi, July 1, 1862 ; Rienzi, Mississippi, August, 1862; Elizabethtown, Ky., September, 1862 ; Perryville, Ky., October 8, 1862; Harrodsburg, Ky., October 10, 1862; Lancaster, Ky., October 12, 1862 ; Rockcastle River, Ky., October, 1862 ; Estillville, Va., December 30, 1862 ; Blountsville, Tenn., December 30, 1862; Zolicoffer, Tenn., December, 1862; Watauga, Tenn., December 30, 1862 ; Jonesville, Va., January 2, 1863 ; Bacon Creek, Ky., December 24, 1862, Glasgow, Ky., December, 1862; Milton, Tenn., February 18, 1863; Cainesville, Tenn., February 19, 1863; Spring Hill, Tenn., February 29, 1863: Columbia, Tenn., March 4 and 5, 1863; Hillsboro, Tenn., March 12, 1863; Brentwood, Tenn , March 25, 1863 ; McGarrick's Ford, Tenn., April, 1863; Triune, Tenn., June 4, 1863; Rover, Tenn., June 23, 1863; Middletown, Tenn., June 24, 1863; Shelbyville, Tenn., June 27, 1863; Elk River Ford, Tenn., July 2, 1863 ; Decherd, Tenn., July 4, 1863; LaFayette, September 17, 1863; Chicamauga, Ga., September 19 and 20, 1863; Anderson Cross Roads, Tenn., October, 1863; Sparta, Tenn., December, 1863 ; Dandridge, Tenn., December 24, 1863 ; Mossy Creek, Tenn., December 29, 1863; Dandridge, Tenn., January 17, 1864 ; Severeville, Tenn., January, 1864; Pigeon River, Tenn., January 27, 1864; Dug Gap, Ga., May 13 and 14, 1864; Red Clay, Ga., May, 1864; Etowah River, Ga., May 24, 26, 27 and 28, 1864; Ackworth, Tenn., June 2 and 5, 1864 ; Nashville, Tenn., August 30, 1864; Campbellville, Tenn., September 5, 1864; Resaca; Franklin,

Tenn., September 27, 1864; Cypress River, Tenn., October 7, 1864; Raccoon Ford, Tenn., October 30, 1864; Shoal Creek, Tenn., November 5, 1864; Florence, Ala.; Lawrenceburg. Tenn., November 24, 1864; Campbellsville, Tenn., November 24, 1864; Columbia, Tenn., November 25, 26 and 27, 1864; Spring Hill, Tenn., November 29, 1864; Bethesda Church, Tenn., November 29, 1864; Franklin, Tenn., November 30, 1864; Nashville, Tenn., December 15 and 16, 1864; Richland Creek, December 24, 1864; Pulaski, Tenn., December 25, 1864; Sugar Creek, Tenn., December 26, 1864; Price's Tanyard, Tenn., January 6, 1865; Corinth, Mississippi, February, 1865; Tuscaloosa, Ala., April 1, 1865; Trion, Ala., April 2, 1865; Bridgeville, Ala., April 6, 1865; Talladega, Ala, April 23, 1865.

ROLL OF HONOR.

We find it impossible to make a perfect record of deaths from wounds. Very many were discharged for disability, and there the record ends. How many of them "went home to die" will never be known. The number wounded does not appear on the rolls, and, therefore, the following is only approximately correct. To die in hospital, or on furlough, while yet in the service of one's country, should be considered as great an honor as to die on the field, if the record was good, and therefore, all such have been included in the Roll of Honor. Some were reported as missing in action who afterwards returned; only a few, however.

COMPANY A.

Stiff, Corporal David D., died at Triune, Tenn., June 11, 1863, of wounds received in action.
Burga, John, died of typhoid fever in hospital at Farmington, Miss., July 9, 1862.
Booth, James L., shot by the enemy while on picket duty near Point Pleasant, Mo., March 7, 1862.
Bartlett, Irwin C., killed in action at Pulaski, Tenn., September 28, 1864. Re-enlisted January 5, 1864.
Oliver, Jerome, wounded. Discharged at Louisville, Ky., December 17, 1862.
Parker, Leonard, wounded. Discharged at St. Louis, Mo., May 27, 1862. Died June 3, 1862, at St. Louis, Mo.
Ross, James, died of disease at New Madrid, Mo., March 24, 1862.
Redson, Thomas, wounded. Discharged for disability at Detroit, August 8, 1862.
Averill, Emerson M., died of chronic diarrhea at Nashville, Tenn., September 20, 1864.
Brangne, Sanders S., died of typhoid fever at Franklin, Tenn., August 25. 1864
Beach, John W., killed in action near Mossy Creek, Tenn., December 29, 1863.
Conklin, John E., died at Nicholasville, March, 1863.
Deming, Orin B, killed in action at Lynnville, Tenn , December 14, 1864.
Gressfell, Abraham, died of disease at Nashville, Tenn., December 14, 1864.
Koster, William, died of measles in hospital at Nashville, Tenn., May 2, 1864.
Richardson, Henry F., died of chronic diarrhea at Jefferson, Mo., May 10. 1865.
Stine, Jacob C., died of typhoid fever at Nashville, Tenn., December 14, 1864.

COMPANY B.

Rogers, First Lieut. Philo W., died of disease at Evansville, Ind., May 17, 1862.
Loveless, Corporal Lewis M., died of typhoid fever at Hamburg, Tenn., June 3, 1862.
Dunn. Corporal Levi, died at Hamburg, Tenn., July 19, 1862.
Fairfield, Elbridge, died of disease at St. Louis, Mo., June 28, 1862.
Bell, Ezra, died of typhoid fever at Hamburg, Tenn., May 1, 1862.
Boyer, Joseph, died of pneumonia at Benton Barracks, St. Louis, Jan'y 18, 1862.
Barnum, Dwight, died of disease at New Madrid, April 14. 1862.
Beers, Uriah, died of pneumonia at St. Louis, December 2, 1862.
Berham, Henry C, died of typhoid fever near Farmington, Miss., July 14, 1862.
Crabtree Charles, died at Evansville, Ind., September 15, 1862.

ROLL OF HONOR.

Dow, Peter, died of typhoid fever near Farmington, Mississippi, August 22, 1862.
Ellis, Eugene, missing in action at Dandridge, Tenn., December 24, 1863. Died of chronic diarrhea at Andersonville, May 20, 1864.
Hull, George, died at Henderson, Ky., May 24, 1862.
Kiche, Francis, died of typhoid fever at Hamburg Landing, Tenn.
Jones, Bratfore B., died at New Albany, Ind., October 8, 1862.
Losely, Lorenzo D., died of measles at St. Louis, December 2, 1861.
Lisco, Rufus, died of typhoid fever near Farmington, Mississippi, June 29, 1862.
O'Neil,, Jerome, died of typhoid fever at Farmington, Mississippi, June 27, 1862.
Olmstead, Morris, died at Nashville, Tenn., July 6, 1864, from accidental shot.
Russell, Reuben O., died of typhoid fever on board hospital boat, May 9, 1862.
Thompson, William, died of consumption at Keokuk, Iowa, July 25, 1862.
Watson, Edward, died of typhoid fever, at Rienzi, Mississippi, July 24, 1862.
Barnum, David, died at Knoxville, Tenn., February 25, 1864.
Beasey, David D., died of disease at Waterloo, Ala., March 16. 1865.
Beasey, Oliver B., died of abscess of the head at Chattanooga, Tenn., July 4, 1864.
Birch, Edwin A., killed in action at Oxford, Ala., April 23, 1865.
Cole, Hiram, died of consumption at Charlotte, Mich., July 20, 1862.
Coon, Andrew B., died of chronic diarrhea at Cahawba, Ala., March 25, 1865.
Hackett, Emory E., died of bronchitis at Jefferson, Ind., January 15, 1865.
Hart, Holland, killed in action at Dandridge, Tenn., December 24, 1863.
Lowe, William, killed in action at Lavergne, Tenn., September 1, 1864.
Shirk, Alfred, died of typhoid fever at New Albany, Ind., September 30, 1862.

COMPANY C.

Bailey, Judson D., died of typhoid fever at Benton Barracks, Mo., February 20, 1862.
Bliss, Rufus W., died of inflammatory rheumatism at St. Louis, Mo., January 24, 1862.
Fifield, William H., killed in action at Shoal Creek, Tenn., November 5, 1864.
Hooper, Joseph E., died of typhoid fever at New Madrid, Mo., April 9, 1862.
Marsac, Franklin R., died of typhoid fever at Evansville, August 16, 1862.
Marsac, Daniel C., re-enlisted January 5, 1864. Died of wounds at Nashville, Tenn., January 10, 1865.
Moon, John D., died of disease of the heart at Rienzi, Mississippi, August 1, 1862.
Olmstead, Harvey, killed in action at Fair Garden, Tenn., January 28, 1864.
Reynolds, Cyrus, died at Chaplin Hill, Ky., October 8,1862, of wounds received in action.
Reid, Henry L, died of typhoid fever at Farmington, July 7, 1862.
Story, George W., died of typhoid fever at New Madrid, Mo., March 24, 1862.
Steele, Elisha, died of chronic diarrhea at Andersonville Prison, Ga., May 20,1864.
Schenck, William J., died at Benton Barracks; Mo., December 11, 1861.
Wilson, Joseph, died of chronic diarrhea at Wyoming, Kent County, May 29, 1862.
Watson, Henry G., died at Chaplin Hill, Ky., October 8, 1862, of gun-shot wound.
Young, Jasper J., died at Benton Barracks, St. Louis, Mo., December 12, 1861.
Young, Franklin E., died at Benton Barracks, St. Louis, Mo., of typhoid fever.
Bonny, Lyman, died of typhoid fever at Nashville, Tenn., September 17, 1864.
Delano, Eben R., died of disease at Nashville, Tenn., July 4, 1864
Dennis, Isaac S., killed in action at Resaca, Ga., May 14, 1864.
Dicker, William H., died at Burnt Hickory, Ga., May 20, 1864, of wounds received in action.
Farnsworth, George W., died of typhoid fever at Chattanooga, May 28, 1864.
Freeland, Charles, died of typhoid fever at Chattanooga, May 28, 1864.
Hiser, Christian, died of disease at Nashville, Tenn., July 13, 1864.
Garrett, Solon H., missing in action at Mossy Creek, Tenn., December 29, 1863. Died at Andersonville, Ga., May 20, 1864.
Kelly, Michael, died of typhoid fever at New Madrid, April 4, 1862.
McNeil, James, died of typhoid fever at Nashville, Tenn., July 15, 1865.
Pike, Benjamin, died at Andersonville, Ga., September 16, 1864.

COMPANY D.

Landon, Q. M. Almon, died of pneumonia at Hamburg, Tenn., May 30, 1862.

Jackson, Sergeant William L., killed in action at Blountsville, East Tenn., December 30, 1862.
Crane, Corporal Charles W., died at Perryville, Ky., October 9, 1862, of wounds received in action, October 8, 1862.
Vandusan, James, died of inflammation of the lungs at Benton Barracks, Mo., December 3, 1861.
Esgett, Corporal Harry J., died at Franklin, Tenn., June 4, 1863, of wounds received in action.
Hicks, Farrier Henry H., died from exposure at Evansville, Ind., May 16, 1862.
Spencer, Wagoner Elmer, died from exposure at New Madrid, Mo., April 22, 1862.
Alden, Justin, killed in action at Perryville, Ky., October 8, 1862.
Blakesly, Levi S., died of disease at Savannah, Tenn., June 25, 1862.
Bom, John, died of pneumonia at St. Louis, Mo., April 8, 1862.
Boer, Peter, died of disease at St. Louis, Mo., August 1, 1862.
Cheney, Rufus, died of erysipelas at New Madrid, Mo., April 12, 1862.
Campbell, James, died of inflammation of the lungs at St. Louis, Mo., January 25, 1862.
Chatfield, James, died of disease at Nashville, Tenn., December 9, 1863.
Degroot, Albert, died at Andersonville, Ga., May 24, 1864.
Kelly, Hiram, died of pneumonia at Farmington, Mississippi, August 15, 1862.
Lesperance, Enos, died of small-pox at Nashville, Tenn., January 23, 1864.
Richards, Charles L., died of inflammation of the lungs at St. Louis, Mo., January 30, 1862.
Shilling, William, died of disease at Nashville, Tenn., November 4, 1863.
Stansbury, Jacob, died of typhoid fever at St. Louis, Mo., April 10, 1862.
Smith, George W., died June 4, 1863, at Franklin, Tenn., of wounds received in action.
Vanhaltren, Benjamin, died at Louisville, Ky., November 17, 1862, of wounds received at Perryville, Ky., October 8, 1862.
White, William H., died of abscess in throat at Farmington, Miss., July 10, 1862.
Braman, Charles, died at Andersonville, May 24, 1864.
Eaton, Joseph M., died of disease at Atlanta, Ga., August 20, 1865.
French, Delos, died of disease at Franklin, Tenn., August 21, 1864.
Fry, Charles, died at Nashville, Tenn., June 11, 1865.
Hanson, Frederick H., died at Nashville, Tenn., December 23, 1864, of wounds received in action.
Hertsman, Adam, killed in action at Lynnville, Tenn., December 24, 1864.
Hill, David, supposed killed by explosion of steamer Sultana, April 28, 1865.
Johnson, John, supposed killed by explosion of steamer Sultana, April 28, 1865.
Losee, Mark, died at Nashville, Tenn., December 3, 1864.
Perrigo, John, missing in action at Dandridge, Tenn., December 24, 1863. Died at Andersonville, Ga., May 24, 1864.
Quant, James, killed in action at Franklin, Tenn., November 30, 1864.
Seymour, Frank, died of disease at Cleveland, Tenn., May 3, 1863.
Vilt, George, died at Andersonville, Ga., May 22, 1864.
Vanhaltren, Gerritt, missing in action at Bent Church, May 30, 1864. Died at Andersonville, Ga.
Vanhaltren, Gismith, died in rebel prison.

COMPANY E.

Mapes, Sergeant Abram, jr., died of disease at St. Louis, March 31, 1862.
Lee, Corporal James, died June 24, 1862, of wounds received in action, at Farmington, Mississippi.
Lanbach, Corporal Edwin H, died of disease at Farmington, Mississippi, July 12, 1862.
Ryan, Saddler Peter, died of disease at St. Louis, Mo., February 7, 1862.
Allen, Andrew, died of disease at Rienzi, Mississippi, August 19, 1862.
Hoag, Wendolin, died of disease at Rienzi, Mississippi, August 8, 1862.
Mellett, Lawrence, died July 3, 1862, at Rienzi, Mississippi, of wounds received in action, July 1, 1862.
Matthew, Charles, died of disease at Nashville, Tenn., March 9, 1864.
Orman, Elon, killed in action at Thomas Station, March 5, 1863.
Oleson, Nelson, died of disease at Nashville, Tenn., July 1, 1864.

ROLL OF HONOR.

Willey, Lewis, died at Louisville, November 5, 1862, of injuries received by being run over by a wagon.
Root, James, died of disease at Hamburg, Tenn., May 20, 1862.
Warren, Trask, died of disease at Jeffersonville, July 19, 1864.
McNaughton, Duncan, died of disease at New Madrid, Mo., April 20, 1862.
Bailey, Alanson B., died of disease at Edgefield, Tenn., July 19, 1865.
Henry, Charles, lost on steamer Sultana, near Memphis, by explosion and burning, April 28, 1865.
Hermich, Charles, lost on steamer Sultana, near Memphis, by explosion and burning, April 28, 1865.
Jacobs, George E., died of typhoid fever at Nashville, Tenn., April 17, 1864.
Kendrick, James, lost on steamer Sultana.
Knight, John, missing in action at Franklin, Tenn., November 30, 1864.
Law, George, died of disease at Nashville, Tenn., March 9, 1864.
Lindsley, William S., lost on steamer Sultana.
Londer, Charles, died of small-pox, May 4, 1865.
McDonald, Donald, died at Mason, July 28, 1865.
Maxon, Charles, died in Southern prison.
Moody, Daniel, killed in action near Louisville, September 30, 1862.
Moody, Watson D., missing in action at Oxford, Ala., April 26, 1865.
Mergan, Martin C, missing in action at Dandridge, December 24, 1864.
Thompson, John, died at Jefferson Barracks, Mo., April 12, 1865.
Wolfram, Chauncy, died in Southern prison, December 20, 1864.

COMPANY F.

Lorenzo, Buckley, died at Keokuk, March, 1863.
Bradford, J. A., missing in action at Blackland, Mississippi, June 24, 1862.
Suel, Amos, died at Rienzi, July 10, 1862.
Bichler, Christian, died at Commerce, Mo., March 11, 1862.
Bates, Austin, died at Evansville, October 4, 1864.
Caswell, John, died of small-pox, March 1, 1862.
Demoray, L. A., died of typhoid fever at Winchester, August 5, 1863.
Davis, John, died at Corinth, October 15, 1882.
Fullington, Lucian B., died at St. Louis, July 6, 1882.
Fitch, Morris E., died of wounds at Franklin, March 26, 1863.
Fullington, George W., missing in action at Spring Hill, November 29, 1864.
Keeney, C. L., died at St. Louis, September 5, 1862.
Moore, Joseph, died in hospital, September 24, 1863.
Norton, George, died at Rienzi, July 28, 1862.
Ravick, W. C., missing in action at Triune, June 11, 1863.
Weaver, Caleb F., died in hospital at Cowan, Tenn., October 2, 1863.
Baxter, Theodore, died at Knoxville, April 2, 1864.
Bradford, Charles, died at Annapolis, March 21, 1865.
Cadwell, A. S., died at Franklin, March 7, 1863.
Clapson, A S., died at Nashville, March 8, 1864.
Core, William, died at Jeffersonville, Ala., January 9, 1865.
Glasson, A, A., died at Nashville, March 8, 1864.
Helmer, George, missing in action at Spring Hill, Tenn., November 29, 1864.
Kellogg, Daniel H , missing in action at Macon, Ga., July 26, 1864.
King, E. H., died at Nashville, February 1, 1864.
Lynch, John, killed in action at Cleveland, Tenn., April 2, 1864.
McCaslin, William, died at Nashville, September 10, 1864.
McIntyre, Arza, died at Mound City, Ill., February 22, 1865.
Murphy, Thomas J., died at Nashville, September 5, 1864.
Myers, Henry E., died at Jeffersonville, June 22, 1864.
Randall, James N., died January 2, 1864, of wounds received in action at Mossy Creek, December 29.

COMPANY G.

Hawley, Captain James, killed at Chicamauga, September 20, 1863.
Ainsworth, James E., died at Rienzi, July 15, 1862.
Allen, LeRoy, died at Franklin, April 13, 1863.
Benedict, Norman, died at Keokuk, August 22, 1862.

ROLL OF HONOR.

Smith, Captain James H., missing in action; left on the field, wounded, at Dandridge, December 24, 1863.
Arnold, Jerry, died at New Madrid, Mo., April 14, 1862.
Brock, William, died of quick consumption at Reading, Mich., May 23, 1862.
Cone, Austin, died at Farmington, Mississippi, June 16, 1862.
Ford, Alton S, died at Jefferson, May 22, 1862.
Fleetwood, Ansel, died at New Madrid, April 11, 1862.
Martin, William B., died at Chattanooga, October 18, 1863.
Tuttle, William, died at Camp Benton, Mo., December 4, 1861.
Wilson, Bradly, died at Libby prison, November 3, 1863.
Adams, Oscar, killed by guerrillas near Sparta, Tenn., November 29, 1863.
Boyle, Charles, killed in action at Dandridge, Tenn., December 24, 1863.
Brown, D. E., died at Keokuk, 1862.
Carry, John A., died at Nashville, April 4, 1864, of wounds received in action.
Groves, William H., died at Nashville, November 12. 1863.
Harwick, George, died at Chattanooga, July 13. 1864.
Norton, Joseph H., died at Nicholasville, January 6, 1863.

COMPANY H.

Harvey, Robert M., died at St. Louis, December 14, 1861.
Beutter, George, drowned in Harpeth river, while on a scout, May 15, 1863.
Bryant, Silas, died at Farmington, Mississippi, August 5, 1862.
Clark, John, died in hospital at St. Louis, February 26, 1862.
Dodge, Albert F., died at Hamburg, Tenn., May 14, 1862.
Morey, Charles B., died on furlough, April 1, 1864.
Smith, Oscar, died at Rienzi, August 4, 1862.
Phillips, James R., missing in action, April 5, 1863.
Donnelly, Daniel, died at Jeffersonville, December 26, 1864.
Johnson, Robert, died at St. Louis, December 8, 1864.
Kinney, Andrew, died at St. Louis, December 26, 1861.
Lewis, A., died at home on furlough.
Pennell, James E., missing in action at Shoal Creek, November 5, 1864.
Scott, Douglas, missing in action at Booneville, Mississippi, July 1, 1862.
Weller, Stafford D., died at Lebanon, Ky., November 10, 1862.

COMPANY I.

Lamkin, Frank H., died at Booneville, Mississippi, June 30, 1862.
Houre, Augustus, died in hospital at Stevenson, September 1, 1863.
Bugbee, John, died at Benton Barracks, February 13, 1862.
Colwell, John M, died at Rienzi, August 13, 1862.
Lamkin, Reuben R., died at Nashville, March, 29, ———, of wounds received in action.
Lewis, Franklin H., died at Farmington, July 13, 1862.
Myers, Friend M., missing in action at Blackland, June 24, 1862.
Simmons, George, died on furlough, May 30, 1862.
Dutcher, William H., died at Nashville, September 17, 1864.
Tallman, Frank, died at Dansville, Ky., August 20, 1863.
Fessenden, William, died at Stevenson, November 2, 1863.
Moon, Henry, died at Chattanooga, July 5, 1864.
Peas, Charles H., died on furlough at Brighton, Mich., October 31, 1864.
Rex, Alfred, missing at Shoal Creek, November 5, 1864.
Wheeler, Richard, died at Knoxville, May 14, 1864.

COMPANY K.

McMillen, Samuel, died at Nashville, January, 1864.
Hill, Robert, died at St. Louis, February 9, 1862.
Allen, Benjamin, died at New Madrid, March 23, 1862.
Cook, Leo, died near Corinth, June 13, 1862.
Evarts, I, died at Jeffersonville, October 25, 1862.
Hiptenberger, Joseph, died at Rienzi, August 11, 1862.
Haywood, Charles, died at Farmington, July 3, 1862.
Haywood, Calvin, died at Farmington, July 5, 1862.

Gamble, Robert C., died at Jeffersonville, January 14, 1865, of wounds received in action.
Lewis, Elisha, died at Murfreesboro. March 25, 1863.
Leonard, John, died at Rienzi, July 7, 1862.
Lewis, Absalom, died on furlough.
Stephen, Lyman, died at Rienzi, July 8, 1862.
Dell, John W., died at Nashville, July 14, 1864.
Dillingham, Stephen, drowned, April 9, 1865.
Maples, Comstock, died at Louisville, December 13, 1864.
Mapes, Charles, died at Nashville, November 15, 1864.
Smith, Recompense, died at Franklin, July 20, 1864.
Smith, Joseph, died of wounds, December 24, 1864.
Snyder, John, missing in action at Franklin, November 30, 1864.
Washburn, ——, died in the service, March 16, 1863.

COMPANY L.

Thomas, William P., died near Farmington, June 25, 1862.
Barnhouse, W. H., missing in action at Booneville, Mississippi, July 1, 1862.
Anderson, Albert P., died July 3, 1862, of wounds received in action at Booneville.
Bee, John, killed at Booneville.
Corwin, N. W., died near Corinth, July 22, 1862.
Eisley, Felix, killed near Mossy Creek, December 29, 1863.
Hunter, John F., died near Rienzi, August 6, 1862.
Park, James, died at Hamburg.
Moore, L. D., missing in action at Booneville. Returned and died of wounds at Shoal Creek, December 1, 1864.
Reed, Albert, died at New Madrid, April 13, 1862.
Turner, A. W., missing at Booneville, July 1, 1862.
Williams, Theodore, died at Andersonville.
Wooden, Timothy, died at St. Louis, January 21, 1862.
Baker, Hiram, died at Louisville, March 22, 1864.
Gadbold, William, died at Andersonville. Missing at Dandridge.
Manchester, George, died at Nashville, June 23, 1864.
Pray, Paris L., died at Nashville, December 28, 1864.
Snyder, Jacob, died at Nashville, April 4, 1864.
Stevens, F. S., died of wounds at Thompson's Station, March 4, 1863.
Stevens, Colonel J., died at Nashville, January 1, 1865.
Thomas, Ezra, died at Nashville, March 31, 1864.
Wightman, Charles, killed at Lynnville, December 24, 1864.

COMPANY M.

Darrow, First Lieutenant Russell T., killed at Cypress Creek, October 7, 1864.
Sweeney, Frank, missing at Chicamauga.
Murdock, Daniel, died at Rienzi, July 15, 1862.
Alexander, Edward, killed at Glasgow, Ky., December 4, 1862.
Birdsell, William, missing at Severeville, January 27, 1864
Bratt, Rufus, died on furlough.
Boyer, Marion, died in hospital at Keokuk, 1862.
Cowan, Robert H., died at New Madrid, April 10, 1862.
Clark, Jetson, died in hospital at Keokuk.
Dooley, Patrick, missing at Brentwood.
Fancher, David, died at Farmington, May 12, 1862.
Gaines, Sullivan, died at Knoxville, February 2, 1864, of wounds received in action.
Harris, Hiram J., died at St. Louis, May 30, 1862.
Hutton, C. C., died at Rienzi, August 9, 1862.
Jenks, George, died at New Madrid, April 13, 1862.
Norcott, E. W., died on furlough, April 3, 1862.
Potter, Charles H., killed at Dandridge.
Ploof, Charles, died on furlough.
Baker, John, died at Nashville, March 18, 1864.
Dean, Silas, died at Chattanooga, June 28, 1864.
Kuhn, James, missing at Dandridge.

Spaulding, A. M., died September 23, 1863, of wounds received at Chicamauga.
Allen, Benjamin F., died at Nashville, September 11, 1864.
Miller, Jacob, died in hospital.
Mickersell, Solomon, died at Waterloo, Ala., March 11, 1865.
Moser, Abraham, killed in action at Fair Garden, January 27, 1864.
Norcutt, Warren B., died at Franklin, August 22, 1864.
Phillips, D. C., died in hospital.
Walters, Charles F., missing at Chicamauga.
Walker, Henry, died on furlough.
Whitn.an, Charles, drowned.
Williams, William H., died of sunstroke.

THE ADJUTANT'S REMARKS.

No returns previous to December, 1861.
December 1861—Stationed at Benton Barracks, St. Louis, Missouri. No remarks.
January, 1862—The same.
February, 1862—In the field en route from St. Louis to New Madrid, Missouri. No remarks.
April 5, 1862—Near New Madrid, Missouri. No remarks.
May 9, 1862—Near Farmington, Mississippi. No remarks.
June 20, 1862—Near Farmington, Mississippi. No remarks.
July 14, 1862—Near Booneville, Mississippi. No remarks.
July, 1862—No station given. No remarks.
August, 1862—Near Rienzi, Mississippi. No remarks.
October 30, 1862—Near Louisville, Kentucky. No remarks.
November 16, 1862—New Market, Kentucky. No remarks.
December 16, 1862—Lebanon, Kentucky. No remarks.
December, 1862—Nicholasville, Kentucky. No remarks.
January, 1863—Louisville, Kentucky. No remarks.
February, 1863—Franklin, Tennessee. No remarks.
March, 1863—Franklin, Tennessee. No remarks.
April, 1863—Franklin, Tennessee. No remarks.
May—10 A. M. May 1—Regiment returned from reconnaissance on Lewisburg pike, etc., result, twelve rebels killed and wounded as far as heard from, twelve others taken prisoners; till 14th, usual camp, picket and scout duty every day; 15th, regiment aroused at 2 A. M., and moved half an hour later to the village of Hillsborough; while crossing the West Harpeth river George Beutter, company H, was drowned; usual camp, picket and scout duty till end of month.
June, 1863—Near Manchester, Tennessee; 2d, move camp to Triune, Tennessee, from Franklin, Tennessee; 4th, reaching there at 6:30 P. M.; had a sharp skirmish; two of our men company D killed, three others wounded; known rebel loss, fifty-three killed, wounded and missing. Returned to Triune 6th; 9th, the rebels attacked camp at Triune; our regiment moved to the front and drove the enemy—no loss; 11th, another reconnaissance to the front, no loss, in the morning picket party lost one sergeant killed, one private taken prisoner, seven horses and equipments lost. Till 22d, usual guard, scout and picket duty; 23d, moved for a long scout, without tents, change of clothing or baggage, along with whole of first division. Engagement at Rover, Tennessee, one man wounded; 24th marched to Middleton; skirmished from noon till dark; one man wounded; 25th, 26th, on the march; 27th, charged the enemy seven miles into Shelbyville, Tennessee; three of our regiment missing. Rebels lost about eight hundred killed, wounded and missing; it is supposed that over one hundred and fifty were drowned in attempting to cross Duck river. Rumor says that about two thousand rebels were lost, one thousand two hundred of the number embracing the opportunity of a general rout to desert to their homes; 28th, Shelbyville and march; 29th, back to Shelbyville and march to Hoover's Gap; 30th, on the march, rained every day and night since starting, 23d inst.

THE ADJUTANT'S REMARKS.

July—Near Winchester, Tennessee; 1st and 2d, on the march; 3d, Decherd, Cowan, Tennessee, drove the rebels, took a number of prisoners; 4th and 5th, two miles out of Decherd; 6th, 7th, 8th and 9th, Franklin, Tennessee, between Salem and Winchester; 10th, 11th and 12th, Salem, Tenn.; 13th, New Market, Ala.; 14th, Huntsville, Ala., and long march; 15th. 16th, 17th, Huntsville, Ala.; 18th, 19th and 20th (two battalions), New Market; 21st, Winchester; 22d, on the march; 23d, 24th, 25th, Fayetteville, Tennessee; 26th, march, Salem, Tennessee; 27th, 28th, Salem (company desks, tents and baggage reached regiment); 29th, march Winchester; 30th, 31st, near Winchester, Tennessee. Two first weeks in the month it rained every day and every night. Government provisions and forage very scarce, stringent orders against leaving camp.

August—Bridgeport, Alabama; 1st, on the march, Salem, Tennessee; 2d, march Fayetteville, Tennessee, remaining there until the 10th, usual guard and picket duties; 11th, march, Walker, Alabama; 12th, march Huntsville, Alabama; 13th, Maysville, Alabama; 14th, Larkinville, Alabama; 15th, on a scout, killed two rebels, wounded one, took two prisoners; 16th, march, Stevenson and Bolivar, Alabama; 17th to 26th, at Bolivar, usual guard and picket duties; 27th, march Bridgeport, Alabama; 28th, forded the Tennessee river, the first regiment without loss of man or horse—lost several guns by horses getting into deep water, and men falling off; 29th to 31st, opposite Bridgeport, scouted in the mountains as far east as Georgia, taking several prisoners.

September—Near Jasper, Tennessee; 1st, bivouacked opposite Bridgeport; 2d, scouted on Raccoon mountain and back twenty miles; 3d, marched down on left bank river to Caperton's Ferry, eighteen miles; 4th, crossed Raccoon mountain to Valley Head, twenty-two miles; 5th, moved down the valley five miles; 6th, 7th, 8th, in same place; 9th crossed Lookout mountain to Alpine, Ga., eighteen miles; 10th, scouted towards Rome six miles and back; 11th, same; 12th, marched toward Lafayette, ten miles; 13th, ninth Pennsylvania in advance, run into a heavy force near Lafayette, our regiment covered the ground while the wounded were removed, then covered the retreat, marched back to Alpine, marched twenty-six miles; 14th, marched to Lookout mountain, eight miles; 15th, crossed down to Little Wills Valley twelve miles; 16th, crossed Lookout mountain to McLamore's Cove, sixteen miles; 17th, marched down the Cove, four miles; 18th, first battalion scouted to Blue Bird Gap; 19th, joined the infantry line at Pond Springs, enemy in view, but little skirmishing; 20th, on the right in the Chicamauga battle, guarded the train to Chattanooga in the night; 21st, crossed the river and went to Harrison's Ferry, fourteen miles; 22d to 27th, guarding fords and ferry, from Harrison's Ferry to Thacher's Ferry, fifteen miles above; sent the scouting parties across the river, one man wounded and three captured; 28th, marched to Chattanooga, fourteen miles; 29th, marched to Rankin's Ferry, twenty-five miles; 30th, at Rankin's Ferry.

October—Winchester, Tennessee; 1st, guarding Rankin's Ferry and fords; 2d, marched up Sequatchee Valley to Anderson's Crossroads, to protect the wagon train; received notice of the enemy burning the train eleven o'clock A. M., learned the enemy were repulsed by Col. McCook; returned to Rankin's Ferry; marched thirty-two miles; 3d, started on the Wheeler chase, marched thirty-two miles; 4th, joined brigade at Walnut Grove, passed through Dunlap, bivouacked on Cumberland mountain, marched thirty miles; 5th, marched through McMinnville and Woodbury, marched fifty-five miles; 6th, marched to Murfreesboro, drew rations, marched near Shelbyville, marched twenty-five miles; 7th; passed through Uniontown, camped on Duck river, marched twenty-seven miles; 8th, passed through Rainy Spring, Lewisburg and Connersville, marched thirty miles; 9th, passed through Pulaski, camped at Rogersville, four miles from Lamb's Ferry, Tennessee river; 10th, left Rogersville and marched ten miles; 11th, marched twenty-one miles; 12th, marched to Huntsville, on provost guard, at this place captured several prisoners, marched twenty-five miles; 13th, passed through New Market after Roddy's rebel brigade, marched twenty-three miles; 14th, marched to Branchville, marched eighteen miles; 15th, passed through Salem, camped five miles from Winchester, marched nine miles; 16th to 19th, in camp at same place; 20th, moved camp to Winchester; 21st to 25th, same place; 26th, moved to Decherd station, three miles; 26th to 30th, same place; 31st, moved to Winchester three miles.

November—Sparta, Tennessee; 1st to 8th, in camp at Winchester doing usual camp and picket duty; 9th to 14th, on scouting and foraging expedition to **Fayetteville**, thirty-five miles west of Winchester, a part of the ninth Pennsylvania accompanying, brought in about four hundred bushels of wheat, sixty-five head of beef cattle, and between five and six hundred head of sheep, also several horses and mules; 15th, in camp; 16th, marched sixteen miles; 17th, passed through Shelbyville, marched fourteen miles; 18th, marched twenty miles, camped at Murfreesboro; 19th, in camp; 20th, marched twenty miles, camped at Milton; 21st, marched fourteen miles, camped at Liberty; 22d to 27th, in camp doing usual camp and picket duty; 28th, marched twenty-three miles, passed through Smithville, camped on Rainy Fork; 29th, marched six miles, one man of company G killed by bushwhackers; 30th, in camp.

December—Near Mossy Creek, Tennessee; 1st, marched east to Sparta, Tennessee, remaining until the 8th, when the regiment moved up the Cumberland mountains, passing over and down the same through Crossville, reaching Kingston, Tennessee, 13th, thence eastwardly; 14th, 15th, 16th, through Knoxville, fording the Holston river, and arriving at Strawberry Plains 17th. On the 18th forded and re-forded the Holston four miles above Strawberry Plains, moving several miles to the northeast and returning to Strawberry Plains on morning of the 19th, remaining in camp there till the 23d, when the regiment removed to New Market, Tennessee; 24th, in connection with the remainder of first brigade marched to Dandridge, and engaged a vastly superior force of the rebels, returning late at night to New Market. In this engagement one officer was wounded and taken prisoner, one other badly wounded in the leg, and one other sprained ankle by horse falling, two enlisted men were killed, nine taken prisoners, and seven wounded—total casualties twenty-one; 25th, marched to Mossy Creek, Tennessee, remained near that place till end of month, On 29th, another skirmish with the rebels. One officer badly wounded, one enlisted man killed, two taken prisoners, and four wounded—total casualties eight.

During 1863 the regiment was engaged in twenty-four battles or important skirmishes, and on each occasion met with losses, in addition to minor actions in which no losses occurred. Marched over two thousand one hundred and forty miles in addition to picketing, scouting and foraging sorties, which were equal at least in length to the regular marches.

January, 1864—Marysville, Tennessee; 1st, 2d and 3d, in camp two miles from Mossy Creek, Tennessee; 4th, marched to the rear two miles; 5th to 13th, in camp near Mossy Creek; 14th, marched twenty-two miles, camped near Dandridge; 15th, in camp; 16th, marched four miles on Indian Creek road; 17th, marched to the front to relieve the second brigade in line of battle until midnight; 18th, marched twenty-seven miles, crossed the Holston, camped near Strawberry Plains; 19th, marched seventeen miles, passed through Knoxville, crossed the Holston river; 20th, marched fifteen miles; 21st, marched twenty-two miles; 22d, in camp: 23d, marched four miles, camped on Flat creek; 24th, marched eight miles; 25th, marched twenty-two miles, camped on Pigeon river; 26th, broke camp at midnight, marched twenty miles; 27th, formed line of battle at daylight, engaged the enemy, eleven wounded, two missing, marched twenty miles; 28th, marched twenty miles. One man of company L captured by rebel infantry; 29th, marched twenty miles, passed through Severeville; 30th, marched ten miles, camped near Marysville.

February—Chestua creek, Monroe county, Tennessee; 1st to 8th, in camp near Marysville, Tennessee; 9th, marched eighteen miles, forded Little Tennessee river, camped on Four Mile creek, Monroe county, Tennessee; 10th to 16th, in camp at last named place; 17th, marched ten miles, camped near Citaco creek, Monroe county, Tennessee; 18th to 22d, in camp at last named place; 23d, marched twenty-three miles, camped near Chestua creek, Monroe county, Tennessee; 24th to 29th, in camp at last named place.

March—Cleveland, Tennessee; 1st, 2d and 3d, in camp at Chestua creek, near Madisonville, Tennessee; 4th, marched twenty-five miles to Calhoun; 5th to 11th, in camp at Calhoun; 12th, marched twelve miles to Cleveland, Tennessee; 13th to 31st, in camp at Cleveland, Tennessee. March 29th about three hundred of the men were mustered into the service as veteran volunteers.

MOVEMENTS OF THE NON-VETERANS.

April—From April 1st to 30th, in camp at Cleveland, Tennessee. April 14th,

THE ADJUTANT'S REMARKS.

three hundred and fifteen re-enlisted veterans left for Michigan on furlough.

May—1st and 2d, in camp at Cleveland, Tennessee; 3d, marched fourteen miles on Dalton road to Mount Pleasant church; 7th, marched seven miles to Varnet Station skirmishing; 8th, marched one and a half miles in line of battle toward Buzzard's Roost; 10th, two miles in line; 11th, marched through Tunnel Hill to Dug Gap, fifteen miles; 12th, in fortifications in front of Dug Gap; 13th, marched through Dug Gap, skirmishing; 14th, advance of division on Tilton road, skirmishing, loss one killed, three wounded, marched twenty five miles; 15th, made breastworks at Tilton; 16th, crossed Coosa waters, ten miles; 17th, four miles; 18th, twelve miles on Cassville road; 19th, marched eight miles on Cassville road, skirmishing, 20th, marched six miles to Cassville Station; 22d, marched ten miles to Etowah river and guarded fords; 23d, forded Etowah, marched ten miles; 24th, advance guard Burnt Hickory road, skirmished enemy, two men wounded, twelve miles; 25th, marched seven miles; 26th, marched four miles, skirmishing, two wounded; 27th, skirmished enemy, one wounded, two missing; 28th, skirmished enemy, two wounded; 31st, in camp near Dallas and Hamilton Crossroads.

June—2d, marched four miles on Ackworth and Dallas road skirmishing; 5th, skirmished enemy at same place, captured one prisoner; 8th, marched eighteen miles; 9th, marched five miles; 10th, patrolling the Marietta road; 14th, marched four miles to Ackworth; 16th, marched eight miles toward Lost mountain; 17th, marched six miles to top of Lost mountain; 20th, scouted to Powder Springs twelve miles; 26th, on scout to Powder Springs; 28th, marched to Ackworth, ten miles.

VETERANS RETURNED.

July—Guarding railroad from Nashville to Rutherford creek.

August—1st to 29th, guarding railroad from Brentwood to Rutherford creek, Tennessee; 29th, marched to Nashville nineteen miles; 30th, marched twelve miles toward Murfreesboro, skirmished Wheeler's raiders, lost one man missing from company C; 31st, marched five miles toward Franklin.

September—1st, marched fifteen miles to Franklin, Tennessee, skirmished Wheeler's raiders; 2d, marched to Columbia. twenty-seven miles; 3d, laid at Columbia; 4th, marched ten miles on Pulaski pike; 5th, marched to near Campbellville, skirmished enemy in afternoon, moved on to Lawrenceburgh, twenty-nine miles; 6th, marched to Military road, twenty-five miles; 7th, marched to Florence, Alabama, ten miles; 8th, marched twenty miles on Military road towards Nashville; 9th, marched to near Pulaski, twenty-five miles; 10th, marched twenty miles; 11th, twenty miles; 12th, thirteen miles to Franklin; 12th to 25th, camped at Franklin; 25th, marched beyond Columbia thirty-three miles; 26th, marched to Pulaski; 27th, fought all day with Forrest's command, lost one man killed; 28th, marched to Connersville, seventeen miles; 29th, marched to Shelbyville, twenty-five miles; 30th, marched via Normandy to Tullahoma, twenty-five miles.

October—1st, marched from near Tullahoma, Tennessee, to Winchester, eight miles; 2d, marched twenty-four miles towards Shelbyville; 3d, marched twenty-nine miles, camped near Lewisburg; 4th, marched twenty-seven miles to within ten miles of Pulaski; 5th, marched eighteen miles on Lewisburg road; 6th, marched thirty-six miles on Military road; 7th, marched fifteen miles, met the enemy and charged on them. Lieutenant Darrow, company M, and three men killed, two wounded; 8th, marched fifteen miles; 9th, marched twenty miles; 10th, marched twenty-five miles, camped on Military road, twelve miles from Halls; 11th, marched thirty-six miles toward Pulaski; 12th, in camp on Hurricane creek; 13th, marched twelve miles, camped near Pulaski pike; 14th. in camp; 15th, marched to Sugar creek, twenty-nine miles; 16th, marched twenty-one miles; 17th, to 30th, in camp one and a half miles from the river; 30th, went out, met the enemy, turned back, went to Rogersville; 31st, marched to Sugar creek, 14 miles.

November—1st, marched from Blue Waters to Col. Huff's, thence to Shoal creek, Alabama, and encamped, fifteen miles; 2d, 3d, 4th, 5th, enemy attacked and forced us back to Four Mile Creek, Alabama; loss heavy; 9th to 14th, in camp; 15th, on reconnaissance to the right, camped at Taylor Springs; 15th to 20th, in camp at Taylor Springs; 20th, marched to Lexington, Tennessee, eight miles; 21st, to Lawrenceburgh, Tennessee, enemy attacked us about four P. M., fell back towards Campbellville to within three miles of Columbia and encamped; 25th, marched across Duck river; 26th, in camp; 27th, marched five miles; 28th marched fourteen miles east of Lewisburg pike, formed line of battle, laid in line all night; 29th, fell back sixteen miles, encamped near Franklin, Tennessee, skirmished with the enemy all day; 30th, engaged enemy all day, lost one killed, seventeen wounded, and three missing.

December—1st, marched eighteen miles from near Franklin to within five miles of Nashville, lay in line of battle all night; 2d, marched through Nashville to Edgefield, seven miles, crossed the Cumberland river; 3d to 11th, in camp at Edgefield; 12th, marched from Edgefield across the Cumberland river through Nashville, four miles, and encamped on Charlotte pike; 13th and 14th, in camp; 15th, advanced two miles, dismounted and skirmished on foot all day, mounted at sunset and marched six miles; 16th, marched twenty miles, one man of company B wounded by General Hammond's command firing into the column by mistake; 17th, crossed the Franklin pike, swam Harpeth river, marched twenty miles; 18th, marched ten miles to Spring Hill; 19th, in camp; 20th, marched ten miles, camped on Rutherford creek; 21st and 22d, in camp; 23d, marched across Duck river through Columbia, ten miles, 24th, regiment in advance on pike, fought all day, made a charge mounted and drove the enemy sixteen miles, two men killed and six wounded; 25th, marched fifteen miles through Pulaski; 26th, marched twelve miles to near Sugar Creek; 27th, in camp; 28th, marched eighteen miles, camped near Taylor Springs; 29th, marched fifteen miles, camped on Little Cypress river; 30th, marched to Waterloo; 31st, in camp, company I and twelve men of company G, with General McCook, in Kentucky after horses and did not return until the last of the month, brought one hundred and thirteen horses.

January, 1865—From 1st to 17th in camp at Waterloo, Ala.; 17th, marched eight miles, across the Tennessee river, passed through Eastport; 18th, marched twenty miles, passed through Iuka and Burnsville, captured six prisoners; 19th, marched twenty-five miles, went into Corinth, and returned to Farmington; 20th, marched twenty miles, camped at Iuka, captured five prisoners; 21st, marched fifteen miles, passed through Eastport, crossed the Tennessee river, returned to old camp; from 21st to 31st, in camp at Waterloo.

February—From 1st to 28th, in camp at Waterloo, Alabama.

March—From 1st to 10th, in camp at Waterloo, Alabama; 11th, moved across the river, marched five miles; from 11th to 22d, in camp at Chickasaw, Alabama; 22d, marched sixteen miles; 23d, marched four miles; 24th, marched thirty miles, passed through Frankfort, and Russellville; 25th, marched thirty miles, crossed Big Ford creek and Buttehatchie river; 26th, marched twenty-five miles on Jasper road, passed through Eldridge; 27th, marched thirty miles, passed through Jasper; 28th, crossed the Mulberry river, marched ten miles; 29th, crossed Black Warrior river, marched sixteen miles; 30th, passed through Elyton, marched fourteen miles; 31st, marched twenty-eight miles on Tuscaloosa road.

April—1st, marched in northward direction thirty miles to Johnston Ferry; 2d, crossed Black Warrior river on a scow, horses swam, marched twelve miles; 3d, marched thirty-five miles to Tuscaloosa, Alabama, surprised and captured the pickets at the bridge, entered the town, captured three cannon and a large number of prisoners; 4th, formed line of battle around Tuscaloosa, remained there until the morning of the 5th, crossed the river, burned some government buildings and the bridge, marched thirty-four miles, crossed Sipsey creek, three battalions remained there until 4 P. M., Co. F was sent out on a scout in the morning, crossed at a ferry twelve miles below town; 6th, marched to Bridgeville, crossed Sipsey creek, met General Adams commanding, started for Tuscaloosa, sixth Kentucky in rear was now pressed hard, second Michigan halted and formed line of battle to relieve sixth Kentucky, repulsed the enemy, three men wounded, marched forty miles; 7th, marched to Northport, twenty miles; 8th, marched north thirteen miles; 9th, in camp; 10th, in camp; 11th, marched to Windham Springs, twenty miles; 12th, marched in a northerly direction; 13th, marched fifteen miles, crossed Wolf creek; 14th, marched twenty-seven miles, crossed Lost creek and Black Warrior river; 15th, marched eight miles to Lindley Ferry; sixteenth, second and third battalions crossed Sipsey river; 17th, marched ten miles; 18th, marched sixteen miles, crossed Mulberry river; 19th, crossed Black Warrior river at Minnter's Ferry, marched sixteen miles to James Valley; 20th, marched twenty miles, easterly direction; 21st, marched thirteen miles to Luf's Ferry; 22d, crossed Coosa river, marched twelve miles to Talladega; 23d, marched thirty miles, skirmished with General Hill's brigade, captured one piece of artillery, two men killed; 24th, marched thirty miles southeast direction, crossed branch of Talladega river; 25th, marched thirty miles, passed through Bowdon, Ga., crossed Tallapoosa river; 26th, marched twenty-four miles, crossed Chattahoochee river; 27th, marched twenty-five miles towards Macon; 28th, marched thirty miles; 29th, marched sixteen miles; 30th, marched eighteen miles, passed through Forsyth.

May—1st, marched eight miles, camped near Macon, Ga.; from May 1st to 31st, in camp.

June—1st to 30th. in camp at Macon, Ga.

July—16th and 17th, companies D and L marched to Perry, sixty miles, to take charge of post, companies G and M to Thomaston, fifty miles, company I to Barnesville, forty miles, company B to Forsyth, twenty-five miles, companies F and K to Milledgeville, thirty-five miles.

FIELD AND STAFF.

NAME.	RANK.	ENTERED SERVICE.	REMARKS.
Gordon Granger	Colonel.	Sept. 7, 1861.	Promoted Brig. Gen'l U. S. Vol's Mar. 26, 1862.
Philip H. Sheridan	"	May 25, 1862.	" Oct. —, 1862, to date July 1, 1862
Archibald P. Campbell	"	Sept. 2, 1861. Port Huron.	Discharged for disability Sept. 29, 1864.
Thomas W. Johnston	"	Aug. 24, 1861, Marshall.	Mustered out as Lieut. Colonel August 29, 1865.
William C. Davies	Lieut. Colonel	Sept. 2, 1861, Grand Rapids.	Resigned March 31, 1862.
Selden H. Gorham	"	" " Port Huron.	" July 7, 1862.
Archibald P. Campbell	"	" " "	Promoted Colonel to rank from July 1, 1862.
Frederick Fowler	"	Aug. 25, 1861, Reading.	Resigned May 9, 1863.
Benjamin Smith	"	" 26, " Grand Rapids.	Mustered out March 6, 1865.
Thomas W. Johnston	"	" 24, " Marshall.	" Aug. 29, 1865.
Marshal. J. Dickinson	"	" 26, " Vermontville.	" as Major Aug. 17, 1865.
Robert H. G. Minty	Major.	Sept. 2, 1861, Grand Rapids.	Promoted Lieut. Col. 3d Mich. Cav. Sept. 7, 1861.
Selden H. Gorham	"	" " "	" " April 1, 1862.
Charles P. Babcock	"	" " "	Resigned Oct. 26, 1862.
Henry A. Shaw	"	Aug. 21, 1861, Eaton Rapids.	" Sept. 25, 1862.
Russell A. Alger	"	Sept. 2, 1861,	Promoted Lieut. Col. 6th Mich. Cav. Oct. 16, 1862.
John C. Godley	"	Aug. 21, 1861, East Saginaw.	Resigned Sept. 12, 1863.
Frank W. Dickey	"	Sept. 2, 1861, Marshall.	" May 7, 1863.
Leonidas Scranton	"	Aug. 26, 1861, Grand Rapids.	" Nov. 19, 1864.
Marshall J. Dickinson	"	" " Vermontville.	Promoted Lieut. Col. July 31, 1865.
Benjamin Smith	"	" " Grand Rapids.	" " Sept. 13, 1863.
Harmon F. Nicholson	"	" " Muskegon.	Mustered out Aug. 17, 1865.
Thomas W. Johnston	"	Aug. 24, 1861, Marshall.	{ Promoted Colonel Dec. 31, 1864, and not mustering for want of the requisite number of men, was made Lieut. Col March 6, '65.
Henry Vance	"	Aug. 30, 1861 Muskegon.	Mustered out as Captain Aug, 17, 1865.
Charles N. Baker	"	Sept. 2. 1861. Port Huron.	" " "
Peter A. Schuyler	Adjutant.	" " Grand Rapids.	Promoted Captain Co. H. April 11, 1862.
George Lee	"	" "	" and A. A. G. U. S. V. March 11, 1863; Maj. and Brevet Lieut. Col U. S. V. Gen'l Sheridan's staff; 1st Lieut. 21st U. S. I. Died at New Orleans Oct. 29, 1867.
Henry C. Whipple	"	" "	Promoted Captain and A. A. G. U. S Vol Sept. 15, 1863.
Edwin Hoyt, Jr	"	" "	Mustered out Nov. 30, 1864
Healy C. Akeley	"	Oct. 28, 1863,	" Aug. 17, 1865.

NAME.	RANK.	ENTERED SERVICE.	REMARKS.
Frank E. Walbridge	Quartermaster.	Sept. 2, 1861, Gr'nd Rapids.	Promoted Captain A. Q. M. U. S. Vol's June 9, 1862.
James B. Scott	"	"	Mustered out Nov. 30, 1864.
Isaac C. Griswold	"	Sept. 9, 1861, Vermontville.	Mustered out Aug. 17, 1865.
Erastus W. Lawrence	Commissary.	Sept. 2, 1861, Gr'nd Rapids.	Absent on detached service at muster out.
Charles L. Henderson	Surgeon.	"	Resigned Oct. 19, 1862.
William Brownell	"	June 6, 1863, Detroit.	Mustered out Nov. 3, 1864; died at Utica, Mich., May 22, '84.
George E. Ranney	Ass't Surgeon.	Sept. 2, 1861, Gr'nd Rapids.	" June 9, '65, to accept Com'n Surgeon 136th U. S. C. T.
William Brownell	"	Oct. 20, 1862,	Promoted Surgeon Oct. 20, '62.
William F. Green	"	Aug. 18, 1862, Gr'nd Rapids.	" 1st East Tenn. Cav. Aug. 15, 1863.
James A. Dunlap	2d "	June 6, 1863, Detroit.	Mustered out Aug. 17, 1865.
George E. Ranney	Chaplain.	Sept. 2, 1861,	Promoted Surgeon Nov. 15, 1864.
Francis Drew	"	Aug. 28, 1861, Hillsdale.	Resigned Sept. 3, 1862.
Robert Taylor	Bat'n Adj't'nt.	Sept. 2, 1861, Gr'nd Rapids.	" for disability Feb'y 10, 1864.
Alphonso Gordon	"	"	1st Lieut. Co. E, Aug. 1, 1862.
Peter A. Weber	"	"	Mustered out June 1, 1862, to accept Captaincy in 6th Mich. Cav. and killed, as Major, at Falling Waters, Md., July 14, 1863. Promoted Regimental Adjutant ———— 1862; served with P. H. Sheridan as A. A. G. till close of was; died at New Orleans as Col.
George Lee	"	"	Promoted Reg. Q. M. Aug. 1, 1862; accidentally shot himself.
James B. Scott	Bat'n Q'rm'ster	"	Mustered out June 1, 1862; Captain and Com. Sub. U. S. V. Oct. 28, 1862; resigned and honorably discharged Oct. 15, 1864; Major and Brevet Lieut. Colonel.
Seymour Brownell	"	"	
John A. Brooks	"	"	Mustered out June 1, 1862.

NON-COMMISSIONED STAFF.

NAME.	RANK.	ENTERED SERVICE.	REMARKS.
Edwin Hoyt, Jr.	Serg'nt. Major.	Sept. 2, 1861, Gr'nd Rapids.	Appointed 2d Lieut. Co. F Sept. 20, 1862.
John G. Crawford	"	"	" Co. L Sept. 9, 1862.
James A. Strong	"	"	" 1st Lieut. 8th Mich. Cav. Nov. 1, 1862.
William H. Tallman	"	Sept. 26, 1861, Port Huron.	" 2d Lieut. Co. D March 1, 1864; re-enlisted Jan. 5, 1864.
Thomas F. Anderson	"	Sept. 10, 1861, Grand Haven.	" 1st Lieut. Co M Dec. 31, 1864.
Henry Gould	"	Sept. 30, 1861, Gr'nd Rapids.	Mustered out at Macon, Ga. Aug. 17, 1865.
John E. Babbitt	Q'm'r Sergeant	Sept. 2, 1861,	Discharged for disability at Hamburg, Ill., April 23, 1862.
William B. Martin	"	"	" Jan'y 31, 1862.
Ezra Beaman	"	"	" Nov. 13, 1861.

NAME.	RANK.	ENTERED SERVICE.	REMARKS.
Franklin N. Eaton	Q'm'r Sergeant	Sept. 20, 1861, Albion.	Appointed 2d Lieut. Co. F Aug. 1, 1863.
Ami A. Brown	"	Aug. 26, 1861, Galesburg.	Discharged at Nashville, Tenn., Oct. 22, 1864.
Henry W. Walker	"	"	Mustered out at Macon, Ga., Aug. 17, 1865, re-enlisted Jan. 5, '64.
Martin S. Williamson	Com. Sergeant.	Sept. 2, 1861, Gr'nd Rapids.	Transferred to Co. A April 10, 1862.
Erastus W. Lawrence	"	"	Appointed 2d Lieut. Co. K Sept. 19, 1862.
Trueman W. Hawley	"	"	Discharged Jan'y 30, 1863.
George Wentworth	"	Oct. 9, 1861, Utica.	On detached service at muster out.
Daniel A. Spicer	Hosp. Steward.	Sept. 2, 1861, Gr'nd Rapids.	Discharged Dec. 11, 1862; appointed Ass't Surgeon 10th Mich. Inf.
William E. Austin	"	"	Discharged for disability near Corinth, Miss., June 14, 1862.
George E. Ranney	"	Aug. 18, 1862, "	Appointed Ass't Surgeon March 1, 1864.
James A. Dunlap	"	Aug. 24, 1861, Fentonville.	Discharged at Franklin, Tenn., March 29, 1863.
William W. Booth	"	Sept. 7, 1861, Homer.	Unaccounted for.
Chandler Redfield	"	Sept. 23, 1861, Gr'nd Rapids.	Discharged for disability at Nashville, Tenn., Jan'y 5, 1865.
Henry H. Henshaw	"	Sept. 1, 1864, Jackson.	Mustered out at Edgefield, Tenn., June 21, 1865.
Adrian B. Coulter	"	Aug. 26, 1861, East Saginaw.	" Macon, Ga., Aug. 17, 1865; re-enlisted Jan. 5, 1864.
Orestes Watkins	Saddler Serg't.	Sept. 2, 1861, Gr'nd Rapids.	Discharged for disability Jan'y 23, 1863.
Jacob Maurer	"	"	" at Louisville Oct. 4, 1862.
Isaac W. Kendrick	"	"	"
James C. Roseback	"	Sept. 12, 1861, Detroit.	Re-enlisted Jan'y 5, 1864; mustered out Aug. 17, 1865.
Frederick Trempler	Veter'y Serg't.	Sept. 2, 1861, Gr'nd Rapids.	Discharged for disability at Farmington, Miss., May 22, 1862.
Peter Haight	"	"	April 2, 1862; Q. M. Sergeant.
Robert A. White	"	"	at Rienzi, Miss., Sept. 9, 1862.
Elder Godley	"	"	Master of transportation; Acting Q. M. Atlanta campaign; transferred to Co. C; mustered out Oct. 22, 1864.
Robert G. Mason	"	Sept. 6, 1861, "	
George B. Whitney	"	"	Discharged for disability May 22, 1865.
William Walker	"	Aug. 22, 1861, East Saginaw.	Mustered out Oct. 22, 1864.

REGIMENTAL BAND.

NAME.	RANK.	ENTERED SERVICE.	REMARKS.
Abner P. Stimpson	Ch. Trumpeter.	Sept. 14, 1861, Niles.	Re-enlisted Jan. 5, '64; mustered out at Macon, Ga., Aug. 17, 1865.
Frank Sylvester	Pr. Musician.	Sept. 2, 1861, Gr'nd Rapids.	Discharged for disability near Farmington, Miss., May 21, 1862.
Benjamin F. Cheesbro	"	"	" Jan'y 30, 1863.

John Richards............	Pr. Musician.	Sept. 2, 1861, Grand Rapids.	Discharged at Keokuk, Iowa, Dec. 11, 1862.
Albert Atkins............	Musician.	Sept. 14, 1861, "	Augustus Akins, died at Runyan, Miss., Aug. 16, 1862.
George P. Balcome.......	"	"	Discharged for disability at St. Louis, Mo., Feb'y 20, 1862.
George W. Davis.........	"	"	" July 18, 1862.
Charles B. Field.........	"	"	" Oct. 10, 1862.
David W. Field...........	"	"	" May 15, 1862.
Joseph Griswold..........	"	"	" Aug. 21, 1862.
Henry W. Hopkins........	"	"	" April 24, 1862.
McCormack Lyon..........	"	"	Mustered out Aug. 31, 1862.
Jefferson Powell..........	"	"	"
John Ranney.............	"	"	Discharged for disability at Detroit July 17, 1862.
John Simons..............	"	"	Mustered out Aug. 31, 1862.
George E. Stevenson......	"	"	Discharged for disability Oct. 10, 1862.
Louis Town...............	"	"	Mustered out Aug. 31, 1862.
Frederick Watkins........	"	"	Died at New Madrid, Mo., April 15, 1862.
John Wild................	"	"	Mustered out Aug. 31, 1862.

COMPANIES.

Co. A. NAME.	RANK.	ENTERED SERVICE.	REMARKS.
John C. Godley.	Captain.	Aug. 21, 1861, E. Saginaw.	Promoted Major Sept. 25, 1862.
George Carter............	"	"	Resigned on account of disability Nov. 5, 1863.
Alphonso E. Gordon......	"	Sept. 2, 1861, Grand Rapids.	June 6, 1864.
John W. Kingscott.......	"	Aug. 24, 1861, Warren.	Transferred to Co. H.
Walter Whittemore.......	1st Lieut.	Sept. 1, 1861, Bay City.	Promoted Major 136th U. S. C. T. June 8, 1865.
George Carter............	"	Aug. 21, 1861, E. Saginaw.	Captain Sept. 25, 1862.
Merrit Blackmer.........	"	Aug. 22, 1861, "	Resigned May 17th, 1863.
Theodore F. Smith.......	"	Sept. 1, 1861, Bay City.	" May 4, 1864, for disability.
Walter Whittemore.......	"	Aug. 28, 1861, E. Saginaw.	Promoted Captain Sept. 23, 1864.
Joseph M Jones..........	2d Lieut.	Aug. 21, 1861, E. Saginaw.	Mustered out Aug. 17, 1865.
Merritt Blackmer.........	"	Aug. 22, 1861, "	Promoted 1st Lieut. Sept. 25, 1862.
Theodore F. Smith.......	"	Sept. 1, 1861, Bay City.	" May 27, 1863.
Walter Whittemore.......	"	Aug. 21, 1861, E. Saginaw.	" May 5, 1864.
Royal Loomis............	1st Sergeant.	Aug. 22, 1861, "	Captain Co. B Dec. 26, 1864.
Theodore F. Smith.	"	Aug. 22, 1861, "	2d Lieut Jan'y 1, 1863.
Royal Loomis............	Q'm'r Sergeant	Aug. 21, 1861, "	" March 1, 1864; re-enlisted Jan'y 5, 1864.

Co. A.

NAME.	RANK.	ENTERED SERVICE.	REMARKS.
Walter Whittemore	Q'm'r Sergeant	Sept. 1, 1861, Bay City.	Promoted 2d Lieut. May 27, 1863.
Hiram J. Jenkins	"	Aug. 28, 1861, "	Re-enlisted Jan. 5, 1864; mustered out at Macon, Ga., Aug. 17, '65.
Thomas Abbott	"	Aug. 21, 1861, E. Saginaw.	
Albert M. Hale	"	Aug. 22, 1861, "	Discharged at Detroit, Nov. 17, 1864.
Thomas C. Gordon	Corporal.	" "	Sergeant; discharged at Nashville Oct. 22, 1864.
Jessup Moorhouse	"	" "	Discharged for disability at Franklin, Tenn., May 5, 1863.
Joseph L. Mead	"	" "	Promoted 1st. Lieut. 7th Mich. Cav. June 11, 1863.
George C. Clement	"	" "	Discharged at Nashville, Tenn., Oct. 22, 1864.
John Bedford	"	Aug. 27, 1861, Saginaw City.	"
David D. Stiff	"	Aug. 28, 1861, Bay City.	Died at Triune, Tenn., June 11, '63, of wounds received in action.
Michael Bever	"	Aug. 26, 1861, E. Saginaw.	Mustered out at Macon, Ga., Aug. 17, 1865.
Erastus S. Kimball	"	" "	Serg't "
John G. Richards	Musician.	Aug. 28, 1861, Saginaw City.	Transferred to N. C. S.; principal musician.
James Hutchinson	"	" Bay City.	Mustered out at Macon, Ga., Aug. 17, 1865.
William Walker	Farrier.	Aug. 22, 1861, E. Saginaw.	Promoted Veterinary Sergeant Dec. 1, 1861.
Daniel Cole	"	Sept. 2, 1861, "	Discharged at Nashville, Tenn., Oct. 22, 1864.
Charles Anthony	Private.	Aug. 23, 1861, Bridgeport.	Mustered out at Macon, Ga., Aug. 17, 1865; re-enlisted Jan'y 5, '64.
John Burga	"	Aug. 27, 1861, E. Saginaw.	Died of typhoid fever in hospital near Farmington, Miss., Jul. 9, '64.
John Ballentine	"	Aug. 28, 1861, Bay City.	Discharged at Nashville, Tenn., Oct. 22, 1864.
James L. Booth	"	Aug. 31, 1861, Saginaw City.	Shot by the enemy while on picket duty, near Point Pleasant, Mo., March 7, 1862.
Alexander Boyd	"	Aug. 28, 1861, Bay City.	Mustered out at Macon, Ga., Aug. 17, '62; re-enlisted Jan'y 5, '64.
William S. Brown	"	Sept. 1, 1861, "	Corporal; transferred to Marine Brigade March 3, 1863.
Irwin C. Bartlett	"	" "	Killed in action at Pulaski, Tenn., Sep. 28, '64; re-enlisted Jan. 5, '64.
Barnard Bourrassa	"	Aug. 31, 1861, "	Mustered out at Detroit July 22, 1865.
Augustus Burling	"	Aug. 22, 1861, E. Saginaw.	Discharged for disability at Stevenson, Ala., Sept. 4, 1863.
Washington Cahoon	"	Aug. 28, 1861, Bay City.	Re-enlisted Jan. 5, '64; mustered out at Macon, Ga., Aug. 17, '65.
Jonas W. Cole	"	Sept. 1, 1861, "	Discharged for disability at Columbus, Ohio, April 15, 1863.
William Clark	"	Aug. 28, 1861, E. Saginaw.	Re-enlisted Jan. 5, '64; in hospital at Jeffer'n Barr'ks at muster out.
Alanson Canfield	"	Sept. 1, 1861, Bay City.	Corporal; transferred to V. R. C. Jan'y 4, 1864.
Albert J. Demaree	"	Aug. 31, 1861, "	Discharged for disability at St. Louis, Mo., June 14, 1862.
William Dalmage	"	Aug. 28, 1861, "	" June 2, 1864.
James W. Davis	"	Aug. 21, 1861, Saginaw City.	Re-enlisted Jan. 5, 1864; mustered out at Macon, Ga., Aug. 17, '65.
Edward Demaw	"	Aug. 31, 1861, "	" "
Charles Douglass	"	Sept. 1, 1861, Bay City.	" "

Alfred Foy.............	Private.	Sept. 1, 1861, Bay City.	Re-enlisted Jan. 5, '64; Serg't, must'd out Macon, Ga., Aug. 17, '65.
William Fisher.........	"	" " "	" " " " " " " "
Charles A. Fricker.....	"	Aug. 30, 1861, "	Corporal; discharged for disability at Louisville, Ky., Oct. 2, '62.
Elias O. Graves........	"	Sept. 2, 1861, "	Re-enlisted Jan. 5, '64; must'd out Macon, Ga., Aug. 17, '65; serg't
Alonzo Gaines.........	"	Aug. 30, 1861, E. Saginaw.	corp.
Walter A. Griffin......	"	Aug. 23, 1861, Bridgeport.	Sergeant; discharged at Nashville, Tenn., Oct. 22, 1864.
James P. Green........	"	Aug. 31, 1861, Bay City.	" " " " " "
Ira Graves.............	"	Sept. 2, 1861, "	" " " " " "
Eben Groover..........	"	Sept. 16, 1861, E. Saginaw.	Re-enlisted Jan. 5, 1865; mustered out at Macon, Ga., Aug. 17, '65.
Thomas Hazzard.......	"	" " "	Discharged for disability at Louisville, Ky., Nov. 7, 1862.
Calvin C. Higgins......	"	Aug. 31, 1861, "	Re-enlisted Jan. 5, '64; mustered out at Macon, Ga., Aug. 17, '65.
Joseph Hoag...........	"	Sept. 12, 1861, "	" " " " " "
Sylvester Hulbert......	"	Aug. 28, 1861, Midland.	Discharged at Nashville, Tenn., Oct. 22, 1864.
Reuben S. Harper......	"	Aug. 21, 1861, E. Saginaw.	{ Re-enlisted Jan. 5, 1864; transferred to V. R. C. April 21, 1865; discharged at Springfield, Ill., Aug. 18, 1865.
William Head..........	"	Aug. 28, 1861, Bay City.	....
James H. Henderson...	"	Sept. 16, 1861, E. Saginaw.	Discharged for disability at St. Louis, Mo., Oct 29, 1862.
Thomas Jameson.......	"	Aug. 28, 1861, Bay City.	Re-enlisted Jan. 5, '65; Corp.; must'd out Macon, Ga., Aug. 17, '65.
Francis Jackson........	"	" " "	Serg't; appointed 1st Lieut. Sept. 23, 1864; re-enlisted Jan. 5, '64.
Joseph M. Jones........	"	Sept. 3, 1861, E. Saginaw.	....
Luther Jones..........	"	Aug. 31, 1861, Bay City.	Re-enlisted Jan. 5, '64; Corp.; must'd out Macon, Ga., Aug. 17, '65.
Henry Lockwood.......	"	Aug. 30, 1861, Saginaw.	Discharged at Nashville, Tenn., Oct. 22, 1864.
John W. Love..........	"	Aug. 21, 1861, E. Saginaw.	Re-enlisted Jan. 5, 1864; mustered out at Macon, Ga., Aug. 17, '65.
Charles Lyon..........	"	Aug. 27, 1861, Saginaw.	{ Re-enlisted Jan'y 5, 1864; died April 4, 1865 at Tuscaloosa, Ala., of wounds received in action.
Ezekiel Lemon.........	"	Sept. 16, 1861, E. Saginaw.	Discharged by order Sept. 13, 1862.
William Lemon........	"	Aug. 31, 1861, Bay City.	Re-enlisted Jan. 5, 1864; mustered out at Macon, Ga., Aug. 17, '65.
Henry Lansing........	"	Sept. 16, 1861, E. Saginaw.	....
Andrew McCann.......	"	Sept. 1, 1861, Bay City.	Transferred to Miss. Marine Brigade Jan'y 1, 1863.
Finley McDonley.......	"	Sept. 2, 1861, "	Discharged at Nashville, Tenn., Oct. 22, 1864.
Alpheus Martindale....	"	" " "	Re-enlisted Jan. 5, 1864; Serg't; must'd out at Detroit June 22, '65.
Marshman Maxon......	"	Sept. 3, 1861, Pine Run.	Discharged at Nashville, Tenn., Oct. 22, 1864.
William W. Middaugh..	"	" " Bay City.	Detroit July 10, 1865.
David D. Manly........	"	Aug. 26, 1861, E. Saginaw.	Re-enlisted Jan. 5, 1864; mustered out at Macon, Ga., Aug. 17, '65.
Rosville D. Miller......	"	Sept. 2, 1861, "	Discharged for disability at St. Louis, Mo., June 27, 1862.
John H. McDonald.....	"		Wounded; discharged at Louisville Ky., Dec. 17, 1862.
Jerome Oliver..........	"		

Co. A.

NAME.	RANK.	ENTERED SERVICE.	REMARKS.
Leonard Parker............	Private.	Aug. 28, 1861, E. Saginaw.	Wounded; discharged at St. Louis, Mo., May 27, 1862; died June 3, 1862, at St. Louis, Mo.
George Peel...............	"	Aug. 29, 1861, Saginaw.	Discharged at Nashville, Tenn., Oct. 22, 1864.
William Parks.............	"	Sept. 2, 1861, E. Saginaw.	" for disability at St. Louis, Mo., Aug. 23, 1862.
John S. Parks.............	"	Sept. 16, 1861, "	Re-enlisted Jan. 5, 1864; on detached service at muster out.
James Ross................	"	Aug. 28, 1861, "	Died of disease at New Madrid, Mo., March 24, 1862.
Thomas Redson............	"	Sept. 2, 1861, "	Wounded; discharged for disability at Detroit, Aug. 8, 1862.
Urbin Reichel.............	"	" "	Re-enlisted Jan. 5, 1864; mustered out at Macon, Ga., Aug. 17, '65.
Frederick Reynor..........	"	Sept. 1, 1861, Bay City.	Missing in action at Chicamauga, Sept. 20, 1863; returned; discharged at Nashville, Tenn., Oct. 22, 1864.
William Rice...............	"	Aug. 25, 1861, Flint.	Discharged for disability, Jan. 20, 1862; kick by a horse.
Robert Sears, Jr...........	"	Aug. 21, 1861, E. Saginaw.	Discharged at Nashville, Tenn., Oct. 22, 1864.
Frank S. Schmeltzer.......	"	Aug. 28, 1861, "	....
Jonathan W. Schnicker....	"	Sept. 16, 1861, Bay City.	Discharged at Nashville, Tenn., Oct. 22, 1864.
Charles Saphy..............	"	Aug. 26, 1861, E. Saginaw.	Re-enlisted Jan. 5, 1864; mustered out at Macon, Ga., Aug. 17, '65.
Orestes Watkins...........	"	Aug. 27, 1861, "	" promoted Hospital Steward March 1, 1865.
Thomas H. Way...........	"	Aug. 29, 1861, "	Discharged Dec. 15, 1862; kick by a horse.
Freeman S. Wolverton.....	"	Aug. 18, 1861, Bay City.	Discharged at Quincy, Ill., Nov. 8, 1862.
Seth Williams..............	"	Sept. 16, 1861, E. Saginaw.	Nashville, Tenn., Oct. 22, 1864.
Lewis Washburn...........	"	Aug. 30, 1861, Bay City.	Re-enlisted Jan. 5, 1864; discharged at Camp Chase, O., June 16, '65.
William W. Wright........	Saddler.	Aug. 22, 1861, Saginaw.	" mustered out at Macon, Ga., Aug. 17, 1865.
Lester H. Vankoughnett...	Wagoner.	Sept. 3, 1861, E. Saginaw.	Discharged for disability at Rienzi, Miss., July 25, 1862.
David G. Walton...........			at Nashville, Tenn., Oct. 22, 1864.
RECRUITS.			
Thomas Adams............	Private.	Nov. 16, 1863, Pontiac.	....
George H. Allhouse........	"	Nov. 20, 1863, Detroit.	Transferred to V. R. C., Jan. 4, 1864; mustered out at Washington, D. C., Sept. 4, 1865.
Friend Alvord..............	"	Nov. 17, 1863, "	Mustered out at Detroit, July 17, 1865.
Washington Ames..........	"	Dec. 9, 1863, Sterling.	Transferred to V. R. C., Jan. 4, 1864.
Lewis Andrews.............	"	Oct. 29, 1863, Grand Rapids.	Mustered out at Macon, Ga., Aug. 17, 1865.
Samuel E. Andrews........	"	Aug. 17, 1863, Allegan.	Discharged by order, Aug. 25, 1865.
Robert Armstrong..........	"	Nov. 18, 1863, Pontiac.	" at Nashville, Tenn., June 20, 1865.
Theodore Arthur...........	"	" "	Mustered out at Macon, Ga., Aug. 17, 1865.
Emerson M. Averill........	"	Dec. 30, 1863, Grand Rapids.	Died of chronic diarrhea at Nashville, Tenn., Sept. 20, 1864.
Sanders L. Bragne.........	"	Oct. 29, 1863, Corunna.	Died of typhoid fever at Franklin, Tenn., Aug. 25, 1864.

Lavinus Babcock	Private.	Nov. 24, 1863, Pontiac.	Mustered out at Madison, Ind., June 8, 1865.
William Bailey	"	Oct. 27, 1863, Grand Rapids.	" Macon, Ga., Aug. 17, 1865.
Charles W. Baker	"	Oct. 29, 1863, Kalamazoo.	" " "
Coradan A. Barrows	"	Aug. 15, 1864, Gr'nd Rapids.	Corporal; mustered out at Macon, Ga., Aug. 17, 1865.
John W. Beach	"	Oct. 29, 1863, Corunna.	Killed in action near Mossy Creek, Tenn., Dec. 29, 1863.
William Bell	"	Nov. 29, 1863, Pontiac.	Mustered out at Nashville, Tenn., May 18, 1865.
Christian Berge	"	Nov. 14, 1863, Detroit.	" Camp Chase, Ohio, June 17, 1865.
Mathew Bezalium	"	Jan. 27, 1864, E. Saginaw.	" Macon, Ga., Aug. 17, 1865.
James R. Bell	"	Aug. 30, 1864, Jackson.	" Springfield, Ill., Sept. 1, 1865.
Theodore A. Blake	"	Oct. 29, 1863, Gr'nd Rapids.	Transferred to V. R. C., Feb. 11, 1865.
David Boswell	"	Nov. 11, 1863, Pontiac.	Discharged for disability, May 19, 1865.
George Brummer	"	Nov. 10, 1863, "	Mustered out at Macon, Ga., Aug. 17, 1865.
Washington Brown	"		" " Nashville, Tenn., Oct. 22, 1864.
William Brown	"	Jan. 18, 1864, Gr'nd Rapids.	" " Jackson, Mich., Aug. 31, 1865.
David Cantine	"	Nov. 10, 1863, Pontiac.	" " Macon, Ga., Aug. 17, 1865.
Taylor R. Chapman	"	Apr. 16, 1863, Franklin, Ten	
John E. Conklin	"	July 31, 1862, Gr'nd Rapids.	Died at Nicholasville, March —, 1863.
Malcom B. Davis	"	Nov. 11, 1861, "	Discharged for disability, Oct. 2, 1862.
Orin B. Deming	"	Nov. 10, 1863, Pontiac.	Killed in action at Lynnville, Tenn., Dec. 14, 1864.
Abram Demay	"		Discharged for disability at Detroit, July 1, 1862.
James Douglass	"	Nov. 17, 1863, Pontiac.	Transferred to V. R. C.
Stewart Drummond	"	Aug. 9, 1863, Jackson.	Mustered out at Macon, Ga., Aug. 17, 1865.
Malcom Dunning	"	Aug. 13, 1862, E. Saginaw.	" " Edgefield, Tenn., June 20, 1865.
John Flinn	"	Nov. 5, 1863, Pontiac.	" " Macon, Ga., Aug. 17, 1865.
Elijah Gibbs	"	Aug. 21, 1862, E. Saginaw.	Corporal; mustered out at Edgefield, Tenn., June 20, 1865.
Abraham Gressfell	"	Dec. 28, 1863, Gr'nd Rapids.	Died of disease at Nashville, Tenn., Dec. 14, 1864.
Benjamin F. Hitchcock	"		Discharged for disability at Detroit, Aug. 30, 1862
Thomas W. Johnston	"		at St. Louis, Mo., Oct. 29, 1862.
Arthur Kidd	"	Aug. 18, 1864, Jackson.	Mustered out at Edgefield, Tenn., June 20, 1865.
William Koster	"	Oct. 25, 1863, Gr'nd Rapids.	Died of measles in hospital at Nashville, Tenn., May 2, 1864.
John Matthews	"	Nov. 11, 1863, Pontiac.	Mustered out at Detroit, Sept. 9, 1865.
Jehile Oliver	"	Aug. 14, 1862, E. Saginaw.	" " Nashville, Tenn., May 20, 1865.
George W. Osborn	"	Nov. 10, 1863, Pontiac.	" " Macon, Ga., Aug. 17, 1865.
Alexander Perry	"		" " "
Alonzo Percival	"	Sept. 1, 1864, Jackson.	" " Edgefield, Tenn., June 20, 1865.
Horace Richardson	"	" "	" " "
Henry F. Richardson	"	" "	Died of chronic diarrhea at Jefferson, Mo., May 10, 1865.

Co. A. NAME.	RANK.	ENTERED SERVICE,	REMARKS.
John G. Schneidman	Private.		Discharged for disability at Detroit, Aug. 25, 1862.
Charles Snyder	"	Aug. 11, 1864, Corunna.	Died of typhoid fever at Nashville, Tenn., Dec. 14, 1864.
Jacob C. Stine	"	Aug. 25, 1864, Jackson.	Discharged by order, June 20, 1865.
George L. Stephens	"	Oct. 24, 1864, Kalamazoo.	Mustered out at Edgefield, Tenn., June 20, 1865.
George L. Stearns	"	Aug. 24, 1864, "	Transferred to V. R. C., Feb. 11, 1865; mustered out at Burnside Barracks, Md., Aug 14, 1865.
Solomon Sutliff	"	Oct. 27, 1863, Corunna.	Re-enlisted Jan. 5, 1864; transferred to N. C. S. as Saddler Sergeant, June 27, 1865; transferred back, July 3, 1865; (no further record.)
Frederick Trempler	"	Sept. 12, 1861, Detroit.	Discharged; (no further record.)
Jehiel Wheeler	"		Discharged at Nashville, Tenn., Oct. 2, 1864.
Martin S. Williamson	"	Sept. 2, 1862, Gr'nd Rapids.	
Co. B.			
Henry A. Shaw	Captain.	Aug. 21, 1861, Eaton Rapids.	Promoted Major Nov. 12, 1861.
Philo W. Rogers	"	Aug. 24, 1861, "	Acted as Captain but never commissioned, see 1st Lieut.
Marshall J. Dickinson	"	Aug. 26, 1861, Vermontville.	Promoted Major Sept. 13, 1863.
Marshall P. Thatcher	"	Sept. 2, 1861, Port Huron.	Mustered out Feb. 8, 1865.
Royal Loomis	"	Aug. 21, 1861, E. Saginaw.	Mustered out Aug. 17, 1865.
Philo W. Rogers	1st Lieut.	Aug. 24, 1861, Eaton Rapids.	Died of disease at Evansville, Ind., May 17, 1862.
Charles A. Witherell	"	Nov. 5, 1862,	Resigned May 29, 1863.
William H. McGraw	"	Sept. 9, 1861, Dansville.	Resigned Aug. 27, 1863.
Edwin Hoyt, Jr.	"	Sept. 2, 1861, Gr'nd Rapids.	Promoted Adjutant March 1, 1864.
James W. Gladding	"	Sept. 9, 1861, Eaton Rapids.	Resigned Feb. 20, 1865.
Isaac Griswold	"	" Vermontville.	Mustered out Aug. 17, 1865.
Marshall J. Dickinson	2nd Lieut.	Aug. 26, 1861, "	Promoted Captain May 17, 1862.
William H. McGraw	"	Sept. 9, 1861, Dansville.	Promoted 1st Lieut. to rank from Jan. 30, 1863,
James W. Gladding	"	" Eaton Rapids.	" " March 1, 1864.
Henry M. Hempstead	"	Aug. 24, 1861, Marshall.	" Captain Co. L to rank from Dec. 22, 1864.
Birney E. Shaw	"	Sept. 9, 1861, Eaton Rapids.	Resigned March 31, 1865.
William H. McGraw	1st Sergeant.	" Dansville.	Appointed 2d Lieut. Sept. 8, 1862.
Willard H. Dickinson	Q'm'r Sergeant	" Vermontville.	Discharged for disability near Corinth, Miss., June 14, 1862.
Martin Montgomery	Sergeant.	" Eaton Rapids.	Discharged at Detroit July 11, 1862.
Jacob M. Perrine	"	" "	Discharged for disability at Franklin, Tenn., May 21, 1863.
James W. Gladding	"	" "	Appointed 2d Lieut. Jan. 30, 1863.
Birney E. Shaw	"	" "	Sept. 20, 1864; re-enlisted Jan. 5, 1864.

Stark Lampman	Corporal.	Sept. 9, 1861,	Charlotte.	Re-enlisted Jan. 5, '64; Com. Serg't; mustered out at Macon, Ga., Aug. 17, 1865.
John Graham	"	"	Eaton Rapids.	Discharged for disability April 23, 1862.
Henry M. Lindsley	"	"	Dansville.	" " " at Nashville, Tenn., Feb. 21, 1864.
Isaac Griswold	"	"	Vermontville.	Re-enlisted Jan. 5, 1864; Q. M. Serg't; appointed 1st Lieut. to rank from Oct. 1, 1864.
John Young	"	"	Sunfield.	Re-enlisted Jan. 5, 1864; Q. M. Serg't; mustered out at Macon, Ga., Aug. 17, 1865.
Lewis M. Loveless	"	"	Grand Ledge.	Died of typhoid fever at Hamburg, Tenn., June 3, 1862.
James McQueen	"	"	Eaton Rapids.	Discharged for disability at New Madrid, Mo., April 3, 1862.
Levi Dunn	"	"	Charlotte.	Died of disease at Hamburg, Tenn., July 19. 1862.
Timothy Boyer	Musician.	Sept. 29, 1861,	Vermontville.	Discharged for disability at Detroit July 9, 1862.
Elbridge Fairfield	"	Sept. 9, "	Eaton Rapids.	Died of disease at St. Louis, Mo., June 28, 1862.
Daniel H. Powers	Farrier.	"	"	Died of disease at Hamburg, Tenn., June 14, 1862.
Michael Belger	"	"	"	Discharged for disability at Corinth, Miss., Dec. 18, 1862.
John Annis	Private.	"	Dansville.	" " " at Louisville, Ky., Dec. 18, 1862.
Joseph Avery	"	"	Eaton Rapids.	Transferred to V. R. C. Dec. 1, 1863.
Augustus Beldon	"	"	"	Re-enlisted Jan. 5, '64; mustered out at Macon, Ga., Aug. 17, '65.
James Buskirk	"	"	Dansville.	Discharged at Nashville, Tenn., Oct. 22, 1864.
Ezra Bell	"	"	Vermontville.	Died of typhoid fever at Hamburg, Tenn., May 1, 1862.
Emery Revard	"	"	Chester.	Discharged for disability May 30, 1863.
William N. Beekman	"	"	Vermontville.	Re-enlisted Jan. 5, '64; mustered out at Macon, Ga., Aug. 17, '65.
John S. Bosworth	"	"	Charlotte.	Discharged for disability at Detroit, July 24, 1862.
Joseph Boyer	"	"	Sunfield.	Died of pneumonia at Benton Barracks, St. Louis, Jan. 18, 1862.
Dwight Barnum	"	"	Eaton Rapids.	" disease at New Madrid, Miss., April 14, 1862.
Uriah Beers	"	"	Dansville.	" pneumonia at St. Louis, Dec. 2, 1862.
Andrew Beers	"	"	"	Re-enlisted Jan. 5, '64; serg't; must'd out at Macon, Ga., Aug. 17, '65.
Johann Bryer	"	"	"	" " " " " "
John Brown	"	Oct 13, 1861,	Gr'nd Rapids.	" " corp. " " "
Henry C. Burham	"	Sept. 9, 1861,	Dansville.	Died of typhoid fever near Farmington, Miss., July 14, 1862.
John Chadwick	"	"	Charlotte.	Transferred to 3d Iowa Cavalry, Jan. —, 1862.
Charles Crabtree	"	"	"	Died at Evansville, Ind., Sept. 15, 1862.
Henry Cramer	"	"	Eaton Rapids.	Discharged at Detroit, July 2, 1862.
Henry Collins	"	"	Dansville.	Re-enlisted Jan. 5, 1864; mustered out at Macon, Ga., Aug. 17, '65.
Leander S. Curtis	"	"	Eaton Rapids.	Discharged for disability at St. Louis, Mo, July 8, 1862.
Daniel Campbell	"	"	Roxand.	Re-enlisted Jan. 5, '64; corp.; must'd out at Macon, Ga, Aug. 17, '65.
Joseph M. Cramer	"	"		

Co. B. NAME.	RANK.	ENTERED SERVICE.		REMARKS.
Peter Dow............	Private.	Sept. 9, 1861,	Sunfield.	Died of typhoid fever near Farmington, Miss., Aug. 22, 1862.
Abraham Dakin........	"	"	Dansville.	Re-enlisted Jan. 5, '64; Corp.; must'd out Macon, Ga., Aug. 17, '65.
Eugene Ellis..........	"	"	Vermontville.	Missing in action at Dandridge, Tenn., Dec. 24, 1863; died of chronic diarrhea at Andersonville, Ga., May 20, 1864.
Leonard Ferris........	"	"	Eaton Rapids.	Discharged at Nashville, Tenn., Oct. 22, 1864.
William H. Francis....	"	"	Dansville.	Corporal; transferred to V. R. C., Jan. 15, 1864.
Hiram Fry............	"	"	Eaton Rapids.	Discharged for disability at Detroit, Sept. 2, 1862.
Elias D. Fowler.......	"	"	"	Discharged at St. Louis, Mo., Jan. 26, 1863.
Henry Graves.........	"	"	Charlotte.	Corporal; discharged at Nashville, Tenn., Oct. 22, 1864.
Henry L. Gould.......	"	Sept. 30, 1861,	Gr'nd Rapids.	Promoted Sergeant Major March 21, 1865; re-enlisted Jan. 5, 1864.
George Hull...........	"	Sept. 9, 1861,	Eaton Rapids.	Died at Henderson, Ky., May 24, 1862.
Seymour Houghton....	"	"	Detroit.	....
Forbes W. Hults......	"	"	Vermontville.	Re-enlisted Jan. 5, '64; mustered out at Macon, Ga., Aug. 17, '65.
Francis Hicke.........	"	"	Dansville.	Died of typhoid fever at Hamburg Landing, Tenn., May 7, 1862.
William F. Hunt.......	"	"	Vermontville.	Discharged at Detroit, Dec. 14, 1864.
Nathan Jennie.........	"	"	Eaton Rapids.	June 28, 1865.
Bratford B. Jones......	"	"	Roxand.	Died at New Albany, Ind., Oct. 8, 1862.
John H. Kimball.......	"	"	Eaton Rapids.	Discharged for disability at Detroit, July 1, 1862.
Warren A. Loveless...	"	"	Grand Ledge.	" at Keokuk, Iowa, Aug. 21, 1862.
Lorenzo D. Losey.....	"	"	Eaton Rapids.	Died of measles at St. Louis, Dec. 2, 1861.
Rufus Lisco...........	"	"	Vermontville.	" typhoid fever near Farmington, Miss., June 29, 1862.
George W. Lawhead...	"	"	Charlotte.	Re-enlisted Jan. 5, 1864; mustered out at Macon, Ga., Aug. 17, '65.
Newell Miller..........	"	"	Dansville.	Re-enlisted Jan. 5, '64; serg't; must'd out at Macon, Ga., Aug. 17, '65.
Robert Means.........	"	"	Bellevue.	Discharged for disability at St. Louis, Mo., June 3, 1862.
William Merritt........	"	"	Eaton Rapids.	" at Mossy Creek, Tenn., Dec. 22, 1863, for promotion.
George D. Nelson.....	"	"	Vermontville.	" at Nashville, Tenn., Oct. 22, 1864.
Jerome O'Neil.........	"	"	Charlotte.	Died of typhoid fever at Farmington, Miss., June 27, 1862.
Morris Olmstead.......	"	"	Eaton Rapids.	Died at Nashville, Tenn., July 6, 1864, from accidental shot.
Henry Perrine.........	"	"	"	Discharged at Grand Rapids, Mich.
Sylvanus Palamtur.....	"	"	"	" for disability at Detroit, July 24, 1862.
Henry W. Palamtur....	"	"	"	" at Nashville, Tenn., Oct. 22, 1864.
William H. Pole.......	"	"	Charlotte.	" at Detroit, July 9, 1862.
Job Reynolds.........	"	"	"	Serg't; died at Danville, Va., April 11. 1864, of scorbutis, in prison.
Reuben O. Russell....	"	"	Bellevue.	Died of typhoid fever on board hospital boat, May 9, 1862.
Charles Reed.........	"	"	Eaton Rapids.	Re-enlisted Jan. 5, 1864; mustered out at Macon, Ga., Aug. 17, '65.

Morris Roger	Private.	Sept. 9, 1861,	Charlotte.	Re-enlisted Jan. 5, 1864.
Willis R. Rogers	"	"	Vermontville.	{ " " sergeant; killed in action at Orford, Ala., April 23, 1865.
Benjamin Root	"	"	Eaton Rapids.	Discharged at Corinth, Sept. 13, 1862.
Zina Snyder	"	"	"	" for disability at Detroit, July 18, 1862.
Lucius Torrey	"	"	"	" " Aug. 18, 1862.
William Thompson	"	"	Roxand.	Died of consumption at Keokuk, Iowa, July 25, 1862.
Charles G. Thompson	"	"	Eaton Rapids.	Discharged for disability at St. Louis, Mo., May 3. 1862.
Munroe Wright	"	"	"	Re-enlisted Jan. 5, '64; Corp ; must'd out Macon, Ga., Aug. 17, '65.
Austin Walker	"	"	"	" " Serg't; " " "
Solomon Wetherell	"	"	"	" " Farrier; " " "
Jerome Wheeler	"	"	"	Discharged for disability at Detroit, Aug. 25, 1862.
Samuel Walters	"	"	"	Died of typhoid fever at Rienzi, Miss., July 24. 1862.
Edward Watson	"	"	Vermontville.	Re-enlisted Jan. 5, 1864; mustered out at Macon, Ga., Aug. 17, '65.
Silas H. Wilson	"	"	"	Discharged at Keokuk, Iowa, Aug. 23, 1862.
David Young	"	Sept. 29, 1861,	Eaton Rapids.	" for disability at St. Louis, May 3, 1862.
Daniel Vickery	Saddler.	Sept. 9, 1861,	"	Re-enlisted Jan. 5, 1864; mustered out at Macon, Ga., Aug. 17, '65.
Charles S. Preston	Wagoner.	"	"	Discharged for disability at Detroit, July 1, 1862.
Allen M. Hobbs				
RECRUITS.				
David Barnum	Private.	Nov. 14, 1863,	Jackson.	Died at Knoxville, Tenn., Feb. 25, 1864.¹
Charles Ballinger	"	Nov. 21, 1863,	Pontiac.	Mustered out at Macon, Ga., Aug. 17, 1865.
Henry Badder	"	Aug. 13, 1864,	Corunna.	
Daniel Beasey	"	Dec. 22, 1863,	Jackson.	Died of disease at Waterloo, Alabama, March 16, 1865.
Robert B. Beasey	"	Dec. 12, 1863,	"	Corporal; mustered out at Macon, Ga., Aug. 17, 1865.
Oliver B. Beasey	"			Died of abscess of head at Chattanooga, Tenn., July 4, 1864.
James M. Berkey	"	Nov. 2, 1863,	Kalamazoo.	Unaccounted for.
Edwin A. Birch	"	Nov. 19, 1863,	Pontiac.	Killed in action at Oxford, Alabama, April 23, 1865.
Emery Rivard	"	Aug. 31, 1864,	Jackson.	Mustered out at Edgefield, Tenn., June 20, 1865.
Francis Bolton	"			Serg't; re-enlisted Jan. 5, '64; must'd out Macon, Ga., Aug. 17, '65.
Reuben D Bowen	"	Oct. 10, 1862,	Allen.	Mustered out at Edgefield, Tenn. June 27, 1865.
Michael Boylen	"	Nov. 23, 1863,	Pontiac.	Mustered out at Macon, Ga., Aug. 17, 1865.
Michael Brennan	"	Nov. 25, 1863,		Transferred to Co. K.
Lyman Bristol	"	Oct. 30, 1863,	Corunna.	Mustered out at Detroit Aug. 31, 1865.
William Burton	"	Aug. 15, 1862,	Grand Rapids.	Unaccounted for.
James Byrne	"	Nov. 14, 1863,	Detroit.	Prisoner of war since Sept. 27, 1864; at muster out.
C. H. Campbell	"	Nov. 10, 1862,	Reading.	Unaccounted for.

Co. B.

NAME.	RANK.	ENTERED SERVICE.	REMARKS.
Henry Casey	Private.	Nov. 17, 1863, Detroit.	Sick at Pulaski, Tenn., since Dec. 24, 1864, at muster out.
William B. Chandler	"	Oct. 27, 1863, Kalamazoo.	Mustered out at Macon, Ga., Aug. 17, 1865.
Timothy Clooman	"	Oct. 29, 1863, "	"
Hiram Cole	"	Nov. 1, 1861, Grand Rapids.	Died of consumption at Charlotte, Mich., July 20, 1862.
James Collins	"	Aug. 24, 1861, Bloomfield.	
Philo Collins	"	Aug. 18, 1864, Jackson.	Mustered out at Nashville, Tenn., June 2, 1865.
Andrew B. Coon	"	Oct. 30, 1863, Grand Rapids.	Died of chronic diarrhea at Cahawba, Alabama, March 25, 1865.
Henry Corkendall	"	Nov. 2, 1863, "	Mustered out at Macon, Ga., Aug. 17, 1865.
Abel Cruson	"	Oct. 28, 1863, Corunna.	Discharged May 3, 1865.
John Craig	"	Nov. 17, 1863, Pontiac.	Killed in action at Cassville, Ga., May 17, 1864.
William D. De Courey	"	....	Transferred to 2d Mich. Battery, Oct. 22, 1862.
Louis Dechard	"	Nov. 7, 1863, Pontiac.	Mustered out at Detroit, May 25, 1865.
James W. Ellis	"	Aug. 18, 1864, Jackson.	" Edgefield, Tenn., June 20, 1865.
Alfred Fay	"	Jan. 4, 1864, "	Transferred to V. R. C., Jan. 2, 1865; discharged Aug. 14, 1865.
Charles Fulkerson	"	Aug. 22, 1862, Gr'nd Rapids.	Discharged at Detroit Sept. 1, 1864.
C. H. Furgeson	"	Aug. 12, 1862, Grand Rapids.	Unaccounted for.
G. E. Gates	"	Nov. 5, 1862, Reading.	
David Gibbs	"	May 27, 1864, Jackson.	Corporal; mustered out at Macon, Ga., Aug. 17, 1865.
Patrick Hays	"	Aug. 15, 1862, Grand Rapids.	Mustered out at Edgefield, Tenn., June 20, 1865.
Duane Hawkins	"	Aug. 31, 1864, Jackson.	" Nashville, Tenn., June 2, 1865.
Emery E. Hackett	"	Aug. 18, 1864, "	Died of bronchitis at Jeffersonville, Ind., Jan. 15, 1865.
Holland Hart	"	Oct. 28, 1863, Corunna.	Killed in action at Dandridge, Tenn., Dec. 24, 1863.
Hans Isaac Hollinbeck	"	Nov. 14, 1863, Jackson.	Transferred to V. R. C., Feb. 11, 1865; mustered out at Burnside Barracks, Md., Aug 14, 1865.
Jerome Hutchinson	"	Aug. 12, 1862, Gr'nd Rapids.	Mustered out at Davenport, Iowa, May 29, 1865.
John Hutt	"	Nov. 4, 1863, Pontiac.	On detached service at muster out.
Merritt Hulse	"	Oct. 1, 1864, "	Mustered out at Macon, Ga., Aug. 17, 1865.
Henry Jones	"	Oct. 27, 1862, Cambria.	" "
Charles Jones	"	Nov. 4, 1863, Pontiac.	Transferred to Co. I, Dec. 10, 1863.
Joseph B. Lamaine	"	Nov. 10, 1863, Jackson.	Mustered out at Macon, Ga., Aug. 17, 1865.
Alexander Ledessimer	"	Nov. 4, 1863, Pontiac.	" "
Andrew J. Lensbaugh	"	Nov. 9, 1863, Gr'nd Rapids.	Transferred to V. R. C., April 21, 1865; mustered out at Springfield, Ill., Aug. 17, 1865.
Frederick Lensbaugh	"	....	Transferred to V. R. C., April 21, 1865.
William Lowe	"	Nov. 2, 1863, Gr'nd Rapids.	Killed in action at Lavergne, Tenn., Sept. 1, 1864.

Patrick McCann	Private.	Dec. 23, 1863, Grand Rapids,	Mustered out at Macon, Ga., Aug. 17, 1865.
Michael Metcalf	"	Nov. 6, 1863, Jackson.	" " " " "
John P. Miller	"		Discharged for disability at Detroit, June 1, 1863.
Edward McIntyre	"	Feb. 4, 1864, Vermontville.	Mustered out at Macon, Ga., Aug. 17, 1682.
Woodruff McMurray	"	Nov. 5, 1863, Jackson.	" " " " "
Jacob I. Ohlar	"	Aug. 14, 1862, Gr'nd Rapids.	" " Nashville, Tenn., June 2, 1865.
Sylvester Olmstend	"	Sept. 27, 1862, Hillsdale.	" " Edgefield, Tenn., June 20, 1865.
James E. Parks	"	Nov. 14, 1863, Jackson.	
A. C. Peterson	"	Oct. 27, 1862, Hillsdale.	Discharged for disability at Franklin, Tenn., April 4, 1863.
C. B. Phelps	"	Nov. 8, 1863, Pontiac.	Missing in action at North Cross Roads, Nov. 30, 1864; returned; discharged at Camp Chase, Ohio, June 16, 1865.
Amasa D. Place	"		Transferred to 2d Mich. Battery, Oct. 22, 1862.
Millard Powell	"	Oct. 28, 1863, Corunna.	Transferred to V. R. C., Feb 4, '65; died at Louisville, June 8, '65.
James E. Roys	"	Jan. 4, 1864, Jackson.	Mustered out at Macon, Ga., Aug. 17, 1865.
George H. Schlappi	"	Oct. 28, 1863, Corunna.	Missing in action at Oxford, Ala., April 23, 1865, mustered out Macon, Ga., Aug. 17, 1865.
Otis Shea	"	Nov. 20, 1863, Jackson.	Discharged at Davenport, Iowa, May 20, 1865.
Alfred Shirk	"	Aug. 12, 1862, Grand Rapids.	Died of typhoid fever at New Albany, Ind., Sept. 30, 1862.
Wilbur Showler	"	Sept. 27, 1862, Hillsdale.	Mustered out at Edgefield, Tenn., June 20, 1865.
Peter Simot	"	Nov. 6, 1863, Jackson.	Sick at Nashville, Tenn., since June 1, 1865, at muster out.
Samuel S. Stout	"	Aug. 14, 1862, Grand Rapids.	Mustered out at Edgefield Tenn., June 20, 1865.
Andrew Stout	"		Discharged at Nicholasville, Ky., Jan. 24, 1863.
Robert Stevenson	"	Nov. 7, 1863, Jackson.	Mustered out at Macon, Ga., Aug. 17, 1865;
J. H. Stage	"	Nov. 5, 1862, Hillsdale.	Unaccounted for.
Samuel Sumwalt	"	Aug. 18, 1864, Jackson.	Mustered out at Edgefield, Tenn., June 20, 1865.
Adolphus Taifer	"	Nov. 4, 1863, Pontiac.	" " Macon, Ga., Aug. 17, 1865.
Hiram Tubbs	"	Oct. 28, 1863, Corunna.	Mustered out at Detroit, June 5, 1865.
Urial B. Walker	"	Oct. 21, 1861, Dansville.	Discharged for disability at Evansville, Ind., Dec. 2, 1862.
Charles W. Watkins	"		" for appointment in U. S. Col'rd Troops, Sept. 14, 1864.
Daniel Williams	"	Aug. 12, 1862, Grand Rapids.	Discharged for disability at Nicholasville, Feb. 2, 1863; reported died at Chattanooga, Tenn., no date.
William C. Young	"	Nov. 6, 1863, Jackson.	Sick at Knoxville, since Jan. 20, 1864.
Co. C.			
Russell A. Alger	Captain.	Sept. 2, 1861, Gr'nd Rapids.	Promoted Major April 2, 1862.
John M. Weatherwax	"	Sept. 25, 1861, "	Mustered out Oct. 22, 1864.
Martin L. Squier	"	Sept. 2, 1861, "	" " Aug. 17, 1865.
Henry C. Whipple	1st Lieut.		Promoted Adjutant April 15, 1863.

Co. C.

NAME.	RANK.	ENTERED SERVICE.	REMARKS.
Alphonso E. Gordon	1st Lieut.	Sept. 2, 1861, Grand Rapids.	Promoted Captain Co. D, May 2, 1863.
Martin L. Squier	"	Sept. 25, 1861, "	" Oct. 22, 1864.
Franklin Perkins	"	Aug. 29, 1861, "	Mustered out Aug. 17, 1865.
John M. Weatherwax	2d Lieut.	Sept. 2, 1861, "	Promoted Captain, July 1, 1862.
John J. McCormick	"	Sept. 1, 1861, "	" 1st Lieut. Co. I, April 15, 1863.
Martin L. Squier	"	Sept. 25, 1861, "	" " " March 1, 1864.
Royal H. Loomis	"	Aug. 21, 1861, E. Saginaw.	" Captain Co. B, Dec. 26, 1864.
Frank N. Eaton	"	Sept. 20, 1861, Albion.	" 1st Lieut Co. T, Oct. 7, 1864.
Frank Burr	1st Sergeant.	Aug. 27, 1861, Grand Rapids.	Discharged July 9, 1862, for promotion 1st Lieut. 4th Mich. Cav.
Adrian Yates	Q'm'r Sergeant	Aug. 28, 1861, "	Transferred to 2d Mich. Cav. Oct. 2, 1861.
William W. Henry	"	Sept. 5, 1861, "	Di-charged July 23, 1862.
James C. Acker	"	Aug. 31, 1861, "	Discharged at Detroit Oct. 2, 1864.
Nelson F. Austin	"	Aug. 27, 1861, "	Discharged near Hamburg, Tenn., May 2, 1862.
Oscar D. Robinson	"	Sept. 12, 1861, "	Absent, sick at Commerce, Mo., March 2, 1862; no further record.
Alfred Fayant	Corporal.	" "	Re-enlisted Jan. 5, '64; serg., must'd out at Macon, Ga., Aug. 17, '65.
John G. Snyder	"	Sept. 2, 1861, "	Re-enlisted Jan. 5, '64; serg., must'd out at Macon, Ga., Aug. 17, '65.
John H. Squier	"	Sept. 25, 1861, "	Discharged at Detroit, Oct. 29, 1862.
Thomas A. Brown	"	Sept. 9, 1861, "	Re-enlisted Jan. 5, '64; serg., must'd out at Macon, Ga., Aug. 17, '65.
Uzel B. McIntyre	"	Sept. 2, 1861, "	Discharged at Franklin, Tenn., March 22, 1863.
James Holpen	"	Sept. 9, 1861, "	Discharged for disability at St. Louis, Mo., Oct. 14, 1862.
Hiram C. Francis	"	Aug. 27, 1861, "	Discharged at Louisville, Ky., Oct. 20, 1862.
Levi Barber	"	Sept. 29, 1861, "	Discharged at Benton Barracks, Mo., Feb. 14, 1863.
Henry P. Adams	Musician.	Sept. 25, 1861, "	Re-enlisted Jan. 5, 1864; mustered out at Macon, Ga., Aug. 17, '65.
Uri M. Nichols	"	Aug. 31, 1861, "	Left sick at New Madrid April 12, 1862.
Andrew J. French	Farrier.	Sept. 9, 1861, "	Discharged at St. Louis, Mo., Sept. 23, 1862.
Herman E. Wood	"	Sept. 3, 1861, "	Discharged at Hamburg, Tenn., May 2, 1862.
Robert G. Mason	Saddler.	Sept. 23, 1861, "	Discharged at Nashville, Tenn., Oct. 22, 1864.
Martin L. Squier	Wagoner.	Sept. 25, 1861, "	Appointed 2d Lieut. April 15, 1863.
Joseph B. Arnold	Private.	Oct. 2, 1861, "	Discharged at Louisville, Ky.
William Brown	"	Sept. 9, 1861, "	Discharged for disability at Keokuk, Wis., Nov. 15, 1862.
Lemuel E. Brooks	"	Sept. 14, 1861, "	Mustered out at Detroit, June 30, 1865.
Jutson D. Bailey	"	Sept. 21, 1861, "	Died of typhoid fever at Benton Barracks, Mo., Feb. 20, 1862.
Rufus W. Bliss	"	Sept. 23, 1861, "	Died of inflammatory rheumatism at St. Louis, Mo., Jan. 24, '62.
Barnett W. Briggs	"	Oct. 2, 1861, "	Discharged at Nashville, Tenn., Oct. 22, 1864.
Robert E. Crotty	"	Aug. 31, 1861, "	Corporal, discharged at Detroit, Jan. 17, 1865.

Name	Rank	Date	Place	Remarks
Joseph B. Copeland	Private.	Sept. 9, 1861,	Grand Rapids.	Discharged at Evansville, Ind., Jan. 20, 1863.
Daniel Chapin	"	Sept. 31, 1861,	"	Re-enliste l Jan. 5, 1864; mustered out at Macon, Ga., Aug. 17, '65.
John S. Corliss	"	Sept. 25, 1861,	"	" sup'd killed by exp. str. Sultana Apr. 28,'65
Truman F. Cook	"	Sept. 14, 1861,	"	" mustered out at Macon, Ga., Aug. 17, '65.
David Dudley	"	Aug. 31, 1861,	"	Unaccounted for.
Samuel L. Duffey	"	"	"	Discharged for disability at Detroit, Feb. 24, 1862.
Charles Dunham	"	Sept. 17, 1861,	"	{ Corporal; missing in action at Chicamauga, Ga., Sept. 20, 1863; discharged at Detroit, May 5, 1865.
Jacob M. Dubois	"	Sept. 19, 1861,	"	Discharged at Nashville, Tenn., Oct. 22, 1864.
William H. Fifield	"	Sept. 17, 1861,	"	{ Re-enlisted Jan. 5, 1864; killed in action at Shoal Creek, Tenn., Nov. 5, 1864.
Buel Gill	"	Sept. 10, 1861,	"	Re-enlisted Jan. 5, '64; serg't; must'd out at Macon, Ga., Aug. 17, '65
Myron Garlick	"	Aug. 13, 1861,	"	Absent sick April 12, 1862; no further record.
James H. Hadden	"	Aug. 28, 1861,	"	Mustered out at Detroit, July 15, 1865; re-enlisted Jan. 5, 1864.
James W. Hotchkiss	"	Sept. 5, 1861,	"	Discharged at Corinth, Miss., Sept. 11, 1862.
George W. Haas	"	Sept. 10, 1861,	"	Re-enlisted Jan. 5, 1864; mustered out at Macon, Ga., Aug. 17, '65.
Jonathan Huntley	"	Sept. 16, 1861,	"	Discharged at St. Louis, Mo., May 13, 1863.
Edward Haslam	"	Sept. 19, 1861,	"	" at Nashville, Tenn., Oct. 22, 1864.
Henry H. Henshaw	"	Sept. 23, 1861,	"	Re-enlisted Jan. 5, 1864; promoted Hospital Steward, April 14, '64.
Melvill Hill	"	Sept. 24, 1861,	"	" absent sick since Dec. 17, '64, at muster out
Joseph E. Hooper	"	"	"	Died of typhoid fever at New Madrid, Mo., April 9, 1832.
Charles Henshaw	"	Sept. 26, 1861,	"	Discharged at Detroit March 17, 1863.
Peter R. Johnson	"	Sept. 23, 1861,	"	at Corinth, Miss., June 14, 1862.
Patrick McNamara	"	Sept. 9, 1861,	"	" for disability at Franklin, Tenn., May 20, 1863.
Marcus H. McCoy	"	Sept. 12, 1861,	"	Corporal; discharged for disability at Quincy, Ill., March 25, '62.
Lemuel Maxfield	"	"	"	Left sick April 26, 1862; no further record
Robert McLenathan	"	Sept. 18, 1861,	"	Unaccounted for.
Franklin R. Marsac	"	Sept. 23, 1861,	"	Died of typhoid fever at Evansville, Aug. 16, 1862.
Daniel C. Marsac	"	"	"	Re-enlisted Jan. 5, 1864; died of wounds at Nashville, Jan. 10, '65.
John J. McCormick	"	Sept. 1, 1861,	"	1st Sergeant; appointed 2d Lieut., Sept 19, 1862.
John D. Moon	"	Oct. 2, 1861,	"	Died of disease of the heart at Rienzi, Miss., Aug. 1, 1862.
Harvey Olmstead	"	Sept. 17, 1861,	"	Killed in action at Fair Garden, Tenn., Jan. 28,1864.
Joseph Palmer	"	Sept. 3, 1861,]	"	Corp.; Serg't; re-enlisted Jan. 5, '64; app. 1st Lieut.Co. E, Oct.22,'64
Covert S. Rosegrant	"	Sept. 16, 1861,	"	Re-enlisted Jan. 5, 1864; mustered out at Macon, Ga., Aug. 17, '65.
Ithamer Rosegrant	"	"	"	Discharged at Nashville, Tenn., Oct. 22, 1864.
Cyrus Reynolds	"	Sept. 7, 1861,	"	Died at Chaplin Hill, Ky., Oct. 8, '63, of wounds received in action.
John Reinshagen	"	Sept. 24, 1861,	"	Mustered out at Edgefield, Tenn., June 20, 1865.

Co. C.

NAME.	RANK.	ENTERED SERVICE.	REMARKS.
Samuel W. Rust	Private.	Sept. 25, 1861, Grand Rapids.	Mustered out at Macon, Ga., Aug. 17, 1865; re enlisted Jan. 5, '64.
Henry S. Reed	"	Sept. 10, 1861, "	Died of typhoid fever at Farmington, July 7, 1862.
John Rust	"	Sept. 25, 1861, "	Re-enlisted Jan. 5, '64; mustered out at Jackson, Mich., Aug 30, '65.
Leroy B. Stowell	"	Oct. 2, 1861, "	Discharged at St. Louis, Mo., Aug. 20, 1862.
Matthew Spencer	"	Sept. 6, 1861, "	Transferred to V. R. C., April 10, 1864.
George W. Story	"	Sept. 3, 1861, "	Died of typhoid fever at New Madrid, Mo., March 24, 1862.
James R. Scadden	"	Sept. 19, 1861, "	Discharged at Detroit, Mich., July 26, 1865.
Elisha Steele	"	Sept. 13, 1861, "	Died of chronic diarrhea at Andersonville prison, Ga., May 20, '64.
George E. Sleight	"	Sept. 16, 1861, "	Re-enlisted Jan. 5, 1864; mustered out at Macon, Ga., Aug. 17, '65.
William F. Schenck	"	"	Died at Benton Barracks, Mo., Dec. 11, 1861.
Ozro J. Smith	"	"	Discharged near Hamburg, Tenn., May 2, 1862.
Eliphalet, Sadler	"	Sept. 17, 1861, "	" at St. Louis, May 30, 1862.
Isaiah Spaulding	"	Sept. 24, 1861, "	Re-enlisted Jan. 5, 1864; must'd out at Macon, Ga., Aug. 17, 1865.
Franklin Torrence	"	Sept. 7, 1861, "	"
David P. Trill	"	Sept. 16, 1861, "	"
Samuel C. Totten	"	Sept. 21, 1861, "	Discharged near Hamburg, Tenn., May 2, 1862.
Peleg Thompson	"	"	Transferred to V. R. C. Sept. 1, 1863.
Daniel W. Vanvalkenburg	"	Sept. 9, 1861, "	Discharged at Benton Barracks, Mo., Feb. 14, 1862.
Leonard Wood	"	Sept. 2, 1861, "	Discharged at Columbus, Ohio, July 22, 1862.
John R. Wyman	"	Sept. 3, 1861, "	Discharged for disability at Cincinnati, Ohio, Nov. 21, 1862.
Samuel T. Welsh	"	Sept. 9, 1861, "	Discharged for disability at Detroit, July 18, 1862
Joseph Willson	"	"	Died of chronic diarrhea at Wyoming, Kent Co., May 29, 1862.
Clayton C. Wood	"	Sept. 14, 1861, "	Discharged for disability at Detroit, July 22, 1862.
John W. Winters	"	"	Re-enlisted Jan. 5, '64; must'd out at Jackson, Mich., Aug. 30, '65.
Thomas Wasson	"	Sept. 16, 1861, "	Re enlisted Jan. 5, 1865; must'd out at Macon, Ga., Aug. 17, 1865.
David M. Winters	"	Sept. 17, 1861, "	Discharged at Detroit, July 23, 1862.
Henry G. Watson	"	Sept. 14, 1861, "	Died at Chaplin Hill, Ky., Oct. 8; 1862, of gunshot wound.
Jasper J. Young	"	Sept. 7, 1861, "	Died at Benton Barracks, St. Louis, Dec. 12, 1861.
Franklin E. Youngs	"	"	Died at Benton Barracks, St. Louis, of typhoid fever, June 21, '62.
RECRUITS.			
Healy C. Akeley	Private.	Oct. 23 1863, Grand Rapids.	Appointed 1st Lieut. and Adjutant, Nov. 30, 1864.
Alonzo Arnold	"	Aug. 30, 1862, "	Mustered out at Edgefield, Tenn., June 20, 1865.
John H. Ashley	"	Aug. 24, 1864, Kalamazoo.	Mustered out at Edgefield, Tenn., June 20, 1865.
George Austin	"	May 16, 1864, "	Unaccounted for.
Frederick Becker	"	Nov. 11, 1863, Pontiac.	Mustered out at Macon, Ga., Aug. 17, 1865.

Marvin Blodgett	Private.	Aug. 8, 1862,	Kalamazoo.	Discharged for disability at Louisville, Ky., Sept. 26, 1863.
Lyman Bonny	"	Jan. 4, 1864,	Gr'nd Rapids.	Died of typhoid fever at Nashville, Tenn., Sept. 17, 1864.
William Burton	"	Aug. 15, 1862,	"	Sent to Camp Chase, Ohio, as paroled prisoner, Dec. 25, 1862; no further record.
William H. Buck	"	Oct. 27, 1863,	Corunna.	Mustered out at Jackson, Mich., Aug. 30, 1865.
William Campbell	"	Nov. 25, 1863,	Detroit.	Missing in action at Burnt Hickory, May 24, '64; no further rec'd.
William Carson	"	"	"	Mustered out at Louisville, Ky., June 6, 1865.
D. J. Chipman	"	Nov. 24, 1863,	"	Unaccounted for.
Monmouth M. Chandler	"	Aug. 16, 1862,	Grand Rapids.	Transferred to V. R. C., Feb. 1, 1865; mustered out at Burnside Barracks, Ind., Aug. 14, 1865.
Jason W. Clark	"	Jan. 4, 1864,	Jackson.	Mustered out at Macon, Ga., Aug. 17, 1865.
Henry Coleman	"	Dec. 7, 1863,	"	Discharged for disability at Detroit, Feb. 27, 1865.
Samuel Collum	"	Nov. 11, 1863,	Pontiac.	Mustered out at Louisville, Ky., July 15, 1865.
Dean Cutler	"	Aug. 31, 1864,	Jackson.	" " St. Louis, Aug. 14, 1865.
Eugene Day	"	Oct. 29, 1863,	Corunna.	" " Macon, Ga., Aug. 17, 1865.
John Daikens	"	Nov. 20, 1863,	Jackson.	
Robert Darlington	"	Nov. 21, 1863,	"	Transferred to V. R. C.
Willard Decker	"	Jan. 18, 1864,	Grand Rap'ds.	Mustered out at Macon, Ga., Aug. 17, 1865.
Eben R. Delano	"	Jan. 11, 1864,	Jackson.	Died of disease at Nashville, Tenn., July 4, 1864.
Isaac S. Dennis	"	Nov. 19, 1863,	Gr'nd Rapids.	Killed in action at Resaca, Ga., May 14, 1864.
William H. Dicker	"	Nov. 16, 1863,	Pontiac.	Died at Burnt Hickory, Ga., May 20, '64, of wounds rec'd in action.
Alonzo W. Dorlin	"	Jan. 11, 1864,	Jackson.	Sergeant; mustered out at Macon, Ga., Aug. 17, 1865.
Patrick Dooling	"	Nov. 24, 1863,	Pontiac.	Mustered out at Detroit, Aug. 25, 1865.
James Doddard	"	"	Detroit.	Taken prisoner at Shoal Creek, Ala., Nov. 8, 1864.
Phares A. Dorland	"	Nov. 13, 1863,	"	Mustered out at Macon, Ga., Aug. 17, 1865.
Jerome Drown	"	May 16, 1864,	St. Clair.	"
Charles Dunn	"	Nov. 20, 1863,	Jackson.	"
Joseph Duse	"	Oct. 27, 1863,	Kalamazoo.	"
Leonard Dye	"	Nov. 11, 1863,	Detroit.	Discharged for disability at Louisville, Ky., Sept. 20, 1864.
John W. Eddy	"	Oct. 30, 1863,	Corunna.	Mustered out at Nashville, Tenn., June 9, 1865.
William Eldridge	"	Nov. 3, 1863,	Pontiac.	Captured near Pulaski, Tenn., Oct. 14, 1864.
John Eller	"	Nov. 17, 1863,	Grand Rapids.	Mustered out at Macon, Ga., Aug. 17, 1865.
John Ellis	"	Nov. 24, 1863,	Detroit.	"
James A. Farr	"	Nov. 30, 1863,	Corunna.	"
Wilson Farnsworth	"	Oct. 27, 1863,	Kalamazoo.	"
George W. Farnsworth	"	Oct. 29, 1863,	Gr'nd Rapids.	Died of typhoid fever at Chattanooga, Tenn., June 19, 1864.
David B. Finn	"	Nov. 24, 1863,	Detroit.	Mustered out at Macon, Ga., Aug. 17, 1865.

Co. C. NAME.	RANK.	ENTERED SERVICE.	REMARKS.
Michael Follen	Private.	Nov. 9, 1863, Jackson.	Mustered out at Macon, Ga., Aug. 17, 1865.
Charles Freeland	"	Nov. 11, 1863, Pontiac.	Died of typhoid fever at Chattanooga, Tenn., May 28, 1864.
Moses W. Fredenburg	"	Jan. 2, 1864, Grand Rapids.	Mustered out at Nashville, Tenn., May 18, 1865.
Solon H. Garrett	"	Aug. 13, 1862, "	Missing in action at Mossy Creek, Tenn., Dec. 29, 1863; died of chronic diarrhea at Andersonville, Ga., May 20, 1864.
Alfred Grant	"	Aug. 25, 1862, "	Mustered out at Edgefield, Tenn., June 20, 1865.
Benjamin F. Haas	"	Aug. 15, 1862, "	Nashville, Tenn., May 16, 1865.
C. R. Harvey	"	Oct. 31, 1863, Kalamazoo.	Absent sick since Oct. 30, 1864, at muster out.
Edwin Hackett	"	Sept. 12, 1864, Jackson.	Mustered out at Edgefield, Tenn., June 20, 1865.
Christian Hiser	"	Oct. 27, 1863, Corunna.	Died of disease at Nashville, Tenn., July 13, 1864.
Ira M. Hotchkiss	"		Discharged at Farmington, Miss., July 19, 1862.
Allen Hovey	"		Transferred to Co. L, April 26, 1864.
Albert Huntley	"	Sept. 2, 1862, Grand Rapids.	Discharged for disability at St. Louis, Mo., March 28, 1865.
John Hunt	"	Feb. 29, 1864, Pontiac.	Mustered out at Macon, Ga., Aug. 17, 1865.
Michael Kelly	"	Oct. 25, 1861, St. Louis.	Died of typhoid fever at New Madrid, April 4, 1862.
Almer Kelley	"	Oct. 27, 1863, Corunna.	Mustered out at Macon, Ga., Aug. 17, 1865.
Charles McClenathan	"	Sept. 18, 1861, Grand Rapids.	Discharged at Cincinnati, Ohio, Nov. 21, 1862.
James McNiel	"	Jan. 4, 1864, "	Died of typhoid fever at Nashville, Tenn., July 15, 1865.
John McNiel	"	Dec. 23, 1863, "	Mustered out at Macon, Ga., Aug. 17, 1865.
Bonaparte Moody	"	Dec. 21, 1863, E. Saginaw.	"
Russell M. Nichols	"	Aug. 5, 1862, Kalamazoo.	Discharged for disability at Louisville, Ky., Oct. 2, 1863.
Benjamin Pike	"	Oct. 12, 1863, Grand Rapids.	Died of chronic diarrhea at Andersonville, Ga., Sept. 16, 1864.
William M. Porter	"	Aug. 13, 1862, "	Mustered out at Edgefield, Tenn., June 20, 1865.
Samuel C. Preston	"	"	" Nashville, Tenn., June 8, 1865.
Edward Rosegrant	"		Discharged for disability at Gallatin, Tenn., Jan. 2, 1863.
George F. Robinson	"	Aug. 31, 1864, Jackson.	Mustered out at Detroit, July 6, 1865.
George Russell	"	Aug. 18, 1862, Grand Rapids.	Discharged for disability at Nashville, Tenn., April 25, 1863.
Alexander Sailers	"	Aug. 12, 1862, "	Mustered out at Louisville, Ky., May 29, 1865.
Hollis Taylor	"	Oct. 23, 1863, "	On detached service with U. S. C. T. at muster out.
John M. Terwilleger	"	Aug. 4, 1862, Kalamazoo.	Mustered out at Edgefield, Tenn., June 20, 1865.
Harlan S. Thorp	"	Aug. 24, 1862, "	"
Benjamin F. Tifft	"	Oct. 27, 1863, Corunna.	"
George W. Town	"	Aug. 31, 1864, Jackson.	"
John Wason	"	Aug. 13, 1862, Grand Rapids.	" Camp Chase, Ohio, June 28, 1865.
Daniel C. Wells	"	Aug. 11, 1862, "	Discharged at Louisville, Ky.,

Name	Rank	Enrolled	Place	Remarks
Nathan Wilkes	Private.	Oct. 23, 1863,	Grand Rapids.	Committed suicide at New Albany, Ind., Sept. 30, 1864.
George Wilkes	"	"	"	{ Transferred to V. R. C., February 1, 1865; mustered out at Louisville, Ky., June 3, 1865.
Co. D.				
Benjamin Smith	Captain.	Aug. 26, 1861,	Grand Rapids.	Promoted Major May 7, 1863.
Alphonso E. Gordon	"	Sept. 2, 1861,	"	Transferred to Co. E, Nov. —, 1863.
Erasmus D. Buddington	"	Aug. 26, 1861,	"	Resigned Oct. 7, 1864.
William H. Tallman	1st Lieut.	Sept. 26, 1861,	Port Huron.	Transferred to 136th U. S. C. T. June 22, 1865.
Stewart B. McCray	1st Lieut.	Aug. 26, 1861,	Gr'nd Rapids.	Resigned April 14, 1862.
James P. Scott	"	Sept. 2, 1861,	"	Promoted R. Q. M. Aug. 1, 1862.
Erasmus D. Buddington	"	Aug. 26, 1861,	"	Promoted Captain March 1, 1864.
Hugo B. Rathbun	"	Sept. 11, 1861,	Paris.	Mustered out February 2, 1865.
John S. Corliss	"	Sept. 3, 1861,	Bowne.	" " Aug. 17, 1865.
Darwin B. Lyon	2d Lieut.	Aug. 26, 1861,	Grand Rapids.	Resigned Jan. 21, 1862.
Erasmus D. Buddington	"			Promoted 1st Lieut. Jan. 1, 1862.
Benjamin F. Bailey	"			Resigned March 13, 1864.
William N. Tallman	"	Sept. 6, 1861,	Holland.	Promoted Captain Oct. 7, 1864.
Erasmus D. Buddington	1st Sergeant.	Sept. 26, 1861,	Port Huron.	Promoted 2d Lieut. April 24, 1862.
Almon London	Q'm'r Sergeant	Aug. 26, 1861,	Grand Rapids.	Died of pneumonia at Hamburg, Tenn, May 30, 1862.
Benjamin F. Bailey	"	Sept. 10, 1861,	Nunica.	Promoted 2d Lieut. Jan. 1, 1863.
Oscar F. Bunker	"	Sept. 6, 1861,	Holland.	
		Aug. 31, 1861,	Bowne.	
David Irwin	"	Sept. 5, 1861,	Byron,	{ Discharged for disability at Cairo, Ill., July 15, 1862. Killed in action at Blountsville, East Tenn., Dec. 30, 1862.
William S. Jackson	"	Sept. 6, 1861,	Holland.	{ Discharged July 18, 1864, to accept com. in 1st U. S. Colored Heavy Artillery.
Daniel Wells	Corporal.	Sept. 10, 1861,	Grand Haven.	Drowned in Ohio river, near Golconda, Sept. 12, 1862.
Samuel B. Osgood	"	Sept. 3, 1861,	Gaines.	Re-enlisted Jan. 5, 1864; promoted 1st Lieut, March 1, 1864.
Hugo B. Rathbun	"	Sept. 11, 1861,	Paris.	{ Died at Perryville, Ky., Oct. 9, 1862, of wound received in action at that place, Oct. 8, 1862.
Charles W. Coane	"	Sept. 6, 1861,	Grand Haven.	Died of inflam. of lungs at Benton Bar'ks, Mo., Dec. 3, 1861.
James Vandusen	"	Sept. 16, 1861,	Bowne.	Re-enlisted Jan. 5, 1864; Serg't, promoted 1st Lieut. Feb. 27, '65.
John S. Corlis	"	Sept. 3, 1861,	"	Died at Franklin, Tenn, June 4, 1863, of wounds rec'd in act'n.
Harry J. Esgett	"	Sept. 10, 1861,	Nunica.	Discharged for disability at Detroit, July 1, 1862.
Wayne T. W. Pardee	"	Sept. 16, 1861,	Bowne.	
John F. Myar	Musician.	Sept. 12, 1861,	Jackson.	Keokuk, Iowa, Nov. 27, 1862.
James A. Stevenson	"	Sept. 20, 1861,	St. Johns.	Re-enlisted Jan. 5, 1864; must'd out at Macon, Ga., Aug. 17, '65.
Henry H. Hickox	Farrier.	Sept. 3, 1861,	Byron.	Died from exposure at Evansville, Ind., May 16, 1862.
David R. Avnillo	"	Sept. 5, 1861,	Dorr.	

Co. D.

NAME.	RANK.	ENTERED SERVICE.	REMARKS.
Luther Richards	Saddler.	Sept. 20, 1861, Grand Rapids.	Discharged for disability at Louisville, Ky., Dec. 17, 1862.
Elmer Spencer	Wagoner.	Sept. 13, 1861, Ravena.	Died from exposure at New Madrid, Mo., April 22, 1862.
Thomas Anderson	Private.	Sept. 10, 1861, Grand Haven.	Re-enlisted Jan. 5, 1864; Sergt., promoted Sergt-Maj. April 3, '64.
Justin Alden	"	Sept. 13, 1861, Eggleston.	Killed in action at Perryville, Ky., Oct. 8, 1862.
Levi S. Blakesly	"	Sept. 11, 1861, Pontiac.	Died of disease at Savannah, Tenn., June 25, 1862.
John Boin	"	Sept. 10, 1861, Paris.	Died of pneumonia at St. Louis, Mo., April 8, 1862.
Nicholas Bloom	"	Sept. 11, 1861, Grand Haven.	Discharged for disability at Stevenson, Ala., Aug. 24, 1863.
William Batson	"	Sept. 13, 1861, Chester.	Louisville, Ky., Nov. 16, 18.2.
Charles H. Blanding	"	Sept. 16, 1861, Lowell.	" " March 10, 1863.
Peter Boes	"	Sept. 11, 1861, H.lland.	
Rufus Cheney	"	" Paris.	Died of disease at St. Louis, Mo, Aug. 1, 1862.
James Campbell	"	Sept. 3, 1861, Byron.	Died of erysipelas at New Madrid, Mo., April 12, 1862.
Peter Conners	"	Sept. 20, 1861, Richmond.	Died of inflammation of lungs at St. Louis, Mo., Jan. 25, 1862.
James Chatfield	"	Sept. 6, 1861, Grand Haven.	Discharged at Nashville, Tenn., Oct. 22, 1864.
Oscar F. Compton	"	Sept. 3, 1861, Eastmanville.	Died of disease at Nashville, Tenn., Dec. 9, 1863.
Jacob Dambacker	"	Sept. 4, 1861, Pt. Betsey.	Discharged at Nashville, Tenn., Oct. 22, 1864.
Marion Davies	"	Sept. 6, 1861, Wright.	Discharged for disability at Evansville, Nov. 16, 1862.
John P. Dohm	"	Sept. 13, 1861, Paris.	Transferred to V. R. C., April 30, 1864.
Theodore J. De Puy	"	" "	Discharged for disability at Detroit July 14, 1862.
Martin Degroot	"	Sept. 16, 1861, Holland.	" "
Albert Degroot	"	Sept. 18, 1861, "	Re-enlisted Jan. 5, '64, Sergt, must'd out at Macon, Ga., Aug.17, '65.
John Degough	"	Sept. 20, 1861, Grand Haven.	Died at Andersonville, May 24, 1864.
Henry Edding	"	Sept. 11, 1861, Holland.	Discharged at Nashville, Tenn., Oct. 22, 1864.
Martin Flasher	"	Sept. 6, 1861, Jamestown.	" Detroit, Feb. 7, 1865.
William H. Finch	"	Sept. 18, 1861, Holland.	
Ami Filley	"	Sept. 20, 1861, Jackson.	Discharged for disability at Corinth, Miss. Sept 11, 1862.
Hiram Filley	"	" "	" Franklin, Tenn., April 9, 1863.
Samuel Garzo	"	Sept. 18, 1861, Richmond.	Died of pneumonia at Farmington, Miss., Aug. 15, 1862.
Eben G. Gale	"	Sept. 6, 1861, Holland.	Transferred to V. R. C., Jan. 15, 1864; discharged Oct. 22, 1864.
Samuel Goodman	"	Sept. 5, 1861, Byron.	Discharged for disability at Holland, Mich. Sept. 5, 1862.
William Hawkins	"	Sept. 4, 1861, Pt. Betsey.	" Detroit, July 25, 1862.
Gerrit Herrink	"	Sept. 11, 1861, Holland.	Re-enlisted Jan. 5, 1864; mustered out at Macon, Ga., Aug. 17, '65.
Levi Harper	"	Sept. 12, 1861, Dorr.	Discharged at Nashville, Tenn., Oct. 22, 1864.
Henry Irons	"	Sept. 16, 1861, Gaines.	Discharged for disability at Louisville, Ky., Nov. 19, 1862.
Samuel C. Johnson	"	Sept. 5, 1861, Nunica.	Re-enlisted Jan.5, '64; corp.; must'd out at Macon, Ga., Aug. 17, '65.

Edwin H. Jackson..........	Private.	Aug. 31, 1861, Eastmanville.	Re-enlisted Jan. 5, '64; mustered out at Macon, Ga., Aug. 17, '65.
Enos Lesperance...........	"	Sept. 10, 1861, Grand Haven.	Died of small-pox at Nashville, Tenn., Jan. 23, 1864.
Elhanon W. Loomis........	"	Sept. 11, 1861, Holland.	Re-enlisted Jan. 5, 1864; mustered out at Macon, Ga., Aug. 17, '65.
Derick Mudima............	"	"	Discharged at Nashville, Tenn., July 18, 1863.
William Mordick...........	"	Sept. 14, 1861, "	Discharged at Louisville, Ky., June 11, 1863.
Andrew P. Myers..........	"	Sept. 16, 1861, Plainfield.	Re-enlisted Jan. 5, '64; mustered out at Macon, Ga., Aug. 17, '65.
Render Meyering..........	"	Sept. 20, 1861, Holland.	Discharged for disability at Keokuk, Iowa, March 10, 1863.
James McLain.............	"	Sept. 20, 1861, Paris.	Re-enlisted Jan. 5, 1864; transferred to V. R. C., Feb. 11, 1865.
David C. McLain...........	"	Sept. 20, 1861, Gaines.	Discharged for disability at Benton Barracks, Mo., Feb. 22, 1862.
John J. McNaughton.......	"	Sept. 16, 1861, Bowne.	Re-enlisted Jan. 5, '64; serg. must'd out at Macon,Ga., Aug. 17, '65.
John Nies.................	"	Sept. 18, 1861, Holland.	Musician; discharged at Nashville, Tenn., Oct. 22, 1864.
Daniel L. Nash............	"	Sept. 16, 1861, Bowne.	Discharged for disability at Detroit, Feb. 15, 1862.
Ezekiel Parker............	"	Sept. 10, 1861, Blendon.	Re-enlisted Jan. 5, '64; mustered out at Jackson, Mich., Aug 30, '65.
Simon Reidesma..........	"	Sept. 18, 1861, Holland.	Missing in action March 25, 1863; re-enlisted Jan. 5, 1864; mustered out at Camp Chase, Ohio, June 9, 1865.
Martin Reidesma..........	"	Sept. 20, 1861, Jamestown.	Discharged for disability at Detroit, Sept. 1, 1862.
Charles L. Richards.......	"	" Bowne.	Died of inflammation of lungs at St. Louis, Mo., Jan. 30, 1862.
Duncan Ross..............	"	" Lowell.	Re-enlisted Jan. 5, '64; serg't; must'd out at Macon, Ga., Aug. 17, '65
John Reimersma...........	"	Sept. 11, 1861, Holland.	Discharged for disability at Franklin, Tenn., April 1, 1863.
William Shilling...........	"	Sept. 20, 1861, "	Died of disease at Nashville, Nov. 4, 1863.
Augustus B. Simmons......	"	Sept. 16, 1861, Bowne.	Discharged at Nashville, Tenn., Oct. 22, 1864.
James K. Stewart..........	"	Sept. 13, 1861, Chester.	Discharged for disability at Louisville, Ky., Jan. 15, 1863.
Chester E. Shader..........	"	" Ravena.	Re-enlisted Jan. 5, '64; serving with 136th U.S.C.T. at muster out.
Jacob Stansbury...........	"	Sept. 10, 1861, Holland.	Died of typhoid fever at St. Louis, Mo., April 10, 1862.
George W. Smith...........	"	Sept. 6, 1861, "	Died June 4, 1863, at Franklin, Tenn., of wounds rec'd in action.
Riley Standish.............	"	Sept. 4, 1861, Jamestown.	Sergeant; discharged at Nashville, Tenn., Oct. 22, 1864.
Eugene Shaw..............	"	Sept. 20, 1861, Wyoming.	"
Ellis Thompson............	"	Sept. 14, 1861, Nunica.	Discharged for disability, July 1, 1863.
James M. Thompson.......	"	Sept. 16, 1861, Bowne.	Discharged at Nashville, Tenn., Oct. 22, 1864.
Christian Thiel............	"	Sept. 18, 1861, Holland.	" for disability at Detroit, Jan. 14, 1864.
William Utter..............	"	Sept. 20, 1861, Byron.	" " July 15, 1862.
William B. Upton..........	"	Aug. 31, 1861, Ottawa Center	
Benjamin Vanhaltren......	"	Sept. 6, 1861, Eastmanville.	Died at Louisville, Nov. 17, 1862, of wounds received at Perryville, Ky., Oct. 8, 1862.
John Vananroy............	"	Sept. 11, 1861, Holland.	Corporal, discharged at Nashville, Tenn., Oct. 22, 1864.
John G. Vanlewven........	"	Sept. 16, 1861, Vergennes.	Re-enlisted Jan. 5. '64; abs't sick since May 25, '64, at must. out.
Philo Valentine............	"	Sept. 18, 1861, Zeeland.	

Co. D.

NAME.	RANK.	ENTERED SERVICE.	REMARKS.
Lucas Vanwil	Private.	Sept. 20, 1861, Holland.	Discharged for disability April 2, 1862.
John Vogle	"	"	Re-enlisted Jan. 5, 1864; absent in hospital at muster out.
William H. White	"	Sept. 16, 1861, Vergennes.	Died of abscess in throat at Farmington, Miss., July 10, 1862.
Henry Westveld	"	Sept. 20, 1861, Holland.	Discharged at Nashville, Tenn., Oct. 22, 1864.
RECRUITS.			
Jesse Ackerman	Private.	Aug. 30, 1862, Grand Rapids.	Discharged for disability at Louisville, Ky., June 30, 1863.
Sidney A. Acker	"	Aug. 27, 1864, Reading.	Absent in hospital at muster out.
John Ashley	"	Nov. 9, 1863, Jackson.	Mustered out at Macon, Ga., Aug. 17, 1865.
James M. Birkey	"	Nov. 2, 1863, Kalamazoo.	"
Merrick G. Blood	"	Oct. 2, 1862, Hillsdale.	Transferred from Co. K; must'd out at Macon, Ga., Aug. 17,1865.
Charles Braman	"	Nov. 9, 1863, Jackson.	Died at Andersonville, Ga., May 24, 1864.
Charles H. Campbell	Musician.	Nov. 10, 1862, Hillsdale.	Mustered out at Chicago, Ill., May 22, 1865.
William M. B. Clifford	Private.	Nov. 7, 1863, Grand Rapids.	Farrier; mustered out at Louisville, Ky., June 12, 1865.
Samuel Coakley	"	Sept. 1, 1864, Jackson.	Mustered out at Edgefield, Tenn., June 20, 1865.
Thomas Cole	"		Transferred to V. R. C., Feb 15, 1865.
Henry Deuret	"	Dec. 28, 1863, Grand Rapids.	Mustered out at Macon, Ga., Aug. 17, 1865.
Nicholas Dittmore	"	Dec. 12, 1862, Pontiac.	"
Michael J. Dunbacker	"	Dec. 12, 1862, Jackson.	Corporal; mustered out at Macon, Ga., Aug. 17, 1865.
John J. Dunelly	"	Feb. 6, 1864, Grand Rapids.	In hospital at Nashville, Tenn., at muster out.
James Dewill	"	Sept. 1, 1864, Jackson.	Discharged for disability at Detroit, July 11, 1862.
Joseph M. Eaton	"	Dec. 9, 1863, Jackson.	Died of disease at Atlanta, Ga., Aug. 20, 1865.
Austin Fellows	"	Nov. 8, 1862, Kalamazoo.	Mustered out at Macon, Ga., Aug. 17, 1865.
Andrew J. Fillikins	"	Sept. 15, 1862, Hillsdale.	Discharged for disability at Nashville, Tenn., March 21, 1863.
James Fitzallen	"	Nov. 11, 1863, Pontiac.	Mustered out at Macon, Ga., Aug. 17, 1865.
Andrew L. Foster	"	Aug. 18, 1864, Jackson.	" Louisville, Ky., July 15, 1865.
George Franklin	"	Nov. 11, 1863, Pontiac.	Transferred to V. R. C., Feb. 11, 1865; mustered out at Burnside Barracks, Ind., Aug. 14, 1865.
Delos French	"	Jan. 5, 1864, Jackson.	Died of disease at Franklin, Tenn., Aug. 21, 1865.
Charles Fry	"	Nov. 19, 1863, Detroit.	Died at Nashville, Tenn., June 11, 1865.
John Frank	"	Aug. 18, 1864, Jackson.	Mustered out at Edgefield, Tenn., June 20, 1865.
George E. Gates	"	Nov. 10, 1862, Hillsdale.	" Macon, Ga., Aug. 17, 1865.
Charles Gardner	"	Oct. 29, 1863, Kalamazoo.	"
John Geiger	"	Corunna.	"
George Gleason	"	Nov. 24, 1863, Pontiac.	" Detroit, July 14, 1865.

Name	Rank	Date	Place	Remarks
Christopher Gordon	Private.	Dec. 28, 1863,	E. Saginaw.	Mustered out at Macon, Ga., Aug. 17, 1865.
Charles W. Griffith	"	Oct. 29, 1863,	Kalamazoo.	" " Jackson, Mich, Aug. 30, 1865.
Charles E. Haines	"	Oct. 10, 1863,	Grand Rapids.	" " Macon, Ga., Aug. 17, 1865.
Henry Hall	"	Nov. 12, 1863,	"	
Michael Hand	"	Nov. 4, 1863,	Kalamazoo.	
Frederick H. Hanson	"	Nov. 18, 1863,	Detroit.	Died at Nashville, Tenn., Dec. 23, '64, of wo'ds rec'd in action.
Adam Hertsman	"	Oct. 29, 1863,	Kalamazoo.	Killed in action at Lynnville, Tenn, Dec, 24, 1864.
Elias Heath	"	Oct. 30, 1863,	Grand Rapids.	Mustered out at Detroit, Aug. 15, 1865.
David Hill	"	Nov. 17, 1863,	Pontiac.	Supposed killed by explosion on steamer Sultana, April 28, 1865.
John Hicks	"	Oct. 30, 1863,	Corunna.	Transferred to V. R. C., April 30 1864.
George Howard	"	Dec. 28, 1863,	Grand Rapids.	Corporal; mustered out at Macon, Ga., Aug. 17, 1865.
Charles C. Hunt	"	Nov. 24, 1863,	Pontiac.	Mustered out at Macon, Ga., Aug. 17, 1865.
Thomas Hunt	"	Oct. 29, 1863,	Corunna.	Transferred to V. R. C., Feb. 11, 1865; mustered out at Burnside Barracks, Ind., Aug 14, 1865.
William W. Hurst	"	Nov. 6, 1863,	Grand Rapids.	Unaccounted for.
James Ingalls	"	Nov. 17, 1863,	Pontiac.	Mustered out at Nashville, Tenn., May 11, 1865.
George Irons	"	Jan. 1, 1862,	St. Louis, Mo.	
Thomas Jackson	"	Nov. 19, 1863,	Detroit.	Mustered out at Nashville, Tenn., May 11, 1865.
Lewis C. James	"	Aug. 12, 1864,	Jackson.	" " Edgefield, Tenn., June 20, 1865.
John Johnson	"	Nov. 23, 1863,	Pontiac.	Supposed killed by explosion of steamer Sultana, April 28, 1865.
Calvin B. Johnson	"	Nov. 25, 1863,	"	Mustered out at Macon, Ga., Aug. 17, 1865.
John Jones	"	Nov. 19, 1863,	"	" " Nashville, Tenn., May 12, 1865.
Julius H. King	"	Dec. 28, 1863,	Grand Rapids.	" " Macon, Ga., Aug. 17, 1865.
Charles King	"	Aug. 31, 1864,	Saline.	" " Edgefield, Tenn., June 20. 1865.
George Kohler	"	Nov. 17, 1863,	Detroit.	" " Macon, Ga., Aug. 17, 1865.
Mark Losee	"	Oct. 24, 1863,	Pontiac.	Died at Nashville, Tenn., Dec. 5, 1864.
Aaron Long	"	Sept. 1, 1864,	Jackson.	Mustered out at Edgefield, Tenn., June 20, 1865.
John F. Mayar	"	Nov. 10, 1864,	Mason.	" " Macon, Ga., Aug. 17, 1865.
W. B. McIntyre	"			Discharged at Franklin, Tenn., Feb. 22, 1862.
John Perrigo	"	Nov. 9, 1863,	Jackson.	Missing in action at Dandridge, Tenn., Dec. 24, 1863; died at Andersonville, Ga., May 24, 1864.
James Phillips	"			Mustered out at Jackson, Mich., Aug. 30, 1865.
James Quant	"	Nov. 24, 1863,	Pontiac.	Killed in action at Franklin, Tenn., Nov. 30, 1864.
Frank Rondon	"			Transferred to V. R. C., April 10, 1864.
Courtland H. Scott	"	Feb. 14, 1862,	St. Louis, Mo.	Transferred to Co. K, June 16, 1863.
Frank Seymour	"	Oct. 27, 1863,	Kalamazoo.	Died of disease at Cleveland, Tenn., May 3, 1864.
Henry Snyder	"	Nov. 14, 1863,	Pontiac.	Mustered out at Macon, Ga., Aug. 17, 1865.

Co. D. NAME.	RANK.	ENTERED SERVICE.	REMARKS.
Dewitt C. Sprague	Private.	Oct. 10, 1863, Grand Rapids.	Missing in action at Dandridge, Tenn., Dec. 24, 1863; transferred to V. R. C. Feb. 11, 1865.
John H. Stage	"	Nov. 5, 1862, Hillsdale.	Discharged for disability at Louisville, Ky., July 14, 1863.
Nicholas Stoka	"	Nov. 9, 1863, Pontiac.	Absent in hospital since Aug. 31, 1864, at muster out.
Moses Strause	"	Nov. 11, 1863, "	Mustered out at Macon, Ga., Aug. 17, 1865.
George Tilt	"	Nov. 5, 1863, "	Died at Andersonville, Ga., May 22, 1864.
Nathan O. Udell	"	Oct. 10, 1863, Grand Rapids.	"
David Upright	"	Sept. 1, 1864, Jackson.	"
Gerritt Vanhaltren	"	Aug. 12, 1862, Grand Rapids.	Mustered out at Edgefield, Tenn., June 20, 1865.
Eugene Van Amburg	"	Oct. 27, 1863, "	Missing in action at Bent Church, May 30, 1864; died at Andersonville, Ga., ——.
Gismith Vanhaltren	"	"	Mustered out at Detroit, July 28, 1865.
Benjamin F. Walker	"	Sept. 1, 1864, Benton.	Died in rebel prison ——.
Gilbert Wood	"	Sept. 10, 1862, Hillsdale.	Mustered out at Edgefield, Tenn., June 20, 1865.
Edwin M. Wood	"	Dec. 27, 1863, Saginaw City.	" Nashville, Tenn., June 2, 1865.
Warren J. Woolman	"	Aug. 9, 1864, Flint.	Mustered out at Edgefield, Tenn., June 20, 1865.
Co. E.			
Benjamin S. Whitman	Captain.	Aug. 26, 1861, Muskegon.	Resigned May 12, 1862.
Harmon F. Nicholson	"	"	Promoted Major March 1, 1864.
Henry Vance	"	Aug. 30, 1861, "	" July 31, 1865.
Henry W. Sears	1st Lieut.	Aug. 26, 1861, "	
Alphonso E. Gordon	"	Sept. 2, 1861, Gr'nd Rapids.	Transferred to Co. C.
Henry Vance	"	Aug. 30, 1861, Muskegon.	Promoted Captain, March 1, 1864.
Simeon F. Dickinson	"	Sept. 13, 1861, Gr'nd Rapids.	Discharged May 15, 1865.
Joseph Palmer	"	Sept. 17, 1861, "	Transferred to Co. I.
Harmon F. Nicholson	2d Lieut.	Aug. 26, 1861, Muskegon.	Promoted Captain, June 1, 1862.
Henry Vance	"	Aug. 30, 1861, "	" 1st. Lieut., Oct. 26, 1862.
Henry Barton	"	Sept. 25, 1861, Gr'nd Rapids.	Resigned Nov. 19, 1864. (had been transferred to Co. L as 1st Lieut., and commis'd Capt. of Co. ——), but refused to muster.
George Bradford	1st Sergeant.	Aug. 26, 1861, "	Discharged for disability at Rienzi, Miss., July 11, 1862.
Simeon F. Dickinson	Q'm'r Serg't.	Sept. 13, 1861, "	Appointed 2d Lieut. Co. I, May 2, 1863.
Henry Vance	"	Aug. 30, 1861, Muskegon.	" June 2, 1862.
William Bingham	"	"	Discharged at Nashville, Tenn., Oct. 24, 1864.
Charles Barton	"	Sept. 21, 1861, Gr'nd Rapids.	Discharged for disability, Sept. 25, 1862.
Abram Mapes, Jr.	"	Sept. 13, 1861, Muskegon.	Died of disease at St. Louis, March 31, 1862.

Name	Rank	Enlistment Date	Place	Remarks
William H. Harrison	Corporal	Aug. 27, 1861	Gr'nd Rapids	Re-enlisted Jan. 5, 1864; must'd out at Macon, Ga., Aug. 17, 1865.
Edson Barrows	"	Sept. 15, 1861	White River	Appointed 2d Lieut. 7th Mich. Cav., Dec. 4, 1864.
John L. Edmonds	"	Sept. 13, 1861	Gr'nd Rapids	Discharged for disability at Farmington, Miss., May 23, 1862.
John B. Robinson	"	Aug. 30, 1861	Muskegon	Discharged at Louisville, Ky., Nov. 5, 1863.
Franklin Perkins	"	Aug. 29, 1861	Grand Rapids	Appointed 1st Lieut. Co. C, Jan. 28, 1865.
James Lee	"	Aug. 30, 1861	Muskegon	Died June 24, '62, of wounds rec'd in action at Farm'gton, Miss.
James W. Barry	"	Aug. 29, 1861	"	Discharged for disability, April 21, 1862.
Edwin H. Laubach	"	Oct. 2, 1861	Grand Rapids	Died of disease at Farmington, Miss., July 12, 1862.
Isaac A. Sanderson	Musician	Aug. 30, 1861	Muskegon	Missing in action March 18, 1863; returned July 28, 1863; discharged at Nashville, Tenn., Oct. 22, 1864.
William E. Murray	"	"	"	Discharged at Nashville, Tenn., Oct. 22, 1864.
Alexander McNaughton	Farrier	Sept. 8, 1861	Grand Rapids	Discharged at Cleveland, Tenn., April 12, 1864.
Truman Young	"	Aug. 30, 1861	Berlin	Died of disease at St. Louis, Mo., Feb. 7, 1862.
Peter Ryan	Saddler	Sept. 13, 1861	Muskegon	Discharged for disability at Franklin, Tenn., April 1, 1863.
Calvin Rogers	Wagoner	Aug. 27, 1861	Grand Rapids	Died of disease at Rienzi, Miss., Aug. 19, 1862.
Andrew Allen	Private	Sept. 9, 1861	Casnovia	Re-enlisted Jan. 5, '64; serg't; must'd out at Macon, Ga., Aug. 17, '65.
Valentine Beach	"	Sept. 16, 1861	Grand Rapids	Discharged Oct. 22, 1864.
Washington Brown	"	"	"	Discharged for disability at Detroit, July 24, 1862.
Robert H. Barton	"	Sept. 25, 1861	"	Appointed 2d Lieut. Co. E, Feb. 1, 1863.
Henry Barton	"	"	"	Re-enlisted Jan. 5, 1864; mustered out at Macon, Ga., Aug. 17, '65.
Christian Brown	"	Sept. 28, 1861	"	Missing in action at Dallas Ford, Tenn. river, Sept. 24, 1863; mustered out at Detroit July 25, 1865.
Gamaliel Carlisle	"	Sept. 3, 1861	Berlin	Re-enlisted Jan. 5, 1864; Sergeant.
James F. Cole	"	Sept. 9, 1861	"	Missing in action March 8, 1862; returned July 8, 1863; re-enlisted Jan. 5, 1864; must'd out at Macon, Ga., Aug. 17, 1865.
George T. Carlisle	"	Sept. 4, 1861	"	Sergeant; discharged at Corinth, Miss., Sept. 11, 1862.
Amos B. Cook	"	Sept. 25, 1861	Grand Rapids	Discharged for disability at Detroit, Sept. 20, 1862.
John Cheeny	"	Oct. 2, 1861	Gr'nd Rapids	St. Louis, Sept. 22, 1862.
John F. Chubb	"	Sept. 14, 1861	White River	
Jacob Davis	"	Sept. 8, 1861	Muskegon	
John Eaton	"	Sept. 9, 1861	Ravena	Discharged at Corinth, Miss., Sept. 11, 1862.
George Eckles	"	Sept. 3, 1861	Grand Rapids	Re-enlisted Jan. 5, 1864; mustered out at Macon, Ga., Aug. 17, '65.
Lewis K. Fenton	"	Sept. 16, 1861	"	
John Fitzmaurice	"	Sept. 14, 1861	White River	
Antoine Gabriel	"	Aug. 27, 1861	Gr'nd Rapids	Discharged at Nashville, Tenn., Oct. 22, 1864.
Napoleon B. Harrison	"	Sept. 9, 1861	"	Discharged for disability at St. Louis, Mo., May 8, 1862.
Daniel Harris n	"			

Co. E. NAME.	RANK.	ENTERED SERVICE.	REMARKS.
Wendolin Hoag	Private.	Sept. 13, 1861, Muskegon	Died of disease at Rienzi, Miss., Aug. 8, 1862.
George Hilton	"	Sept. 16, 1861, Grand Rapids.	" " St. Louis, Mo., June 22, 1862.
Charles Hutchinson	"	Sept. 14, 1861, "	Discharged at Nashville, Tenn., Oct. 22, 1864.
David Herren	"	Oct. 2, 1861, "	Re-enlisted Jan. 5, 1864; mustered out at Detroit, July 3, 1865.
George R. Jones	"	Sept. 8, 1861, Muskegon.	Discharged for disability at Cairo, Ill., April 14, 1862.
Ephraim Kellum	"	Sept. 9, 1861, Casnovia.	Re-enlisted Jan. 5, 1864; mustered out at Macon, Ga., Aug. 17, '65.
James Keating	"	Sept. 13, 1861, Muskegon.	Re-enlisted Jan. 5, '64; must'd out at Detroit, July 6, 1865.
Decatur Knickerbocker	"	Sept. 23, 1861, Gr'nd Rapids.	Discharged at Nashville, Tenn., Oct. 22, 1864.
Abraham M. Kocher	"	Aug. 30, 1861, Muskegon.	Sergeant; discharged at Nashville, Tenn., Oct. 22, 1864.
Nathan Lovell	"	Sept. 23, 1861, Grand Rapids.	Re-enlisted Jan. 5, 1864; must'd out at Macon, Ga., Aug. 17, 1865.
Charles Lafond	"	Sept. 10, 1861, Muskegon.	Discharged for disability at Rienzi, Miss., Aug. 22, 1862.
Frank Murray	"	Aug. 30, 1861, "	Farmington, Miss., June 11, 1862.
Lawrence Millett	"	Sept. 6, 1861, "	Died July 3, '62, at Rienzi, Miss., of w'ds rec'd in act'n July 1, '62.
Charles Matham	"	Aug. 30, 1861, "	Died of disease at Nashville, Tenn., March 9, 1864.
Eleazer B. Mason	"	Sept. 9, 1861, Gr'nd Rapids.	Re-enlisted Jan. 5, '64; mustered out at Macon, Ga., Aug. 17, '65.
Archibald McMillan	"		Discharged at Nashville, Tenn., Oct. 22, 1864.
James McKey	"	Sept. 25, 1861,	Transferred to V. R. C., Feb. 15, 1864; transferred back Aug. 2, 1864; discharged Oct. 8, 1864.
Alexander McDonald	"	"	Discharged for disability at St. Louis, Mo., Feb. 1, 1862.
Daniel S. Monroe	"	"	" March 16, 1863.
William H. Millard	"	"	
Thomas Newcomb	"	Aug. 30, 1861, Muskegon.	Transferred to V. R. C., Sept. 1, 1863.
Elon Omans	"	Oct. 2, 1861, Gr'nd Rapids.	Discharged for disability at St. Louis, Mo., Jan. 11, 1862.
Nelson Oleson	"	Aug. 30, 1861, Muskegon.	Killed in action at Thompson's Station, March 5, 1863.
John Olney	"	Sept. 16, 1861, "	Died of disease at Nashville, Tenn., July 1, 1864.
Thomas O'Brien	"	Sept. 14, 1861, White River.	Re-enlisted Jan. 5, 1864; mustered out at Detroit, June 24, 1865.
William M. Pierson	"	Sept. 9, 1861, Grand Rap'ds.	Missing in action at Crawfish Spgs, Sept. 20, '63; disch'd Oct. 22, '64.
Francis M. Perkins	"	Sept. 3, 1861, "	Discharged for disability at Benton B'ks, St. Louis, Mo., Feb. 1, '62.
Martin Petit	"	Sept. 13, 1861, Muskegon.	Re-enlisted Jan. 5, 1864; must'd out at Detroit, June 27, '65; sergt.
William Post	"	Sept. 23, 1861, Gr'nd Rapids.	" " June 29, '65.
Philip Post	"	"	Discharged for disability at St. Louis, Mo., Aug. 15, 1862.
			Re-enlisted Jan. 5, 1864; missing in action at Oxford, Ala., April 23, 1865; sergeant; mustered out at Macon, Ga., Aug. 17, '65.
Dennis Rafferty	"	Aug. 30, 1861, Muskegon.	Re-enlisted Jan. 5, 1864; mustered out at Macon, Ga., Aug. 17, '65.
Jacob Post	"	Sept. 23, 1861, Gr'nd Rapids.	Discharged at Detroit, March 31, 1865.
Lansing Post	"		Corporal; discharged at Nashville, Tenn., Oct. 22, 1864.

Name	Rank	Date	Place	Remarks
James Root	Private.	Oct. 2, 1861,	Grand Rapids.	Died of disease at Hamburg, Tenn., May 20, 1862.
Thomas Ryan	"	Aug. 30, 1861,	Muskegon.	Discharged for disability at Columbus, Ohio, July 18, 1862.
John Rowling	"	Sept. 4, 1861,	Berlin.	" Corinth, Miss., Sept. 11, 1862.
Thomas Rowling	"	Aug. 30, 1861,	Muskegon.	Re-enlisted Jan. 5, 1864; on detached service at muster out.
William H. Russell	"	Sept. 14, 1861,	White River.	Discharged at Nashville, Tenn., Oct. 22, 1864.
Julius P. Smith	"	Sept. 13, 1861,	Muskegon.	Discharged for disability at St. Louis, Mo., May 5, 1862.
Joseph Scholes	"	Sept. 9, 1861,	Grand Rapids.	" " Oct. 1, 1862.
Isaac M. Sines	"	Sept. 4, 1861,	"	Transferred to V. R. C., April 6, 1864.
John W. Snyder	"	Sept. 13, 1861,	Muskegon.	{Re-enlisted Jan. 5, 1864; missing in action April 28, 1865; mustered out at Macon, Ga., Aug. 17, 1865.
Volney Trask	"	Sept. 11, 1861,	Grand Rapids.	Discharged at Nashville, Tenn., Oct. 22, 1864.
Warren Trask	"	Sept. 25, 1861,	"	Died of disease at Jeffersonville, July 19, 1864.
Thomas Terry	"	"	"	Discharged Oct. 20, 1864.
James Tompkins	"	Aug. 30, 1861,	Muskegon.	Discharged for disability at Detroit, July 1, 1862.
John J. Waters	"	Sept. 7, 1861,	Grand Rapids.	{Missing in action March 18, 1863; returned Nov. 15, 1863; discharged at Nashville, Tenn., Oct. 22, 1864.
Thomas Wall	"	Sept. 8, 1861,	Muskegon.	{Missing in action at Booneville, Miss., July 1, 1862; discharged for disability at Portsmouth Grove, R. I., March 27, 1863.
Ferdinand W. Wardle	"	"	"	{Died at Louisville, Nov. 5, 1862, of injuries received by being run over by a wagon.
Lewis Willey	"	Sept. 9, 1861,	Grand Rapids.	Died of disease at New Madrid, Mo., April 20, 1862.
Duncan McNaughton	"	Oct. 2, 1861,	"	
RECRUITS.				
Nathaniel Allen	Private.	Aug. 4, 1862,	Kalamazoo.	Mustered out at Nashville, Tenn., June 8, 1865.
George W. Arnold	"	Aug. 31, 1864,	Jackson.	" Edgefield, Tenn., June 21, 1865.
Elias Aulspaugh	"	Sept. 1, 1864,	"	" St. Louis, Mo., May 31, 1865.
Samuel H. Barton	"	Oct. 27, 1863,	Corunna.	" Macon, Ga., Aug. 17, 1865.
Alanson B. Bailey	"	Aug. 18, 1864,	Jackson.	Died of disease at Edgefield, Tenn., July 19, 1865.
Oliver S. Bailey	"	"	"	Mustered out at Camp Chase, Ohio, June 16, 1865.
Joseph J. Bennett	"	Aug. 31, 1864,	"	" Edgefield, Tenn., June 21, 1865.
Jacob Blakely	"	Oct. 27, 1863,	Corunna.	" Detroit, June 30, 1865.
John Bowman	"	Aug. 17, 1864,	Flint.	" Edgefield, Tenn., June 21, 1865.
Archibald Catney	"	Nov. 9, 1863,	Pontiac.	{Missing in action at Dandridge, Tenn., Dec. 24, 1863; died at Andersonville, Ga., July 17, 1864.
Thomas Connor	"	Oct. 27, 1863,	Corunna.	Mustered out at Macon, Ga., Aug. 17, 1865.
Francis Crandall	"	Nov. 20, 1863,	Pontiac.	"
Daniel Curry	"	Nov. 9, 1863,	"	"

Co. E. NAME.	RANK.	ENTERED SERVICE.	REMARKS.
Henry Davidson	Private.	Oct. 28, 1863, Corunna.	Mustered out at Macon, Ga., Aug. 17, 1865.
McKenzie Dingman	"	Aug. 12, 1862, Grand Rapids.	Missing in action at Pulaski, Tenn., Nov. 30, 1864; mustered out at Detroit, July 7, 1865.
James W. Dingman	"		Transferred to V. R. C., April 10, 1864; discharged June 29, '65.
John Estey	"	Nov. 7, 1863, Pontiac.	Mustered out at Macon, Ga., Aug. 17, 1865.
Charles C. Ferguson	"	Aug. 12, 1862, Grand Rapids.	Transferred to V. R. C., Dec. 1, 1863; discharged June 17, 1865.
Anson Finch	"	May 18, 1864, "	Mustered out at Macon, Ga., Aug. 17, 1865.
James Hawkins	"	Oct. 28, 1863, Corunna.	Discharged for disability at Detroit, _____
Orville Hamlin	"	Dec. 7, 1863, Jackson.	Mustered out at Macon, Ga., Aug. 17, 1865.
Ogilva E. Hamlin	"	" "	At Parole camp at muster out.
Ward Hamlin	"	" "	Mustered out at Macon, Ga., Aug, 17, 1865.
Charles Henry	"	Oct. 28, 1863, Corunna.	Mustered out at Macon, Ga., Aug, 17, 1865.
Charles Hermich	"		Lost on steamer Sultana, April 28, 1865.
George E. Jacobs	"	Nov. 2, 1863, Grand Rapids.	Died of typhoid fever at Nashville, Tenn., April 17, 1864.
William Jones	"	Nov. 23, 1863, Pontiac.	Mustered out at Macon, Ga., Aug. 17, 1865.
William E. Johnson	"	Nov. 4, 1862, Hillsdale.	
James Kendrick	"	Nov. 23, 1863, Corunna.	Killed by explosion of steamer Sultana, April 28, 1865.
John Knight	"	Nov. 20, 1863, Pontiac.	Missing in action at Franklin, Tenn., Nov. 30, 1864; mustered out at Jackson, Mich., Sept. 2, 1865.
Joseph Krozier	"	" "	Mustered out at Chattanooga, Tenn., April 22, 1865.
George Law	"	Oct. 29, 1863, Corunna.	Died of disease at Nashville, Tenn., March 9, 1864.
Wilson S. Langley	"	Sept. 10, 1864, Huntsv., Ala.	Mustered out at Detroit, July 8, 1865.
William S. Lindsley	"	Oct. 30, 1863, Corunna.	Lost on steamer Sultana, April 28, 1865.
William J. Logie	"	Nov. 2, 1863, Kalamazoo.	Mustered out at Macon, Ga., Aug. 17, 1865.
Charles H. Louder	"	Aug. 12, 1862, Grand Rapids.	Died of small-pox in hospital at Nashville, Tenn., May 4, 1865.
Samuel C. Logan	"	Nov. 20, 1863, Jackson.	Unaccounted for.
James J. May	"	Oct. 27, 1863, Corunna.	Mustered out at Macon, Ga., Aug. 17, 1865.
William P. McDonald	"	Aug. 12, 1862, Grand Rapids.	" " " Edgefield, Tenn., June 21, 1865.
Donald McDonald	"	Nov. 9, 1863, Pontiac.	Died of disease at Macon, Ga., July 28, 1865.
Hubble Middlebrook	"		Transferred to V. R. C., May 15, 1864.
Charles Moxon	"		Died in Southern prison
Francis Monroe	"	Sept. 15, 1864, Huntsv., Ala.	Mustered out at Detroit, July 5, 1865.
Daniel Moody	"	Oct. 28, 1861, Grand Rapids.	Killed in action near Louisville, Ky., Sept. 30, 1862.
Watson D. Moody	"	Aug. 12, 1862, " "	Missing in action at Oxford, Ala. April 23, 1865; sergeant, mustered out at Nashville, Tenn., June 9, 1865.

Name	Rank	Date	Place	Remarks
Martin C. Morgan	Private.			Missing in action at Dandridge, Tenn., Dec. 24, 1863.
Chauncey Parmenter	"	Aug. 17, 1864, Grand Rapids.		Mustered out at Edgefield, Tenn., June 21, 1865.
Roderick C. Phillips	"	Nov. 1, 1862, Hillsdale.		" " Macon, Ga., Aug. 17, 1865.
Miner Picket	"	Aug. 12, 1862, Grand Rapids.		" " Edgefield, Tenn., June 21, 1865.
Lucius W. Picket	"			Discharged for disability, Aug. 9, 1863.
Eugene K. R. Roberts	"			Discharged for disability at Detroit ———
Christian Rupert	"	Nov. 9, 1863, Pontiac.		Mustered out at Macon, Ga., Aug. 17, 1865.
Stephen H. Shippey	"	Aug. 18, 1864, Jackson.		" " Nashville, Tenn., June 21, 1865.
Lafayette Skinner	"	Aug. 12, 1862, Gr'nd Rapids.		" " Edgefield, Tenn., June 21, 1865.
William H. Soper	"	Nov. 9, 1863, Pontiac.		
Philo Taylor	"	Oct. 28, 1863, Corunna.		Mustered out at Macon, Ga., Aug. 17, 1865.
John Thompson	"	Feb. 24, 1864, Pontiac.		Died at Jefferson Barracks, Mo., April 12, 1865.
Horace H. Turner	"	Oct. 3, 1862, Hillsdale.		Discharged for disability at Nashville, Tenn., May 15, 1864
Absalom L. Ward	"	Oct. 28, 1863, Corunna.		Mustered out at Macon, Ga., Aug. 17, 1865.
John Welsh	"	Aug. 15, 1864, Gr'nd Rapids.		"
Isaac Whitbanks	"	Aug. 25, 1864, Jackson		" " Edgefield, Tenn., June 21, 1865.
Dexter M. Wilson	"	Aug. 12, 1862, Gr'nd Rapids.		Transferred to V. R. C., Nov. 28, 1864.
Daniel B. Wooley	"	Oct. 28, 1863, Corunna.		Mustered out at Macon, Ga., Aug. 17, 1865.
Chauncey Wolfram	"	Sept. 1, 1864, Jackson.		Died in Southern prison, Dec. 20, 1864.
Co. F.				
Arvine Peck	Captain.	Sept. 7, 1861, Lowell.		Resigned April 29, 1862.
Leonidas S. Scranton	"	Aug. 26, 1861, Gr'nd Rapids.		Promoted Major Oct. 26, 1862.
Daniel T. Fargo	"	Sept. 4, 1861, Greenville.		Mustered out Dec. 15, 1864.
Marvin H. Creager	"	Aug. 30, 1861, Gr'nd Rapids.		Mustened out Aug. 17, 1865.
Leonidas S. Scranton	1st Lieut.	Aug. 26, 1861, "		Promoted Captain, April 29, 1862.
John J. McCormick	"	Sept. 21, 1861, "		Mustered out Oct. 22, 1864.
William Tenney	"	Sept. 30, 1861, "		" " Aug. 17, 1865.
Daniel T. Fargo	2d Lieut.	Sept. 4, 1861, Greenville.		Promoted Captain Oct. 26, 1862.
Edwin Hoyt, Jr.	"	Sept. 2, 1861, Gr'nd Rapids.		" 1st. Lieut. Co. B, Aug. 1, 1863.
Franklin N. Eaton	"	Sept. 20, 1861, Albion.		" " Co. I, Aug. 7, 1864.
Marvin H. Creager	"	Aug. 30, 1861, Gr'nd Rapids.		" Captain, Dec. 15, 1864.
Marvin H. Creager	1st Sergeant.			Re-enlisted Jan. 5, 1864; appointed 2d Lieut. Co. I, March 1, '64.
George Rossman	Q'm'r Sergeant	Sept. 10, 1861, Greenville.		Discharged for disability at Cleveland, Tenn., April 1, 1864.
William R. Mason	"	Sept. 12, 1861, Lowell.		Benton Barracks, Mo., Feb. 16, 1862.
Lorenzo Buckley	"	Sept. 9, 1861, "		"
George D. Wood	"	Sept. 12, 1861, Greenville.		Died of disease at Keokuk, Iowa, March 18, 1863.
Jacob J. Finney	"	Sept. 9, 1861, Gr'nd Rapids.		Discharged at Nashville, Tenn., Oct. 22, 1864.

Co. F.

NAME.	RANK.	ENTERED SERVICE.	REMARKS.
William E. Root............	Corporal.	Sept. 10, 1861, Greenville.	Re-enlisted Jan. 5, '64; sergt.; must'd out at Macon,Ga.,Aug.17,'65.
Burdick M. Winegar........	"	Sept. 11, 1861, Lowell.	Discharged for disability at Detroit, July 16, 1862.
Philo T. Peck..............	"	Sept. 13, 1861, Gr'nd Rapids.	Discharged at Nashville, Tenn., Oct. 22, 1864.
Isaac Brannan..............	"	Sept. 14, 1861, Lowell.	Transferred to V. R. C., April 30, 1864.
Jacob A. Bradford..........	"	Sept. 5, 1861, Greenville.	{ Missing in action at Blackland, Miss., June 24, 1862; returned Sept. 28, 1862; sergeant; discharged Oct. 22, 1864.
Benjamin F. Norton........	"	Sept. 9, 1861, Gr'nd Rapids.	Discharged at Nashville, Tenn., Oct. 22, 1864.
Martin V. Carlisle	"	Sept. 14, 1861, Lowell.	Discharged July 28, 1862.
Henry B. Williams.........	"	Aug. 28, 1861, Greenville.	" July 25, 1862.
Carlos G. Wilson...........	Musician.	Sept. 14, 1861, Lowell.	Discharged at Nashville, Tenn., Oct. 22, 1864.
John H. Loomis............	"	Sept. 2, 1861, "	Discharged for disability at Hamburg, Tenn., April 28, 1862.
Thomas J. McCulloch......	Farrier.	Sept. 9, 1861, Grand Rapids.	Discharged at Nashville, Tenn., Oct. 22, 1863.
George Pettit..............	"	Sept. 12, 1861, Lowell.	Discharged for disability at Detroit, July 10, 1862.
Joel S. Beamon............	Saddler.	" Grand Rapids.	Re-enlisted Jan. 5, '64; sergt, must'd out at Macon, Ga., Aug.17,'65.
Selah Cook................	Wagoner.	Sept. 10, 1861, Lowell.	Discharged Aug. 9, 1862
Suel Ames.................	Private.	Sept. 9, 1861, Grand Rapids.	Died of typhoid fever at Rienzi, Miss., July 10, 1832.
George Avery	"	Sept. 12, 1861, Lowell.	Discharged at Nashville, Tenn., Oct. 22, 1864.
George Bowen..............	"	Sept. 7, 1861, Grand Rapids.	Sergeant; appointed 2d Lieut. Co. K, March 1, 1864.
Christian Bichler..........	"	Oct. 7, 1861, Lowell.	Died of typhoid fever at Commerce, Mo., March 11, 1862.
Joseph Baranoski...........	"	Sept. 4, 1861, Grand Rapids.	Re-enlisted Jan. 5, '64; mustered out at Macon, Ga., Aug. 17, '65.
Martin Barnard............	"	Sept. 10, 1861, Lowell.	" " Detroit, Sept. 4, 1865.
Austin Bates...............	"	Sept. 12, 1861, "	Died of disease at Evansville, Ind., Oct. 4, 1864.
John C. Burgess............	"	Sept. 26, 1861, Greenville.	Re-enlisted Jan. 5, 1864; mustered out at Macon, Ga., Aug. 17, '65.
Charles Barnum............	"	Sept. 5, 1861, "	Discharged for disability at Detroit, July 16, 1862.
George S. Bishop...........	"	Sept. 10, 1861, Greenville.	Transferred to V. R. C., April 30, 1864
Augustus M. Barnes........	"	Sept. 25, 1861, Grand Rapids.	Discharged at Nashville, Tenn., Oct. 22, 1864.
Alonzo Bryant.............	"	Sept. 15, 1861, Greenville.	
George Corbin..............	"	Sept. 12, 1861, "	Appointed 2d Lieut. 4th Mich. Cav., Aug. 13, 1862.
William W. Campbell......	"	Aug. 27, 1861, Gr'nd Rapids.	Discharged at Detroit, Feb. 25, 1865.
John C. Cook..............	"	Aug. 31, 1861, "	Discharged at St. Louis, May 30, 1862.
Thales L. Chapin...........	"	Sept. 2, 1861, "	Re-enlisted Jan. 5, '64;corp ; must'd out at Macon,Ga.,Aug.17,'65.
John Caswell...............	"	Sept. 9, 1861, Lowell.	Died of small-pox, March 1, 1862
William J. Cheesbro.......	"	Sept. 12, 1861, "	Discharged Oct. 22, 1864.
Cyrus M. Duncan..........	"	Sept. 30, 1861, Gr'nd Rapids.	Discharged for disability near Farmington, Miss., June 20, 1862.
Lorenzo M. Demoray......	"	Sept. 5, 1861, Greenville.	Died of typhoid fever at Winchester, Tenn., Aug, 5, 1863.

Name	Rank	Enlisted	Remarks
Dwight T. Devendorf	Private.	Aug. 27, 1861, Greenville.	Discharged for disability at Hamburg, Tenn., April 20, 1862.
John Jones	"	Sept. 11, 1861, "	Died of disease at Corinth, Miss., Oct. 15, 1862.
Lucien B. Fullington	"	Sept. 26, 1861, Lowell.	" St. Louis, Mo., July 6, 1862.
Morris E. Fitch	"	Aug. 31, 1861, Gr'nd Rapids.	Died of wounds at Franklin, Tenn., March 26, 1863.
Philo Fitch	"	Aug. 30, 1861, "	Discharged at Nashville, Tenn., Oct. 22, 1864.
Erastus Fox	"	Sept. 11, 1861, "	Discharged for disability at Winchester, Tenn., July 29, 1863.
George W. Fullington	"	Sept. 9, 1861, Lowell.	Sergeant; missing in action at Spring Hill, Tenn., Nov. 29, 1864; mustered out Aug. 17, 1865; re-enlisted Jan. 5, 1864.
Enerson H. Galba	"	" "	Discharged for disability at Louisville, Dec. 27, 1862.
Julius Gardner	"	Aug. 30, 1861, Gr'nd Rapids.	" Corinth, Oct. 24, 1862.
Warner Green	"	Sept. 16, 1861, Lowell.	Re-enlisted Jan. 5, 1864; sergt.; died at Nashville, Tenn., Dec. 4, 1864, of gunshot wound.
Frank W. Gee	"	Sept. 3, 1861, Gr'nd Rapids.	Discharged at Nashville, Tenn., Oct. 22, 1864.
William G. Horning	"	Sept. 10, 1861, "	Discharged for disability at Detroit, July 22, 1862.
Seymour Hall	"	Sept. 9, 1861, "	Re-enlisted Jan. 5, '64; serg't; must'd out at Macon, Ga., Aug. 17, '65.
Homer H. Hanry	"	Sept. 3, 1861, "	
George P. Hall	"	Aug. 27, 1861, "	Transferred to V. R. C.
James Heaton	"	Aug. 29, 1861, "	Re-enlisted Jan. 5, '64; mustered out at Jackson, Mich., Aug. 31, '65.
John C. Jaques	"	Oct. 23, 1861, "	
George Jestious	"	Sept. 12, 1861, Lowell.	Discharged for disability, Jan. 18, 1862.
Henry Knight	"	" "	Discharged at Nashville, Tenn., Oct. 22, 1864.
Curtis L. Keeney	"	Aug. 28, 1861, Grand Rapids.	Reported died of disease at St. Louis, Mo., Sept. 5, 1862.
Joseph W. Lamoreaux	"	Oct. 5, 1861, "	Re-enlisted Jan. 5, '64; serg., must'd out at Macon, Ga., Aug. 17, '65.
George R. Lewis	"	Oct. 17, 1861, "	Corporal; discharged at Nashville, Tenn., Oct. 22, 1864.
Charles McMurray	"	Sept. 16, 1861, Lowell.	Discharged for disability at Benton Barracks, Mo., Feb. 19, 1862.
Joseph Morse	"	" "	Died in hospital at Nashville, Tenn., Sept. 24, 1863.
Peter Morse	"	Sept. 14, 1861, Grand Rapids.	Discharged for disability at Hamburg, Tenn., May 4, 1862.
James M. McCullah	"	Sept. 16, 1861, "	Discharged at Nashville, Tenn., Oct. 22, 1864.
Shirk Miller	"	Sept. 9, 1861, "	Re-enlisted Jan.5, '64; sergt.; must'd out at Macon,Ga., Aug. 17, '65.
George Norton	"	Sept. 12, 1861, Lowell.	Died of typhoid fever at Rienzi, Miss., July 28, 1862.
William H. Osborn	"	Oct. 23, 1861, Grand Rapids.	
Ira Purdy	"	Sept. 9, 1861, "	Transferred to Marine Brigade, March 13, 1863.
Horace Peck	"	Sept. 14, 1861, "	Discharged for disability at Rienzi, Miss., July 12, 1862.
Mansa W. Peck	"	Sept. 11, 1861, "	" Detroit, June 21, 1862.
William H. Pearsall	"	" "	Transferred to V. R. C.
William H. Rarick	"	Aug. 31, 1861, "	Missing in action at Triune, Tenn., June 11. 1863; returned Nov. 5, 1863; transferred to V. R. C; disch'd at Detroit, Oct. 7, 1864.

Co. F.

NAME.	RANK.	ENTERED SERVICE.	REMARKS.
Alfred Robbin	Private.	S:pt. 12, 1861, Lowell.	
Hiram S. Race	"	Sept. 11, 1861, Greenville.	Discharged at Nashville, Tenn., Oct. 22, 1864.
George B. Race	"	"	"
Charles F. Smith	"	Oct. 10, 1861, Gr'nd Rapids	Re-enlisted Jan. 5, 1864; mustered out at Macon, Ga., Aug. 17, '65.
Washington L. Stinson	"	Aug. 27, 1861, "	Discharged for disability at Louisville, Dec. 27, 1862.
Francis Skinner	"	Sept. 10, 1861, Lowell.	" at Sparta, Tenn., Dec. 3, 1863.
James B. Sabin	"	Aug. 29, 1861, Greenville.	" for disability at Franklin, Tenn., April 12, 1863.
Kenneth W. Tubbs	"	Aug. 26, 1861, Grand Rapids.	" Sept. 11, 1862.
Abram S. Tuttle	"	Sept. 14, 1861, "	" July 3, 1862, for disability.
William Tenney	"	Sept. 30, 1861, "	Re-enlisted Jan. 5, 1864; sergeant; appointed 1st Lieut. Oct. 22,'64.
William Vanlien	"	Sept. 2, 1861, "	" corp; must'd out at Macon, Ga, Aug.17,'65.
Horace P. Woodman	"	Sept. 9, 1861, "	Discharged at Nashville, Tenn., Oct. 22, 1864.
Elijah Walcott	"	Sept. 6, 1861, "	" for disability at Detroit, Oct. 20, 1862.
Henry Wendover	"	Sept. 12, 1861, Lowell.	" " Nov. 20, 1862.
William R. Ward	"	Sept. 5, 1861, Grand Rapids	" Jan. 5, 1862.
Caleb F. Weaver	"	Sept. 6, 1861, Greenville.	Died in hospital at Cowan, Tenn., Oct. 2, 1863.
William W. Wheeler	"	Sept. 16, 1861, Gr'nd Rapids.	Discharged at Nashville, Tenn., Oct. 22, 1864.
Merritt Wilson	"	S:pt. 19, 1861, Lowell.	" Detroit, July 5, 1862.
RECRUITS.			
Philip Arthur	Private.	Aug. 19, 1862, Detroit.	
Harvey Averill	"	Aug. 25, 1862, Gr'nd Rapids.	Mustered out at Edgefield, Tenn., June 21, 1865.
Theophilus Baxter	"	Aug. 31, 1862, "	Died of rheumatism at Knoxville, Tenn., April 2, 1864.
Corydon A. Barrows	"	Aug. 15, 1864, "	Transferred to Co. A, Dec. 7, 1864.
Jeremiah Blackman	"	Oct. 27, 1863, Corunna.	Mustered out at Macon, Ga, Aug. 17, 1865.
Andrew Bradford	"	Aug. 11, 1862, Gr'nd Rapids.	Mustered out at Edgefield, Tenn., June 21, 1865.
Chrales Bradford	"	Oct. 27, 1863, Corunna.	Died at Annapolis, Md, March 21, 1865.
William Brown	"	Feb. 29, 1864, Pontiac.	Transferred to Co. A, Dec. 7, 1864.
Edward Butler	"	Nov. 11, 1863, Gr'nd Rapids.	Discharged for disability, May 18, 1865.
Colonel C. Burgess	"	Nov. 4, 1863, Jackson.	Mustered out at Macon, Ga., Aug. 17, 1865.
Anson S. Cadwell	"	Sept. 12, 1862, Gr'nd Rapids.	Died at Franklin, Tenn.. March 7, 1863.
Andrew Call	"	Oct. 27, 1863, Corunna.	Mustered out at Macon, Ga., Aug. 17, 1865.
Frank Chamberlin	"	Dec. 30, 1863, Gr'nd Rapids.	" "
Edgar B. Chase	"	Jan. 23, 1864, "	" "
Amos S. Clapson	"		Died of disease at Nashville, Tenn., March 8, 1864.
William Core	"	Dec. 28, 1863, Gr'nd Rapids.	" Jeffersonville, Ala., Jan. 9. 1866.

Name	Rank	Date	Place	Remarks
George Dart	Private.	Aug. 31, 1864,	Jackson.	Mustered out at Edgefield, Tenn., June 21, 1865.
Osborn DeGraw	"	Nov. 11, 1863,	Gr'nd Rapids.	" " Macon, Ga., Aug. 17, 1865.
Thomas Dixon	"	Aug. 22, 1862,	"	" " Nashville, Tenn., June 3, 1865.
James Eddy	"	Aug. 11, 1862,	"	" " Camp Chase, Ohio, June 16, 1865.
Dudley Fox	"	Nov. 14, 1863,	Jackson.	" " Macon, Ga., Aug. 17, 1865.
Theron J. Fox	"	Jan. 4, 1864,	Gr'nd Rapids.	" " " " "
Amos A. Glasson	"	Nov. 2, 1863,	"	Died of disease at Nashville, Tenn., March 8, 1864.
Rix Hammond	"	Oct. 28, 1863,	"	Absent sick since Aug. 25, 1864, at muster out.
Lionel W. Harris	"	Dec. 30, 1863,	Corrunna.	Mustered out at Macon, Ga., Aug. 17, 1865.
George Helmer	"	Oct. 28, 1863,	"	{ Missing in action at Spring Hill, Tenn., Nov. 29, 1864; mustered out at Louisville, Ky., July 18, 1865.
George Howard	"	Dec. 28, 1863,	Gr'nd Rapids.	See Co. D.
George Howard	"	Oct. 28, 1863,	"	Mustered out at Detroit, Sept. 6, 1865.?
Peter Keefer	"	Aug. 23, 1862,	Detroit.	" " Nashville, Tenn., June 3, 1865.
Andrew I. Kenney	"	Nov. 4, 1863,	Gr'nd Rapids.	" " Detroit, Sept. 16, 1865.
Daniel H. Kellogg	"	Dec. 8, 1863,	Jackson.	{ Missing in action at Macon, Ga., July 26, 1864; mustered out at Camp Chase, Ohio, June 8, 1865.
John H. Kellogg	"	....	....	Discharged ———
David S. Kidd	"	Aug. 7, 1862,	Detroit.	Mustered out at Edgefield, Tenn., June 21, 1865.
Edward H. King	"	Dec. 28, 1863,	Gr'nd Rapids.	Died of disease at Nashville, Tenn., Feb. 1, 1864.
Joseph Labino	"	Nov. 14, 1863,	Detroit.	On detached service at muster out.
John Lamon	"	Nov. 18, 1863,	"	{ Transferred to V. R. C., April 30, 1864; transferred back Sept. 10, 1864, but never reported.
George G. Lambertson	"	Nov. 2, 1863,	Pontiac.	Mustered out at Camp Dennison, June 2, 1865.
Lorenzo Livingstone	"	Aug. 26, 1862,	Kalamazoo.	" " Edgefield, Tenn., June 21, 1865.
John Lynch	"	Sept. 13, 1862,	Gr'nd Rapids.	Killed in action at Cleveland, Tenn., April 2, 1864.
Alonzo Mattison	"	Oct. 27, 1863,	Corunna.	Mustered out at Macon, Ga., Aug. 17, 1865.
William Marion	"	Oct. 29, 1863,	Kalamazoo.	" " " " "
William McCaslin	"	" "	Grand Rapids.	Died of disease at Nashville, Tenn., Sept. 10, 1864.
Azra McIntyre	"	Nov. 20, 1863,	Jackson.	" " Mound City, Ill. Feb. 22, 1865.
Levi Miller	"	Nov. 24, 1863,	Pontiac.	Mustered out at Camp Chase, Ohio, June 16, 1865.
Nathan Miner	"	Jan. 26, 1864,	Gr'nd Rapids.	" " Nashville, Tenn., May 20, 1865.
Solomon Mikesell	"	Aug. 18, 1864,	Jackson.	Died of disease at Waterloo, Ala., May 13, 1865.
Hugh McKay	"	Dec. 22, 1863,	Zilwaukee.	Mustered out at Macon, Ga., Aug. 17, 1865.
George McNiel	"	Oct. 29, 1863,	Grand Rapids.	Transferred to V. R. C. April 30, 1864.
Thomas J. Murphy	"	Nov. 17, 1863,	Detroit.	Died of disease at Nashville, Tenn., Sept. 5, 1864.
Marvin Murray	"	Nov. 23, 1863,	Pontiac.	Mustered out at Macon, Ga., Aug. 17, 1865.|

Co. F. NAME.	RANK.	ENTERED SERVICE.	REMARKS.
Henry E. Myers	Private.	Nov. 19, 1863, Pontiac.	Died of remittent fever at Jeffersonville, Tenn., June 22, 1864.
Julius C. Otto	"	Aug. 15, 1862, Kalamazoo.	Mustered out at Edgefield, Tenn., June 20, 1865.
Michael H. Powers	"	Mar. 31, 1864, Gr'nd Rapids.	" Macon, Ga., Aug. 17, 1865.
George Quant	"	Nov. 18, 1863, Pontiac.	Absent sick since May 1, 1864, at muster out.
James N. Randall	"	Oct. 27, 1863, Corunna.	Died Jan. 2, 1864, at Mossy Creek, Tenn., of wounds received in action, Dec. 29, 1863.
Richard W. Rowe	"	Jan. 27, 1862, St. Louis, Mo.	Discharged at St. Louis, Mo., April 17, 1863.
George Ruthardt	"	Nov. 10, 1863, Gr'nd Rapids.	Mustered out at Macon, Ga., Aug. 17, 1865.
George Schaub	"	Nov. 12, 1863, Pontiac.	Discharged for disability at Detroit, June 13, 1865.
Sydney M. Shelley	"	Oct. 27, 1863, Corunna.	Mustered out at Macon, Ga., Aug. 17, 1865.
William Sherwood	"	Aug. 31, 1864, Jackson.	" Edgefield, Tenn., June 21, 1865.
Paul Snider	"	Dec. 30, 1863, Grand Rapids.	" Macon, Ga., Aug. 17, 1865.
John Thurston	"	Aug. 11, 1862,	" Edgefield, Tenn., June 21, 1865.
John Thompson	"	Feb. 20, 1864, Pontiac.	Discharged ————
Samuel H. Vleet	"	Dec. 30, 1863, Ithaca.	Mustered out at Macon, Ga., Aug. 17, 1865.
Henry C. Worden	"	Dec. 9, 1863, Grand Rapids.	"
Henry Zuppy	"	Dec. 22, 1863, Cambria.	Discharged for disability at Detroit, July 28, 1864.
Co. G.			
Frederick Fowler	Captain.	Aug. 25, 1861, Reading.	Promoted Lieut.-Col., July 13, 1862; resigned June —, 1863.
James Hawley	"	" Hillsdale.	Killed in action at Chicamauga, Ga., Sept. 20, 1863.
James H. Smith	1st Lieut.	Sept. 2, 1861, Port Huron.	Mustered out Aug. 31, 1865; left on the field at Dandridge.
Jasper A. Waterman	"	Aug. 25, 1861, Reading.	Resigned Sept. 8, 1862.
James Hawley	"	" Hillsdale.	Promoted Captain, Jan. 30, 1863.
James H. Smith	"	Aug. 2, 1861, Port Huron.	" March 1, 1864.
Samuel V. Robertson	"	Aug. 21, 1861, Hillsdale.	" Co. I, Dec. 31, 1864.
Henry Woodruff	2d Lieut.	Aug. 3, 1861, Marshall.	Transferred to 136th U. S. C. T., June 22, 1865.
James Hawley	"	Aug. 25, 1861, Hillsdale.	Promoted 1st Lieut. Sept. 8, 1862.
F. Byron Cutler	"	Aug. 14, 1861, North Adams.	Resigned for disability May 2, 1863.
James H. Smith	"	Aug. 2, 1861, Port Huron.	Promoted 1st Lieut., May 29, 1863.
Samuel V. Robertson	"	Aug. 21, 1861, Hillsdale.	" March 1, 1864.
Collatinus D. Warner	1st Sergeant.	Sept. 14, 1861, Reading.	Discharged at Corinth, Miss., Aug. 4, 1862.
F. Byron Cutler	Q'm'r Serg't.	" North Adams.	Appointed 2d Lieut., Co. K. June 9, 1862.
Homer H. Kidder	"	" Reading.	Discharged at Louisville, Ky., Oct. 3, 1862.
George W. Baker	"	" Hillsdale.	Transferred to 2d Mich. Battery.
Samuel V. Robertson	"	Sept. 21, 1861,	Appointed 2d Lieut. May 2, 1863.

Name	Rank	Date	Place	Remarks
Jerry Arnold	Q'm'r Sergeant	Aug. 29, 1861,	Hillsdale.	Died of typhoid fever at New Madrid, Mo., April 14, 1862.
William H. VanHorn	Corporal.	Sept. 14, 1861,	"	Discharged at Corinth, Miss., Sept. 11, 1862.
James A. Taylor	"	Sept. 5, 1861,	Jonesville.	" " " 9, 1862.
George A. Douglass	"	Sept. 6, 1861,	Wheatland.	Sergeant; discharged at Jackson, Oct. 1, 1864.
Wells W. Gates	"	Sept. 14, 1861,	Hillsdale.	Re-enlisted Jan. 5,'64; sergt.; must'd out at Macon, Ga., Aug.17,'65.
Irvin Eddy	"	"	Cambria.	Sergeant; appointed 2d Lieut. Co. M, March 1, 1864.
J. Byron Day	"	Aug. 29, 1861,	Hillsdale.	Discharged at Cincinnati, Nov. 21, 1862.
Clarence H. Chapman	"	Sept. 5, 1861,	Reading.	Discharged for disability at Detroit, July 22, 1862.
James Thompson	"	Sept. 17, 1861,	Hillsdale.	Sergeant; discharged at Detroit, Oct. 1, 1864.
Nathan F. Ellis	Musician.	Aug. 30, 1861,	"	Discharged for disability at Cincinnati, Jan. 9, 1862.
William C. Campbell	"	Sept. 11, 1861,	Reading.	" at Nashville, Tenn., Oct. 22, 1864.
Frank K. Proctor	Farrier.	Sept. 16, 1861,	Hillsdale.	Re-enlisted Jan. 5, 1864; discharged for disability May 3, 1865.
Abram F. Pierce	"	Sept. 2, 1861,	Allen.	" abs't in hos'l since Aug.8,'65,at mus'r out.
Michael Barnhart	Saddler.	Sept. 16, 1861,	Litchfield.	Discharged at Keokuk, Iowa, Nov. 6, 1862.
Liberty Straw	Wagoner.	Sept. 20, 1861,	Adams.	" for disability at Farmington, Miss. June 6, 1862.
James E. Ainsworth	Private.	Sept. 23, 1861,	Hillsdale.	Died of cholera morbus near Rienzi, Miss., July 15, 1862.
LeRoy Allen	"	Sept. 14, 1861,	"	Died of typhoid pneumonia at Franklin, Tenn., April 13, 1863.
Royal B. Ames	"	"	"	Discharged Oct. 28, 1862.
John Alsbro	"	Sept. 20, 1861,	Adams.	{ Re-enlisted Jan. 5, 1864; on detached service since June 21, 1865, at muster out.
William Ashley	"	Sept. 18, 1861,	Hillsdale.	Died of pneumonia at Camp Benton, Mo., Feb. 14, 1862.
James Appleton	"	Sept. 23, 1861,	Allen.	Discharged at Corinth, Miss., Sept. 11, 1862.
Grove S. Bartholomew	"	Sept. 16, 1861,	Reading.	" for disability at St. Louis, Mo., March 16, 1862.
Ralph Bailey	"	Sept. 23, 1861,	"	" at Louisville, Nov. 13, 1862.
John A. Bailey	"	Sept. 17, 1861,	"	
Israel P. Bates	"	Sept. 23, 1861,	Hillsdale.	{ Transferred to V. R. C., April 6, 1864; discharged at Alexandria, Va., Oct. 3, 1864.
William H. Barrett	"	Aug. 29, 1861,	"	Discharged at Louisville, Ky., Nov. 13, 1862.
Charles S. Beckwith	"	Sept. 16, 1861,	Reading.	Re-enlisted Jan. 5,'64; absent w'nded since Dec.5,'64,at mus'r out.
Norman Benedict	"	Sept. 19, 1861,	Woodbridge.	Died of disease at Keokuk, Ia., Aug. 22, 1862.
Warren Bowen	"	Sept. 16, 1861,	Hillsdale.	Re-enlisted Jan.5,'64; sergt.; must'd out at Macon, Ga., Aug.17,'65.
Washington Bulson	"	Sept. 1, 1861,	Algansee.	" left mortally wounded at Pulaski, Tenn., Nov. 23, 1864; mustered out at Macon, Ga, Aug. 17, 1865.
James Burt	"	Sept. 23, 1861,	Ransom.	Re-enlisted Jan. 5, '64; mustered out at Macon, Ga., Aug. 17, '65.
Ephraim B. Briggs	"	Sept. 6, 1861,	Reading.	Discharged Oct. 22, 1864. 3
William Brock	"	Aug. 31, 1861,	"	Died of consumption at Reading, Mich., May 23, '62. [June 10, '65.
Henry H. Brown	"	Sept. 23, 1861,	"	Re-enlisted Jan. 5, '64; discharged for disability at Nashville, Tenn.,

Co. G.

NAME.	RANK.	ENTERED SERVICE.	REMARKS.
Leander Birdsall	Private.	Sept. 14, 1861, Reading.	Re-enlisted Jan. 5, '65; serg.; must'd out at Macon, Ga., Aug. 17, '65.
Austin Cone	"	" Hillsdale.	Died of typhoid fever at Farmington, Miss., June 16, 1862.
William Davenport	"	Sept. 11, 1861, "	Discharged at Bowling Green, Ky., Jan. 24, 1863.
Ebben H. Dunton	"	Sept. 23, 1861, Reading.	Re-enlisted Jan. 5, '64; must'd out at Jackson, Mich., Aug. 30, '65.
Orson W. Fisk	"	Sept. 16, 1861, Hillsdale.	Discharged at Nashville, Tenn., Oct. 22, 1864.
Alton S. Ford	"	Sept. 23, 1861, Jefferson.	Died of typhoid fever at Jefferson, Mich., May 22, 1862.
Eli R. Forquer	"	Sept. 14, 1861, Camden.	Re-enlisted Jan. 5, '64; on detached service since June 21, 1865, at muster out.
John Forquer	"	" Reading.	Discharged for disability at Detroit, Sept. 15, 1862.
Joseph Fitzgerald	"	Sept. 20, 1861, Hillsdale.	Re-enlisted Jan. 5, '64; must'd out at Jackson, Mich., Aug. 30, '65.
Ansel Fleetwood	"	Sept. 14, 1861, Pulaski.	Died of typhoid fever at New Madrid, Mo., April 11, 1862.
Henry H. Ferris	"	" Reading.	Discharged for disability at Benton Barracks, Mo., Feb. 14, 1862.
Cornelius M. Gregory	"	Sept. 23, 1861, Adams.	" Detroit, Sept. 6, 1862.
John B. Herrington	"	Sept. 16, 1861, Reading.	" Franklin, Tenn., May 3, 1863.
Chauncey L. Howell	"	Sept. 20, 1861, Hillsdale.	Re-enlisted Jan.5, '64; serg.; must'd out at Macon, Ga., Aug. 17, '65.
John F. Howell	"	Sept. 21, 1861, "	" "
William Hughes	"	Sept. 16, 1861, Reading.	Discharged for disability at Benton Barracks, Mo., March 17, '62.
William A. Keyes	"	Sept. 14, 1861, Hillsdale.	Discharged for disability at Cincinnati, Sept. 2, 1862.
Sylvester H. Kellogg	"	" Reading.	" Benton Barracks, Mo., Feb. 17, '62.
Nelson E. Kidder	"	" "	" at Nashville, Tenn., Oct. 22, 1864.
Hugh Loughrey	"	Sept. 23, 1861, Hillsdale.	
Joseph L. Long	"	Aug. 28, 1861, Wheatland.	Re-enlisted Jan 5, '64; sergeant; killed in action at Tuscaloosa, Ala., April 3, 1865.
William B. Martin	"	Sept. 20, 1861, Moscow.	Died of chronic diarrhea at Chattanooga, Tenn., Oct. 18, 1863.
Isaac McCurdy	"	" Adams.	Re-enlisted Jan. 5, '64; corp.; must'd out at Macon, Ga., Aug.17, '65.
Robert McDougall	"	Sept. 7, 1861, Woodbridge.	" discharged at Detroit, June 13, 1865.
James Y. Mesick	"	Sept. 19, 1861, Hillsdale.	" must'd out at Louisville, Ky., Aug. 31, 1865.
Richard Morrison	"	Sept. 14, 1861, Pulaski.	" " Macon, Ga., Aug. 17, 1865.
Alonzo S. Mulliken	"	Sept. 23, 1861, Hillsdale.	" serg.; must'd out at Macon, Ga., Aug. 17, '65.
George A. Munger	"	Aug. 31, 1861, "	" must'd out at Jackson, Mich., Aug. 30, '65.
Oscar D. Nutton	"	Sept. 23, 1861, Moscow.	Discharged at Nashville, Tenn., June 2, 1863.
Otis F. Packard	"	Sept. 14, 1861, Litchfield.	" St. Louis, Mo., Jan. 7, 1863.
John Pease	"	Sept. 12, 1861, Hillsdale.	" Corinth, Miss., Sept. 9, 1862.
George Perkins	"	Sept. 10, 1861, Amboy.	" Keokuk, Iowa, Oct. 3, 1862.
William Price	"	Sept. 14, 1861, Allen.	Re-enlisted Jan.5, '64; killed in act'n at Franklin,Tenn., Nov.30, '64.

Judah Reed	Private.	Sept. 14, 1861,	Reading.	Discharged at Nashville, Tenn., Oct. 22, 1864.
Gabriel See	"	Sept. 7, 1861,	"	{ Re-enlisted Jan. 5, '64; on detached service since June 27, 1865, at muster out.
Aymour R. Shannon	"	Sept. 14, 1861,	Hillsdale.	Discharged for disability at Detroit, July 12, 1862.
Jonathan B. Sommers	"	Sept. 23, 1861,	"	" at St. Louis, Sept. 26, 1862.
Henry B. Standard	"	Sept. 14, 1861,	Reading.	
Joseph Sturdevant	"	" 1861,	Hillsdale.	Discharged at Nashville, Tenn., Oct. 22, 1864.
Robert Taylor	"	Aug. 28, 1861,	Cambria.	Appointed Chaplain, Sept. 4, 1862.
Horace W. Titus	"	Sept. 7, 1861,	Pittsford.	Discharged at Detroit, July 22, 1862.
Stephen Turner	"	Sept. 14, 1861,	Hillsdale.	Corporal; discharged at Nashville, Tenn., Oct. 29, 1863.
William Tuttle	"	Sept. 2, 1861,	Cambria.	Died of measles and cong'n of lungs at Cp. Benton, Mo., Dec. 4, '61.
Charles Vandenburg	"	Sept. 14, 1861,	Reading.	Discharged at Nashville, Tenn., Oct. 22, 1864.
William H. Vandewarker	"	Sept. 6, 1861,	Hillsdale.	"
Berdette S. Waldo	"	Sept. 14, 1861,	Cambria.	Re-enlisted Jan. 5, '64; serg.; must'd out at Mrcon, Ga., Aug. 17, '65.
Theron D. Waters	"	Sept. 4, 1861,	"	Discharged at Jackson, Oct. 1, 1864.
Frank L. Weston	"	Sept. 16, 1861,	"	Re-enlisted Jan. 5, '64; corp.; must'd out at Macon, Ga., Aug. 17, '65.
Samuel Wheaton	"	Sept. 14, 1861,	Ransom.	Discharged at Keokuk, Iowa, Sept. 10, 1862.
Harvey Wilson	"	"	Litchfield.	Discharged at Detroit, Dec. 18, 1862.
Bradley Wilson	"	"	Hillsdale.	Died of disease in Richmond, Va., prison, Nov. 3, 1863.
Charles Wooster	"	Sept. 2, 1861,	Wheatland.	Re-enlisted Jan. 5, '64; corp.; must'd out at Macon, Ga., Aug. 17, '65.
Joshua Winney	"	Sept. 16, 1861,	Hillsdale.	Unaccounted for.
RECRUITS.				
Oscar Adams	Private.	Nov. 7, 1863,	Pontiac.	Killed by guerrillas near Sparta, Tenn., Nov. 29, 1863.
Alonzo Alsbrow	"	Aug. 25, 1862,	Detroit.	Mustered out at Edgefield, Tenn., June 21, 1865.
Andrew Armdon	"	Sept. 4, 1862,	Hillsdale.	" Nashville, Tenn., June 8, 1865.
Francis E. Bird	"	Sept. 3, 1862,	"	" Edgefield, Tenn., June 21, 1865.
Philip R. Bowen	"	Sept. 9, 1862,	"	" "
Charles Boyle	"	Oct. 31, 1863,	Pontiac.	Killed in action at Dandridge, Tenn., Dec. 24, 1863.
Maxim Boisvert	"	Nov. 24, 1863,	"	Mustered out at Macon, Ga., Aug. 17, 1865.
William A. Brown	"	Nov. 13, 1861,	Hillsdale.	Discharged for disability at St. Louis, Mo., April 5, 1832.
Darwin E. Brown	"			Died of disease at Keokuk, Iowa, —— 1862.
Lyman T. Brown	"	Aug. 15, 1862,	Grand Rapids.	Discharged June 21, 1865.
George W. Burt	"	Sept. 14, 1862,	Hillsdale.	Mustered out at Edgefield, Tenn., June 21, 1865.
John A. Carry	"	Sept. 12, 1862,	"	Died at Nashville, Tenn., April 4, '64, of wounds rec'd in action.
Jefferson N. Campbell	"	Aug. 25, 1862,	"	Discharged for disability at Cleveland, Ohio, July 17, 1865.
Jackson Cartwright	"	Sept. 8, 1862,	"	Mustered out at Edgefield, Tenn., June 21, 1865.
Curtis S. Camp	"	Nov. 5, 1863,	Pontiac.	" Macon, Ga., Aug. 17, 1865.

Co. G.

NAME.	RANK.	ENTERED SERVICE.	REMARKS.
John Codger	Private.	Oct. 27, 1863, Corunna.	Transferred to U. S. Navy, April —, 1864.
David Emery	"	Nov. 6, 1863, Jackson.	Mustered out at Davenport, Iowa, Sept. 11, 1865.
Daniel Emery	"		Absent wounded since Dec. 20, 1864, at muster out.
Michael Fitzgerald	"	Nov. 9, 1863, Corunna.	Mustered out at Detroit, July 11, 1865.
William H. Groves	"	Sept. 9, 1862, Hillsdale.	Died of disease at Nashville, Nov. 12, 1863.
James C. Graham	"	Nov. 6, 1863, Corunna.	Transferred to Co. I, Dec. 10, 1863.
Charles M. Hannah	"	Aug. 14, 1862, Detroit.	Mustered out at Edgefield, Tenn., June 21, 1865.
John Harrington	"	" Hillsdale.	" Macon, Ga., Aug. 17, 1865.
George Harwick	"	Dec. 31, 1864, Grand Rapids	Died of disease at Chattanooga, Tenn., July 13, 1864.
James Hawkins	"	Oct. 28, 1863, Corunna.	Discharged at Detroit, Nov. 22, 1864.
Michael Helwick	"	Sept. 30, 1862, Hillsdale.	" Louisville, Jan. 15, 1863.
Joshua Henry	"		" Jackson, Oct. 1, 1864.
William C. Howell	"	Aug. 14, 1862, Detroit.	Mustered out at Edgefield, Tenn., June 21, 1865.
William Howe	"	Aug. 25, 1862, Hillsdale.	" "
Miles B. Hunt	"	Aug. 15, 1862, Grand Rapids.	Discharged for disability, May 17, 1865.
Henry G. Johnson	"	Sept. 4, 1862, Reading.	Mustered out at Nashville, Tenn., June 3, 1865.
Nathaniel Keith	"	Sept. 10, 1863, "	Transferred to V. R. C., Feb. 15, 1864.
Zachariah Kemp	"	Dec. 23, 1863, Cambria.	Mustered out at Macon, Ga., Aug. 17, 1865.
Patrick Leonard	"	Nov. 5, 1863, Pontiac.	Killed in camp ——.
Charles Martin	"	Nov. 6, 1863, "	Mustered out at Macon, Ga., Aug. 17, 1865.
David McDuffee	"	Sept. 4, 1862, Hillsdale.	" Cleveland, Ohio, May —, 1865.
Archibald McHenry	"	Nov. 7, 1863, Corunna.	" Macon, Ga., Aug. 17, 1865.
James K. P. McLain	"	Jan. 2, 1864, Grand Rapids.	" Detroit, Aug. 1, 1865.
John O. McNair	"	Aug. 30, 1862, Hillsdale.	" Edgefield, Tenn., June 21, 1865.
Jabez H. Moses	"	Sept. 11, 1865,	Discharged at Franklin, Tenn., March 3, 1863.
John B. Mulliker	"	Aug. 11, 1862, Detroit.	Mustered out at Nashville, Tenn., June 8, 1865.
Jerome McWithey	"	Dec. 9, 1863, Pontiac.	" Macon, Ga., Aug. 17, 1865.
Tibits Nichols	"	Sept. 6, 1862, Hillsdale.	Discharged for disability at Nashville, Tenn.
Joseph H. Norton	"	Sept. 4, 1863,	Died of typhoid fever at Nicholasville, Ky., Jan. 6, 1863.
James O'Connor	"	Nov. 4, 1863, Pontiac.	Mustered out at Macon, Ga., Aug. 17, 1865.
Eugene K. Roberts	"	Nov. 13, 1861, Hillsdale.	Discharged at Detroit, Nov. 22, 1864.
Smith Seymour	"	Nov. 5, 1863, Corunna.	Discharged ——.
F. Small	"		Mustered out at Burnside Barracks, Md., Aug. 14, 1865.
Seymour F. Smith	"	Feb. 5, 1863, Allen.	" Detroit, May 17, 1865.
Edward C. Smith	"	Sept. 4, 1862, Hillsdale.	" Edgefield, Tenn., June 21, 1865.

Walter Straw	Private.	Aug. 18, 1862,	Detroit.	Discharged for disability at Detroit, Aug. 11, 1863.
William W. Taylor	"	Sept. 8, 1862,	Hillsdale.	Mustered out at Edgefield, Tenn., June 21, 1865.
Reuben Vickers	"	Sept. 28, 1862,	"	"
Thaddeus D. Walters	"	Aug. 15, 1862,	Grand Rapids.	Mustered out at Camp Chase, Ohio, June 16, 1865.
Arthur Waiters	"	Sept. 1, 1862,	Hillsdale.	Discharged for disability at Nashville, Tenn., Aug. 24, 1863.
Christopher Wamsley	"	Sept. 8, 1862,	"	Mustered out at Nashville, Tenn., June 3, 1865.
George E. Weston	"	Aug. 30, 1862,	"	" Edgefield, Tenn., June 21, 1865.
John A. White	"	Aug. 22, 1862,	"	" " "
Oscar Whitney	"	Jan. 18, 1864,	Grand Rapids.	" Detroit, May 17, 1865.
Erasmus Wilber	"	Sept. 15, 1862,	Hillsdale.	" Nashville, Tenn., June 3, 1865.
Lanson Woodworth	"	Nov. 10, 1863,	Jackson.	" Detroit, Sept. 7, 1865.
Richard Wrikter	"	Aug. 15, 1862,	Grand Rapids.	" Edgefield, Tenn., June 21, 1865.
Porter Yates	"	Aug. 9, 1862,	Hillsdale.	" " "
Co. H.				
Chester E. Newman	Captain.	Aug. 24, 1861,	Gr'nd Rapids.	Resigned, ———— 1862.
Peter A. Schuyler	"	Sept. 2, 1861,	Warren.	Resigned Sept. 23, 1864.
John W. Kingscott	1st Lieut.	Aug. 24, 1861,	"	Mustered out Dec. 27, 1865.
George E. Adair	"	"	Warren.	Resigned Sept. 3, 1862.
John W. Kingscott	"	"	"	Promoted Captain Co. A, June 7, 1864.
William G. Kingscott	2d Lieut.	Sept. 8, 1861,	"	Transferred to 136th U. S. C. T., June 22, 1865.
Alexander Grant	"	Aug. 24, 1861,	"	Resigned Feb. 4, 1862.
John W. Kingscott	"	"	Warren.	Promoted 1st Lieut. Oct. 1, 1862.
Myron A. Johnson	1st Sergeant.	Aug. 27, 1861,	Utica.	Resigned Nov. 19, 1864.
John W. Kingscott	Q'm'r Serg't.	Aug. 24, 1861,	Warren.	Appointed 2d Lieut. Jan. 4, 1862.
William W. Booth	"	"	Fentonville.	Promoted hospital steward, Nov. 1, 1862.
Charles Barnes	"	Sept. 5, 1861,	Almont.	Re-enlisted Jan. 5, 1864; corporal; mustered out at Jackson, Mich., Aug. 30, 1865.
Myron A. Johnson	"	Aug. 27, 1861,	Utica.	Appointed 2d Lieut., Oct. 1, 1862.
George St. John	"	Aug. 26, 1861,	"	Discharged at Detroit, Oct. 1, 1864.
Ernest Lorenze	Corporal.	Sept. 3, 1861,	Erin.	Mustered out at Nashville, Tenn., Oct. 22, 1864.
James C. Scott	"	Sept. 7, 1861,	Utica.	Re-enlisted Jan. 5, 1864; on detached service with 136th U. S. C. T., at muster out.
James McCaffry	"	Sept. 9, 1861,	Warren.	Re-enlisted Jan. 5, '64; serg.; mus'd out at Macon, Ga., Aug. 17, '65.
Benjamin F. Hitchcock	"	"	"	Discharged for disability Oct. 19, 1862.
Robert M. Harvey	"	Sept. 7, 1861,	Utica.	Died of measles at Benton Barracks, Mo., Dec. 14, 1861.
Joshua Terry	"	Sept. 5, 1861,	Almont.	Discharged at Nashville, Tenn., Oct. 22, 1864.
David Worden	Musician.	Sept. 9, 1861,	Utica.	Re-enlisted Jan. 5, '64; must'd out at Detroit, July 17, 1865.

Co. H.

NAME.	RANK.	ENTERED SERVICE.	REMARKS.
Abraham Demay	Musician.	Sept. 27, 1861, Parshallville.	Discharged for disability at Detroit, July 1, 1862.
Erastus D. McKay	Farrier.	Sept. 5, 1861, Almont.	Re-enlisted Jan. 5, '64; must'd out at Jackson, Mich., Aug. 30, '65.
George B. Whitney	"	Sept. 6, 1861, Gr'nd Rapids.	promoted veterinary sergeant Dec. 11, '64.
Frederick Trempler	Saddler.	Sept. 12, 1861, Detroit.	promoted saddler sergeant, March 1, 1863.
Samuel Atwood	Private.	Sept. 9, 1861, Vassar.	Re-enlisted Jan. 5, '64; serg.; must'd out at Macon, Ga., Aug. 17, '65.
Charles H. Beard	"	Sept. 8, 1861, Almont.	Re-enlisted Jan. 5, '64; sergt.; must'd out at Macon, Ga, Aug. 17, '65.
Irvin W. Benson	"	Sept. 7, 1861, Warren.	Drowned in West Harpeth river, Tenn., May 15, 1863, while
George Beutter	"	" Utica.	on a scout.
Charles Bittner	"	Sept. 9, 1861, "	Discharged for disability at Keokuk, Oct. 31, 1862.
George Black	"	Sept. 6, 1861, Watrousville.	Re-enlisted Jan. 5, '64; corp.; must'd out at Macon, Ga., Aug. 17, '65.
Silas Bryant	"	" 6, 1861, "	Died in hospital near Farmington, Miss., Aug. 5, 1862.
David M. Black	"		Discharged for disability July 18, 1862.
John Clark	"	Sept. 24, 1861, Warren.	Died in hospital at St. Louis, Feb. 26, 1862.
Charles Clark	"	Sept. 9, 1861, "	Re-enlisted Jan. 5, '64; corp.; must'd out at Macon, Ga., Aug. 17, '65.
Henry Clark	"	Sept. 20, 1861, "	" " " " " "
Albert F. Dodge	"	Sept. 30, 1861, Fentonville.	Died of fever at Hamburg, Tenn., May 14, 1862.
John Duff	"	Sept. 6, 1861, Vassar.	
Rodolph Eggerman	"	Sept. 4, 1861, Detroit.	
Joseph Findley	"	Sept. 5, 1861, Almont.	Discharged at Nashville, Tenn., Oct. 22, 1864.
Jacob M. H. Finch	"	Sept. 8, 1861, Utica.	Tranffered to Co. B, 3d Mich. Cav., Nov. 13, 1861.
Benjamin C. Gamble	"	Sept. 24, 1861, Warren.	Discharged for disability at Detroit, Jan. 15, 1864.
Frederick Guthrie	"	Sept. 5, 1861, Almont.	Re-enlisted Jan. 5, 1864; mustered out at Detroit, June 17, 1865.
Jerome B. Harvey	"	Sept. 7, 1861, "	{ " " wagoner; mustered out at Macon, Ga., Aug. 17, 1865.
Linus W. Harwood	"	Sept. 4, 1861, Warren.	Re-enlisted Jan. 5, '64; must'd out at Macon, Ga., Aug. 17, '65.
Henry J. Holstein	"	Sept. 3, 1861, "	Discharged for disability at Keokuk, Oct. 1, 1862.
Jacob Heipple	"	Sept. 9, 1861, Utica.	
Calvin Hills	"	Sept. 6, 1861, Akron.	Discharged for disability at Gallatin, Tenn., March 11, 1863.
Henry Howard	"	Sept. 21, 1861, Warren.	Re-enlisted Jan. 5, '64; serg.; must'd out at Macon, Ga., Aug. 17, '65.
Edgar Johnson	"	Sept. 2, 1861, Utica.	" " " " " "
Henry Johnson	"	Sept. 9, 1861, Tuscola.	" corp.; serg.: app'd 1st Lieut. Sept. 20, '64.
William G. Kingsctt	"	Sept. 7, 1861, Warren.	
Jacob B. Loyer	"	Sept. 27, 1861, Parshallville.	
Florell C. McCoy	"	Sept. 3, 1861, Warren.	Re-enlisted Jan. 5, 1864; mustered out at Macon, Ga., Aug. 17, '65.

Charles B. Morey	Private.	Sept. 1, 1861,	Gr'nd Rapids.	Died on furlough in Michigan, April 1, 1864.
Albert C. Parker	"	Sept. 25, 1861,	Utica.	Discharged for disability July 29, 1862.
Alfred Powers	"	Sept. 5, 1861,	Vassar.	" at Cairo, Ill., March 17, 1862.
Delos Pennell	"	Sept. 11, 1861,	"	Re-enlisted Jan. 5, '64; died at Jeffersonville, Ind., Dec. 26, '64, of gunshot wound.
William B. Paap	"	Sept. 6, 1861,	Detroit.	Discharged for disability Sept. 9, 1862.
Henry C. Rice	"	Sept. 9, 1861,	Utica.	" at New Madrid, Mo., March 10, 1862.
Alois Rasch	"	Sept. 4, 1861,	Warren.	Re-enlisted Jan. 5, '64; serg.; must'd out at Macon,Ga.,Aug. 17, '65.
Richard M. Ross	"	Sept. 6, 1861,	Watrousville.	Discharged for disability at St. Louis, May 30, 1862.
William H. Scott	"	Sept. 25, 1861,	Utica.	Transferred to V. R. C., Feb. 15, 1864; discharged at Nashville, Tenn., Oct. 22, 1864.
Charles J. Stevens	"	Sept. 3, 1861,	Warren.	Discharged at Nashville, Tenn., Oct. 22, 1864.
Charles Stead	"	Sept. 7, 1861,	Utica.	
Godfried Schreader	"	Sept. 3, 1861,	"	Transferred to V. R. C. April 30, 1864; discharged at Washington, D. C.. Oct. 4, 1864.
Henry Shuster	"	Sept. 4, 1861,	Warren.	Re-enlisted Jan. 5, '64; serg.; must'd out at Macon, Ga., Aug.17, '65.
John G. Schnidman	"	Sept. 6, 1861,	Tuscola.	Discharged for disability, Oct. 31, 1862.
Owen Summerson	"	" "	Watrousville.	Re-enlisted Jan. 5, '64; corp.;must'd out at Macon,Ga., Aug. 17, '65.
Jacob Smith	"	Sept. 26, 1861,	Grand Rapids.	Discharged for disability at Detroit, June 21, 1862.
Oscar Smith	"	Sept. 29, 1861,	Utica.	Died at Rienzi, Miss., Aug. 4, 1862.
George W. Tripp	"	Sept. 3, 1861,	"	Re-enlisted Jan. 5, 1864; mustered out at Macon, Ga., Aug. 17, '65.
William Thomas	"	Sept. 13, 1861,	"	Discharged for disability at St. Louis, Jan. 20, 1862.
Francis Tatro	"	Sept. 3, 1861,	Warren.	Mustered out Oct. 22, 1864.
Stephen E. Taylor	"	Sept. 19, 1861,	Almont.	Re-enlisted Jan. 5, 1864; corporal; mustered out at Jackson, Mich., Aug. 30, 1865.
Henry Williams	"	Oct. 9, 1861,	Watrousville.	Re-enlisted J.n. 5,'64; promoted com. sergt. March 1, 1863.
George Wentworth	"			Re-enlisted Jan. 5, 1864; mustered out at Macon, Ga., Aug. 17, '65.
Henry Westerhouse	"	Oct. 16, 1861,	Jamestown.	Mustered out Oct. 22, 1864.
Charles W. Finch	"	Oct. 19, 1861,	Romeo.	Discharged for disability May 23, 1863.
Frederick Hartman	"	Sept. 6, 1861,	Casco.	Discharged at Nashville, Tenn., Oct. 22, 1864.
Julius Hurd	"	Oct. 9, 1861,	Watrousville.	"
Maurice Kealler	"	Sept. 10, 1861,	Grand Haven.	
James Mason	"	Sept. 20, 1861,	Utica.	Discharged for disability at Evansville, Ind., May 4, 1863.
James R. Phillips	"	Oct. 7, 1861,	Clarkston.	Missing in action April 5, 1863; returned Oct. 31, 1863; mustered out at Nashville, Tenn., Oct. 22, 1864.
Reuben Page	"	Oct. 11, 1861,	Burks Corn'rs.	Discharged for disability at Franklin, Tenn., April 22, 1863.
Thomas M. Price	"	Oct. 9, 1861,	Watrousville.	" St. Louis, Mo., Feb. 18, 1862.

Co. H. NAME.	RANK.	ENTERED SERVICE.	REMARKS.
William Spethoff	Private.	Sept. 6, 1861, Detroit.	Transferred to V. R. C., Nov. 1, 1863.
RECRUITS.			
George Barth	Private.		" " Feb. 15, 1865.
Max Bates	"	Nov. 6, 1863, Pontiac.	Discharged for disability at Detroit, Feb. 28, 1865.
Lewis Banditt	"	Oct. 30, 1863, Pontiac.	Mustered out at Macon, Ga., Aug. 17, 1865.
Frederick Binkey	"	Jan. 14, 1864, Saginaw.	" "
Samuel B. Briggs	"	Jan. 23, 1864, Kalamazoo.	Re-enlisted Jan. 5, '64; far'r; must'd out at Macon,Ga.,Aug. 17,'65.
Philip Bramen	"	Sept. 12, 1861, Detroit.	Died at Red Clay, Tenn., May 5, 1864; poisoned accidentally.
Oscar Crandall	"	Nov. 9, 1863, Pontiac.	Mustered out at Macon, Ga., Aug. 17, 1865.
John E. Culver	"	Nov. 14, 1863, Jackson.	" " Jackson, Mich, Aug. 30, 1865.
Russell Davis	"	Nov. 20, 1863, "	" " Edgefield, Tenn, June 21, 1865.
Daniel Donelly	"	Aug. 25, 1864, "	Died of disease at Jeffersonville, Ind., Dec. 26, 1864.
Michael Enos	"	Sept. 3, 1861, Dixborough.	
Hugh W. Gibson	"	Aug. 31, 1864, Jackson.	Discharged for disability March 3, 1864.
Cyrus Harvey	"	Sept. 4, 1861, St. Louis.	Transferred to V. R. C., Jan. 15, 1864.
Arthur D. Harman	"	Aug. 21, 1862, E. Saginaw.	Mustered out at Edgefield, Tenn., June 21, 1865.
Henry Hengstebeck	"	Aug. 20, 1864, Flint.	" Macon, Ga., Aug. 17, 1865.
John S. Hovey	"	Nov. 7, 1863, Pontiac.	Discharged for disability July 1, 1862.
Gilbert Hurd	"	Oct. 28, 1861, Watrousville.	Mustered out at Edgefield, Tenn., June 21, 1865.
James W. Hubbard	"	Aug. 21, 1852, E. Saginaw.	Mustered out at Macon, Ga., Aug. 17, 1865.
William W. Hurst	"	Oct. 29, 1863, Pontiac.	" "
Robert Johnson	"	Nov. 6, 1863, Grand Rapids.	Died of disease at St. Louis, Mo., Dec. 8, 1864.
Andrew Kinney	"	Aug. 25, 1864, Pontiac.	Died at Benton Barracks, Dec. 26, 1861.
John R. Kingman	"	Nov. 11, 1861, Gr'nd Rapids.	Absent sick at Detroit since May 1, 1865, at muster out.
Henry Koth	"	Sept. 1, 1864, Jackson.	Mustered out at Nashville, Tenn., Oct. 22, 1864.
John Herman Kuhn	"	Nov. 1, 1861, Erin.	
A. Lewis	"	Nov. 9, 1863, Jackson.	Died at Livingston, Mich.————
Richard Millage	"	Nov. 20, 1863, Jackson.	Mustered out at Macon, Ga., Aug. 17, 1865.
Charles M. Morris	"	Nov. 1, 1861, Warren.	
Charles Morehead	"	Sept. 19, 1863, Sterling.	Mustered out at Macon, Ga., Aug. 17, 1865.
Amel Mullet	"	Oct. 27, 1863, Corunna.	" "
Silas W. Newman	"		
Henry Newman	"	Oct. 29, 1863, "	Mustered out at Detroit, Sept. 2, 1865.
James A. Newman	"	Feb. 9, 1864, Jackson.	" Macon, Ga., Aug. 17, 1865.
Nelson Norton	"	Oct. [30, 1863, Kalamazoo.	" Jackson, Mich., Aug. 30, 1865.

Name	Rank	Date	Place	Notes
Anson Olmsted	Private.	Oct. 23, 1861,	Georgetown.	Re-enlisted Jan. 5, '64; corp., must'd out at Macon,Ga., Aug. 17, '65.
Charles Olmstead	"	Oct. 28, 1863,	Kalamazoo.	Mustered out at Camp Chase, Ohio, June 23, 1865.
Henry Osgood	"	Nov. 17, 1863,	Pontiac.	Mustered out at Macon, Ga., Aug 17, 1865.
Owen Otto	"	Oct. 29, 1863,	Corunna.	" " " " "
Henry Parker	"	"	Kalamazoo.	" Nashville, Tenn., May 13, 1865.
Henry A. Parker	"	Oct. 31, 1863,	Grand Rapids.	" Louisville, Ky., July 25, 1865.
W. B. Pack	"			Discharged at Corinth, Miss., Sept. 7, 1862.
Edward Pennell	"	Nov. 21, 1863,	Pontiac.	Mustered out at Macon, Ga., Aug. 17, 1865.
James E. Pennell	"			Missing in action at Shoal Creek, Ala., Nov. 5, 1864.
Joseph Perry	"	Nov. 14, 1863,	Pontiac.	Mustered out at Macon, Ga., Aug. 17, 1865.
Charles V. Pierce	"	Sept. 1, 1864,	Jackson.	" Louisville, Ky., July 15, 1865.
William J. Piper	"	Dec. 7, 1863,	"	Mustered out at Macon, Ga., Aug. 17, 1865.
Reuben M Price	"	Oct. 7, 1861,	Tuscola.	Discharged for disability March 18. 1862.
Marion Renniff	"	Oct. 27, 1863,	Kalamazoo.	Mustered out at Macon, Ga., Aug. 17, 1865.
John S. Riggs	"	Nov. 6, 1863,	Grand Rapids.	" " " " "
Andrew Rousseau	"	Nov. 18, 1863,	Detroit.	....
Robert S. Redwood	"	Nov. 19, 1863,	Pontiac.	Transferred to V. R. C. Feb. 15, 1865.
John Rutledge	"	Oct. 28, 1863,	Grand Rapids.	" April 30, 1864.
William B. Sawers	"	Nov. 14, 1863,	Detroit.	Mustered out at Macon, Ga., Aug. 17, 1865.
Chandler Scott	"			" " " " "
Douglas Scott	"	Sept. 3, 1861,		{ Missing in action at Booneville, Miss., July 1, 1862; discharged for disability at Washington, Dec. 13, 1862.
Frank Schrader	"	Nov. 7, 1863,	Pontiac.	Mustered out at Macon, Ga., Aug. 17, 1865.
Amos Smith	"	Nov. 20, 1863,	"	" Detroit, May 15, 1865.
George Smith	"	Dec. 9, 1863,	Detroit.	Corporal; mustered out at Macon, Ga., Aug. 17, 1865.
Roswell Squiers	"	Sept. 1, 1864,	Jackson.	Mustered out at Edgefield, Tenn., June 21, 1865.
James R. Stevens	"	Aug. 28, 1861,	Kalamazoo.	{ Transferred from Co. M., Jan. 1, 1862; discharged for disability March 8, 1862.
William Stagg	"	Nov. 14, 1863,	Jackson.	Mustered out at Macon, Ga., Aug. 17, 1865.
Jesse Thorp	"	Sept. 13, 1861,	Port Huron.	Discharged for disability at St. Louis, Mo., March 3, 1862.
William Thomas	"	Nov. 30, 1863,	Pontiac.	Mustered out at Macon, Ga., Aug. 17, 1865.
Hiram Tibbetts	"	Oct. 23, 1861,	Georgetown.	{ Transferred to V. R. C. Sept. 1863; transferred back March 14, 1864; mustered out at Nashville, Tenn., Oct. 22, 1864.
William Walin	"	Nov. 25, 1863,	Pontiac.	Mustered out at Macon, Ga., Aug. 17, 1865.
Henry W. Walker	"	Oct. 1, 1861,	Clinton.	Re-enlisted Jan. 5, 1864; promoted Reg. Q. M. Serg. Nov. 1, 1864.
Stafford D. Weller	"	Aug. 18, 1862,	Grand Rapids.	Died at Lebanon, Ky., Nov. 10, 1862.

Co. I. NAME.	RANK.	ENTERED SERVICE.	REMARKS.
Co. I.			
Charles H. Goodale	Captain.	Aug. 24, 1861, Kalamazoo.	Resigned May 17, 1863.
Milo W. Barrows	"	Aug. 26, 1861, "	" May 27, 1863.
George S. Hodges	"	Sept. 21, 1861, Galesburg.	Mustered out Dec. 26, 1864, died since leaving the service.
Samuel N. Robertson	"	Sept. 21, 1861, Hillsdale.	" Aug. 17, 1865.
Milo W. Barrows	1st Lieut.	Aug. 26, 1861, Kalamazoo.	Promoted Captain May 17, 1862.
George S. Hodges	"	Sept. 12, 1861, Galesburg.	" May 27, 1863.
John Robinson	"	Sept. 12, 1861, Kankakee.	Resigned Oct. 7, 1864.
Frank H. Eaton	"		" March 27, 1865.
Joseph Palmer	"	Sept. 17, 1861, Grand Rapids.	Mustered out Aug. 17, 1865.
George S. Hodges	2d Lieut.	Aug. 26, 1861, Galesburg.	Promoted 1st Lieut. May 17, 1862.
John Robinson	"	Sept. 12, 1861, Kankakee.	" May 27, 1863.
Simeon T. Dickinson	"	Sept. 13, 1861, Gr'nd Rapids.	" Co. E, March 1, 1864.
Marvin H. Creager	"	Aug. 30, 1861, Galesburg.	Transferred to Co. F.
Alonzo W. McCarty	1st Sergeant.	Sept. 11, 1861, Galesburg.	Resigned March 28, 1865.
John Robinson	Q'm'r Serg't.	Sept. 12, 1861, Kankakee.	Appointed 2d Lieut. Sept. 19, 1862.
Ami A. Brown	"	Aug. 26, 1861, Galesburg.	Promoted Q. M. Sergeant March 29, 1864.
Frank H. Lamkin	"	Sept. 11, 1861, Paw Paw.	Died in camp near Booneville, Miss, June 30, 1862.
Oscar Caldwell	"	Sept. 1, 1861, Cooper.	Discharged for disability at Farmington, Miss., May 18, 1862.
Alonzo W. McCarty	"	Sept. 11, 1861, Galesburg.	Re-enlisted Jan. 5, 1864; appointed 2d Lieut. Sept. 24, 1864.
Gilbert Mitchell	"	Sept. 13, 1861, Kalamazoo.	" appointed 1st Lieut. Co. L, Feb. 20,1865.
George L. Stuart	Corporal.	Sept. 7, 1861, Texas.	" serg.; discharged May 17, 1865.
Alonzo Mapes	"	Sept. 3, 1861, Martin.	{ sick in hospital at Nashville, Tenn., at muster out.
George Stannard	"	Sept. 15, 1861, Galesburg.	
Joseph Lindsley	"	" 1861, Otsego.	Discharged for disability at Detroit, July 31, 1862.
Francisco Barrett	"	Sept. 5, 1861, Galesburg.	
Daniel W. Parsons	"	" 1861, "	Unaccounted for.
Abraham Jones	"	Sept. 15, 1861, Grand Rapids.	Re-enlisted Jan. 5, '64; sergt, must'd out at Macon, Ga., Aug.17,'65.
Milford Vosburgh	"	Sept. 4, 1861, Galesburg.	" wag'r; must'd out at Macon,Ga., Aug. 17,'65.
Silas B. Taintor	Musician.	Sept. 12, 1861, Kalamazoo.	{ on detached service with 136th U. S. C. T. at muster out.
Charles H. Bronson	"	" Galesburg.	Re-enlisted Jan. 5, 1864; mustered out at Macon, Ga, Aug. 17, '65.
Franklin T. Edgerly	Farrier.	Sept. 2, 1861, Alamo.	Discharged for disability Dec. 11, 1862.
Horace Cross	"	Sept. 25, 1861, Kalamazoo.	" Feb. 17, 1862.

Name	Rank	Enlisted	Place	Remarks
Augustus House	Saddler	Sept. 5, 1861	Pavillion	Died in hospital at Stevenson, Ala., Sept. 1, 1863.
Walter Guile	Wagoner	Sept. 13, 1861	Galesburg	
Franklin Austin	Private	Sept. 6, 1861	Orangeville	Transferred to V. R. C. Nov. 15, 1863.
Robert Bols	"	Aug. 27, 1861	Augusta	Re-enlisted Jan. 5, '64; far'r; must'd out at Macon, Ga., Aug. 17, '65.
Albert Brewer	"	Sept. 20, 1861	Holland	Discharged for disability at St. Louis, Mo., March 23, 1862.
William A. Buck	"	Aug. 26, 1861	Galesburg	Discharged for disability Sept. 2, 1862.
John Bughee	"	Oct. 10, 1861	Orangeville	Died at Benton Barracks, Mo., Feb. 13, 1862.
Leonard Cambout	"	Sept. 20, 1861	Holland	Discharged for disability April 1, 1863.
Mortimer Crittenden	"	Aug. 26, 1861	Battle Creek	" Aug. 15, 1862.
William Crittenden	"	Sept. 28, 1861	"	Re-enlisted Jan. 5, '64; corp.; must'd out at Macon, Ga., Aug. 17, '65.
William L. Curtiss	"	Sept. 6, 1861	Detroit	Discharged for disability Oct. 4, 1862.
Wesley G. Clapp	"	Sept. 12, 1861	Battle Creek	Mustered out at Nashville, Tenn., Oct. 22, 1864.
William Carpenter	"		Kalamazoo	Missing in action at Dandridge, Tenn., Dec. 24, 1863; died in Andersonville prison, March 17, 1864.
James E. Cummings	"		Augusta	Re-enlisted Jan. 5, 1864; mustered out at Macon, Ga., Aug. 17, '65.
Myron S. Cook	"	Sept. 15, 1861	Prairieville	Transferred to V. R. C., March 13, 1864.
Jerome C. Chadwick	"	Sept. 13, 1861	Kalamazoo	Discharged for disability at Franklin, Tenn., May 23, 1863.
Joseph D. Crane	"	Sept. 11, 1861	"	Re-enlisted Jan. 5, '64; mustered out at Macon, Ga., Aug. 17, '65.
John M. Colwell	"	Oct. 15, 1861	Wheatland	Died of typhoid fever at Rienzi, Miss., Aug. 13, 1862.
George R. Davy	"	Sept. 26, 1861	Battle Creek	Discharged for disability July 3, 1862.
Ellie Ellickson	"	Sept. 20, 1861	Holland	Re-enlisted Jan. 5, 1864; must'd out at Macon, Ga., Aug. 17, 1865.
Charlemagne Francis	"	Sept. 7, 1861	Texas	Sergeant; mustered out at Nashville, Tenn., Oct. 22, 1864.
Abel B. Fowler	"	Oct. 10, 1861	Kalamazoo	Discharged for disability Nov. 7, 1862.
Munson Gage	"	Sept. 6, 1861	Climax	Mustered out at Nashville, Tenn., Oct. 22, 1864.
Joseph Gage	"	Sept. 15, 1861	"	Re-enlisted Jan. 5, 1864; mustered out at Detroit, July 1, 1865.
Richard Haffenden	"	Sept. 23, 1861	Prairieville	Re-enlisted Jan. 5, '64; mustered out at Macon, Ga., Aug. 17, '65.
Robert M. Harvey	"	Sept. 4, 1861	Dearborn	Mustered out at Nashville, Tenn., Oct. 22, 1864.
Seth W. Hoag	"	Aug. 26, 1861	Galesburg	Re-enlisted Jan. 5, 1864; muster'd out at Macon, Ga., Aug. 17, '65.
Charles E. Hope	"	Sept. 5, 1861	Texas	Mustered out at Nashville, Tenn., Oct. 22, 1864.
William C. Hildreth	"	Sept. 17, 1861	Wyoming	Discharged for disability May 17, 1862.
Highland H. Honeywell	"	Sept. 25, 1861	Prairieville	Corporal; mustered out at Nashville, Tenn., Oct. 22, 1864.
John Hending	"	Sept. 5, 1861	Kalamazoo	Discharged for disability at Stevenson, Ala., July 6, 1863.
Asa Harmon	"	Sept. 15, 1861	Paw Paw	Unaccounted for.
Leonard Herrington	"	Sept. 7, 1861	Saugatuck	Re-enlisted Jan. 5, '64; sad'l'r.; must'd out at Macon, Ga., Aug. 17, '65.
Smith Jones	"	Sept. 1, 1861	Augusta	Re-enlisted Jan. 5, '64; far'r; must'd out at Macon, Ga., Aug. 17, '65.
George Kershaw	"	Sept. 23, 1861	Prairieville	Mustered out at Nashville, Tenn., Oct. 22, 1864.
Alonzo Kidder	"	Sept. 28, 1861	Galesburg	Discharged for disability April 21, 1862.

Co. I.

NAME.	RANK.	ENTERED SERVICE.	REMARKS.
Henry Linzo	Private.	Oct. 10, 1861, Galesburg.	Discharged at Detroit, Oct. 3, 1864.
Reuben R. Lamkin	"	Sept. 25, 1861, Paw Paw.	Died at Nashville, Tenn., March 29, 1863, of w'ds rec'd in action.
Maxson Lewis	"	Sept. 28, 1861, Galesburg.	Re-enlisted Jan. 5, '64; mustered out at Detroit, July 25, 1865.
Franklin H. Lewis	"	Sept. 10, 1861, Texas.	Died of typhoid fever at Farmington, Miss., July 13, 1862.
Friend M. Meyers	"	Sept. 2, 1861, ...	{ Missing in action at Blackland, June 24, 1862; discharged at Detroit, Oct. 3, 1864.
William Manning	"	Sept. 23, 1861, Augusta.	Discharged for disability March 21, 1862.
Jeremiah Mahoney	"	Sept. 3, 1861, Dearborn.	Re-enlisted Jan.5,'64; corp.; must'd out at Detroit, June 30, 1865.
Reuben G. Martin	"	Sept. 15, 1861, Galesburg.	Discharged for disability at N. Albany, Ind. Aug. 5, 1863.
Lewis H. McGin	"	Sept. 7, 1861, Texas.	St. Louis, Sept. 19. 1863.
Adelbert L. Pond	"	Sept. 23, 1861, Galesburg.	Detroit, May 16, 1863.
Samuel Peer	"	Sept. 3, 1861, Augusta.	" " Dec. 10, 1862.
Reuben Page	"	Sept. 4, 1861, Texas.	" " Oct. 2, 1862.
Ebenezer Page	"	Sept. 10, 1861, "	" " Dec. 12, 1862.
Daniel P. Rice	"	Sept. 19, 1861, Leroy.	" " Nov. 10, 1862.
Daniel P. Randall	"	.........., Galesburg.	Unaccounted for.
Elam W. Reynolds	"	Aug. 28, 1861, Orangeville.	Re-enlisted Jan. 5, '64; killed in action near Salem, Ala. Ap.1,'65.
Eli Russell	"	Sept. 23, 1861, Comstock.	Re-enlisted Jan.5, '64; corp.; must'd out at Macon, Ga., Aug.17,'65.
Stillman Shepard	"	Sept. 21, 1861, Ganges.	Unaccounted for.
George Smith	"	Sept. 28, 1861, Gainesville.	Died in Michigan, May 30, 1862, while on furlough.
Horace Skutt	"	" " Galesburg.	Re-enlisted Jan. 5, '64; mustered out at Macon, Ga., Aug. 17, '65.
Joseph B. Sawyer	"	Oct. 15, 1861, Gainesville.	" " serg.; " " " "
Clark P. Tabor	"	Sept. 13, 1861, Kalamazoo.	Discharged for disability at Franklin, Tenn., May 23, 1863.
Nelson Thompson	"	Oct. 10, 1861, "	Transferred to V. R. C., March 2, 1864.
James M. Vose	"	Sept. 13, 1861, Galesburg.	Re-enlisted Jan. 5,1864: serg.; must'd out at Macon,Ga.,Aug.17,'65.
Walter W. Vansicklar	"	Aug. 26, 1861, Galesburg.	{ on detached service with 136th U. S. C.
Samuel N. Woodman	"	Sept. 15, 1861, Prairieville.	T., at muster out.
Joseph Winans	"	Sept. 14, 1861, Galesburg.	....
Samuel Winans	"	Oct. 10, 1861, "	Sergeant; mustered out at Nashville, Tenn., Oct. 22, 1864.
RECRUITS.			
John H. Adams	"	Sept. 2, 1862, Grand Rapids.	{ Transferred to V. R. C., March 2, 1864; mustered out at Annapolis, Md., July 27, 1865.
Almond D. Austin	"	..........,	Discharged for disability at St. Louis, Mo., July 8, 1865.

Thomas D. Ayers	Private.	Nov. 5, 1863, Pontiac.	Discharged at Nashville, Tenn., Sept. 3, 1865.
Paul M. Blake	"	Sept. 1, 1862, Kalamazoo.	Mustered out at Nashville, Tenn., June 8, 1865.
Silas S. Butler	"	Nov. 2, 1863, Jackson.	Discharged for disability Oct. 22, 1864.
Samuel Busson	"	Nov. 8, 1863, Pontiac.	" at Detroit, March 10, 1865.
Reuben A. Butler	"		Mustered out at Nashville, Tenn., Oct. 22, 1864.
Alphonzo Case	"	Nov. 7, 1863, Jackson.	" Macon, Ga., Aug. 17, 1865.
Giles Collins	"	Aug. 14, 1862, Kalamazoo.	Discharged for disability at Louisville, Ky., Oct. 2, 1863.
Homer Cross	"		Benton Barracks, Mo., Feb. 23, 1862.
William Congdon	"	Aug. 15, 1862, Texas, Mich.	Mustered out at Edgefield, Tenn., June 21, 1865
William H. Dutcher	"	Nov. 7, 1863, Jackson.	Died of typhoid fever at Nashville, Tenn., Sept. 17, 1864.
John Dubois	"	Pontiac.	Transferred to V. R. C., April 3, 1865.
Frank Fallman	"	Aug. 24, 1862, Kalamazoo.	Died of throat disease at Dansville, Ky., Aug. 20, 1863.
William Fesenden	"	Aug. 13, 1862, "	Died of disease at Stevenson, Ala., Nov. 2, 1863.
Martin Forward	"	Nov. 4, 1863, Pontiac.	Mustered out at Louisville, Ky., June 6, 1865.
John Galliger	"	Oct. 27, 1863, Kalamazoo.	Transferred to V. R. C., April 22, 1864; discharged Aug. 14, '65.
Henry Gardner	"	Aug. 31, 1864, Jackson.	Mustered out at Edgefield, Tenn., June 21, 1865.
George T. Gardner	"		"
James N. Gilbert	"	Aug. 24, 1864, Kalamazoo.	"
Harrison Gleim	"	Aug. 8, 1862, St. Louis, Mo.	Transferred Asst. Adjutant-General to Gen. Hamilton.
John Grunsden	"	Nov. 4, 1863, Pontiac.	Mustered out at Macon, Ga., Aug. 17, 1865.
James C. Graham	"	Nov. 6, 1863, Corunna.	"
Nathaniel Harrington	"	Nov. 10, 1863, Grand Rapids.	"
James H. Hayes	"	Nov. 14, 1863, Pontiac.	Mustered out at Jackson, Mich., Aug. 31, 1865.
Samuel M. Holmes	"	Aug. 12, 1862, Prairieville.	Discharged for disability April 9, 1864.
Samuel Horne	"	Dec. 19, 1863, Eagle.	" at Nashville, Tenn., April 9, 1864.
John Hughes	"	Nov. 16, 1863, Pontiac.	Transferred to V. R. C. Feb.15,'65; must'd out at Detroit, Aug.15, '65.
Franklin Jones	"	Nov. 9, 1863, "	
Charles Jones	"	Nov. 4, 1863, "	
Adam Littlejohn	"	Dec. 1, 1863, "	Re-enlisted Jan.5, '64; serg.; must'd out at Macon, Ga., Aug. 17, '65.
William Light	"	Oct. 27, 1863, Grand Rapids.	Mustered out at Macon, Ga., Aug. 17, 1865.
George W. Mallory	"	Nov. 4, 1863, Jackson.	"
Raymond Mather	"	Nov. 2, 1861, "	"
Thomas Meaker	"	Nov. 1, 1861, St. Louis, Mo.	Nashville, Tenn., Oct. 22, 1865.
Perry Manning	"	Nov. 18, 1863, Grand Rapids.	Detroit, July 6, 1865.
Ramire Mapes	"	Nov. 9, 1863, Jackson.	Macon, Ga., Aug. 17, 1865.
Henry Mitchell	"	Nov. 7, 1863, Pontiac.	Absent sick at muster out.
Henry Moon	"	Nov. 4, 1863, Jackson.	Died of fever at Chattanooga, Tenn., in hospital, July 5, 1864.

Co. I. NAME.	RANK.	ENTERED SERVICE.	REMARKS.
Frank M. Osgood	Private.	Aug. 26, 1862, Kalamazoo.	Corporal; discharged May 23, 1865.
Ebenezer Page, Jr	"	Sept. 12, 1861, Texas.	Discharged for disability Oct. 7, 1862.
Wilson Pangburn	"	Aug. 18, 1864, Jackson.	Mustered out at Edgefield, Tenn., June 21, 1865.
Charles H. Pease	"	Nov. 7, 1863, Pontiac.	Died of disease at Brighton, Mich., Oct. 13, '64; while on furlough.
Thomas E. Pilcher	"	Nov. 10, 1861, St. Louis.	Discharged for disability at St. Louis, Mo., Nov. 1, 1863.
Charles E. Plant	"	Dec. 28, 1863, Grand Rapids.	Sick in hospital at Detroit at muster out.
Charles Randall	"		Mustered out at Nashville, Tenn., Oct. 22, 1864.
Thomas Randall	"		Mustered out Oct. 28, 1864.
Alfred Rex	"	Sept. 19, 1861, Galesburg.	Taken prisoner at Shoal Creek, Ala., Nov. 5, 1864.
Adolphus Rickett	"	Aug. 24, 1864, Kalamazoo.	Mustered out at Nashville, Tenn., Oct. 22, 1864.
Artemus Richards	"	Dec. 1, 1861, St. Louis, Mo.	" Louisville, Ky., June 10, 1865.
Theophilus Rose	"	Sept. 1, 1864, Jackson.	
Orin M. Rogers	"	Nov. 4, 1863, "	
Henry Rowe	"	Jan. 5, 1864, "	Mustered out at Detroit, Aug. 8, 1865.
Silas B. Sperry	"	Dec. 12, 1863, "	" Macon, Ga., Aug. 17, 1865.
George L. Stephens	"	Nov. 5, 1863, Pontiac.	" Detroit, Sept. 7, 1865.
John Stetson	"	Aug. 24, 1864, Kalamazoo.	Transferred to Co. A, Dec. 7, 1864.
Charles M. Talmage	"	Sept. 1, 1864, Jackson.	Mustered out at Edgefield, Tenn., June 21, 1865.
John C. Thorp	"	Aug. 6, 1862, Kalamazoo.	" Nashville, Tenn., May 29, 1865.
Edwin Townsend	"	Aug. 18, 1862, "	Discharged for disability at Lebanon, Ky., April 18, 1863.
James Tomkiel	"	Sept. 1, 1862, "	Mustered out at Nashville, Tenn., June 3, 1865.
Henry Travis	"	Oct. 30, 1863, Pontiac.	" Macon, Ga., Aug. 17, 1865.
John F. Tuttle	"	Nov. 25, 1863, Grand Rapids.	" Louisville, Ky., June 13, 1865.
George N. Wheeler	"	Aug. 31, 1864, Jackson.	Absent sick at muster out.
Richard Wheeler	"	Nov. 5, 1863, "	Died of disease at Knoxville, Tenn., May 14, 1864.
John Woodman	"	Nov. 9, 1863, Pontiac.	Mustered out at Edgefield, Tenn., June 21, 1865.
Co. K.		Sept. 1, 1862, Kalamazoo.	
Archibald P. Campbell	Captain.	Sept. 12, 1861, Port Huron.	Promoted Lieut. Col. July 18, 1862.
Thomas W. Johnston	"	Aug. 24, 1861, Marshall.	Transferred Captain Co. M, March 13, 1863.
Charles N. Baker	"	Sept. 2, 1861, Port Huron.	Mustered out Aug. 17, 1865.
Moses R. Smith	1st Lieut.	"	Resigned June 8, 1862.
Marshall P. Thatcher	"	"	Promoted Captain Co. B, March 1, 1864.
Henry H. Sanborn	"	"	
George Buchanan	"	"	Mustered out Aug. 17, 1865.
Marshall P. Thatcher	2d Lieut.	"	Promoted 1st Lieut. June 8, 1862.

Name	Rank	Enlisted	From	Remarks
F. Byron Cutler	2d Lieut.	Sept. 14, 1861,	North Adams.	Transferred 2d Lieut. Co. G, Sept. 19, 1862.
Charles N. Baker	"	Sept. 2, 1861,	Port Huron.	Promoted Captain Oct. 16, 1862.
James H. Smith	"	"	"	Transferred 2d Lieut. Co. G, June 1, 1863.
Harry H. Sanborn	"	"	"	Promoted 1st Lieut. March 1, 1864.
Erastus W. Lawrence	"	"	Grand Rapids.	Transferred Regimental Commissary, Sept. 20, 1862.
George Bowen	1st Sergeant.	Sept. 7, 1861,	"	Resigned Nov. 19, 1864.
John Davidson	Q'm'r Serg't.	Sept. 2, 1861,	Port Huron.	Discharged for disability at Detroit, June 11, 1862.
Harry H. Sanborn	"	"	"	Apppointed 2d Lieut. May 29, 1863.
James H. Smith	"	"	"	Oct. 16, 1862.
Joseph Armstrong	"	"	"	Discharged for disability at Detroit, Oct. 2, 1862.
George Buchanan	"	"	"	Re-enlisted Jan. 5, 1864; appointed 1st Lieut. April 9, 1864.
Noah T. Farr	"	"	"	Discharged for disability at Detroit, Aug. 8, 1862.
Henry Kingsley	Corporal.	Sept. 10, 1861,	"	Benton Barracks, Feb. 19, 1862.
William H. Tallman	"	Sept. 26, 1861,	"	Re-enlisted Jan. 5, '64; promoted sergeant major July 26, 1862.
Horace Plaisted	"	Sept. 2, 1861,	"	" serg.; must'd out at Macon, Ga., Aug. 17, '65.
James Lewis	"	"	"	
William Cole	"	"	"	Discharged for disability at Detroit, Aug. 30, 1862.
Anthony Cline	"	"	"	
Solomon Bean	"	"	"	Discharged for disability at Detroit, Sept. 26, 1862.
Samuel McMillan	"	"	"	Died of disease at Nashville, Jan. —, 1864.
Wenzel Euting	Musician.	Sept. 14, 1861,	"	Supposed to have fallen overboard at Cairo, April, 1862.
Adolphus Lang	"	Sept. 2, 1861,	"	Mustered out at Detroit, Sept. 7, 1865.
John Ashley	Farrier.	"	"	Mustered out at Nashville, Tenn., Oct. 22, 1864.
Samuel B. Carl	"	"	"	Appointed 2d Lieut. 7th Mich. Cav., March 2, 1863.
Robert D. Hill	Wagoner.	"	"	Died at St. Louis, Mo., Feb. 19, 1862.
Charles Ambrook	Saddler.	"	"	Promoted hospital steward in regular army.
Benjamin Allen	Private.	"	"	Died at New Madrid, Mo., March 23, 1862.
Charles N. Baker	"	"	"	2d Lieut. Sept. 19, 1862; promoted from 1st sergeant.
Wesley Brown	"	"	"	Re-enlisted Jan. 5, 1864.
Charles Brockway	"	"	"	" must'd out at Macon, Ga., Aug. 17, 1865.
Mark Beach	"	"	"	" accid'ly kil'd at Carter Creek, June 19, '64.
Henry Burnham	"	"	"	Discharged for disability Sept. 9, 1862.
Franklin Barker	"	"	"	Re-enlisted Jan. 5, '64; sergeant; missing in action at Shoal Creek, Ala., Oct. 30, 1864; must'd out at Detroit, July 19, '65.
William Craig	"	"	"	Died at Scraggs Farm, Tenn., Jan. —, 1865, of gunshot wound.
John Chambers	"	"	"	Re-enlisted Jan. 5, '64; mustered out at Macon, Ga., Aug. 17, '65.
Samuel Campbell	"	Sept. 20, 1861,	"	

9

Co. K.

NAME.	RANK.	ENTERED SERVICE.	REMARKS.
Lego Cook	Private.	Sept. 20, 1861, Port Huron.	Died near Corinth, Miss., June 13, 1862.
Iris Everts	"	Sept. 2, 1861, "	Died at Jeffersonville, Ind., Oct. 25, 1862.
William H. Edmison	"	Sept. 20, 1861, "	Discharged for disability at New Madrid, Mo., April 10, 1862.
Alexander Edmison	"	"	Re-enlisted Jan. 5, 1864.
Daniel Fleming	"	Sept. 2, 1861, "	Re-enlisted Jan. 5, '64; corp.; must'd out at Macon, Ga., Aug. 17, '65.
William Fry	"	Sept. 20, 1861, "	" died at Shoal Creek, Ala., Oct. 30, 1864 of wounds received in action.
Joseph Gamble	"	"	Re-enlisted Jan. 5, '64; mustered out at Detroit, Aug. 16, 1865.
Nathaniel Henry	"	Sept. 2, 1861, "	" " Macon, Ga., Aug. 17, '65.
Joseph Hiptenberger	"	"	Died at Rienzi, Miss., Aug. 11, 1862.
Archer B. Hunter	"	"	Re-enlisted Jan. 5, '64; serg.; must'd out at Macon, Ga., Aug. 17, '65.
Charles Hayward	"	Sept. 20, 1861, "	Died near Farmington, Miss., July 3, 1862.
Calvin M. Hayward	"	"	" " July 5, 1862.
Jerome Inman	"	Oct. 2, 1861, Grand Rapids.	Re-enlisted Jan. 5, '64; mustered out at Macon, Ga., Aug. 17, '65.
Samuel Jacobs	"	Sept. 2, 1861, Port Huron.	" " " "
James Jewell	"	Sept. 20, 1861, "	Mustered out at Nashville, Tenn., Oct. 22, 1864.
Jackson Kimball	"	Sept. 2, 1861, "	
Andrew Kitchen	"	"	Re-enlisted Jan. 5, '64; serg.; mus'd out at Macon, Ga., Aug. 17, '65.
John Lang	"	"	
Levi Lewis	"	"	Discharged at Winchester, Tenn., Nov. 16, 1863.
Elisha Lewis	"	Sept. 10, 1861, "	Died of disease at Murfreesboro, March 25, 1863.
Columbus Lewis	"	Sept. 26, 1861, "	Re-enlisted Jan. 5, '64; mustered out at Macon, Ga., Aug. 17, 1865
Shepherd Lee	"	"	Discharged at St. Louis, Sept. 19, 1862.
Ferdinando D. Loop	"	"	Re-enlisted Jan. 5, 1864; mustered out at Macon, Ga., Aug. 17, 1865.
John Leonard	"	Oct. 7, 1861, "	Died at Rienzi, Miss., July 7, 1862.
Absalom Lewis	"	Sept. 20, 1861, "	Died at Lexington, Mich.,
James Lewis	"	Oct. 2, 1861, "	Discharged for disability
Sanford Mills	"	"	Re-enlisted Jan. 5, '64; must'd out at Macon, Ga., Aug. 17, 1865.
Charles Moak	"	"	" corp.; must'd out at Macon, Ga., Aug. 17, '65.
Charles P. Mills	"	Sept. 20, 1861, "	" serg.; must'd out at Macon, Ga., Aug. 17, '65.
Diogenes Mallory	"	"	" corp.; must'd out at Macon, Ga., Aug. 17, '65.
Augustus Menkee	"	"	" must'd out at Macon, Ga., Aug. 17, 1865.
John F. Myres	"	"	" died in hospital at Detroit, Sept. 15, 1864.
George J. Millard	"	"	" must'd out at Macon, Ga., Aug. 17, 1865.
George Mann	"	Sept. 2, 1861, "	" corp.; must'd out at Macon, Ga., Aug. 17, '65.

Name	Rank	Date, Place	Remarks
Nathan Magoonaugh	Private.	Sept. 2, 1861, Port Huron.	Re-enlisted Jan. 5, '64; mustered out at Macon, Ga., Aug. 17, '65.
Robt. K. M. McCulloch	"	"	bl'ksm.; must'd out at Macon, Ga., Aug. 17, '65.
Ronald R. McDonald	"	Oct. 10, 1861, Detroit.	Discharged for disability July 20, 1862.
George Parker	"	Sept. 2, 1861, Port Huron.	Re-enlisted Jan. 5, '64; mustered out at Macon, Ga., Aug. 17, '65.
Jacob Rohr	"	Sept. 20, 1861, "	" " "
Adam Reid	"	"	farr'r; " "
William Robinson	"	"	
Joseph H. Smith	"	Sept. 2, 1861, "	Discharged for disability July 23, 1862.
Lyman Stephen	"	Sept. 20, 1861, "	Died of disease at Rienzi, Miss, July 8, 1862.
James Sanders	"	"	Re-enlisted Jan. 5, '64; serg.; must'd out at Macon, Ga., Aug. 17, '65.
William J. Spencer	"	"	
Benjamin Teeple	"	Sept. 12, 1861, "	Discharged for disability Aug. 23, 1862.
Joseph Utley	"	Sept. 20, 1861, "	Re-enlisted Jan. 5, 1864; mustered out at Detroit, Aug. 30, 1865.
Nelson Utley	"	Sept. 12, 1861, "	
George Vanorman	"	"	Discharged at St. Louis, Oct. 18, 1862.
William Valentine	"	Sept. 2, 1861, "	Discharged for disability at Detroit, Sept. 15, 1863.
Amos Wiggins	"	Sept. 12, 1861, "	Re-enlisted Jan. 5, '64; mustered out at Macon, Ga., Aug. 17, '65.
Robert Wixon	"	"	Detroit, Aug. 30, 1865.
Joseph B. Wixon	"	Sept. 27, 1861, "	Reported died at Burchville, Mich., July 2, 1862; reported discharged for disability
Henry Welch	"	Sept. 2, 1861, "	Discharged for disability at Detroit, July 17, 1862.
Amos C. Welch	"	Sept. 10, 1861, "	Re-enlisted Jan. 5, '64; serg.; must'd out at Macon, Ga., Aug. 17, '65.
Aaron Winchester	"	"	Discharged for disability June 26, 1862.
Alonzo Worden	"	Sept. 20, 1861, "	Re-enlisted Jan. 5, 1864; died at Macon, Ga., June 30, '65, of w'ds.
George Washburn	"	"	must'd out at Jackson, Mich., Aug. 31, '65.
Hiram Wetherall	"	"	kil'd in ac'n at Shoal Cr'k, Ala., Oct. 30, '64.
Abraham Walker	"	Oct. 4, 1863, "	
William Whalin	"	Sept. 20, 1861, "	Re-enlisted Jan. 5, '64; corp.; must'd out at Macon, Ga., Aug. 17, '65.

RECRUITS.

Name	Rank	Date, Place	Remarks
John Armsberger	Private.	Nov. 2, 1863, Grand Rapids.	Mustered out at Macon, Ga., Aug. 17, 1865.
M. Blood	"	Oct. 7, 1862, Hillsdale.	Tranferred to Co. D, June 16, 1863.
William Brotherton	"	Nov. 4, 1863, Grand Rapids.	Mustered out at Macon, Ga., Aug. 17, 1865
Michael Brown	"	"	"
Michael Brennan	"	Nov. 25, 1863, Pontiac.	Transferred to V.R.C., Jan. 6, 1865; disch'd for disab'ty July 13, '65.
Ervin Brown	"	Mar. 27, 1864, Jackson.	Mustered out at Indianapolis, Ind., May 19, 1865.
George Burger	"	Jan. 4, 1864, Grand Rapids.	Absent sick since June, 1865, at muster out.
Henry Cain	"	Nov. 4, 1863, Jackson.	Mustered out at Jackson, Aug. 31, 1865.

Co. K. NAME.	RANK.	ENTERED SERVICE.	REMARKS.
Lewis Chappell	Private.	Feb. 18, 1864, E. Saginaw.	Mustered out at Nashville, Tenn., May 21, 1865.
William Collins	"	Nov. 9, 1863, Pontiac.	Absent sick at Detroit since Dec. 1, 1863, at muster out.
Joseph Creamer	"	Feb. 29, 1864, St. Clair.	Mustered out at Macon, Ga., Aug. 17, 1865.
Stephen Curran	"	Aug. 8, 1864, Pontiac.	" " St. Louis, Mo., Jan. 9, 1865.
John W. Dell	"	Feb. 9, 1864, St. Clair.	Died of disease at Nashville, Tenn., July 14, 1864.
Christopher Deitz	"	Nov. 27, 1864, Jackson.	Mustered out July 12, 1865.
Stephen Dillingham	"	Aug 5, 1862, Kalamazoo.	Sergeant; drowned in North River, Ala., April 9, 1865.
Spencer Eaton	"	Jan. 30, 1864, Pontiac.	Mustered out June 25, 1865.
Stephen Erwin	"		Discharged June 6, 1865.
Michael Folts	"	Feb. 23, 1864, St. Clair.	Mustered out at Macon, Ga., Aug. 17, 1865.
James Freeman	"	Nov. 3, 1863, Kalamazoo.	" "
Ira Garfield	"	Aug. 8, 1862, "	Discharged for disability May 4, 1865.
Robert C. Gamble	"	Feb. 23, 1864, Pontiac.	Died at Jeffersonville, Ind., Jan. 14, '65, of w'nds rec'd in action.
Samuel Gassaway	"	Nov. 14, 1863, Jackson.	Absent sick at Nashville, since Dec. 12, 1864. at muster out.
Marion C. Harris	"	Oct. 21, 1862, Fayette.	Mustered out at Jackson, Mich., Aug. 31, 1865.
William Hamilton	"	Nov. 18, 1863, Pontiac.	" " Macon, Ga., Aug. 17, 1865.
Wells G. Hickox	"	Nov. 1, 1862, Hillsdale.	" "
Martin Hogan	"	Nov. 11, 1863, Grand Rapids.	" "
Josiah W. Johnston	"	Aug. 14, 1863, Pontiac.	" "
Jesse Jones	"	Feb. 23, 1864, "	" "
Comstock Maples	"	Nov. 1, 1862, Hillsdale.	Died of disease at Louisville, Ky., Dec. 13, 1861.
Charles Mapes	"	Feb. 9, 1864, Corunna.	" " Nashville, Tenn., Nov. 15, 1864.
Thomas McCutcheon	"	Sept. 8, 1862, Cairo, Ill.	Mustered out at Edgefield, Tenn., June 21, 1865.
William Norvell	"	Nov. 13, 1863, Pontiac.	Mustered out at Macon, Ga., Aug. 17, 1865.
William Reed	"	Feb. 10, 1864, Lexington.	Mustered out at Nashville, Tenn., May 20, 1865.
David H. Rogers	"	Jan. 16, 1864, Hampden.	Mustered out at Macon, Ga., Aug. 17, 1865.
Henry Sales	"	Nov. 13, 1863, Pontiac.	Re-enlisted Jan. 5, 1864; mustered out at Macon, Ga., Aug. 17, '65.
Courtland H. Scott	"	Sept. 6, 1861,	Mustered out at Macon, Ga., Aug. 17, 1865.
Alfred Sheldon	"	Nov. 20, 1863, Pontiac.	Transferred to Co. B.
Otis Shay	"		Mustered out at Macon, Ga., Aug. 17, 1865.
George Shultz	"	Oct. 30, 1863, Corunna.	Transferred to V. R. C.
Robert Slengerland	"	Feb. 7, 1864, Hampton.	Mustered out at Nashville, Tenn., May 16, 1865.
John Smith	"	Nov. 19, 1863, Pontiac.	Died of typhoid fever at Franklin, Tenn., July 29, 1864.
Recompense Smith	"	Nov. 12, 1863, "	Died Dec. 25, 1864, of wounds received in action Dec. 24, 1864.
Joseph Smith	"	Nov. 20, 1863,	

John Snyder	Private.	Oct. 28, 1863, Grand Rapids.	Missing in action at Franklin, Tenn., Nov. 30, 1864; mustered out at Camp Chase, Ohio, June 16, 1865.
Martin Spencer	"	Oct. 29, 1863, Corunna.	Mustered out at Macon, Ga., Aug. 17, 1865.
Abraham Stocker	"	Oct. 31, 1862, Hillsdale.	"
Aaron Stocker	"	Nov. 2, 1862, "	"
Alva Stevens	"	Feb. 23, 1864, Pontiac.	Absent sick since Dec. 12, 1864, at muster out.
John Steel	"	Nov. 13, 1863, Detroit.	Mustered out at Nashville, Tenn., May 25, 1865.
Lewis Strawser	"	Nov. 19, 1863, Pontiac.	Must'd out May 24, '65; mis'g in act'n at Shoal Cr'k, Ala., Aug. 30, '64.
John Sutter	"		Transferred to V. R. C. Dec. 30, 1864.
— Washburne	"	Aug. 29, 1862, Brockway.	Died of disease March 16, 1863.
Lewis Wheelock	"	Oct. 28, 1863, Corunna.	Mustered out at Macon, Ga., Aug. 17, 1865
Austin Winney	"	Nov. 12, 1862, Allen.	Discharged for disability at Louisville, Ky., May 27, 1863.
George W. Youngs	"	Nov. 1, 1862, Hillsdale.	Mustered out at Macon, Ga., Aug. 17, 1865.
Co. L.			
Bezaleel P. Wells	Captain.	Aug. 24, 1861, Niles.	Mustered out Oct. 22, 1864.
Henry M. Hempstead	"	"	Transferred to Co. M.
Richard Williams	"	Sept. 14, 1861, Marshall.	Mustered out Aug. 17, 1865.
Andrew J. Foster	1st Lieut.	Aug. 24, 1861, Niles.	Resigned August 31, 1862.
John H. Hutton	"	"	Resigned April 9, 1864, for disability.
Gilbert Mitchell	"	Sept. 13, 1861, Kalamazoo.	Transferred to 136th U. S. C. T. June 22, 1865.
John H. Hutton	2d Lieut.	Aug. 24, 1861, Niles.	Promoted 1st Lieut. Sept. 9, 1862.
John G. Crawford	"	Sept. 2, 1861, Grand Rapids.	Resigned March 31, 1863.
Joseph N. Stevens	"	Aug. 24, 1861, Niles.	Mustered out Oct. 22, 1864.
Richard Williams	"	Sept. 14, 1861, "	Promoted Captain May 14, 1865.
Joseph N. Stevens	1st Sergeant.	Aug. 24, 1861, "	Appointed 2d Lieut. April 15, 1863.
William P. Thomas	Q'm'r Serg't.	Sept. 12, 1861, "	Died of typhoid fever near Farmington, Miss., June 25, 1862.
Mark A. H. Chipman	"	Sept. 7, 1861, "	Discharged at Franklin, Tenn., April 2, 1863.
William H. Barnhouse	"	Sept. 14, 1861, "	Missing in action near Booneville, Miss., July 1, 1862; returned May 2, 1863, mustered out Oct. 22, 1864.
John Lamoure	"	Sept. 7, 1861, "	Re-enlisted Jan. 5, '64; mustered out at Macon, Ga., Aug. 17, '65.
Jay Blodgett	"	Sept. 16, 1861, "	Discharged at Corinth, Miss., Sept. 11, 1863.
Franklin H. Cross	Corporal.	Sept. 13, 1861, "	Mustered out at Nashville, Tenn., Oct. 22, 1834.
John K. Stark	"	Sept. 17, 1861, "	Discharged for disability at Cairo, Ill., Aug. 14, 1862.
Harvey L. Drew	"	Sept. 16, 1861, "	Transferred to 3d Mich. Cav. Nov. 2, 1861.
Albert P. Anderson	"	Sept. 14, 1861, "	Died July 3, '62, of w'ds rec'd in ac'n near Booneville, Mis., J'ly 1, '62
Orville D. Carlisle	"	Sept. 17, 1861, "	Discharged for disability at Keokuk, Iowa, Nov. 14, 1862.
Ira Hagarty	"	Sept. 6, 1861, "	Mustered out at Nashville, Tenn., Oct. 22, 1864.

Co. L.

NAME.	RANK.	ENTERED SERVICE.	REMARKS.
James Schram	Corporal.	Sept. 14, 1861, Niles.	Mustered out at Nashville, Tenn., Oct. 22, 1864.
William H. Todd	"	Sept. 16, 1861, "	Discharged for disability at Evansville, Ind., Dec. 9, 1862.
Samuel Maxham	Musician.	Sept. 18, 1861, "	St. Louis, Dec. 6, 1862.
Abner P. Stimpson	"	Sept. 14, 1861, "	Re-enlisted Jan. 5, '64; promoted regimental trumpeter Ap. 1, '64.
Daniel Hobbs	Farrier.	Sept. 17, 1861, Vermontville.	Re-enlisted Jan. 5, 1864; must'd out at Macon, Ga., Aug. 17, 1865.
Freeman Hitchcock	"	Sept. 11, 1861, Niles.	Mustered out at Nashville, Tenn., Oct. 22, 1864.
John Bee	Saddler.	Sept. 7, 1861, "	Killed in action near Booneville, Miss., July 1, 1862.
Robert Lingrell	Wagoner.	Sept. 8, 1861, "	Re-enlisted Jan. 5, '64; sergt. must'd out at Macon, Ga., Aug.17,'65.
Ransom Birdsell	Private.	Sept. 14, 1861, "	Mustered out at Nashville, Tenn., Oct. 22, 1864.
Isaac Bone	"	"	
Henry D. Benson	"	"	Mustered out at Nashville, Tenn., Oct. 22, 1864.
Lawrence Burns	"	"	Re-enlisted Jan.5,'64;killed in action near Florence,Ala.,Oct.6,'64.
Roger Burns	"	"	Re-enlisted Jan. 5, 1864; mustered out at Macon, Ga., Aug. 17, '65.
John C. Barker	"	Oct. 4, 1861, "	"
John B. Cisna	"	Sept. 16, 1861, "	Discharged for disability at Keokuk, Oct. 3, 1862.
William Carlisle	"	Sept. 16, 1861, "	Discharged Oct. 2, 1864.
Ashley Carlisle	"	Sept. 16, 1861, "	Mustered out Oct. 22, 1864.
Nelson W. Corwin	"	"	Died of chronic diarrhea near Farmington, Tenn., July 22, 1862.
Augustus Conrad	"	Sept. 14, 1861, "	Re-enlisted Jan. 5, '64; mustered out at Macon, Ga., Aug. 17, '65.
James Corman	"	Sept. 16, 1861, "	
Nelson Crippen	"	Sept. 14, 1861, "	Discharged for disability at Detroit, Dec. 27, 1862.
James Dunn	"	Sept. 16, 1861, "	Mustered out at Nashville, Tenn., Oct. 22, 1864.
William H. Dodge	"	Sept. 7, 1861, "	Discharged for disability at Louisville, Dec. 4, 1862.
James Dewitt	"	Sept. 18, 1861, "	Detroit, July 14, 1862.
Delos Ells	"	Sept. 11, 1861, "	Mustered out at Nashville, Tenn., Oct. 22, 1864.
Felix Eiseley	"	Sept. 24, 1861, "	Killed in action near Mossy Creek, Tenn., Dec. 29, 1863.
Martin Eiseley	"	"	Re-enlisted Jan. 5, '64; mustered out at Macon, Ga., Aug. 17, '65.
Fretterick Gooding	"	Oct. 21, 1861, Memphis.	
Charles W. Granger	"	Sept. 14, 1861, Niles.	Discharged for disability at Detroit, Dec. 4, 1862.
John W. Griffith	"	Sept. 7, 1861, "	Re-enlisted Jan.5,'64; must'd out at Jackson, Mich., Aug. 31, '65.
Charles Hudson	"	Sept. 6, 1861, "	Re-enlisted Jan.5,'64; k'd in ac'n at Fr'kin,Tenn.,Sept.2,'64.
Edwin Hollister	"	Sept. 14, 1861, "	corp.; k'd in ac'n at Fr'kin,Tenn.,Sept.2,'64.
Jacob Hand	"	Sept. 16, 1861, "	Discharged for disability at St. Louis, Nov. 27, 1862.
Henry W. Hewitt	"	"	Re-enlisted Jan. 5, '64; corp.; dro'd in Sopsie Riv., Ala., Ap.16,'65.
John Hanson	"	"	Discharged for disability at Franklin, Tenn, May 30, 1863.
			Discharged at Nashville, Tenn., Oct. 22, 1864.

John F. Hunter	" Sept. 7, 1861, Niles.	Died of typhoid fever at Rienzi, Aug. 6, 1862.
William Kelley	" Sept. 18, 1861, "	Discharged Jan. 5,1864; muster'd out at Macon, Ga., Aug. 17, '65.
Alonzo Ketchum	" Sept. 14, 1861, "	Re-enlisted Jan. 5,1864; muster'd out at Macon, Ga., Sept. 5, 1862.
Charles Kennicutt	" Sept. 16, 1861, "	Discharged for disability at Detroit, Sept. 5, 1862.
Civillian S. Lee	" Sept. 7, 1861, "	Re-enlisted Jan. 5,1864; mustered out at Macon, Ga., Aug. 17,1865.
Andrew Loveland	" Sept. 21, 1861, "	Mustered out at Nashville, Tenn., Oct. 22, 1864.
Jesse M. Lester	" Sept. 24, 1861, "	Re-enlisted Jan. 5, '64; discharged at Keokuk, Iowa, June 7, '65.
Wiliam S. Lowrey	" Sept. 20, 1861, "	Re-enlisted Jan. 5, 1864; mustered out at Macon, Ga., Aug. 17, '65.
Theodore Manco	" Sept. 13, 1861, "	Missing in action at Booneville, Miss., July 1, 1862; returned
		May 2, 1863; re-enlisted Jan. 5,1864; died at Shoal Creek, Ala.,
Lorenzo D. Moore	" Sept. 24, 1861, "	Dec. 1, 1864, of gunshot wound.
		Discharged at Nashville, Tenn., Oct. 22, 1864.
Marquis D. Mealoy	" Oct. 1, 1861, "	Discharged at Detroit, August 16, 1862.
William H. Manering	" Oct. 10, 1861, "	Re-enlisted Jan. 5, '64; discharged at Nashville, Tenn., May 19, '65.
Edgar Nelson	" Sept. 16, 1861, "	Discharged for disability at Detroit, July 15, 1863.
Chester Niles	" Sept. 30, 1861, "	Died of chronic diarrhea at Hamburg, Tenn.
James Park	" Sept. 16, 1861, "	Discharged for disability at St. Louis, Mo., July 13, 1862.
Benjamin F. Rugg	" Sept. 7, 1861, "	Re-enlisted Jan. 5, 1864; discharged at Macon, Ga., July 4, 1865.
Franklin H. Rice	" Sept. 16, 1861, "	Died of chronic diarrhea at New Madrid, Mo., April 13, 1862.
Albert Reed	" Oct. 3, 1861, "	Discharged for disability at St. Louis, Mo., May 14, 1862.
Marvin Scott	" Sept. 16, 1861, "	Discharged at Nashville, Tenn., Oct. 22, 1864.
Frank Stephens	" " "	
Henry Smith	" Sept. 21, 1861, "	Re-enlisted Jan. 5, 1864; absent in hospital w'nde'l at muster out
George Shari	" Sept. 17, 1861, "	must'd out at Jackson, Mich., Aug. 31, '65.
Walter Smith	" Sept. 14, 1861, "	"
Alfred Shockley	" Sept. 24, 1861, "	
Edward Stark	" "	Discharged for disability at Keokuk, Oct. 20, 1862.
George Smith	" "	Re-enlisted Jan. 5, '64; mustered out at Macon, Ga., Aug. 17, 1865.
John W. Stone	" Sept. 7, 1861, "	Discharged for disability at Louisville, Ky., May 14, 1863.
Edgar Sanford	" "	Keokuk, Oct. 20, 1862.
Anthony W. Turner	" Oct. 16, 1861, "	Missing in action at Booneville, Miss., July 1, 1862; discharged
		at Nashville, Tenn., Oct. 22, 1864.
Edgar Talmadge	" Oct. 21, 1861, Memphis.	....
Lorenzo D. Thomas	" Sept. 14, 1861, Niles.	Discharged for disability at Keokuk, Oct. 10, 1862.
Almer Taggart	" Sept. 18, 1861, "	Re-enlisted Jan. 5, '64; mustered out at Macon, Ga., Aug. 17, '65.
Charles Vallean	" Sept. 14, 1861, "	Discharged at Wills Valley, Ala., May 30, 1863.
Robert Warren	" Oct. 21, 1861, Memphis.	

Co. L. NAME.	RANK.	ENTERED SERVICE.	REMARKS.
William Wynn	Private.	Sept. 1, 1861, Niles.	Re-enlisted Jan. 5, 1864; must'd out at Macon, Ga., Aug. 17, '65.
Richard Williams	"	Sept. 14, 1861, "	" " appointed 2d Lieut. Sept. 20, 1864.
Theodore Williams	"	Sept. 18, 1861, "	Died of chronic diarrhea at Andersonville, Ga., Aug. 15, 1864, while a prisoner of war.
Jacob Wieting	"	Sept. 24, 1861, "	Discharged for disability at Quincy, Ill, March 25, 1863.
Timothy Wooden	"	Sept. 16, 1861, "	Died of chronic diarrhea at Benton Barracks, Mo., Jan. 21, 1862.
Cornelius H. Young	"	Sept. 7, 1861, "	Discharged for disability at Corinth, Miss., Aug. 9, 1862.
RECRUITS.			
James H. Andrews	Private.	Aug. 27, 1864, Kalamazoo.	Discharged June 3, 1865.
Hiram Baker	"	Oct. 30, 1863, Grand Rapids.	Died of typhoid pneumonia at Louisville, Ky., March 22, 1864.
Patrick Brewer	"	Oct. 28, 1863, Corunna.	Mustered out at Macon, Ga., Aug. 17, 1865.
Herman Chapman	"	Aug. 24, 1864, Kalamazoo.	Chicago, Ill., May 24, 1865.
Hiram Dalley	"	Nov. 14, 1861, Pontiac.	Re-enlisted Jan. 5, 1864; mustered out at Macon, Ga., Aug. 17, '65.
John Fitzgerald	"	Nov. 14, 1863, Pontiac.	Mustered out at Macon, Ga., Aug. 17, 1865.
William Ford	"	" " Jackson.	" " Camp Dennison, Ohio, June 22, 1865.
Hiram C. Francis	"		Discharged for disability at Detroit. Oct. 29, 1862.
William Gadbold	"	Nov. 13, 1863, Pontiac.	Missing in action at Dandridge Tenn., Jan. 28, 1864; died at Andersonville, Ga., May 12, 1864.
Jonathan F. Goodrich	"	Nov. 1, 1861, "	Re-enlisted Jan. 5, '64; mustered out at Macon, Ga., Aug. 17, 1865.
George Hamlin	"	Nov. 24, 1863, Pontiac.	Absent in hospital at Nashville since April 18, '64, at muster out.
Thomas Haslette	"	Aug. 18, 1864, Jackson.	Mustered out at Edgefield, Tenn., June 21, 1865.
James Haslette	"		" " Madison, Ind., May 27, 1865.
Hampton Haggarty	"	Nov. 1, 1861, Niles.	Corporal; discharged Dec. 13, 1864.
Alton Horey	"	Nov. 19, 1863, Detroit.	Mustered out at Detroit, Aug. 17, 1865.
Albert W. Howard	"	July 28, 1864, Kalamazoo.	Transferred to V. R. C., Feb. 11, 1865.
John Johnson	"	Feb. 5, 1864, Detroit.	Mustered out at Louisville, Ky., Aug. 20, 1865.
James L. Layton	"	Sept. 17, 1864, Kalamazoo.	" " Camp Chase, Ohio, June 20, 1865.
James L. Lee	"	Dec. 31, 1863, "	" " Jackson, Mich., Aug. 31, 1865.
Porter A. Lybacker	"	Aug. 14, 1862, Cassopolis.	" " Detroit, July 5, 1865.
James M. Marshall	"	Aug. 19, 1862, "	Discharged at Franklin, Tenn., March 30, 1863.
George H. Mann	"	Aug. 14, 1862, "	Mustered out at Edgefield, Tenn., June 21, 1865.
Lewis Mark	"	Nov. 11, 1863, Pontiac.	" " Camp Chase, Ohio, June 17, 1865.
George Manchester	"	Nov. 14, 1863, Jackson.	Died of disease at Nashville, Tenn., June 23, 1864.
Frank Maxwell	"	Aug. 9, 1864, Kalamazoo.	Mustered out at Detroit, June 19, 1865.
Azariah Martin	"	" " Flint.	" " Nashville, Tenn., June 3, 1865.

Anson Noble	Private.	Aug. 18, 1864, Jackson.	Discharged May 3, 1865; see Co. M.
Chandler F. Parker	"	Nov. 1, 1861, ...	Re-enlisted Jan. 5, '64; must'd out at Jackson, Mich., Aug. 31, '65.
Paris L. Pray	"	Nov. 21, 1863, Pontiac.	Died of typhoid fever at Nashville, Tenn., Dec. 28, 1864.
Whitman Randall	"	Aug. 21, 1862, E. Saginaw.	
Loren A. Rice	"	Jan. 9, 1863, Niles.	Mustered out at Macon, Ga., Aug. 17, 1865.
Josiah Rumball	"	Aug. 24, 1864, Flint.	"
Henry H. Rymer	"	Nov. 9, 1863, Jackson.	"
Abraham Scranton	"	Nov. 25, 1863, Detroit.	Transferred to V. R. C., Feb. 11, 1865.
Edward M. Shipman	"	Aug. 22, 1864, Grand Rapids.	Mustered out at Edgefield, Tenn., June 21, 1865.
Frank Shipman	"	Aug. 18, 1864, "	"
Seth Smith	"	Nov. 4, 1861, Niles.	Discharged for disability at Keokuk, Oct. 20, 1862.
George Smith	"	Apr. 30, 1864, Grand Rapids.	Mustered out at Macon, Ga., Aug. 17, 1865.
Jacob Snyder	"	Nov. 14, 1863, Jackson.	Died at Nashville, Tenn., April 4, '64, of congestion of the brain.
John C. Spencer	"	Dec. 29, 1863, Grosse Point.	Discharged at Detroit, June 16, 1865.
Hiram Stilson	"	Aug. 14, 1862, Cassopolis.	Transferred to V. R. C., Feb. 11, 1865.
Franklin S. Stevens	"	....	Sergeant; died at Thompson's Station, March 4, 1863, of wounds.
Joseph Stoner	"	Dec. 7, 1863, Jackson.	Mustered out at Macon, Ga., Aug. 17, 1865.
Hubbard Steadman	"	Oct. 27, 1863, Kalamazoo.	"
Georgé Streeter	"	Oct. 29, 1863, Corunna.	Absent in hospital at muster out.
Henry A. Stewart	"	Nov. 25, 1863, Detroit.	Mustered out at Jackson, Mich., Aug. 31, 1865.
William S. Striker	"	Nov. 2, 1863, Grand Rapids.	" Macon, Ga., Aug. 17, 1865.
Colonel J. Stephens	"	Aug. 6, 1864, Niles.	Died of chronic diarrhea at Nashville, Tenn., Jan. 1, 1865.
William N. Stillson	"	Aug. 24, 1864, Kalamazoo.	Mustered out at Detroit, July 12, 1865.
Jeremiah Sullivan	"	Nov. 2, 1863, Grand Rapids.	" Macon, Ga., Aug. 17, 1865.
George F. Sweeney	"	Aug. 22, 1864, Jackson.	" " "
William C. Sweeney	"	Aug. 18, 1864, "	" Edgefield, Tenn., June 21, 1865.
Lyman S. Thrasher	"	Oct. 30, 1863, Corunna.	" Macon, Ga., Aug. 17, 1865.
Ezra Thomas	"	Oct. 29, 1863, Kalamazoo.	Died of typhoid fever at Nashville, Tenn., March 31, 1864.
Henry Tinman	"	....	Transferred to V. R. C., April 30, 1863.
Alexander Truckey	"	Nov. 19, 1863, Pontiac.	Mustered out at Macon, Ga., Aug. 17, 1865.
Suretus H. Tucker	"	Aug. 24, 1864, Kalamazoo.	" Jackson, Mich., Aug. 31, 1865.
John T. Tuttle	"	Aug. 30, 1864, Jackson.	" Macon, Ga., Aug. 17, 1865.
Jackson S. Tucker	"	Nov. 16, 1863, Pontiac.	" Detroit, Aug. 25, 1865.
Seneca B. Vaughn	"	Oct. 27, 1863, Kalamazoo.	" Louisville, Ky., June 26, 1865.
Nathan A. Vaughn	"	....	" Macon, Ga., Aug. 17, 1865.
Charles Vanalstein	"	Oct. 29, 1863, Corunna.	" Louisville, Ky., May 30, 1865.
James Welch	"	Nov. 25, 1863, Pontiac.	" Macon, Ga, Aug. 17, 1865.

Co. L. NAME.	RANK.	ENTERED SERVICE.	REMARKS.
Richard Welch	Private.	Nov. 24, 1863, Pontiac.	" " Annapolis, Md., June 27, 1865.
Jeremiah Welch	"	Nov. 2, 1863, "	" " Macon, Ga., Aug. 17, 1865.
Charles S. Wightman	"	Nov. 14, 1863, Jackson.	Killed in action near Linnville, Tenn., Dec. 24, 1864.
Edward Wilkins	"	Nov. 11, 1863, Pontiac.	Mustered out at Macon, Ga., Aug. 17, 1865.
Charles L. Wisener	"	Aug. 18, 1864, Jackson.	Edgefield, Tenn., June 21, 1865.
Co. M.			
Frank W. Dickey	Captain.	Sept. 2, 1861, Marshall.	Promoted Major Oct. 16, 1862.
Thomas W. Johnston	"	Aug. 24, 1861, "	Promoted Major Dec. 22, 1864.
Henry M. Hempstead	"		Mustered out Aug. 24, 1865.
Abram D. VanGordon	1st Lieut.		
Russell T. Darrow	"	Sept. 7, 1861, "	Killed in action at Cypress River, Ala., Oct. 7, 1864.
Thomas F. Anderson	"	Sept. 10, 1861, Grand Haven.	Mustered out Aug. 17, 1865.
Thomas W. Johnston	2d Lieut.	Aug. 24, 1861, Marshall.	Promoted Captain Co. K., Aug. 1, 1862.
Russell T. Darrow	"	Sept. 7, 1861, "	Promoted 1st Lieut. March 1, 1864.
Irwin Eddy	"	Sept. 14, 1861, Cambria.	Resigned Nov. 19, 1864.
Russell T. Darrow	1st Sergeant.	Sept. 7, 1861, Marshall.	Appointed 2d Lieut. June 1, 1862.
Henry M. Hempstead	Q'm'r Serg't.	Aug. 24, 1861, "	" Co. B, March 1, 1864; re-enlisted Jan. 5, '64.
Frank Sweeney	"		Missing in action at Chicamauga, Ga., Sept. 20, 1863; exchanged Dec. 31, 1864; discharged June 26, 1865.
Elihu Agnew	"	Sept. 16, 1861, "	Discharged at Nashville, Tenn., Oct. 22, 1864.
James H. Howey	"	Aug. 24, 1861, "	Re-enlisted Jan. 5, 1864; appointed 1st Lieut. 136th U. S. C. T.
Joseph Sykes	"	Sept. 2, 1861, Clarence.	Discharged for disability Nov. 21, 1862.
Chauncey Alexander	Corporal.	Aug. 20, 1861, Marshall.	Re-enlisted Jan. 5, '64; serg.; must'd out at Macon, Ga., Aug. 17, '65.
Edward Knapp	"	Sept. 20, 1861, Parma.	Discharged at Nashville, Tenn., Oct. 22, 1864.
Daniel Murdock	"	Sept. 9, 1861, Marshall.	Died of typhoid fever at Rienzi, Miss., July 15, 1862.
James Harrington	"	Sept. 10, 1861, "	Discharged for disability near Farmington, Miss., June 20, 1862.
Othniel Keyes	"		" " at Corinth, Miss., Sept. 11, 1862.
Henry French	"	Sept. 7, 1861, Homer.	" " St. Louis, Mo., March 13, 1862.
John Smith	"	Aug. 27, 1861, Marshall.	" " Evansville, March 11, 1863.
Warren B. Norcott	"	Sept. 16, 1861, Hillsdale.	" " Franklin, Tenn., May 1, 1863.
George A. Tyler	Musician.	Sept. 2, 1861, Marshall.	" " Corinth, Miss., Sept. 13, 1862.
Stephen W. Lester	"	Sept. 19, 1861, "	Re-enlisted Jan. 5, 1864; mustered out at Macon, Ga., Aug. 17, '65.
Charles Harrington	Farrier.	Sept. 13, 1861, "	Transferred to 3d Mich. Cav. Nov. 1, 1861.
Johnson Watt	"	" Newton.	Re-enlisted Jan. 5, '64; serg.; must'd out at Macon, Ga., Aug. 17, '65.
Mason F. Smith	Saddler.	Sept. 2, 1861, Marshall.	

Name	Rank	Enlisted	Place	Remarks
Joseph Keemer	Wagoner.	Sept. 12, 1861,	Marshall.	Discharged at Detroit Jan. 26, 1865.
Charles H. Ackley	Private.	Sept. 2, 1861,	Convis.	" Nashville, Tenn., Oct. 22, 1864.
Dewitt C. Abell	"	Sept. 5, 1861,	Burlington.	Discharged for disability at St. Louis, Mo., Aug. 22, 1862.
Alonzo Austin	"	Sept. 2, 1861,	Marshall.	" Keokuk, Dec. 6, 1862.
Edward Alexander	"	Sept. 12, 1861,	"	{ Killed in a skirmish at Glasgow, Ky., with John Morgan's command, Dec. 24, 1862.
William Birdsell	"	Sept. 16, 1861,	Hillsdale.	{ Missing in action at Severeville, Tenn., Jan. 27, 1864; discharged at Detroit, April 17, 1865.
Albert Buckingham	"	Sept. 18, 1861,	"	Discharged at Nashville, Tenn. Oct. 22, 1864.
Rufus Bratt	"	Sept. 13, 1861,	Newton.	Died of diarrhea at Newton, Mich., June 3, 1862.
Marion Boyer	"	Sept. 7, 1861,	Burlington.	Died of chronic diarrhea at Keokuk, Aug. 24, 1862.
Andrew Boyce	"	"	"	Discharged at Nashville, Tenn., Oct. 22, 1864.
Nathan Boyce	"	"	"	Mustered out at Detroit, July 3, 1865.
David Barringer	"	Aug. 31, 1861,	Marshall.	Re-enlisted Jan.5, '64; must'd out at Jackson, Mich., Aug. 31, '65.
Richard Brown	"	Sept. 20, 1861,	"	" d'd of chronic diarr'a at Parma, Mich., Oct. 2, '64
Robert H. Cowan	"	Sept. 16, 1861,	Hillsdale.	Died of diarrhea at New Madrid, Mo., April 10, 1862.
William A. Case	"	"	"	Re-enlisted Jan. 5, 1864; mustered out at Macon. Ga., Aug. 17, '65.
Jetson Clark	"	Aug. 31, 1861,	Marshall.	Died of chronic diarrhea at Keokuk, Iowa, July 24, 1862.
Patrick Dooley	"	Sept. 12, 1861,	"	{ Missing in action at Brentwood, Tenn., March 25, 1863; re-enlisted Jan.5,1864; mustered out at Camp Chase, O., June 20, '65.
Le Grand Dean	"	"	"	Discharged at Keokuk, Oct. 17, 1862.
Franklin Eaton	"	Sept. 20, 1861,	Albion.	Promoted Q. M. Sergeant May 15, 1862.
David Fancher	"	Sept. 12, 1861,	Homer.	Died of typhoid fever near Farmington, Miss., May 12, 1863.
Julius Gregory	"	Sept. 16, 1861,	Parma.	Re-enlisted Jan.5,'64; farr'r; must'd out at Macon, Ga., Aug.17,'65.
Burt Gaines	"	Sept. 2, 1861,	Athens.	Discharged at Nashville, Tenn., Oct. 22, 1864.
Sullivan Gaines	"	"	Saranac.	Died at Knoxville, Tenn., Feb. 2, '64, of w'ds rec'd Jan. 27, 1864.
Earl Hoisington, Jr.	"	Sept. 3, 1861,	Marshall.	Reported captured by John Morgan, parolled and sent to Canada.
Hiram J. Harris	"	Sept. 16, 1862,	Hillsdale.	Died of typhoid fever in hospital at St. Louis, May 30, 1862.
Clement C. Hutton	"	"	"	" at Rienzi, Miss., Aug. 9, 1862.
Gerrit Hall	"	"	Marshall.	{ Re-enlisted Jan. 5, 1864; sergeant; killed in action at Martin's Mills, near Florence, Ala., Oct. 7, 1864.
Ira Hutchinson	"	Sept. 7, 1861,	Homer.	Discharged for disability at Corinth, Miss., Sept. 15, 1862.
Frank Hooker	"	"	Marshall.	" Cairo, Ill. May 15, 1862.
Veit Hildenger	"	Sept. 20, 1861,	"	" Quincy, Ill., April 3, 1863.
Thomas Howard	"	Sept. 18, 1861,	"	
Norman Hotchkiss	"	Sept. 12, 1861,	"	Re-enlisted Jan. 5, 1864; must'd out at Macon, Ga., Aug. 17, '65.
George Hudson	"	Sept. 20, 1861,	Burlington.	Discharged for disability at Louisville, Ky., Oct. 17, 1862.

Co. M. NAME.	RANK.	ENTERED SERVICE.	REMARKS.
Frank Holmes	Private.	Sept. 12, 1861, Marshall.	Died of fever at New Madrid, Mo., April 13, 1862.
George Jenks	"	Sept. 16, 1861, Newton.	Re-enlisted Jan. 5, '64; corp.; appointed 1st Lieut. 136th U.S.C.T.
Lucius Johnston	"	" 16, 1861, Marshall.	Discharged for disability at St. Louis, Nov. 7, 1862.
James Johnston	"	"	Re-enlisted Jan.5,'64; corp.; must'd out at Macon, Ga., Aug. 17,'65.
William Kidney	"	Sept. 10, 1861, "	Transferred to 3d Mich. Cav. Nov. 1, 1861.
Michael McIntyre	"	" " 1861, Hillsdale.	
Owen McManus	"	Sept. 14, 1861, "	Re-enlisted Jan. 5, '64; killed in action at Martin's Mills, near Florence, Ala., Oct. 7, 1864.
Sylvester McLain	"	Sept. 19, 1861, Burlington.	Saddler; discharged for disability at Gallatin, Tenn., Jan. 30, '63.
John Marsh	"	" 16, 1861, Marshall.	Re-enlisted Jan. 5, '64; serg.; must'd out at Macon, Ga., Aug. 17, '65.
Amos Merrill	"	" 26, 1861, Parma.	Discharged to accept appointment in U. S. C. T., March 10, '64.
Samuel Markle	"	" 27, 1861, Marshall.	Re-enlisted Jan.5,'64; mustered out at Jackson, Mich.,Aug.30,'64.
John Myers	"	" 2, 1861, Hillsdale.	" " Macon, Ga., Aug. 17, 1865.
Ezra W. Norcott	"	" 16, 1861, "	Died in Michigan of typhoid fever, April 3, 1862.
Thomas O'Brien	"	" 17, 1861, "	Discharged for disability at Woodsonville, Ky., Jan., 1863.
James Osborn	"	" 16, 1861, Marshall.	Re-enlisted Jan. 5, '64; must'd out at Jackson, Mich., Aug. 30, '65.
Charles Ploof	"	Aug. 30, 1861, "	Died of consumption in Eaton Co., Mich., Aug. 25, 1862.
Frank Pratt	"	Sept. 16, 1861, Burlington.	Discharged at Nashville, Tenn., Oct. 22, 1864.
Charles H. Potter	"	" " 1861, Homer.	Sergeant; killed in action at Dandridge, Tenn., Dec. 24, 1863.
Erastus Reynolds	"	Sept. 4, 1861, Marshall.	Re-enlisted Jan.5,'64; must'd out at Detroit, Aug. 15, 1865.
Chandler Redfield	"	" 7, 1861, Homer.	Promoted hospital steward Nov. 28, 1863.
Lorentz Stamples	"	" 12, 1861, Marshall.	Re-enlisted Jan.5,'64; serg.; must'd out at Macon, Ga., Aug. 17, '65.
Thaddeus M. Southworth	"	" 16, 1861, Hillsdale.	Discharged for disability at Hamburg, Tenn., May 20, 1862.
James R. Stephens	"	Aug. 28, 1861, Kalamazoo.	Transferred to Co. H, Jan. 1, 1862.
Benjamin F. Smith	"	Sept. 10, 1861, Marshall.	Discharged at Nashville, Tenn., Oct. 22, 1864.
Gabriel Smith	"	" 12, 1861, "	
James Smith	"	Aug. 28, 1861, "	Discharged for disability at Evansville, Ind., March 16, 1864.
Emery R. Stembell	"	Sept. 12, 1861, "	Re-enlisted Jan. 5, '64, mustered out at Macon, Ga., Aug. 17, '65.
Thomas Sutherland	"	" "	
William Sayles	"	Sept. 5, 1861, "	
Lyman Sayles	"	" "	Discharged for disability at Detroit, July 1, 1862.
Albert M. Spaulding	"	Sept. 9, 1861, "	Died Sept. 23, 1863, of wounes received in action at Chicamauga.
Stephen R. Travis	"	" 5, 1861, "	Supposed discharged.
William Wickham	"	" " 1861, Newton.	Discharged for disability at Cairo, Ill., April 20, 1862.
William Waltz	"	Sept. 12, 1861, Marshall.	Re-enlisted Jan.5,'64; mustered out at Camp Chase,O.,June 20,'65.

Name	Rank	Date	Remarks
Norcas Williams	Private.	Sept. 5, 1861, Marshall.	Discharged for disability at Corinth, Miss., Sept. 9, 1862.
Franklin Wallace	"	Sept. 7, 1861, Athens.	Re-enlisted Jan. 5, '64; serg ; must'd out at Macon, Ga., Aug.17,'65.
Henry Woodruff	"	Sept. 3, 1861, Marshall.	Re-enlisted Jan. 5, 1864; serg.,app. 1st Lieut. Co. G, Oct, 7, 1864.
Lewis Waterman	"	Sept. 9, 1861, Homer.	Discharged Oct. 8, 1864.
Robert Wilson	"	Sept. 16, 1861, Hillsdale.	Discharged for disability at St. Louis, Mo , Sept. 17, 1862.
Charles Phelps	"	Aug. 27, 1861, Marshall.	Discharged at Nashville, Tenn., Oct. 22, 1864.
RECRUITS.			
Benjamin F. Allen	Private.	Dec. 28, 1863, Marshall.	Died of diarrhea at Nashville, Tenn., Sept. 11, 1864.
Norman R. Ayres	"	Feb. 16, 1864, Allen.	Discharged at Detroit, May 26, 1865.
John Baker	"	Nov. 21, 1863, Pontiac.	Died of diarrhea at Nashville, Tenn., March 18, 1864.
James Beddow	"	Feb. 23, 1864, Allen.	Mustered out at Jackson, Mich., Aug. 30, 1865.
Patrick Burns	"	Jan. 4, 1864, Hampden.	Corporal; mustered out at Macon, Ga., Aug. 17, 1865.
William Clark	"	Nov. 24, 1863, Pontiac.	Mustered out at Macon, Ga., Aug. 17, 1865.
Charles Cowles	"	Nov. 13, 1863, Detroit.	" Detroit, Aug. 31, 1865.
Thomas Coles	"	Aug. 10, 1864, Kalamazoo.	Corporal; mustered out at Macon, Ga., Aug. 17, 1865.
Alexander H. Darrow	"	Aug. 12, 1862, "	Mustered out at Louisville, Ky., June 14, 1865.
A. Davidson	"		Discharged at Keokuk, Oct. 16, 1862.
Silas Dean	"	Nov. 16, 1863, Detroit.	Died of chronic diarrhea at Chattanooga, Tenn., June 28, 1864.
Charles M. Dyke	"	Mar. 25, 1864, Watertown.	Discharged for disability at Detroit, June 15, 1865.
Charles Farrington	"	Sept. 1, 1864, Jackson.	Mustered out at Edgefield, Tenn., June 21, 1865.
Samuel Fowler	"	Dec. 22, 1863, E. Saginaw.	" Macon, Ga., Aug. 17, 1865.
Joseph Gauntlett	"	Sept. 1, 1864, Jackson.	" Edgefield, Tenn., June 21. 1865.
James Glanney	"	Aug. 16, 1864, Pontiac.	" Macon, Ga., Aug. 17, 1865.
Robert Gordon	"	Feb. 19, 1864, Hampton.	Corporal; mustered out at Macon, Ga, Aug. 17, 1865.
Chauncy R. Hayes	"	Aug. 19, 1862, Kalamazoo.	Mustered out at Edgefield, Tenn., June 21, 1865.
George W. Hand	"	Oct. 30, 1863,	" Macon, Ga., Aug. 17, 1865.
James Kuhn	"		Missing in action at Dandridge, Tenn., Dec. 24, 1863.
John Malloy	"	Nov. 19, 1864, Pontiac.	Absent sick since May 26, 1864, at muster out.
James McDermot	"	Nov. 11, 1863, "	Mustered out at Macon,Ga., Aug. 17,1865.
Emanuel Miller	"	Sept. 30, 1862, Marshall.	" " "
Jacob Miller	"		Died of typhoid fever at Camp Chase, Ohio, July 21, 1863.
Solomon Mikersell	"	Aug. 18, 1864, Jackson.	Died of chronic diarrhea at Waterloo, Ala., March 11, 1865.
Horatio A. McKee	"	Nov. 1, 1861, Marshall.	Discharged for disability Nov. 1, 1862.
Alonzo Morey	"	Oct. 28, 1863, Grand Rapids.	Mustered out at Macon, Ga., Aug. 17, 1865.
Abraham Moser	"	Sept. 8, 1862, Detroit.	Killed in action at Fair Garden, Tenn., Jan. 27, 1864.
Warren B. Norcutt	"	Feb. 14, 1864, Allen.	Died of cholera morbus at Franklin, Tenn., Aug. 22, 1864.
Anson Nobles	"	Aug. 18, 1864, Jackson.	Mustered out at Nashville, Tenn., May 16, 1865. See Co. L.

Co. M. NAME.	RANK.	ENTERED SERVICE.	REMARKS.
Richard Phillips	Private.	Feb. 10, 1864, Allen.	" Detroit, Sept. 7, 1865.
Dewitt C. Phillips	"	Sept. 1, 1864, Jackson.	Died of chronic diarrhea at Madison, Ind. Jan. 16, 1665.
James A. Powell	"	Nov. 13, 1863, Pontiac.	Mustered out at Camp Chase, Ohio, June 16, 1865.
Solomon M. Price	"	Aug. 25, 1864, Jackson.	" Edgefield, Tenn, June 21, 1865.
John Raill	"	Nov. 14, 1863, "	Discharged for disability at Nashville, Tenn., June 29, 1865.
Jesse Redman	"	Sept. 1, 1864, "	Mustered out at Edgefield, Tenn., June 21, 1865.
William E. Rowe	"	Oct. 27, 1863, Grand Rapids.	" Macon, Ga., Aug. 17, 1865.
Sydney R. Smith	"	Feb. 5, 1864, Allen.	
Myron C. Tice	"	Aug. 19, 1861, Dowagiac.	Discharged July 18, 1865.
Charles E. Tone	"	Nov. 1, 1861, ...	Re-enlisted Jan.5,'64; mustered out at Camp Chase, O., June 28,'65
George Truslar	"	Aug. 18, 1864, Jackson.	Discharged for disability Feb. 23, 1865.
Charles F. Walters	"	Sept. 8, 1862, Detroit.	Missing in action at Chicamauga, Ga., Sept. 20, 1863; mustered out at Detroit, June 30, 1865.
George Wangart	"	Oct. 29, 1863, Corunna.	Mustered out at Macon, Ga., Aug. 17, 1865.
Robert Wade	"	Oct. 24, 1863, "	"
Henry Walker	"	Nov. 24, 1863, Pontiac.	Died of chronic diarrhea at Detroit, Oct. 15, 1864.
Harvey D. Wardwell	"	Oct. 30, 1863, Corunna.	Mustered out June 3, 1865.
Henry Ward	"	Nov. 19, 1863, Pontiac.	Transferred to V. R. C., April 30, 1864.
Jonathan Wade	"	Aug. 23, 1864, Marshall.	Mustered out at Macon, Ga., Aug. 17, 1865.
Amos Welsh	"	Oct. 28, 1863, Kalamazoo.	Mustered out at Nashville, Tenn., May 18, 1865.
Thomas Welborn	"	Oct. 30, 1863, Grand Rapids.	Drowned March 6, 1864, at Nashville, Tenn.
Charles Whittman	"	Jan. 4, 1864, Jackson.	Mustered out at Louisville, Ky., June 10, 1865.
William White	"	Nov. 27, 1863, Pontiac.	Corporal; mustered out at Macon, Ga., Aug. 17, 1865.
Joseph Wilber	"	Dec. 7, 1863, Jackson.	Died of sunstroke at Nashville, Tenn., Sept. 8, 1864.
William H. Williams	"	Sept. 29, 1863, Corunna.	Mustered out at Macon, Ga., Aug. 17, "
John H. Williams	"		"
Samuel Williams	"	Nov. 24, 1863, Detroit.	"
Reuben Williams	"	Oct. 28, 1863, Grand Rapids.	"
Samuel Willard	"	Oct. 29, 1863, Corunna.	" Detroit, May 15, 1865.
William Wilson	"	Oct. 28, 1863, Grand Rapids.	" Aug. 25, 1865.
Henry Wilson	"	Oct. 29, 1863, Corunna.	"
Elias Worden	"	Oct. 27, 1863, "	" Macon, Ga., Aug. 17, 1865.
Frank Zahringer	"	Oct. 30, 1863, Kalamazoo.	" Camp Chase, Ohio, June 17, 1865.